THE COMPLETE JUDY GARLAND

THE COMPLETE

★ ★ ★ ★ THE ULTIMATE GUIDE TO HER CAREER IN FILMS,

JUDY GARLAND

RECORDS, CONCERTS, RADIO, AND TELEVISION, 1935–1969

EMILY R. COLEMAN

1817

HARPER & ROW, PUBLISHERS, NEW YORK

GRAND RAPIDS, PHILADELPHIA, ST. LOUIS, SAN FRANCISCO
LONDON, SINGAPORE, SYDNEY, TOKYO, TORONTO

THE COMPLETE JUDY GARLAND. Copyright © 1990 by Emily R. Coleman. All rights reserved. Printed in the United States of America. No part of this book may be used or reproduced in any manner whatsoever without written permission except in the case of brief quotations embodied in critical articles and reviews. For information address Harper & Row, Publishers, Inc., 10 East 53rd Street, New York, N.Y. 10022.

FIRST EDITION

Designer: JOEL AVIROM

Library of Congress Cataloging-in-Publication Data

Coleman, Emily R.
    The complete Judy Garland : the ultimate guide to
her career in films, records, concerts, radio, and
television, 1935–1969/Emily R. Coleman.—1st ed.
        p.   cm.
    Includes bibliographical references and indexes.
    ISBN 0-06-016333-X
    1. Garland, Judy—Criticism and interpretation.
I. Title.
ML420.G253C64   1990
782.42164′092—dc20   89-38325

90 91 92 93 94 DT/MPC 10 9 8 7 6 5 4 3 2 1

CONTENTS

★

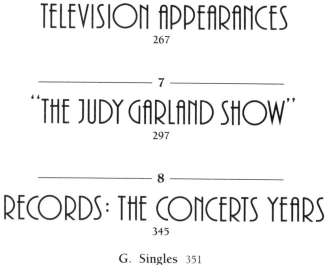

PREFACE

★

Hundreds of thousands of words have been written about Judy Garland's life, about her MGM-imposed and -fostered barbiturate addiction, about her increasing emotional problems toward the end. I have no intention of reviewing them yet again. The purpose of this book is to explore her career as a performer and her development as an artist.

One can only assume that so much has been written about her personal life not because it was unique in the annals of Hollywood—it was not—nor because she was typical—Garland's career hit uncommon heights in a variety of entertainment media—but because the continuing fascination with Judy Garland is with her performing greatness and her enduring ability to attract new fans and admirers even decades after her death.

Yet for all the attention paid to the woman, during her life and after, strangely enough, there has been no systematic attempt to understand the artist. No one has looked at Judy Garland on her own terms, on her own ground.

This book is an attempt to begin that process, to get behind the myths and the "legend." For Judy Garland was not merely a unique talent. She was an artist who developed that talent with intelligence, sensitivity, and skill. She was, moreover, an artist who drew insight from each of the entertainment media in which she performed and transformed these separate lessons into a complex, subtle, and dynamic whole. To understand how Judy Garland could move people so deeply, as she incontrovertibly did and does, is to appreciate artistic balances, fine shadings, and penetrating distinctions.

The chapters that follow are designed to be used in a variety of ways. Each begins with an analysis of that aspect of Garland's career, be it films, radio, concerts, and so forth. These sections may be read separately, by those interested in, say, Judy's television career or her singing, or they may be read consecutively.

For those with the time and interest to form their own systematic opinions of

Garland's professional development, the record of her activities that makes up the bulk of each chapter is more than a more-or-less-complete Garland encyclopedia: It provides the raw data. With this in mind, I have provided cross references and a listing of relevant recordings where they exist; where there is little or no extant material to hear or view, as with her concert appearances, in particular, I have quoted more extensively from contemporary reviews.

Finally, the addenda sections of each chapter provide a cursory look—a trivia trove, if you will—of the context in which Garland performed and the context from which her material was derived. Thus, film buffs will find such miscellanea as how the effect of the Munchkins' voices was achieved and which of Judy's movies were top grossers. (Do you know what Cole Porter thought of *The Pirate?*) Popular music buffs, similarly, can find the origins and original artists on Garland's nonmovie recordings. (Do you know the story behind "Fly Me to the Moon"?) And so on. This material is designed to be dipped into at your leisure, and I hope you find it fun.

Of course, this is not truly the "complete" Garland. There are, for example, Armed Forces Radio Service broadcasts I have not been able to track down, nor have I been able to pinpoint every concert appearance or each concert's production personnel. Undoubtedly, too, between the time I write this and the time you read it, new Garland reissues will have appeared. I would be grateful for any information, or corrections, readers could supply.

After viewing and listening to, quite literally, thousands of hours of Judy Garland, I find that my admiration for her artistry is far more profound now than it was when I began. I have, obviously, formed some strong personal views on her professional development; and the opinions which follow are wholly my own, as are any errors.

Yet this book would have been a great deal less complete than it is without the extraordinary assistance I have received. Thus, I wish to thank John Behrens and Nancy Delaney of CBS Program Information; Cathy Lim of NBC Records Administration; Don McCormick, Curator of the Rodgers and Hammerstein Archives of Recorded Sound at the Performing Arts Research Center (at Lincoln Center, New York City); Wynn Matthias and Sam Brylawski of the Recorded Sound Reference Center and Madeline Matz of the Film and Television Reference Center of the Library of Congress; Terry Geesken of the Museum of Modern Art Stills Archive; Larry Hathaway, formerly Director of Catalogue Development and Jazz, and Pete Welding, Producer, Special Markets Division, of Capitol Records; Van-John Sfiridis, Director, A & R, of DRG Records; Louis B. Marino, Program Information Manager for Warner Bros. Television Distribution; and Larry Ashmead and John Michel, my editor and associate editor at Harper & Row. Each one of these generous individuals went way beyond the call of duty, and there is no adequate way to express my appreciation for their time, patience, courtesy, and invaluable assistance during my research.

1

"MISS SHOW BUSINESS"

★

*"Miss Show Business she has been called and if you think that's merely a
selling gimmick, just go and see her."*

Tony Brown, *Melody Maker*, October 19, 1957
(review of Garland concert)

★

*"It must take a strange sort of person not to be moved by this giant talent. I believe that
people cry at Judy for the same reason they do at sunsets or symphonies or cathedrals;
when one is confronted with overwhelming greatness, it is impossible not to be moved."*

Gordon Jenkins, *Melody Maker*, November 16, 1957

★

Judy Garland, perhaps more than any entertainer in modern history, personified what a mixed blessing extraordinary talent can be. She reached professional heights virtually unparalleled in range and scope. But her personal lows were never private. They were emblazoned in newspapers throughout the country—in some cases, throughout the world.

Born Frances Ethel Gumm on June 10, 1922, Judy spent her formative years on the road as part of a marginal act in the fading world of vaudeville and within the precincts of the MGM studios. (George Jessel gave her the name "Garland" in Chicago in 1934 when audiences giggled at his introduction of the "Gumm Sisters"; she took the name "Judy" from the Hoagy Carmichael song.) She was signed by Metro-Goldwyn-Mayer in September 1935; and Louis B. Mayer, the authoritarian head of the studio, replaced the emotional support she had received from her father, who died suddenly barely two months later.

Her film career at Metro typified the personal and professional benefits and burdens of stardom during the golden age of the Hollywood studios. In many ways a typical child star in the thirties, her normal maturing processes were blunted and perverted by the studio system, and by an ambitious stage mother who happily acquiesced in any emotional or physical sacrifices show business demanded of her daughter.

Despite the "Coogan law," which theoretically protected children from the avarice of their parents, most child stars found their financial affairs managed by their parents or their parents' chosen advisers. Judy's money was managed by her mother and the stepfather she never liked or trusted. Typically, there wasn't an extraordinary amount left when Judy reached maturity. Like most other Hollywood youngsters of the era, she never learned to manage her own income, nor was she taught how. It was a lack of education, the consequences of which would shadow her throughout her life.

Judy was the youngest of the three daughters to marry early to escape their maternal home. But unlike her sisters, she found her mother living with, and on, her and enjoying all the benefits of her financial success, a pattern that would follow her through her later years and relationships as well. Indeed, when they were estranged, Judy's mother threatened to sue her for support. In the interim, however, Ethel Gumm supported any studio dictum and used threats of disrupting her daughter's relationship with the studio in attempts to keep Judy under control.

Both Ethel and Mayer were determined to keep her a child long after it was healthy for an adolescent girl. It was the studio, with Ethel's support, that put Judy

Garland on a diet too stringent for a young growing body in order to reduce her baby fat, and on pills: diet pills, for Judy even as a young woman had a tendency to gain weight; "pep" pills, to keep her functioning before the cameras despite extraordinary working hours; and sleeping pills, to counteract the effect of the amphetamines or help her take naps on the set.

Mayer had a clear and idealized concept of motherhood and family for the screen. But he had a decidedly different vision for his stars. Both he and Ethel disapproved of Judy's first marriage, to David Rose. It would diffuse their control and conflict with her assigned screen parts. They induced her to have an abortion, threatening that a full-term pregnancy would ruin her career. It helped destroy the marriage. It was their pressure, too, that forced Judy to terminate her sessions with a psychiatrist after it had become apparent to her that she needed help and, encouraged by Joseph Mankiewicz, had sought it. The reasoning was the same: They wanted control of the young Garland. (Mankiewicz's confrontation with Mayer over this issue was one of the reasons he left MGM.)

By the late forties, Judy Garland was an established star. She was also a young woman with some rather severe personal problems. Judy's postwar Metro career was played out in the context of the decline of the Hollywood studio system, a far less private and forgiving world than the stars of the past had known. Trying desperately to revitalize its box-office receipts and staunch the flow of red ink, MGM vigorously pursued the expensive musicals that had marked its most prosperous years. All Metro employees were under increased pressure to perform, perform well and on schedule. Yet, in some ways, the studio was at its most understanding with Garland then, buying and designing vehicles expressly for her, financing her hospitalization in Boston in 1949.

But the studio was a different place than it had been in its heyday, and even Mayer was under threat. New executives had been brought in. It was decided that Judy's costs to Metro-Goldwyn-Mayer exceeded her assets. With no attempt at finesse or delicacy, she was simply fired in 1950, after completing *Summer Stock*.

If Judy Garland's career had ended here, as many expected it to, hers would be a sad but not particularly noteworthy story. What makes Garland special, to her fans and to entertainment history, was her unusual mix of personal attractiveness to the public, the extraordinary artistic talent she developed with intelligence and skill, and the sheer strength and raw courage she evidenced to battle both her private demons and overcome the repeated public proclamations of her professional demise. Against all the odds, and against the common wisdom, she created an unparalleled new career as a vocalist and concert artist of world-class dimensions.

The Garland legend, and many of the nastier elements of the Garland mythology, begin with Judy's unasked-for declaration of independence from MGM.

Among the more well covered aspects of Judy Garland's career was her ability to transcend entertainment media. What is equally remarkable, however, was her ability to transcend quite distinct eras in entertainment history and tastes. Garland acquired new fans and admirers through profoundly different epochs in America's history. And Judy Garland was never a fad. She was never passé. Her "comebacks" were never a matter of being "rediscovered."

She was a screen star in the forties, a major box-office draw for MGM during World War II and the years following. Between the vehicles Metro fashioned for her and the down-to-earth ingenuousness of her vocal and film characterizations, she appealed to a public yearning for simple verities. She reflected an honest friendliness, tied to a sense of humor, that evoked nostalgia for a simpler time, a time before America had to deal with the complexities of vast economic devastation and modern global war. Indeed, Judy's one specifically dramatic, nonmusical film, *The Clock,* looked at World War II from a gentle, home-front perspective. (*For Me and My Gal* was safely framed in the First World War, using it primarily as a backdrop to a vaudeville story and, for the most part, approached the subject with cartoonlike simplicity.)

The fifties was an era of emotional disengagement. It was almost as if people were taking a breathing space after the upheavals of the preceding decades. It was the era in which television took hold, and almost everyone seemed to be pursuing the American Dream of a house in the suburbs, two cars, two kids, one spouse, and one job. Economic security and social stability were in.

By the early fifties, Judy's second marriage, to Vincente Minnelli, had failed.

She'd had well-publicized emotional problems and a suicide attempt. She'd been fired from MGM. And it was precisely in the early fifties that she deepened and darkened her vocal style, imbuing her performances with a power and dramatic artistry that left both reviewers and audiences breathless. Her return to the screen, too, in 1954 in *A Star Is Born,* carried with it a potency that continues to reverberate, even upon repeated viewings more than three decades later.

Judy Garland riveted audiences in the fifties because of the extraordinary beauty of her singing. But she riveted them, too, because of the intensity of her style. Garland concerts were regularly reported to be experiences, emotional experiences beyond simple entertainment. Audiences read into Judy's vocal renditions their knowledge of her life; and they felt that she was communicating with them. She seemed to be putting into words, in a public forum, what so many felt (and feel) and can't express. Garland's intensity, in the era of emotional distancing, provided a socially acceptable form of catharsis, a release of pent-up emotions, while providing the audience with a consummately professional show.

The sixties were the activist era, the era of youth, of "never trust anyone over thirty," of social conscience and social conflict. The Kennedy presidency seemed to symbolize the reinvigoration of America's "can do" spirit and a sense of commitment. The sixties, too, were the years when the search for freedom of expression and self-determination turned, for many of that generation, into what has

been described as a "culture of narcissism," an individualized, brooding self-absorption that made interior reality more important than social integration.

In this radically different era and context, Garland continued to pack 'em in. More than that, she acquired new fans, and many members of the "sixties generation" became her most ardent admirers. Critics noted time and again that the standing ovations, the rush to the stage at the end of a performance to touch her hand, crossed all normal generational lines. The very young were as enthusiastic as those who had seen *The Wizard of Oz* as adults on its initial release in 1939.

Judy hadn't changed her act or her style. They both continued to work, on multiple levels. In the early part of the decade, her voice and control were superb, her vocal artistry unsurpassed. In addition, however, the emotional integrity with which she rendered each song, film characterization, and live appearance, taking each performance on its own terms unencumbered by flashy technique, reverberated anew with a generation seeking to understand itself, to be understood, striving to be better, more open, more honest.

She personified a level of seeking that people, of whatever era, could understand, and personalize. The very publicity surrounding her personal life—her increasingly tempestuous relationship with her third husband, Sid Luft; her periodically erratic behavior and failure to appear or perform; later, her conflicting statements as to whether she'd married Mark Herron or not—humanized the awesome greatness of her talent for those publicly exposed to it. Audiences could see her as another human being, confused by a confusing world, as they were.

By the late sixties, Garland's voice was not what it had once been. (Her throat had been damaged during emergency medical procedures in Hong Kong in May 1964.) Her audiences didn't care. They came to see her anyway, and they continued to enjoy and applaud her performances.

This clearly enraged a certain element among the professional critics. Indeed, some were so incensed that they devoted entire reviews and articles to reviewing the fans, attacking them as virtually mindless enthusiasts or strange people peculiarly lacking in socially adjusted values. Some found it particularly galling that Judy should have a following in the gay community. By implication, they made it manifest that any performer attracting such a collection of admirers was hardly worthy of their or any normal person's attention. Thus, the famous Garland "cult" has acquired a patina of peculiarity through the years.

Yet Garland audiences were not musically insensitive. If you listen consecutively to recordings of Judy's 1951 Palace show, her 1958 Cocoanut Grove appearance, the 1961 Carnegie Hall concert, the 1964 Judy/Liza performance at the London Palladium, and her 1967 Palace engagement, you find significant continuity in audience response. Despite quite different voices over the years, despite notable variations in the quality of the backup she received from her orchestras, despite different audiences, there were always three

points of applause: There was applause at the beginning of numbers that came with recognizing a Garland standard. There was applause at the end of each song. But consistently, whenever there was applause during a rendition, it coincided with a particularly telling point of vocal artistry. If Garland audiences had been graded on music appreciation, critics to the side, they would not have done badly.

Nor were they a strange collection of social deviants. After Judy died in London, on June 22, 1969, of an accidental overdose of the drugs to which she'd been addicted so many years before, her body was brought back to New York for the funeral. Thousands lined up to pay their respects. *Variety* called it Judy's "last standing ovation." No one was particularly surprised at the numbers who mourned her. But many members of the press, who had so cheerfully commented on the "cult" and its membership during her lifetime, were chagrined to note how respectable a crowd it seemed to be. They commented on the men in business suits, the middle-aged matrons, the youths, all of whom were visibly moved.

Few enough are the generally happy performers who lead placid private lives; fewer still are those whose lives are retailed decade after decade. It is a cliché, of course, that "sex sells." Yet perhaps more apt is the fact that most people enjoy seeing the underside of a glamour they cannot share, the feet of clay among the mighty.

This is not generally so for Garland fans. Their protectiveness of Judy is noteworthy. Beyond the self-invested priest-hood, the true cult, those who consider themselves the protectors of her memory and the scourge of the uninitiated's errors, lies a vast, quiet army of people who found and continue to find themselves moved by her: by her performing great-ness, by her wealth of talent, and by the complex woman who seemed to reach out to them with charm and humor.

"Miss Show Business" she was called, and certainly she was a consummately professional entertainer of formidable range and depth. But the fans remember her as Judy, a human being who, for mo-ments at a time, brought beauty into their lives.

2

FILMS

───────── ★ ─────────

"Personality is the most important thing to an actress's success. You can sing like Flagstad or dance like Pavlova or act like Bernhardt, but if you haven't personality you will never be a real star. Personality is the glitter that sends your little gleam across the footlights and the orchestra pit into that big black space where the audience is."

Mae West, *Goodness Had Nothing to Do with It*

───────── ★ ─────────

"Judy's uncanny knowledge of showmanship impressed me more than ever as I worked with her."

Fred Astaire, *Steps in Time*

───────── ★ ─────────

Judy Garland's film career spanned the years 1936 to 1963. In twenty-eight years, she appeared in thirty-two major films, two sound-tracks, and a series of short subjects.

There are artists who have had longer careers. There are those whose work is generally more critically revered. There are those whose contemporary popularity was as great or greater. But there are few whose range was so wide, who could sing, dance, and act with equal facility. There are few who excelled at both musical comedy and drama, who could move comfortably from the broad comedy or slapstick routines of an *Easter Parade* or *The Pirate* to the intensity, depth, and dramatic skill of *A Star Is Born* or a *Judgment at Nuremberg*. There are few who could move an audience with humor, whimsy, tenderness, pathos, and tragedy —in a variety of roles or within the space of one—the way Garland could.

Judy Garland quite literally grew up on the screen in public view. She became a "star" at seventeen with *The Wizard of Oz,* but her talents were clear from the beginning. In *Every Sunday*, a Metro short to test audience reaction to newcomers Judy Garland and Deanna Durbin, her telegenic charm and ability to sell a song were obvious. They kept her a contract at MGM when it was initially in doubt.

But Mayer and company had some difficulty in deciding how best to use Judy Garland now that they had kept her. Initially, they simply lent her to Twentieth Century-Fox for *Pigskin Parade*. It was only with strong support from Roger Edens, Judy's musical mentor, and Ida Koverman, Mayer's personal assistant, that she finally got noticed at home and was given an opportunity in *Broadway Melody of 1938*. Her facial expressions and "business" with a lollipop draws audience attention to her in a scene otherwise dominated by the redoubtable Sophie Tucker; she danced well with Buddy Ebsen; and her "Dear Mr. Gable" was a hit.

But having showcased singing, dancing, and acting talent, the studio found no clear direction. In *Thoroughbreds Don't Cry, Everybody Sing, Listen, Darling,* and *Love Finds Andy Hardy,* she was given flyweight material and tentatively teamed with Freddie Bartholomew, Ronald Sinclair, and Mickey Rooney. The teaming with Rooney clicked.

After *The Wizard of Oz,* MGM had a new star—and a new team and formula. Her next three pictures were with Mickey Rooney. True to Mayer's view of her as his ugly "little hunchback," Judy Garland played second fiddle and a puppy-love role supporting a not always interested Mickey Rooney in *Babes in Arms, Andy Hardy Meets Debutante,* and *Strike Up the Band.* Garland's charm, singing talent, and

ability to add depth and spice to her roles through facial expressions and tones of voice saved her good-pal, good-sport characters from being a hazard to diabetics.

Little Nellie Kelly, with George Murphy, was Garland's first adult role. It was also her first solo starring vehicle. And MGM was back in the quandary of what to do with Judy Garland. *Ziegfeld Girl* emphasized an artificial glamour and starred her with Lana Turner and Hedy Lamarr. In *Life Begins for Andy Hardy* and *Babes on Broadway,* the studio tried returning to its former formula, one that its talented and increasingly lovely star had outgrown.

For Me and My Gal reteamed her with George Murphy and introduced Gene Kelly. It was clear that Judy was an acceptable object of male interest. Further, she could dance and hold her own when teamed with professional dancers. So, in *Presenting Lily Mars,* MGM included a long production sequence at the end of the film, reminiscent of a Fred Astaire–Ginger Rogers routine, to see if Judy Garland's real strength was in her feet rather than her singing voice and acting talent. The experiment was not repeated. In fact, she lampooned this type of routine elegantly with Fred Astaire in *Easter Parade.*

In 1943, seven years after making *Every Sunday,* Metro finally found the formula for Garland's screen alchemy. Judy Garland was an unusually gifted singer. Judy Garland could dance (although ballroom dancing was not her forte). Judy Garland could act. She communicated vulnerability and strength, wistfulness and snap. She was an attractive woman. And Judy

Garland had a telegenically infectious sense of humor and fun.

It came together in *Girl Crazy*.

Girl Crazy was a major transition movie in Judy Garland's MGM film career. She finally had a plot, script, and songs that supported her unerring instinct for balancing romance and humor, wistful vulnerability and broad comedy. In *Girl Crazy*, Mickey chased Judy. And her calculated and restrained disdain for him in the "Bidin' My Time" and "Could You Use Me?" numbers made the scenes hers and hers alone despite Rooney's frenetic mugging. They also gave her, for the first time, a chance to use her dancer's skill and grace to comic effect. The effect was not lost on the studio.

The six major musicals Judy Garland made between *Girl Crazy* and leaving Metro in 1950 relied increasingly on her ability to alternate delicacy and tenderness with humor and physical comedy. In *Meet Me in St. Louis, The Harvey Girls, The Pirate, Easter Parade, In the Good Old Summertime,* and *Summer Stock,* there was always a love story. There were always touching ballads. But in each successive film, there was a more generous dose of sheer physical fun. Indeed, in these movies, Judy's dancing enhanced the comedy as often as the romance.

In *Meet Me in St. Louis,* she beats up a bewildered Tom Drake, whom she believes has harmed her youngest sister, and she endures a series of enthusiastically unskilled partners at the Christmas Ball. One of the visual highlights of *The Harvey Girls* is a full-scale brawl between Judy and the Harvey girls and the saloon girls. Brawling was continued in *The Pirate,*

where Judy throws everything that isn't nailed down at a beleaguered Gene Kelly. And their campy "Be a Clown" finale, in full clown make-up, became famous on its own and as a precursor to the "A Couple of Swells" number in *Easter Parade.* The latter, in fact, became one of Garland's best-remembered numbers.

In the Good Old Summertime relied less on musical sequences and broad routines, being closer to a straight comedy performance. But here, too, the nonballad intervals, particularly "I Don't Care," contained an element of burlesque. In *Summer Stock,* MGM planned on revisiting the "Be a Clown"/"A Couple of Swells" successes with "Heavenly Music." Unfortunately, Garland was too ill to perform it, and Phil Silvers took her place. There is no hint of illness, however, in Judy's rousing competitive dance sequence with Gene Kelly at the barn dance. And it is this routine that delineates her character as essentially unconventional, high-spirited, and good-humored, effectively lending some credibility to the rather tired plot development.

Without question, Metro had found another formula that worked. Put Judy Garland in the role of a likable and attractive woman, give her songs and a romance, and leaven the mix with a mischievous sense of humor.

It was these qualities that encouraged Metro to purchase the film rights for *Annie Get Your Gun* for her and to plan on putting her in *Royal Wedding* when June Allyson had to drop out due to pregnancy. Existing footage of Garland doing the "Doin' What Comes Natur'lly" and "I'm an Indian, Too" numbers and her rendition of "How Could You Believe Me?" with Bing Crosby on his radio show in 1951 indicate that the roles were a natural for her.

Unhappily, Judy's illnesses were causing increasing delays on the set at the same time that the studio's patience was disappearing. She was fired from MGM in 1950, after fourteen years and twenty-seven feature-length films.

At twenty-eight, Judy Garland was a battle-scarred veteran of Hollywood. She did not appear in another film for four years.

When she did reappear on screen, it was in *A Star Is Born,* with James Mason, a film over which, for the first time, she exerted significant creative control. It was produced by Transcona Enterprises, a company owned by Garland and her husband, Sid Luft.

She had been interested in a remake of the Janet Gaynor–Fredric March film for over a decade. In 1942, she had played the Gaynor role opposite Walter Pidgeon for "Lux Radio Theatre." But MGM had been unwilling to allow her the part on the screen. The studio felt that the public would never accept Judy Garland as the wife of an alcoholic.

In 1954, what many consider a cinematic masterpiece was released. Garland's performance was hailed as the greatest one-woman show in modern film history.

Elements of her performance were presaged during her Metro career. In *The Clock,* with Robert Walker, her one purely dramatic, nonsinging role at MGM, the essential qualities she showed in *The Wizard of Oz* had grown to maturity. Dorothy's wide-eyed wonder became a tremulous hopefulness, tinged with an adult knowledge that most hopes never materialize, and the waif's wistfulness became a woman's vulnerability. In *The Ziegfeld Follies of 1946,* her "Great Lady Has an Interview" segment was a witty and skilled piece of occupational satire.

But nothing she had done at MGM predicted the controlled intensity, depth, and finely honed precision of observation and characterization that Judy Garland brought to *A Star Is Born.* The MGM formula elements were all there in the first half of the film. The production number sequence, "Someone at Last," was certainly in the tradition of "Great Lady Has an Interview." But the satire was sharpened in *Star.* There was not only caricature; there were almost literal replays of the Hollywood commonplace that became parody in context. The make-up department scene, for example, was virtually an exact description of the studio's approach to Garland's looks early in her career and her wardrobe tests for *The Wizard of Oz.*

Garland used subtle bits to bring a realistic edge to her character. The look in her eyes and the set of her jaw, for instance, when, early on, she explains to James Mason that she will never again wait on tables shows an element of steel in Esther/Vicki that makes her later willingness to renounce her career for him an act of strength rather than sentimentality. It is that strength, too, that makes the impotent desperation she conveys in the dressing room scene with Charles Bickford almost overwhelming.

A Star Is Born is a tragedy in the classical sense of a character doomed by an internal, fatal flaw. Garland's ability to play off the role of a tragic character while fighting the inevitability of the situation makes her performance profound.

Just as her voice had deepened and acquired new layers of richness over the years, so, too, her ability to evoke multi-leveled characterizations had ripened. Where her later Metro performances are alluring for the effortless sense of fun they convey, Garland's post-MGM dramatic performances are compelling for the sense of the real.

In *Judgment at Nuremberg,* she played a woman being virtually reaccused and re-tried for a Nazi-defined crime of intimacy with a Jew. The role was a supporting one, but critical to the film. For without the horror, the pain, the outrage, and the courage that she evokes, her former Nazi judge's unwillingness to continue his defense would have been, quite simply, un-believable.

Garland's last film, *I Could Go On Sing-ing,* with Dirk Bogarde, had quasi-auto-biographical aspects—a famous American singer on a concert tour in England—that imbued her performance with concentrated discernment. There is an almost cinéma vérité feel to the scene in which she stands behind the curtains readying herself to appear onstage at the Palladium. The growing sense of focused energy is palpable. And her angry refusal to appear onstage despite a full house is fully evocative of the complex of conflicting responsibilities, needs, and emotions that assault a public figure.

Bogarde, commenting on the scene in a Garland retrospective, said: "That is the actual woman saying the actual truth. Acting it—brilliantly—and being it, which is a very different thing. . . . She was . . . capable, I think, of being one of the most profound actresses that we had."

The songs in the following section are designed as a fun guide for fans. An attempt was made to note not only all the songs she sang or reprised but song snippets and short melodic interludes that aren't technically songs—for example, "Lions and Tigers and Bears" from The Wizard of Oz. In the occasional instance where scholars might argue over a precise title, common usage was followed for easy recognition.

1 The Big Revue

Warner Bros.
Released: 1929
Running time: One-reel short
Cast includes the Gumm Sisters singing in the chorus and featured "In the Sunny South" sequence.
Songs: "That's the Good Old Sunny South"

2 A Holiday in Storyland

First National Vitaphone
Released: 1930
Running time: One-reel short
Cast: Vitaphone Kiddies
Songs: "Blue Butterfly"

3 The Wedding of Jack and Jill

First National Vitaphone
Released: 1930
Running time: One-reel short
Cast: Vitaphone Kiddies
Songs: "Hang On to a Rainbow"

4 Bubbles

First National Vitaphone
Released: 1930
Running time: One-reel short
Directed by Roy Mack
Music and lyrics by N. K. Jerome, Harold Berg
Cast: Vitaphone Kiddies
Songs: "Lady Luck"

5 La Fiesta de Santa Barbara

Metro-Goldwyn-Mayer
Released: 1936
Running time: Two-reel short
A "shop window" film featuring the Gumm Sisters.
Songs: "La Cucaracha" (The Gumm Sisters)

6 Every Sunday

Metro-Goldwyn-Mayer
Released: 1936
Running time: One-reel short
Written by Mauri Grashin
Directed by Felix E. Feist
Screenplay by Mauri Grashin

CAST

Judy Garland
Deanna Durbin

SYNOPSIS

Two girls decide to save the weekly bandshell concerts the town council wants to shut down because of poor attendance.

SONGS

unidentified aria (Deanna Durbin)
"Americana" (Judy Garland)
"Americana" reprise (Judy Garland, Deanna Durbin)

ADDENDA

★ Judy Garland's and Deanna Durbin's official film debut.

RECORDINGS

"Americana" is available on *The Wit and Wonder of Judy Garland,* DRG SL 5179 (33⅓).

Deanna Durbin and Judy Garland preparing for the Band Concert in *Every Sunday*.

7 Pigskin Parade

20th Century-Fox
Released: November 1936
Running time: 95 minutes
Produced by Darryl F. Zanuck
Directed by David Butler
Screenplay by Harry Tugend, Jack Yellen, William Conselman, based on a story by Art Sheekman, Nat Perrin, Mark Kelly
Music and lyrics by Lew Pollack, Sidney Miller, The Yacht Club Boys
Musical direction: David Buttolph
Photography: Arthur Miller
Editor: Irene Morra

CAST

Amos Dodd .... Stuart Erwin
Bessie Winters .... Patsy Kelly
Slug Winters .... Jack Haley
Chip Carson .... John Downs
Laura Watson .... Betty Grable
Sally Saxon .... Arline Judge
Ginger Jones .... Dixie Dunbar
Sairy Dodd .... Judy Garland
Tommy Baker ... Anthony (Tony) Martin
with

The Yacht Club Boys	Fred Kohler, Jr.
Grady Sutton	Elisha Cook, Jr.
Eddie Nugent	Julius Tannen
Pat Flaherty	Si Jenks

SYNOPSIS

A campus musical. A hillbilly football team from Texas is mistakenly invited to New Haven to play against Yale.

SONGS

"T.S.U. Alma Mater" (chorus)
"You're Slightly Terrific" (Tony Martin)
"Woo Woo" (The Yacht Club Boys, Judy Garland)
"We'd Rather Be in College" (The Yacht Club Boys)
"Down with Everything" (Elisha Cook, Jr., The Yacht Club Boys, chorus)
"Balboa" (Judy Garland)
"You Do the Darndest Things, Baby" (Jack Haley)
"The Texas Tornado" (Judy Garland)
"It's Love I'm After" (Judy Garland)
"The Texas Sunshine" (The Yacht Club Boys)

ADDENDA

★ This was Judy Garland's feature film debut. She received ninth billing.

★ *Pigskin Parade* was Garland's only loan-out during her career at MGM.
★ "Hold That Bulldog" was recorded by Judy Garland but deleted from the final print.
★ *Pigskin Parade* was one of the top moneymakers of the year.
★ In 1969, CBS News produced a special report on the first 100 years of football. The program included a film clip of Judy Garland in *Pigskin Parade*.

AWARDS/NOMINATIONS

Stuart Erwin was nominated for a Best Supporting Actor Academy Award. This was a new category for 1936.

RECORDINGS

The soundtrack for *Pigskin Parade* is available on Pilgrim 4000 (33⅓). "It's Love I'm After," "Balboa," and "The Texas Tornado" are available on *The Judy Garland Scrapbook,* Star-Tone ST 208 (33⅓).

CONTEMPORARY COMMENTS

Variety, November 18, 1936
In the newcomer category is Judy Garland, about 12 or 13 now, about whom the West Coast has been enthusing as a vocal find. . . .She's a cute, not too pretty but pleasingly fetching personality, who certainly knows how to sell a pop.

8 Broadway Melody of 1938

Metro-Goldwyn-Mayer
Released: August 1937
Running time: 113 minutes
Produced by Jack Cummings

Judy Garland and Sophie Tucker in *Broadway Melody of 1938.*

Directed by Roy Del Ruth

Screenplay by Jack McGowan, based on a story by Jack McGowan and Sid Silvers

Music and lyrics by Nacio Herb Brown and Arthur Freed

Musical presentations: Merrill Pye

Music arrangements: Roger Edens

Music direction: Georgie Stoll

Vocal and orchestral arrangements: Leo Arnaud and Murray Cutter

Dance ensembles by Dave Gould

Photography: William Daniels

Editor: Blanche Sewell

Art direction: Cedric Gibbons

CAST

Steve Raleigh .... Robert Taylor
Sally Lee .... Eleanor Powell
Sonny Ledford .... George Murphy
Caroline Whipple .... Binnie Barnes
Alice Clayton .... Sophie Tucker
Peter Trot .... Buddy Ebsen
Betty Clayton .... Judy Garland
Nicki Simonini .... Charles Igor Gorin
Herman Whipple ...... Raymond Walburn
Duffy .... Robert Benchley
with

Willie Howard   Charles Grapewin
Robert Wildhack   Billy Gilbert
Barnett Parker   Helen Troy

SYNOPSIS

All-star revue. What story line there is concerns a young woman's dreams of saving her racehorse from a villainous owner and becoming a star on Broadway.

SONGS

"Yours and Mine" (behind the titles) (Judy Garland)

"Largo al Factotum" aria from *Barber in Seville* (Charles Igor Gorin)

"Follow in My Footsteps" (Eleanor Powell, George Murphy, Buddy Ebsen)

"Yours and Mine" (Eleanor Powell)

"Everybody Sing" (Judy Garland, Sophie Tucker, chorus)

"Some of These Days" (Sophie Tucker)

"I'm Feeling Like a Million" (Eleanor Powell, George Murphy)

"Dear Mr. Gable (You Made Me Love You)" (Judy Garland)

"Yours and Mine" (danced by Eleanor Powell and George Murphy)

"Yours and Mine" (danced by Judy Garland and Buddy Ebsen)

"Your Broadway and My Broadway" (Sophie Tucker, chorus)

"Broadway Rhythm" (Eleanor Powell [dancing], chorus)

ADDENDA

★ *Broadway Melody of 1938* was Garland's MGM feature debut. A previously completed scenario and screenplay were reworked to accommodate her talents when, at the last minute, she was put into the picture.

★ Garland's "You Made Me Love You" is generally considered the highlight of the film, and the song became a permanent part of her repertoire.

★ "I'm Feeling Like a Million" was recorded by Judy but cut from the film prior to release.

★ *Broadway Melody of 1938* was one of the top moneymakers of the year.

RECORDINGS

"Dear Mr. Gable" was released in 1937 on Decca 1463 (78).

"Everybody Sing" was released in the same year on Decca 1332 (78) and Decca 1432 (78).

The complete soundtrack, including "I'm Feeling Like a Million," is available on Motion Picture Soundtracks International MPT 3 (33⅓). "I'm Feeling Like a Million" is also available on *Cut! Out-Takes from Hollywood's Greatest Musicals,* vol. 3, Out-Take Records OFT 3 (33⅓).

CONTEMPORARY COMMENTS

The New York Times, September 3, 1937
There are individual successes in the film which are more successful than the film itself: . . . the amazing precocity of Judy Garland—Metro's challenge to Deanna Durbin.

Miss Garland particularly has a long tour-de-force in which she addresses lyrical apostrophes to a picture of Clark Gable. The idea and words are almost painfully silly, yet Judy falters no more than Miss Shearer doing the balcony scene; she put it over, in fact, with a bang.
—Bosley Crowther

Variety, August 18, 1937
No use getting into the details until Sophie Tucker and Judy Garland are disposed of. . . . You can hear what the others are saying, but Miss Tucker is the only one you see. . . . Then she steps back and pushes Judy Garland, still in her teens, into the camera foreground. Young

Right: Judy serenades Mickey Rooney and Ronald Sinclair in *Thoroughbreds Don't Cry.*

Miss Garland gives them "Everybody Sing," with a Tucker undertone, and it's worth a letter to the homefolks. . . . Most of the rest is just filler in between the Tucker and the Garland numbers.

---

9 Thoroughbreds Don't Cry

Metro-Goldwyn-Mayer
Released: November 1937
Running time: 80 minutes
Produced by Harry Rapf
Directed by Alfred E. Green
Screenplay by Lawrence Hazard, based on a story by Eleanore Griffin and J. Walter Ruben

Music and lyrics by Nacio Herb Brown and Arthur Freed
Photography: Leonard Smith
Editor: Elmo Vernon

CAST

Cricket West . . . . Judy Garland
Tim Donahue . . . . Mickey Rooney
Mother Ralph . . . . Sophie Tucker
Sir Peter Calverton . . . . . . C. Aubrey Smith
Roger Calverton . . . . Ronald Sinclair
Hilda . . . . Helen Troy
"Click" Donahue . . . . Charles D. Brown
Dink Reid . . . . Frankie Darro
"Doc" Godfrey . . . . Henry Kolker
Wilkins . . . . Forrester Harvey

SYNOPSIS

An English boy tries to win an important race with his horse.

SONGS

"Got A Pair of New Shoes" (Judy Garland)

ADDENDA

★ "Sun Showers," sung by Judy Garland, was recorded but not used.
★ This was the first teaming of Judy Garland and Mickey Rooney.
★ This was also the first feature to give Garland top billing.

CONTEMPORARY COMMENTS

The New York Times, November 26, 1937
Judy Garland is the puppy love interest who tosses off some scorchy rhythm singing.

—Bosley Crowther

---

10 **Christmas Trailer**

Metro-Goldwyn-Mayer
Released: 1937
Running time: One-reel short
A ten-minute short to be run in the theaters during the holidays.
Garland song: "Silent Night"

---

11 **Everybody Sing**

Metro-Goldwyn-Mayer
Released: February 1938
Running time: 80 minutes
Produced by Harry Rapf
Directed by Edwin L. Marin

Fanny Brice, Allan Jones, and Judy Garland featured in a publicity release for *Everybody Sing* in *Lowe's Weekly* (movie playbill, March 31, 1938).

Screenplay by Florence Ryerson and Edgar Allan Woolf, with additional dialogue by James Gruen
Music and lyrics by Bronislau Kaper and Walter Jurmann, Gus Kahn, Bert Kalmar and Harry Ruby
Musical interpolations and vocal arrangements: Roger Edens
Musical direction: Dr. William Axt
Photography: Joseph Ruttenberg
Editor: William S. Gray

CAST

Ricky Saboni . . . . .Allan Jones
Judy Bellaire . . . . Judy Garland
Olga Chekaloff . . . . .Fanny Brice
Hillary Bellaire . . . . Reginald Owen
Diana Bellaire. . . . . Billie Burke
Jerrold Hope . . . . .Reginald Gardiner
Sylvia Bellaire . . . . Lynne Carver

Hillary's secretary	Helen Troy
John Fleming	Monty Woolley
Boris	Adia Kuznetzoff
Signor Vittorino	Henry Armetta
Mme. La Brouchette	Michelette Burani
Miss Colvin	Mary Forbes

SYNOPSIS

A household full of theater people whose fortunes are on the wane are given a chance to shine again through the efforts of the younger daughter.

SONGS

"Swing, Mr. Mendelssohn, Swing" (Judy Garland, chorus)

"The First Thing in the Morning" (Allan Jones)

"Cosi Cosa" (Allan Jones, chorus)

"Down On Melody Farm" (Judy Garland)

"Bus Sequence" (Judy Garland, Allan Jones, Lynne Carver, Reginald Gardiner, chorus)

"The One I Love" (Allan Jones)

"Quainty Dainty Me" (Fanny Brice)

"The Show Must Go On" (Allan Jones)

"Why? Because" (Judy Garland, Fanny Brice)

"I Wanna Swing" (Judy Garland)

ADDENDA

★ The title originally assigned to this film was *The Ugly Duckling*.

RECORDINGS

The soundtrack from *Everybody Sing* is available on Pilgrim 4000 (33⅓).

CONTEMPORARY COMMENTS

The New York Times, March 11, 1938
Judy Garland of the rhythm, writin' and 'rithmetic age is a superb vocal technician, despite her not exactly underemphasized immaturity.

—Bosley Crowther

Variety, January 26, 1938
The diminutive Judy Garland takes a long leap forward to stardom. She has what it takes.

12 Listen, Darling

Metro-Goldwyn-Mayer
Released: October 1938
Running time: 70 minutes
Produced by Jack Cummings
Directed by Edwin L. Marin
Screenplay by Elaine Ryan and Anne Morrison Chapin, based on a story by Katherine Brush
Music and lyrics by Al Hoffman, Al Lewis and Murray Mencher, Joseph McCarthy, Milton Ager and James F. Henley
Musical arrangements: Roger Edens
Musical direction: Georgie Stoll
Photography: Charles Lawton, Jr.
Editor: Blanche Sewell
Art direction: Cedric Gibbons

CAST

Buzz Mitchell	Freddie Bartholomew
Pinki Wingate	Judy Garland
Dottie Wingate	Mary Astor
Richard Thurlow	Walter Pidgeon
J. J. Slattery	Alan Hale
Billie Wingate	Scotty Beckett
Abercrombie	Barnett Parker
Uncle Joe	Charley Grapewin

SYNOPSIS

Two children, disapproving of their widowed mother's choice of a new father for them, set off with her on a cross-country search to find her a more suitable partner.

SONGS

"Zing! Went the Strings of My Heart" (Judy Garland)

"Ten Pins in the Sky" (Judy Garland)

"On the Bumpy Road to Love" (Judy Garland, with Freddie Bartholomew, Mary Astor, Walter Pidgeon, Scotty Beckett)

RECORDINGS

"Zing! Went the Strings of My Heart" was released in 1939 on Decca 18543 (78).

"Ten Pins in the Sky" was released in 1938 on Decca 2017 (78) and Brunswick 02656 (78).

CONTEMPORARY COMMENTS

The New York Times, November 24, 1938
Besides being a charming little miss, Judy Garland has a fresh young voice which she uses happily.

—Frank S. Nugent

Variety, October 19, 1938
Handicapped by an illogical and unconvincing story, initial effort of Metro to team Judy Garland and Freddie Bartholomew is a light-weight offering . . . Has little to offer aside from three good song numbers handled capably by Miss Garland which have been nicely routined in the action.

13 Love Finds Andy Hardy

Metro-Goldwyn-Mayer
Released: July 1938
Running time: 90 minutes
Produced by Carey Wilson (although not credited on screen)
Directed by George B. Seitz
Screenplay by William Ludwig, based on stories by Vivien R. Bretherton and characters created by Aurania Rouverol
Music and lyrics by Mack Gordon and Harry Revel, Roger Edens
Vocal arrangements: Roger Edens
Musical arrangements: David Snell
Photography: Lester White
Editor: Ben Lewis

CAST

Judge James Hardy	Lewis Stone
Andy Hardy	Mickey Rooney
Betsy Booth	Judy Garland
Marian Hardy	Cecilia Parker
Mrs. Hardy	Fay Holden
Polly Benedict	Ann Rutherford
Aunt Milly	Betty Ross Clarke
Cynthia	Lana Turner
Augusta	Marie Blake
Dennis Hunt	Don Castle
Jimmy McMahon	Gene Reynolds
Beezy	George Breakston
Peter Dugan	Raymond Hatton

SYNOPSIS

Andy Hardy's romantic life is complicated by the need to earn the final eight dollars he needs to purchase a car in time for the Christmas dance.

SONGS

"It Never Rains, But It Pours" (Judy
    Garland)
"Meet the Beat of My Heart" (Judy
    Garland)
"In Between" (Judy Garland)

ADDENDA

★ "Easy to Love," sung by Judy Garland,
    was cut from the film prior to release.
★ "Bei Mir Bist Du Schoen," sung by Judy
    Garland, was cut from the film prior to
    release.
★ This fourth installment of the Hardy
    family saga outgrossed 1938 releases
    that cost ten times as much to produce.

RECORDINGS

"It Never Rains, But It Pours" was released
    in 1938 on Decca 2017 (78).
"In Between" was released in 1939 on
    Decca 15045 (78).
"Bei Mir Bist Du Schoen" is available on
    *Judy Garland: The Golden Years at
    MGM,* MGM SDP 1-2, 2-record set
    (33⅓), and *The Judy Garland Story,*
    vol. 2: *The Hollywood Years,* MGM E
    4005P (33⅓).
"Easy to Love" is available on *Cut! Out-
    Takes from Hollywood's Greatest Musi-
    cals,* vol. 1, DRG SBL 12586 (33⅓).
"Meet the Beat of My Heart" is available
    on *Cut! Out-Takes from Hollywood's
    Greatest Musicals,* vol. 3, Out-Take
    Records OFT 3 (33⅓).

CONTEMPORARY COMMENTS

Variety, July 13, 1938
Newcomer to the Hardy group of players
. . . is Judy Garland, who tops off a slick
performance by singing three good
songs. . . . Based on her showing, they
will have to find a permanent place for
Miss Garland in the future Hardys.

---

14 The Wizard of Oz

Metro-Goldwyn-Mayer
Released: August 1939
Running time: 100 minutes
Produced by Mervyn LeRoy
Directed by Victor Fleming
Screenplay by Noel Langley, Florence
    Ryerson, and Edgar Allan Woolf,
    adapted from the book by L. Frank
    Baum
Music by Harold Arlen
Lyrics by E. Y. Harburg
Musical adaptation by Herbert Stothart
Musical numbers: Bobby Connolly
Special effects: Arnold Gillespie
Photography: Harold Rosson
Editor: Blanche Sewell
Art direction: Cedric Gibbons, William
    Horning

CAST

Dorothy . . . . Judy Garland
Professor Marvel/The Wizard
    of Oz . . . . Frank Morgan
Hunk/The Scarecrow . . . . Ray Bolger
Zeke/The Cowardly Lion . . . . Bert Lahr
Hickory/The Tin Man . . . . Jack Haley
Miss Gulch/The Wicked Witch
    of the West . . . . Margaret Hamilton
Glinda . . . . Billie Burke
Uncle Henry . . . . Charley Grapewin
Auntie Em . . . . Clara Blandick
Nikko . . . . Pat Walshe
The Singer Midgets
Toto

SYNOPSIS

Dorothy, a Kansas farm girl caught in a tornado, finds herself stranded in Munchkin Land. Having been told that only the Wizard of Oz can help her return home, she and her dog, Toto, set off for Emerald City to ask his help. On the way, she meets and befriends the Scarecrow, the Tin Man, and the Cowardly Lion as the Wicked Witch tries to prevent her from reaching the Wizard and returning home with the ruby slippers.

SONGS

"Over the Rainbow" (Judy Garland)

"Come Out, Come Out, Wherever You Are" (Billie Burke)

"It Really Was No Miracle" (Judy Garland)

"Ding Dong, the Witch Is Dead" (Judy Garland, Billie Burke, The Munchkins)

"We Welcome You to Munchkin Land" (The Munchkins)

"Follow the Yellow Brick Road" (Judy Garland, The Munchkins)

"We're Off to See the Wizard" (Judy Garland, Ray Bolger, Jack Haley, Bert Lahr)

"If I Only Had a Brain (a Heart, the Nerve)" (Ray Bolger, Jack Haley, Bert Lahr)

"Lions and Tigers and Bears" (Judy Garland, Ray Bolger, Jack Haley)

"You're Out of the Woods" (Chorus)

"The Merry Old Land of Oz" (Chorus)

"If I Were King of the Forest" (Bert Lahr)

ADDENDA

★ MGM wanted Shirley Temple to play Dorothy. An attempt to borrow her from Twentieth Century-Fox failed, and Judy Garland was given the role.

★ MGM originally wanted Jerome Kern, not Harold Arlen, to write the music. Kern, however, suffered a mild heart attack and stroke before he started, and his doctors forbade him to work for several months.

★ *The Wizard of Oz* was MGM's most expensive production in its fifteen-year history. Aljean Harmetz, in *The Making of the Wizard of Oz,* reports that there were 9,200 actors, 3,200 costume designs, 8,428 separate make-ups, and 68 sets.

★ It was one of the first films shot in Technicolor. The estimated lighting cost if it had been shot in black and white was $86,000. The actual cost was over $226,000. In all, it cost nearly $3,000,000 to produce.

★ The Munchkins' voices were achieved by recording speaking voices slowly and speeding up the playback during filming. Ken Darby, the vocal arranger, remembers two groups as recording the Munchkins' vocals: the King's Men Quartet and the Debutantes. However, Steven Cox in *The Munchkins Remember* cites the MGM Daily Music Report for December 15, 1938, "which seems to indicate that the little people themselves were involved in the dubbing."

★ It is generally agreed that after the preview L. B. Mayer removed "Over the Rainbow" from the film. Arthur Freed is now credited with forcing the song's return; Mervyn LeRoy, who had more studio clout, took credit at the time.

★ On preview, *Variety* reported that " 'Oz' is aimed for the masses and will require heavy advance buildup in all spots and out of routine approach." (8/16/39)

★ "The Jitterbug," originally with Judy Garland, Ray Bolger, Buddy Ebsen, and Bert Lahr, was filmed with Jack Haley replacing Ebsen, but was cut from the film after the preview.

★ *The Wizard of Oz* has not been off release since 1939, the longest continual exposure of any picture ever made.

★ According to John Lahr in his biography of his father, *Notes on a Cowardly Lion,* after *The Wizard of Oz,* Jack Haley and Bert Lahr were released from MGM studios. Lahr's agent, Louis Shurr, had told Lahr " 'Metro [is] going to stop making musicals at the moment for financial reasons. They're dropping your contract as well as Haley's. . . .' "

★ The first television showing of *The Wizard of Oz* was on CBS on November 3, 1956, on "Ford Star Jubilee." (Judy Garland inaugurated "Ford Star Jubilee" series with her first TV special on September 24, 1955.)

AWARDS/NOMINATIONS

"Over the Rainbow" won an Academy Award for best song of 1939. Herbert Stothart won for the best original score. *The Wizard of Oz* was nominated for Best Picture but lost to *Gone with the Wind.* Cedric Gibbons and William Horning were nominated for Art Direction and Arnold Gillespie and Douglas Shearer for Special Effects (a new category). Judy Garland won a special Oscar for "an outstanding performance by a juvenile." She received a miniature statuette, the only Academy award she ever received.

RECORDINGS

"Over the Rainbow" was originally released on Decca 2672 (78), MGM KGC 166 (45), Decca 2-3962 (78), Decca 9-23961 (45).

"The Jitterbug" was released in 1939 on Decca 2672 (78).

The Wizard of Oz album was released on Decca DL 8387 (33⅓). It is available on CBS AK 45356 (CD); the CD includes "The Jitterbug."

CONTEMPORARY COMMENTS

The New York Times, August 18, 1939
Judy Garland's Dorothy is a pert and fresh faced miss with the wonder-lit eyes of a believer in fairy tales.

—Frank S. Nugent

Variety, August 16, 1939
Judy Garland as the little girl is an appealing figure as the wandering waif.

15 Babes in Arms

Metro-Goldwyn-Mayer
Released: September 1939
Running time: 91 minutes
Produced by Arthur Freed
Directed by Busby Berkeley
Screenplay by Jack McGowan and Kay Van Riper, based on a play by Richard Rodgers and Lorenz Hart
Music and lyrics by Richard Rodgers and Lorenz Hart, Nacio Herb Brown and Arthur Freed, and Harold Arlen and E. Y. Harburg
Musical adaptation: Roger Edens
Musical direction: Georgie Stoll

Orchestral arrangements by Leo Arnaud and George Bassman
Photography: Ray June
Editor: Frank Sullivan
Art direction: Cedric Gibbons

CAST

Mickey Moran	Mickey Rooney
Patsy Barton	Judy Garland
Joe Moran	Charles Winninger
Judge Black	Guy Kibbee
Rosalie Essex	June Preisser
Florrie Moran	Grace Hayes
Molly Moran	Betty Jaynes
Don Brice	Douglas McPhail
Jeff Steele	Rand Brooks
Dody Martini	Leni Lynn
Bobs	John Sheffield
Mr. Maddox	Henry Hull
William	Barnett Parker
Mrs. Barton	Ann Shoemaker
Martha Steele	Margaret Hamilton
Mr. Essex	Joseph Crehan
Brice	George McKay
Shaw	Henry Roquemore
Mrs. Brice	Lelah Tyler

SYNOPSIS

Vaudevillians past their prime attempt to revive their careers by taking a show on the road. While they are out of town, their children decide to stage a revue to prove their talents and ameliorate their parents' financial difficulties.

SONGS

"Ja Da" (Charles Winninger)
"Good Morning" (Judy Garland, Mickey Rooney)
"I Like Opera, I Like Swing" (Judy Garland, Betty Jaynes)
"You Are My Lucky Star" (Betty Jaynes)
"Figaro" (Judy Garland)
"Broadway Rhythm" (Judy Garland, Betty Jaynes)
"Babes in Arms" (Judy Garland, Mickey Rooney, Douglas McPhail, chorus)
"Where or When" (Douglas McPhail, Betty Jaynes, Judy Garland)
"I Cried for You" (Judy Garland)
"My Daddy Was a Minstrel Man" (Judy Garland)
"Downtown Strutters' Ball" (Chorus)
"Oh! Susannah" (Judy Garland, Mickey Rooney, chorus)
"Minstrel Routine" (Douglas McPhail, Mickey Rooney, Judy Garland)
"Ida, Sweet as Apple Cider" (Mickey Rooney)
"Moonlight Bay" (Chorus)
"I'm Just Wild about Harry" (Judy Garland, Mickey Rooney, chorus)
"God's Country" (Judy Garland, Mickey Rooney, Douglas McPhail, Betty Jaynes, chorus)

ADDENDA

★ *Babes in Arms* started the "Come on, let's put on a show!" cycle.
★ *Babes in Arms* was the first film produced by Arthur Freed and the first directed in its entirety for MGM by Busby Berkeley.
★ It was a top moneymaker for 1939.

AWARDS/NOMINATIONS

Mickey Rooney was nominated for Best Actor for his role in *Babes in Arms*. Roger Edens and Georgie Stoll were nominated for Best Score.

RECORDINGS

"Figaro" was released in 1939 on Brunswick 2953 (78) (U.K.).

"I'm Just Wild about Harry" is available on *Judy Garland: From the Decca Vaults,* MCA 907 (33⅓).

The soundtrack for *Babes in Arms* is available on Curtain Calls CC 100/6-7 (33⅓).

CONTEMPORARY COMMENTS

The New York Times, October 20, 1939

Judy Garland . . . does a beautiful imitation of Mrs. Roosevelt's broadcasting manner.

—Bosley Crowther

Variety, September 20, 1939

Despite the Rooney dominance throughout, there are several sterling performances by the younger talent. Judy Garland most effectively carries the adolescent romantic interest opposite him.

---

16 Andy Hardy Meets Debutante

Metro-Goldwyn-Mayer
Released: July 1940
Running time: 87 minutes
Produced by Carey Wilson (uncredited)
Directed by George B. Seitz
Screenplay by Annalee Whitmore and Thomas Selier, based on characters created by Aurania Rouverol
Photography: Sidney Wagner, Charles Lawton
Editor: Harold F. Kress

CAST

Judge Hardy	Lewis Stone
Andy Hardy	Mickey Rooney
Marian Hardy	Cecilia Parker
Mrs. Hardy	Fay Holden
Betsy Booth	Judy Garland
Polly Benedict	Ann Rutherford
Dyanne Fowler	Diana Lewis
Beezy	George Breakston
Aunt Milly	Sara Haden

with

Harry Tyler	Cy Kendall
Addison Richards	George Lessey
Gladys Blake	Clyde Willson

SYNOPSIS

Andy Hardy flirts with a debutante before returning to his tried and true sweetheart.

SONGS

"Alone" (Judy Garland)
"I'm Nobody's Baby" (Judy Garland)

ADDENDA

★ "All I Do Is Dream of You" and "Buds Won't Bud" were recorded by Judy Garland but not used in the film.

★ In 1940, Judy Garland made the select list of "Top Ten" stars audiences most wanted to see.

RECORDINGS

"I'm Nobody's Baby" and "Buds Won't Bud" were released in 1940 on Decca 3174 (78).

CONTEMPORARY COMMENTS

Time, July 22, 1940

Mickey Rooney thrives on his ability and determination to steal anything up to a death scene from a colleague. Some of cinemactor Stone's heartiest chuckles may be explained by the fact that 17 year old Judy Garland, growing prettier by the picture and armed for this one with two good songs, "Alone" and "I'm Nobody's Baby," treats Mickey with a dose of his own medicine.

Variety, July 3, 1940

With second reappearance of Judy Garland in the series indicating that she might move in for regular assignment later, if the Rooney-Garland duo might be required to strengthen later issues.... Miss Garland is prominent and lovely as the adoring girl friend in the big city.

---

17 **Strike Up the Band**

Metro-Goldwyn-Mayer
Released: September 1940
Running time: 120 minutes
Produced by Arthur Freed
Directed by Busby Berkeley
Screenplay by John Monks, Jr., and Fred Finklehoffe
Music and lyrics by Roger Edens, George and Ira Gershwin, and Arthur Freed
Musical direction: Georgie Stoll
Chorals and orchestrations: Leo Arnaud, Conrad Salinger
Photography: Ray June
Editor: Ben Lewis
Art direction: Cedric Gibbons

CAST

Jimmy Connors .... Mickey Rooney
Mary Holden .... Judy Garland
Paul Whiteman .... Himself
Barbara Frances Morgan ..... June Preisser
Philip Turner .... William Tracy
Willie Brewster .... Larry Nunn
Annie .... Margaret Early
Mrs. Connors .... Ann Shoemaker
Mr. Judd .... Francis Pierlot
Mrs. Mary Holden .... Virginia Brissac
with
George Lessey   Enid Bennett
Howard Hickman   Sarah Edwards
Milton Kibbee   Helen Jerome Eddy

SYNOPSIS

A high school brass band reorganizes into a dance band and attempts to finance its entry into a nationwide band contest.

SONGS

"Our Love Affair" (Judy Garland)
"La Conga" (Judy Garland, Mickey Rooney, Six Hits and A Miss)
"Nobody" (Judy Garland)
"Dear Gay Nineties" (Judy Garland, Mickey Rooney, ensemble)
"Nell of New Rochelle" (Judy Garland, Mickey Rooney, Larry Nunn, William Tracy)
"Heaven Will Protect the Working Girl" (Judy Garland, Mickey Rooney, chorus)
"Ta-Ra-Ra-Boom-Te-Re" (June Preisser, chorus)
"Father, Dear Father" (Larry Nunn, Judy Garland)
"When Day Is Done" (Paul Whiteman Orchestra)
"Drummer Boy" (Judy Garland, Six Hits and A Miss)
"Strike Up the Band" (Judy Garland, Mickey Rooney, Six Hits and A Miss, chorus)

ADDENDA

★ The "Fruit Orchestra" sequence was suggested by Vincente Minnelli.

AWARDS/NOMINATIONS

Douglas Shearer won the Academy Award for the Best Sound Recording. Georgie Stoll and Roger Edens were nominated for Best Score. Roger Edens was also nominated for Best Song for "Our Love Affair."

RECORDINGS

"Our Love Affair" was released in 1940 on Decca 3593 (78). The soundtrack for *Strike Up the Band* is available on Hollywood Soundstage 5009 (33⅓).

CONTEMPORARY COMMENTS

The New York Times, September 30, 1940
The music is rollicking, especially "Strike Up the Band" and "La Conga," sung with a good deal of animal spirits by Miss Garland.
—Theodore Strauss (T.S.)

Variety, September 18, 1940
"Strike Up the Band" is Metro's successor to "Babes in Arms," with Mickey Rooney, assisted by major trouping on the part of Judy Garland. . . . Picture is overall smacko entertainment . . . and Mickey Rooney teamed with Judy Garland is a wealth of effective entertainment.

---

18 Little Nellie Kelly

Metro-Goldwyn-Mayer
Released: November 1940
Running time: 96 minutes
Produced by Arthur Freed
Directed by Norman Taurog
Screenplay by Jack McGowan, based on a musical comedy by George M. Cohan
"Singin' in the Rain" written by Arthur Freed and Nacio Herb Brown
"It's a Great Day for the Irish" written by Roger Edens
Musical adaptation: Roger Deems
Musical direction: Georgie Stoll
Photography: Ray June
Editor: Frederick Y. Smith
Art direction: Cedric Gibbons

CAST

Little Nellie/her mother .... Judy Garland
Jerry Kelly .... George Murphy
Michael Noonan ...... Charles Winninger
Dennis Fogarty .... Douglas McPhail
Timothy Fogarty .... Arthur Shields
Mary Fogarty .... Rita Page
Moriarity .... Forrester Harvey
Sergeant McGowan .... James Burke
with
George Watts   Robert Homans
Thomas P. Dillon   Henry Blair

SYNOPSIS

A young Irish girl marries the man she loves against the wishes of her father.

SONGS

"A Pretty Girl Milking Her Cow" (Judy Garland)
"Nellie Is a Darlin' " (Charles Winninger)
"It's a Great Day for the Irish" (Judy Garland, Douglas McPhail, chorus)
"Singin' in the Rain" (Judy Garland)
"Nellie Kelly, I Love You" (Douglas McPhail, Judy Garland, George Murphy, Charles Winninger, chorus)

ADDENDA

★ *Little Nellie Kelly* is the only film in which Judy Garland dies on screen. (MGM softened the blow by having Garland come back as her own daughter.)
★ This film was Garland's first "solo-starrer."
★ "Danny Boy" was recorded by Judy Garland but cut from the release print.

RECORDINGS

"It's a Great Day for the Irish" and "A Pretty Girl Milking Her Cow" were released in 1940 on Decca 3604 (78), Decca 25043 (78), and Decca 9-25043 (45).

"Danny Boy" is available on *Judy Garland: The Golden Years at MGM,* MGM Records SDP 1-2, 2-record set (33⅓), and *The Judy Garland Story,* vol. 2: *The Hollywood Years,* MGM E 4005P (33⅓).

"Singin' in the Rain" is available on *The Judy Garland Story,* vol. 2, MGM E 4005P (33⅓).

The soundtrack for *Little Nellie Kelly* is available on Cheerio 5000 (33⅓).

CONTEMPORARY COMMENTS

Variety, November 16, 1940
Miss Garland romps through the role of Nellie Kelly in grand style, emphasizing her stature as a top notch actress with plenty of wholesome charm and camera presence.

19 Ziegfeld Girl

Metro-Goldwyn-Mayer
Released: April 1941
Running time: 135 minutes
Produced by Pandro S. Berman
Directed by Robert Z. Leonard
Screenplay by Marguerite Roberts and Sonya Levien, based on a story by William Anthony McGuire
Music and lyrics by Nacio Herb Brown, Gus Kahn, Roger Edens, Harry Carroll, Joseph McCarthy, Edward Gallagher, and Al Shean
Vocal arrangements and orchestrations: Leo Arnaud, George Bassman, Conrad Salinger
Musical direction: Georgie Stoll
Photography: Ray June
Editor: Blanche Sewell

CAST

Gilbert Young	James Stewart
Susan Gallagher	Judy Garland
Sandra Kolter	Hedy Lamarr
Sheila Regan	Lana Turner
Frank Merton	Tony Martin
Jerry Regan	Jackie Cooper
Geoffrey Collis	Ian Hunter
"Pop" Gallagher	Charles Winninger
Noble Sage	Edward Everett Horton
Franz Kolter	Philip Dorn

with

Paul Kelly	Bernard Newell
Al Shean	Dan Dailey
Rose Hobart	Felix Bressart
Eve Arden	Ed McNamara
Fay Holden	

Judy performing "Minnie from Trinidad."

SYNOPSIS

The lives and loves of three Ziegfeld girls.

SONGS

"Laugh? I Thought I'd Split My Sides" (Judy Garland, Charles Winninger)

"You Stepped Out of a Dream" (Tony Martin)

"I'm Always Chasing Rainbows" (Judy Garland)

"Caribbean Love Song" (Tony Martin)

"Minnie from Trinidad" (Judy Garland)

"Mr. Gallagher and Mr. Shean" (Charles Winninger, Al Shean)

"Ziegfeld Girls" (Judy Garland, chorus)

"You Gotta Pull Strings" (Judy Garland, chorus)

"You Never Looked So Beautiful Before" (Judy Garland, chorus)

ADDENDA

★ "We Must Have Music," sung by Judy Garland and Tony Martin, was cut from the film prior to release.

★ *Ziegfeld Girls* was one of the top moneymakers of 1941.

★ Garland again made the list of the biggest ticket-selling stars, for 1941.

RECORDINGS

"I'm Always Chasing Rainbows" was released in 1940 on Decca 3593 (78).

The soundtrack for *Ziegfeld Girl* is available on Classic International Filmusicals 3006 (33⅓).

"We Must Have Music" is on *Cut! Out-Takes from Hollywood's Greatest Musicals,* vol. 1, DRG SBL 12586 (33⅓), and the soundtrack, Classic International Filmusicals 3006.

CONTEMPORARY COMMENTS

Time, May 5, 1941
Although their [Garland, Lamarr, Turner] tribulations are never worth the length that . . . producer Pandro Berman devotes to them, Miss Garland warbles a torrid tropical tune, "Minnie from Trinidad," with true professional gusto.

Variety, April 16, 1941
Judy Garland, as the show wise youngster, carries the sympathetic end most capably and delivers her vocal assignments in great style.

20 Life Begins for Andy Hardy

Metro-Goldwyn-Mayer
Released: August 1941
Running time: 100 minutes
Produced by Carey Wilson (uncredited)
Directed by George B. Seitz
Screenplay by Agnes Christine Johnston, based on characters created by Aurania Rouverol
Music direction: Georgie Stoll
Photography: Lester White
Editor: Elmo Vernon
Art direction: Cedric Gibbons

CAST

Judge Hardy . . . . Lewis Stone
Andy Hardy . . . . Mickey Rooney
Betsy Booth . . . . Judy Garland
Mrs. Hardy . . . . Fay Holden
Polly Benedict . . . . Ann Rutherford
Aunt Milly . . . . Sara Haden
Jennitt Hicks . . . . Patricia Dane
Jimmy Frobisher . . . . Ray McDonald
Beezy . . . . George Breakston
Dr. Waggoner . . . . Pierre Watkin

SYNOPSIS
Andy Hardy's adventures in the "big city."

ADDENDA

★ Judy Garland recorded four songs for this film: "Easy to Love," "Abide with Me," "The Rosary," and "America." None were used.
★ This was Garland's third, and last, appearance in the Hardy series.

RECORDINGS
"America" is available on *Judy Garland, 1935–1959,* Star-Tone ST 201 (33⅓). "Easy to Love" is on *Cut! Out-Takes from Hollywood's Greatest Musicals,* vol. 1, DRG SBL 12586 (33⅓).

CONTEMPORARY COMMENTS
Variety, August 6, 1941
Judy Garland, the New York girl friend . . . , clicks solidly in getting Mickey out of romantic trouble.

21 Babes on Broadway

Metro-Goldwyn-Mayer
Released: December 1941
Running time: 118 minutes
Produced by Arthur Freed
Directed by Busby Berkeley
Screenplay by Fred Finklehoffe and Elaine Ryan, based on a story by Fred Finklehoffe
Music and lyrics by E. Y. Harburg, Burton Lane, Ralph Freed, Roger Edens, and Harold Rome
Music direction: Georgie Stoll
Photography: Lester White
Editor: Frederick Y. Smith

CAST

Tommy Williams..........Mickey Rooney
Penny Morris...............Judy Garland
Miss Jones....................Fay Bainter
Barbara Jo...............Virginia Weidler
Ray Lambert................Ray McDonald
Morton Hammond........Richard Quine
Mr. Stone....................Donald Meek
Alexander Woollcott..............Himself
Thornton Reed.............James Gleason
Mrs. Williams................Emma Dunn
Mr. Morris.............Frederick Burton
Inspector Moriarity...........Cliff Clark
Secretary....................Donna Reed
with

Luis Alberni   Ava Gardner
William Pool, Jr. Roger Moore
Vocal Group: Six Hits and A Miss

SYNOPSIS

A group of youngsters get together to put on a show to send underprivileged children to the country.

SONGS

"Anything Can Happen in New York" (Mickey Rooney, Ray McDonald, Richard Quine)
"How About You?" (Judy Garland, Mickey Rooney)
"Hoe Down" (Judy Garland, Mickey Rooney, Six Hits and A Miss, Five Musical Maids)
"Chin Up, Cheerio, Carry On" (Judy Garland)
"Mary's a Grand Old Name" (Judy Garland)
"She's Ma Daisey" (Mickey Rooney)
"Yankee Doodle Boy" (Mickey Rooney)
"I've Got Rings on My Fingers" (Judy Garland)
"Bombshell from Brazil" (Judy Garland, Mickey Rooney, Richard Quine, Ray McDonald, Virginia Weidler, Annie Rooney)
"Mama, Yo Quiero" (Judy Garland, Mickey Rooney)
"Blackout over Broadway" (Judy Garland, Mickey Rooney, Richard Quine, Ray McDonald, Virginia Weidler, Annie Rooney)
"Minstrel Show" (Judy Garland, Mickey Rooney)
"By the Light of the Silvery Moon" (chorus)
"Swanee River" (banjo solo)
"Alabamy Bound" (banjo solo)
"Franklin D. Roosevelt Jones" (Judy Garland)
"Waiting for the Robert E. Lee" (Judy Garland, Virginia Weidler, Annie Rooney)
"Babes on Broadway" (Judy Garland, Mickey Rooney, Richard Quine, Ray McDonald, Virginia Weidler, Annie Rooney)

ADDENDA

★ "Ballad for Americans" was recorded but not used.

AWARDS/NOMINATIONS

"How About You?" was nominated for Best Song of 1942.

RECORDINGS

"How About You?" and "F.D.R. Jones" were released in 1941 on Decca 4072 (78).
The soundtrack for *Babes on Broadway* is available on *Curtain Calls*, CC 100/6-7 (33⅓).

The New York Times, January 1, 1942
Judy Garland . . . stand[s] out in the musical interludes.

—Thomas M. Pryor (T.M.P.)

Time, January 19, 1942
Mickey Rooney, who would rather be caught dead than underplaying, has his hands full when he encounters bright-eyed Judy Garland. . . . Miss Garland, now 19 and wise to her co-star's propensity for stealing scenes, neatly takes the picture away from him.

Variety, December 3, 1941
Both Rooney and Miss Garland, the child wonders of several years back, are fast outgrowing, at least in appearance, this type of presentation, which depends largely on the ah's and oh's that spring from watching precocious children.

22 We Must Have Music

Metro-Goldwyn-Mayer
Released: 1942
Running time: Short subject

SYNOPSIS

A documentary short. The film explained the workings and importance of a movie studio music department.

SONGS

"We Must Have Music" (Judy Garland, Tony Martin)

ADDENDA

★ *We Must Have Music* consists of a musical sequence cut from *Ziegfeld Girl.*

RECORDINGS

"We Must Have Music" is available on *Cut! Out-Takes from Hollywood's Greatest Musicals,* vol. 1, DRG SBL 12586 (33⅓).

23 For Me and My Gal

Metro-Goldwyn-Mayer
Released: October 1942
Running time: 104 minutes
Produced by Arthur Freed
Directed by Busby Berkeley
Screenplay by Richard Sherman, Fred Finklehoffe, Sid Silvers, based on a story by Howard Emmett Rogers
Music and lyrics for "For Me and My Gal" by George W. Meyer, Edgar Leslie, E. Ray Goetz
Musical adaptation: Roger Edens
Musical direction: Georgie Stoll
Dance direction: Bobby Connolly
Vocals and orchestrations: Conrad Salinger, George Bassman, Leo Arnaud
Photography: William Daniels
Editor: Ben Lewis
Art direction: Cedric Gibbons

CAST

Jo Hayden . . . . Judy Garland
Jimmy Metcalf . . . . George Murphy
Harry Palmer . . . . Gene Kelly
Eve Minard . . . . Marta Eggerth
Sid Simms . . . . Ben Blue
Danny Hayden . . . . Richard Quine
Bert Waring . . . Horace (Stephen) McNally
Lily . . . . Lucille Norman
Eddie Melton . . . . Keenan Wynn
with Ben Lessy

SYNOPSIS

A love triangle using a World War I and vaudeville setting as three young troupers, determined to play the Palace, find their lives and careers changed by the war.

SONGS

"Oh, Johnny, Oh" (danced by Gene Kelly)

"They Go Wild, Simply Wild over Me" (danced by Gene Kelly)

"The Doll Shop" (Lucille Norman, George Murphy)

"Don't Leave Me, Daddy" (Judy Garland)

"Oh, You Beautiful Doll!" (George Murphy)

"Sailors' Hornpipe" (danced by Ben Blue)

"By the Beautiful Sea" (Judy Garland, George Murphy, and Girls)

"For Me and My Gal" (Judy Garland, Gene Kelly)

"When You Wore a Tulip" (Judy Garland, Gene Kelly)

"Do I Love You?" (Marta Eggerth)

"After You've Gone" (Judy Garland)

"Tell Me" (Lucille Norman)

"'Til We Meet Again" (Lucille Norman)

"We Don't Want the Bacon" (Ben Lessy)

"Ballin' the Jack" (Judy Garland, Gene Kelly)

"What Are You Gonna Do for Uncle Sammy?" (Ben Blue, Chorus)

"How You Gonna Keep 'Em Down on the Farm?" (Judy Garland)

"Where Do We Go from Here?" (Judy Garland and quartet)

"It's a Long Way to Tipperary" (Judy Garland, chorus)

"Goodbye Broadway, Hello France" (Chorus)

"Smiles" (Judy Garland)

"Oh, Frenchy" (Gene Kelly, Ben Blue)

"Pack Up Your Troubles" (Judy Garland)

"When Johnny Comes Marching Home" (Judy Garland, chorus)

ADDENDA

★ *For Me and My Gal* was the first film in which Judy Garland was the only star billed above the title.

★ This was Gene Kelly's screen debut, due in large part to Garland's spirited support.

★ Marta Eggerth made her American screen debut in this film.

AWARDS/NOMINATIONS

Roger Edens and Georgie Stoll were nominated for an Academy Award for Best Scoring of a Musical Picture.

RECORDINGS

"For Me and My Gal" and "When You Wore a Tulip" (with Gene Kelly) were released on Decca 9-25115 (45), Decca 18480 (78), and Decca 25225 (78).

The soundtrack for *For Me and My Gal* is available on Soundtrak STK 107 (33⅓).

A finale, written and arranged by Roger Edens, for Judy Garland, Gene Kelly, and George Murphy but not used in the film, is available on *Cut! Out-Takes from Hollywood's Greatest Musicals,* vol. 3, Out-Take Records OFT 3 (33⅓).

CONTEMPORARY COMMENTS

The New York Times, October 22, 1942
Miss Garland is a saucy little singer and dances passably. She handles such age flavored ballads as "After You've Gone," "Till We Meet Again" and "Smiles" with music hall lustiness, and sings and dances nicely with Mr. Kelly in the title song. She also teams with George Murphy to do quite well by "Oh, You Beautiful Doll!" But she is not a dramatic actress. She still sniffles and pouts like a fretful child.

—Bosley Crowther

24 Presenting Lily Mars

Metro-Goldwyn-Mayer
Released: April 1943
Running time: 105 minutes
Produced by Joe Pasternak
Directed by Norman Taurog
Screenplay by Richard Connell and Gladys Lehman, based on a novel by Booth Tarkington
Music and lyrics by Walter Jurmann, Paul Francis Webster, E. Y. Harburg, Burton Lane, Roger Edens
Musical adaptation: Roger Edens
Music direction: Georgie Stoll
Dance direction: Ernst Matray
Photography: Joseph Ruttenberg
Editor: Albert Akst
Art direction: Cedric Gibbons

CAST

Lily Mars	Judy Garland
John Thornway	Van Heflin
Mrs. Thornway	Fay Bainter
Owen Vail	Richard Carlson
Mrs. Mars	Spring Byington
Isobel Rekay	Marta Eggerth
Frankie	Connie Gilchrist
Leo	Leonid Kinskey
Poppy	Patricia Barker
Violet	Janet Chapman
Rosie	Annabelle Logan
Davey	Douglas Croft
Charlie Potter	Ray McDonald

with
Tommy Dorsey and his orchestra
Bob Crosby and his orchestra
Specialty dancer: Charles Walters

SYNOPSIS

The story of an ambitious girl's rise from small-town obscurity to Broadway fame and her romance with a Broadway producer.

SONGS

"Is It Really Love?" (Marta Eggerth)
"Tom, Tom, the Piper's Son" (Judy Garland)
"Russian number" (Chorus)

"Every Little Movement" (Judy Garland, Connie Gilchrist)

"When I Look at You" (Marta Eggerth)

"Baby, Think of Me" (Bob Crosby Orchestra)

"When I Look at You" (Judy Garland)

"When I Look at You" (satiric version) (Judy Garland)

"Russian Rhapsody" (Judy Garland)

"Russian Rhapsody" (Marta Eggerth)

"Where There's Music" (Judy Garland, chorus)

"Three O'Clock in the Morning" (Judy Garland, chorus)

"Broadway Rhythm" (Judy Garland, chorus, Tommy Dorsey Orchestra)

ADDENDA

★ Recorded but not used in the picture were "Cara Mona," sung by Judy Garland, and "Paging Mr. Greenback," sung by Judy Garland and chorus.

★ Annabelle Logan, who played one of Judy Garland's younger sisters, became the jazz singer Annie Ross.

★ Joe Pasternak made his directorial debut at MGM with *Presenting Lily Mars*.

★ "St. Louis Blues," "In the Shade of the Old Apple Tree," and "Don't Sit Under the Apple Tree" were recorded for the film but cut prior to release.

RECORDINGS

The complete soundtrack, including dialogue, for *Presenting Lily Mars* is available on Soundtrak STK 117, 2-record set (33⅓). The cut numbers are available on *Cut! Out-Takes from Hollywood's Greatest Musicals,* vol. 2, DRG SBL 12587 (33⅓).

CONTEMPORARY COMMENTS

The New York Times, April 30, 1943
Metro-Goldwyn-Mayer, which dotes on young Judy Garland, is again having her show off her best points. . . . Miss Garland is fresh and pretty, she has a perky friendliness that is completely disarming, and she sings and dances according to the mood—sometimes raucous jive, sometimes sweet little ballads that turn out to be quite enchanting. No doubt about it, Miss Garland is a gifted young lady.

—T.S.

Variety, April 27, 1943
Songs are about equally divided between Judy Garland and Marta Eggerth, with both putting over respective numbers in scintillating fashion.

25 Girl Crazy

Metro-Goldwyn-Mayer
Released: July 1943
Running time: 100 minutes
Produced by Arthur Freed
Directed by Norman Taurog
Screenplay by Fred Finklehoffe, based on a musical by Guy Bolton and Jack McGowan
Music and lyrics by George and Ira Gershwin
"I Got Rhythm" number directed by Busby Berkeley
Musical adaptation: Roger Edens
Orchestration: Conrad Salinger, Axel Stordahl, Sy Oliver
Arrangements: Hugh Martin, Ralph Blane

Music direction: Georgie Stoll
Dance direction: Charles Walters
Photography: William Daniels and
    Robert Planck
Editor: Albert Akst
Art direction: Cedric Gibbons

CAST

Danny Churchill, Jr. . . . . . . Mickey Rooney
Ginger Gray . . . . Judy Garland
Bud Livermore . . . . Gil Stratton
Henry Lathrop . . . . Robert E. Strickland
"Rags" . . . . Rags Ragland
(Specialty) . . . . June Allyson
Polly Williams . . . . Nancy Walker
Dean Phineas Armour . . . . Guy Kibbee
Marjorie Tait . . . . Frances Rafferty
Governor Tait . . . . Howard Freeman
Mr. Churchill, Sr. . . . . Henry O'Neill
Tommy Dorsey and his orchestra

SYNOPSIS

A girl-crazy New York playboy is sent to
an all-male college in Arizona, where he
meets the dean's granddaughter. To prevent the closing of the college due to
inadequate enrollments, they stage a west-
ern rodeo and Queen of the Rodeo contest
to publicize the school.

SONGS

"Treat Me Rough" (June Allyson, Mickey
    Rooney, chorus, Tommy Dorsey
    Orchestra)
"Bidin' My Time" (Judy Garland, The
    King's Men, chorus)
"Could You Use Me?" (Mickey Rooney,
    Judy Garland, Tommy Dorsey
    Orchestra)
"Embraceable You" (Judy Garland,
    Tommy Dorsey Orchestra)
"Cactus Time in Arizona" (Tommy
    Dorsey and orchestra)
"Fascinating Rhythm" (Tommy Dorsey
    and orchestra)
"But Not for Me" (Judy Garland)
"I Got Rhythm" (Judy Garland, Tommy
    Dorsey and orchestra)

ADDENDA

★ *Girl Crazy* was one of the top money-
    making films of 1943.
★ "Bronco Busters," sung by Judy Gar-
    land, Mickey Rooney, Nancy Walker,
    and chorus, was recorded but cut from
    the film before release.

RECORDINGS

"Embraceable You" and "Could You Use
    Me?" were released in 1943 on Decca
    23303 (78). "Could You Use Me?" is
    available on *Hollywood Sings,* vol. 3:
    The Boys and the Girls, Ace of Hearts 69
    (33⅓).
"Bidin' My Time" and "I Got Rhythm"
    were released in 1943 on Decca 23310
    (78). "Bidin' My Time" is on *The Young
    Judy Garland,* MCA MCL 1731 (33⅓).
"But Not for Me" was released in 1943 on
    Decca 23309 (78).
"Bronco Busters" is available on *Holly-
    wood Soundstage,* HS 5008 (33⅓), and
    *Cut! Out-Takes from Hollywood's Great-
    est Musicals,* vol. 2, DRG SBL 12587
    (33⅓).
"Girl Crazy" (with Mickey Rooney) is
    available on Decca A 362 (78), Decca
    DL 5412 (33⅓), and *Hollywood Sound-
    stage* HS 5008 (33⅓).

CONTEMPORARY COMMENTS

The New York Times, December 3, 1943
Mickey Rooney and Judy Garland . . . are the most incorrigibly talented pair of youngsters in movies . . . Judy . . . sings and acts like an earthbound angel.

—T.S.

Time, December 27, 1943
As sung by cinemactress Judy Garland, "Embraceable You" and "Bidin' My Time" become hits all over again and the new "But Not for Me" sounds like another. Her presence is open, cheerful, warming. If she were not so profitably good at her own game, she could obviously be a dramatic cinema actress with profit to all.

Variety, August 4, 1943
Miss Garland is a nifty saleswoman of the numbers, right down to the overproduced "Rhythm" finale which was Busby Berkeley's special chore. Her "Embraceable You" delivery is a standout; ditto "Bidin' My Time" and "Not for Me." She's also got two nice dancing sessions.

26 Thousands Cheer

Metro-Goldwyn-Mayer
Released: October 1943
Running time: 126 minutes
Produced by Joe Pasternak
Directed by George Sidney
Original story and screenplay by Paul Jarrico and Richard Collins
Music and lyrics by Ferde Grofé, Harold Adamson, Lew Brown, Ralph Freed, Burton Lane, Walter Jurmann, Paul Francis Webster, Earl Brent, E. Y. Harburg, Dmitri Shostakovich, Harold Rome
Music direction: Herbert Stothart
Photography: George Folsey
Editor: George Boemler
Art direction: Cedric Gibbons

CAST

Kathryn Jones . . . . Kathryn Grayson
Eddie Marsh . . . . Gene Kelly
Hyllary Jones . . . . Mary Astor
Colonel William Jones . . . . John Boles
Chuck Polansky . . . . Ben Blue
Marie Corbino . . . . Frances Rafferty
Helen . . . . Mary Elliott
Sgt. Kozlack . . . . Frank Jenks
Alan . . . . Frank Sully
Captain Fred Avery . . . . Dick Simmons
Pvt. Monks . . . . Ben Lessy
José Iturbi . . . . Himself

GUEST APPEARANCES

Judy Garland
Red Skelton
Lucille Ball
Virginia O'Brien
Lena Horne
Marilyn Maxwell
Margaret O'Brien
Gloria DeHaven
Sara Haden
Maxine Barrat
Mickey Rooney
Eleanor Powell
Ann Sothern
Frank Morgan
Marsha Hunt
Donna Reed
June Allyson
John Conte
Don Loper
Kay Kyser and his orchestra
Bob Crosby and his orchestra
Benny Carter and his band

SYNOPSIS

A romance between a colonel's daughter and a circus aerialist turned soldier. MGM turned it into a star-studded extravaganza under the guise of the colonel's daughter orchestrating a show for the camp.

SONGS

"Caprice Español" (conducted by José Iturbi)

"Sempre Libera" (from Verdi's *La Traviata*) (Kathryn Grayson)

"Daybreak" (Kathryn Grayson)

"Three Letters in a Mailbox" (Kathryn Grayson)

"I Dug a Ditch" (Kathryn Grayson, chorus)

"Let There Be Music" (Kathryn Grayson)

"Hungarian Rhapsody No. 2" (Franz Liszt) (piano solo by José Iturbi)

"Let Me Call You Sweetheart" (Gene Kelly)

"American Patrol" (José Iturbi conducting)

"Boogie Woogie" number (danced by Eleanor Powell)

"In a Little Spanish Town" (Virginia O'Brien, June Allyson, Gloria DeHaven, Bob Crosby and his orchestra)

"I Dug a Ditch" (Kay Kyser and his orchestra)

"Should I?" (Georgia Carroll, with Kay Kyser and his orchestra)

"Tico Tico" (danced by Maxine Barrat and Don Loper)

"Honeysuckle Rose" (Lena Horne, played by Benny Carter and his band)

"The Joint Is Really Jumpin' in Carnegie Hall" (Judy Garland, accompanied by José Iturbi)

"The United Nations (Victory Song)" (Kathryn Grayson, United Nations Chorus, José Iturbi)

ADDENDA

★ *Thousands Cheer* was one of the top moneymaking films of the year.

AWARDS/NOMINATIONS

George Folsey was nominated for an Academy Award for Color Cinematography. Cedric Gibbons and Daniel Cathcart, Edwin Willis and Jacques Mersereau were nominated for Art Direction. Herbert Stothart was nominated for best Scoring of a Musical Picture.

RECORDINGS

The soundtrack for *Thousands Cheer* is available on *Hollywood Soundstage* No. 409 (33⅓) and on Cheerio 5000 (33⅓).

CONTEMPORARY COMMENTS

Newsweek, September 27, 1943
The famous pianist [José Iturbi] swings skillfully into the boogie woogie groove as Judy Garland prophetically chants: "The joint is really jumpin' at Carnegie Hall."

27 Meet Me in St. Louis

Metro-Goldwyn-Mayer
Released: December 1944
Running time: 114 minutes
Produced by Arthur Freed
Directed by Vincente Minnelli
Screenplay by Irving Brecher and Fred Finklehoffe, based on stories by Sally Benson
Music and lyrics by Ralph Blane and Hugh Martin

Leon Ames and Judy.

Song "You and I" written by Arthur Freed
   and Nacio Herb Brown
Musical adaptation: Roger Edens
Music direction: Georgie Stoll
Orchestrations: Conrad Salinger
Dance direction: Charles Walters
Photography: George Folsey
Editor: Albert Akst
Art direction: Cedric Gibbons

CAST

Esther Smith	Judy Garland
"Tootie" Smith	Margaret O'Brien
Anna Smith	Mary Astor
Rose Smith	Lucille Bremer
John Truett	Tom Drake
Katie	Marjorie Main
Alonzo Smith	Leon Ames
Granpa	Harry Davenport
Lucille Ballard	June Lockhart
Lon Smith, Jr.	Henry Daniels, Jr.
Agnes Smith	Joan Carroll
Colonel Darly	Hugh Marlowe
Warren Sheffield	Robert Sully
Mr. Neely	Chill Wills

SYNOPSIS

A year in the life of a prosperous St. Louis family.

SONGS

"Meet Me in St. Louis" (Judy Garland, Lucille Bremer, Joan Carroll, Harry Davenport)

"The Boy Next Door" (Judy Garland)

"Meet Me in St. Louis" (Judy Garland, Lucille Bremer)

"Skip to My Lou" (Judy Garland, Lucille Bremer, Henry Daniels, Jr., Tom Drake)

"I Was Drunk Last Night" (Margaret O'Brien)

"Under the Bamboo Tree" (Judy Garland, Margaret O'Brien)

"Over the Banister" (Judy Garland)

"The Trolley Song" (Judy Garland)

"You and I" (Leon Ames, Mary Astor— dubbed by Arthur Freed and D. Markas)

"Have Yourself a Merry Little Christmas" (Judy Garland)

ADDENDA

★ Judy Garland initially resisted appearing in *Meet Me in St. Louis*. Arthur Freed and Vincente Minnelli convinced her that the picture would not be the setback to her career that "friends" had warned her it would.

★ The scene in which John Truett helps Esther turn out the lights in the house was a continuous shot, requiring special set construction and particularly difficult lighting to achieve its delicacy. It is one of the highlights of the film and took a full day of rehearsal to orchestrate.

★ "Boys and Girls Like You and Me," sung by Judy Garland, was recorded but not used in the film.

★ *Life* featured Judy Garland on the cover of its December 11, 1944, issue, which reviewed *Meet Me in St. Louis*.

AWARDS/NOMINATIONS

Irving Brecher and Fred Finklehoffe were nominated for Best Screenplay for 1944 for *Meet Me in St. Louis*. George Folsey was nominated for Color Cinematography. "The Trolley Song" was nominated for Best Song. Georgie Stoll was nominated for Scoring. Margaret O'Brien was given a special award as "outstanding child actress of 1944." The film was named one of the year's ten best by the New York Film Critics.

RECORDINGS

"Meet Me in St. Louis" was released in 1944 on Decca 23360 (78) and Decca 9-25494 (45).

"The Trolley Song" was released in 1944 on Decca 23361 (78), Decca 25494 (78), and Decca 9-25494 (45).

"The Boy Next Door" was released in 1944 on Decca 23362 (78).

"Skip to My Lou" was released in 1944 on Decca 23360 (78).

Soundtrack selections are available on Decca A 380 (78), Decca DL 8498 (33⅓), AEI 3101 (33⅓).

"Boys and Girls Like You and Me" is available on AEI 3101 (33⅓).

CONTEMPORARY COMMENTS

The New York Times, November 29, 1944
Miss Garland is full of gay exuberance as the second sister and sings . . . with a rich voice that grows riper and more expressive in each new film.

—Bosley Crowther

Newsweek, December 11, 1944
All the members of . . . [the] cast are good enough, or better. Miss Garland sings and acts in fine fettle as the teenage Smith in love.

---

28 The Clock

Metro-Goldwyn-Mayer
Released: May 1945
Running time: 90 minutes
Produced by Arthur Freed
Directed by Vincente Minnelli
Screenplay by Robert Nathan and Joseph Schrank, based on a story by Paul and Pauline Gallico
Score by George Bassman
Special effects: A. Arnold Gillespie
Photography: George Folsey
Editor: George White
Art direction: Cedric Gibbons, William Ferrari

CAST

Alice Mayberry . . . . Judy Garland
Corporal Joe Allen . . . . Robert Walker
Al Henry . . . . James Gleason
Drunk . . . . Keenan Wynn
Bill . . . . Marshall Thompson
Mrs. Al Henry . . . . Lucille Gleason
Helen . . . . Ruth Brady
Woman in restaurant . . . . . Moyna Macgill

SYNOPSIS

A soldier and girl meet, fall in love, and marry during the space of his 48-hour pass.

ADDENDA

★ *The Clock* was Garland's first purely dramatic, nonsinging role.
★ The background music, "If I Had You," was recorded by Judy Garland and The Merry Macs for Decca.
★ Garland was again named one of the "Top Ten Box Office Stars," for 1945.

RECORDINGS

"If I Had You" (with The Merry Macs) was released in 1945 on Decca 23436 (78).

CONTEMPORARY COMMENTS

Time, May 14, 1946
[Vincente Minnelli] . . . has brought the budding dramatic talents of . . . Judy Garland into unmistakable bloom.

Newsweek, May 14, 1945
Walker and Miss Garland (playing her first nonsinging role) are completely persuasive as the two anonymities drawn together in an overwhelming and disinterested metropolis.

---

29 The Harvey Girls

Metro-Goldwyn-Mayer
Released: January 1946
Running time: 101 minutes
Produced by Arthur Freed
Associate producer: Roger Edens
Directed by George Sidney

Screenplay by Edmund Beloin, Nathaniel Curtis, Harry Crane, James O'Hanlon, Samson Raphaelson, based on a story by Samuel Hopkins Adams; based on an original story by Eleanore Griffin and William Rankin, with additional dialogue by Kay Van Riper

Music and lyrics by Johnny Mercer and Harry Warren

Musical direction: Lennie Hayton

Orchestration: Conrad Salinger

Musical arrangements: Kay Thompson

Musical numbers staged by Robert Alton

Special effects: Warren Newcombe

Photography: George Folsey

Editor: Albert Akst

Art direction: Cedric Gibbons, William Ferrari

After the brawl is over . . .

CAST

Susan Bradley	Judy Garland
Ned Trent	John Hodiak
Chris Maule	Ray Bolger
Em	Angela Lansbury
Judge Sam Purvis	Preston Foster
Alma	Virginia O'Brien
Terry O'Halloran	Kenny Baker
Sonora Cassidy	Marjorie Main
H. H. Hartsey	Chill Wills
Miss Bliss	Selena Royle
Deborah	Cyd Charisse
Ethel	Ruth Brady

with

Jack Lambert	Edward Earle
Morris Ankrum	William Phillips
Ben Carter	Norman Leavitt

Horace (Stephen) McNally

SYNOPSIS

A group of waitresses employed by restaurateur Fred Harvey contend with the Wild West.

SONGS

"In the Valley" (Judy Garland)

"Oh, You Kid" (Angela Lansbury)

"On the Atchison, Topeka and the Santa Fe" (Judy Garland, Ray Bolger, Harvey Girls)

"The Train Must Be Fed" (Ensemble)

"It's a Great Big World" (Judy Garland, Cyd Charisse—dubbed by Betty Russell, Virginia O'Brien)

"In the Wild, Wild West" (Virginia O'Brien)

"Wait and See" (Kenny Baker)

"Round and Round" (Judy Garland, Ray Bolger, Marjorie Main, ensemble)

ADDENDA

★ *The Harvey Girls* was one of the top moneymakers of the year.

- ★ "March of the Doagies," sung by Judy Garland, Kenny Baker, and chorus, was cut from the film prior to release.
- ★ "Hayride," sung by Judy Garland and Ray Bolger, was cut prior to release.
- ★ "My Intuition," sung by Judy Garland and John Hodiak, was cut prior to release.

AWARDS/NOMINATIONS

"On the Atchison, Topeka and the Santa Fe" won the Academy Award for 1946 for Best Song. Lennie Hayton was nominated for Best Scoring of a Musical Picture.

RECORDINGS

"On the Atchison, Topeka and the Santa Fe" (with The Merry Macs) was released in 1945 on Decca 23436 (78).

"In the Valley" was released in 1945 on Decca 23438 (78).

"Round and Round" was released in 1945 on Decca 23459 (78).

"It's a Great Big World" (with Virginia O'Brien) was released in 1945 on Decca 23460 (78).

The Harvey Girls is available on Decca A 388 (78) and selections on Decca DL 8498 (78) and AEI 3101 (33⅓).

"March of the Doagies" is available on *Judy Garland: From the Decca Vaults,* MCA 907 (33⅓) and *Cut! Out-Takes from Hollywood's Greatest Musicals,* vol. 1, DRG SBL 12586 (33⅓).

"Hayride" and "My Intuition" are available on *Cut!,* vol. 1, DRG SBL 12586 (33⅓).

CONTEMPORARY COMMENTS

The New York Times, January 25, 1946
Miss Garland, of course, is at the center of most of the activity and handles herself in pleasing fashion . . .

—Bosley Crowther

Time, January 28, 1946
Miss Garland doesn't seem as recklessly happy as she was in St. Louis but she still appears to be having a pretty fine time.

30 Ziegfeld Follies of 1946

Metro-Goldwyn-Mayer
Released: March 1946
Running time: 109 minutes
Produced by Arthur Freed
Sequences directed by Vincente Minnelli, George Sidney, Robert Lewis, Lemuel Ayers, and Roy Del Ruth
Musical adaptation: Roger Edens
Musical direction: Lennie Hayton
Dance direction: Robert Alton
Judy Garland's sequence:
   Songs by Kay Thompson, Roger Edens
Dance direction: Charles Walters
Director: Vincente Minnelli
Photography: George Folsey and Charles Rosher
Editor: Albert Akst
Art direction: Cedric Gibbons, Merrill Pye, Jack Martin Smith

CAST

Edward Arnold	Kathryn Grayson
Fred Astaire	Lena Horne
Lucille Ball	Gene Kelly
Marion Bell	Robert Lewis
Lucille Bremer	James Melton
Fanny Brice	Victor Moore
Bunin's Puppets	Virginia O'Brien
Cyd Charisse	William Powell

Hume Cronyn
William Frawley
Judy Garland

Red Skelton
Esther Williams
Keenan Wynn

SYNOPSIS

A no-story musical.

SONGS

"Bring on the Beautiful Girls" (Fred
Astaire, Lucille Ball, Cyd Charisse)
"Bring on Those Wonderful Men"
(reprise) (Virginia O'Brien)
"This Heart of Mine" (Orchestra—Esther
Williams sequence)
"The Drinking Song" (from Verdi's *La
Traviata*) (James Melton, Marion Bell)

"Love" (Lena Horne)
"Limehouse Blues" (danced by Fred
Astaire and Lucille Bremer)
"A Great Lady Has an Interview" (Judy
Garland, chorus)
"The Babbitt and the Bromide" (Fred
Astaire, Gene Kelly)
"There's Beauty Everywhere" (Kathryn
Grayson)

ADDENDA

★ Judy Garland recorded "Liza" for the
film, but it was cut prior to release.
★ *Ziegfeld Follies* was one of the top
moneymakers of the year.

RECORDINGS

The soundtrack for *The Ziegfeld Follies of 1946* is available on Curtain Calls CC 100/15-16 (33⅓).

"Liza" is available on *Born in a Trunk: 1945–1950,* AEI 2110 (33⅓).

CONTEMPORARY COMMENTS

Time, March 25, 1946

Among the best [segments]: Pert Judy Garland . . . burlesquing a world weary but oh so cordial movie queen in a dance and doggerel brush with the press.

Newsweek, April 1, 1946

In "A Great Lady Has an Interview," Judy Garland with sixteen leading men displays an unexpected flair for occupational satire.

---

31 Till the Clouds Roll By

Metro-Goldwyn-Mayer
Released: November 1946
Running time: 120 minutes
Produced by Arthur Freed
Directed by Richard Whorf, Judy Garland's numbers directed by Vincente Minnelli
Screenplay by Myles Connolly and Jean Halloway, based on a story by Guy Bolton, adapted by George Wells
Music by Jerome Kern
Musical direction: Lennie Hayton
Vocal arrangements: Kay Thompson
Orchestration: Conrad Salinger
Musical numbers staged and directed by Robert Alton
Photography: Harry Stradling, George Folsey
Editor: Albert Akst
Art direction: Cedric Gibbons

CAST

Jerome Kern . . . . Robert Walker
Marilyn Miller . . . . Judy Garland
Sally . . . . Lucille Bremer
James I. Hessler . . . . Van Heflin
Oscar Hammerstein . . . . Paul Langton
Mrs. Jerome Kern . . . . Dorothy Patrick
Mrs. Muller . . . . Mary Nash
Bandleader . . . . Van Johnson
Julie Sanderson . . . . Dinah Shore
Charles Frohman . . . . Harry Hayden
Victor Herbert . . . . Paul Macey
Sally, as a girl . . . . Joan Wells
with

June Allyson	Kathryn Grayson
Lena Horne	Tony Martin
Frank Sinatra	Gower Champion
Cyd Charisse	Angela Lansbury
Ray McDonald	Virginia O'Brien
Caleb Peterson	William Phillips
The Wilde Twins	

SYNOPSIS

A loosely based biography of Jerome Kern.

SONGS

"Cotton Blossom" (Chorus)
"Who Cares If My Boat Goes Upstream" (Tony Martin)
"Make Believe" (Kathryn Grayson, Tony Martin)
"Life Upon the Wicked Stage" (Virginia O'Brien)
"Can't Help Lovin' Dat Man" (Lena Horne)
"Ol' Man River" (Caleb Peterson)

"Kalua" (Orchestra)

"How'd You Like to Spoon with Me?" (Angela Lansbury)

"They Didn't Believe Me" (Dinah Shore)

"Till the Clouds Roll By" (June Allyson, Ray McDonald)

"Leave It to Jane" (June Allyson)

"Cleopatterer" (June Allyson)

"Who?" (Judy Garland)

"Sunny" (Chorus)

"Look for the Silver Lining" (Judy Garland)

"One More Dance" (Lucille Bremer—dubbed by Trudy Erwin)

"I Won't Dance" (Van Johnson, Lucille Bremer—dubbed by Trudy Erwin)

"She Didn't Say Yes" (The Wilde Twins)

"Smoke Gets in Your Eyes" (danced by Cyd Charisse, Gower Champion)

"The Last Time I Saw Paris" (Dinah Shore)

"The Land Where the Good Songs Go" (Lucille Bremer—dubbed by Trudy Erwin)

"Yesterdays" (Chorus)

"Long Ago and Far Away" (Kathryn Grayson)

"A Fine Romance" (Virginia O'Brien)

"All the Things You Are" (Tony Martin)

"Why Was I Born?" (Lena Horne)

"Ol' Man River" (Frank Sinatra)

ADDENDA

★ Garland was pregnant during the shooting and her scenes were moved up in the shooting schedule as her pregnancy became increasingly obvious. This being so, she found it highly amusing to dance among a myriad of men and sing "Who?"

★ "D'Ye Love Me?," sung by Judy Garland, was cut from the film prior to release.

RECORDINGS

"Look for the Silver Lining" was released on MGM 30002 (78), MGM 30431 (78), and MGM 30212 (X-45).

"Who?" was released in 1946 on MGM 30003 (78).

The soundtrack for *Till the Clouds Roll By* is available on MGM E 3231 (33⅓), MGM E 501 (33⅓), and Sandy Hook SH 2080 (33⅓).

"D'Ye Love Me?" is available on *Cut! Out-Takes from Hollywood's Greatest Musicals,* vol. 1, DRG SBL 12586 (33⅓).

CONTEMPORARY COMMENTS

The New York Times, December 6, 1946
Why couldn't it simply have given us more such enjoyable things as Judy Garland playing Marilyn Miller and singing the melodious "Sunny" [*sic*] and "Who?"
—Bosley Crowther

Time, January 6, 1947
Judy Garland is charming as the late Marilyn Miller and still more charming when she sings "Who?"

Dance Film Notes, April 1947
After raising quizzical eyebrows several times at the casting of Judy Garland as Marilyn Miller in *Till Clouds Roll By,* I must now admit that she plays the part astonishingly well. . . . I must say in all honesty that it is difficult to think of anyone who could have done so more successfully.
—John K. Newnham

32 The Pirate

Metro-Goldwyn-Mayer
Released: June 1948
Running time: 102 minutes
Produced by Arthur Freed
Directed by Vincente Minnelli
Screenplay by Albert Hackett and Frances Goodrich, based on a play by S. N. Behrman
Music and lyrics by Cole Porter
Musical direction: Lennie Hayton
Instrumental arrangements: Conrad Salinger
Dance direction: Robert Alton and Gene Kelly
Photography: Harry Stradling
Editor: Blanche Sewell
Art direction: Cedric Gibbons, Jack Martin Smith

CAST

Manuela	Judy Garland
Serafin	Gene Kelly
Don Pedro Vargas	Walter Slezak
Aunt Inez	Gladys Cooper
Advocate	Reginald Owen
Viceroy	George Zucco
Specialty dancers	The Nicholas Brothers
Capucho	Lester Allen
Isabella	Lola Deem
Mercedes	Ellen Ross
Lizarda	Mary Jo Ellis
Casilda	Jean Dean

with

Marion Murray	Ben Lessy
Jerry Bergen	Val Setz
The Goldsmith Brothers	Cully Richards

SYNOPSIS

A strolling player pretends to be a famous bloodthirsty pirate to win the love of a young woman betrothed to the town mayor.

SONGS

"Nina" (Gene Kelly)
"Mack the Black" (Judy Garland)
"The Pirate Ballet" (danced by Gene Kelly)
"You Can Do No Wrong" (Judy Garland)
"Love of My Life" (Judy Garland)
"Be a Clown" (Judy Garland, Gene Kelly)

ADDENDA

★ "Voodoo," sung by Judy Garland, was cut from the film prior to release.
★ Cole Porter called *The Pirate* "a $5,000,000 Hollywood picture that was unspeakably wretched, the worst that money could buy," quoted in *The Cole Porter Story,* as told to Richard C. Hubler (Cleveland: World Publishing Co., 1965).

AWARDS/NOMINATIONS

Victor Young was nominated for an Academy Award for Best Scoring of a Musical Picture.

RECORDINGS

"Be a Clown" was released in 1948 on MGM 30097 (78).
"Love of My Life" and "You Can Do No Wrong" were released in 1948 on MGM 30098 (78).
"Mack the Black" was released in 1948 on MGM 30099 (78).

The Pirate is available on MGM E 3234
(33⅓), MGM C 763 (33⅓) (U.K.),
MGM 21 (78), MGM E 21 (33⅓), and
MCA MCAD 5950 (CD).

"Voodoo" is available on *Cut! Out-Takes
from Hollywood's Greatest Musicals,* vol.
1, DRG SBL 12586 (33⅓).

CONTEMPORARY COMMENTS

The New York Times, May 21, 1948
Miss Garland teams nicely with Mr. Kelly,
singing or dancing, and she throws herself
with verve into a wild, slapstick exercise,
tossing everything that's not nailed down
at the dashing trouper. It's funny.
—T.M.P.

Time, June 21, 1948
Miss Garland's tense, ardent straightfor-
wardness is sometimes very striking.

Newsweek, June 7, 1948
With Judy Garland and Gene Kelly pitch-
ing energetically into the lead roles, the
new *Pirate* is one of the most delightful
musicals to hit the screen in a month of
Sundays.

---

33 Easter Parade

Metro-Goldwyn-Mayer
Released: July 1948
Running time: 104 minutes
Produced by Arthur Freed
Directed by Charles Walters
Screenplay by Sidney Shelton, Frances
Goodrich and Albert Hackett, based on
a story by Frances Goodrich and Albert
Hackett
Music and lyrics by Irving Berlin

Musical numbers staged and directed by
Robert Alton
Musical direction: Johnny Green
Orchestration: Conrad Salinger,
Van Cleave, Leo Arnaud
Vocal arrangements: Robert Tucker
Photography: Harry Stradling
Editor: Albert Akst
Art direction: Cedric Gibbons,
Jack Martin Smith

CAST

Hannah Brown . . . . Judy Garland
Don Hewes . . . . Fred Astaire
Jonathan Harrow III . . . . Peter Lawford
Nadine Gale . . . . Ann Miller
François, the Headwaiter . . Jules Munshin
Mike, the Bartender . . . . Clinton Sundberg
Essie . . . . Jeni Le Gon

SYNOPSIS

A dancer is ditched by his partner for a
starring role in a new Ziegfeld show. To
prove he can make a star out of anyone,
he picks a girl from a chorus line and sets
out to groom her.

SONGS

"Happy Easter" (Fred Astaire)
"Drum Crazy" (Fred Astaire)
"It Only Happens When I Dance with
You" (Fred Astaire, danced by Fred
Astaire and Ann Miller)
"Everybody's Doin' It" (Judy Garland,
chorus)
"I Wish I Were in Michigan" (Judy
Garland)
"Beautiful Faces Need Beautiful Clothes"
(danced by Fred Astaire, Judy Garland)
"A Fella with an Umbrella" (Peter
Lawford, Judy Garland)

"Shaking the Blues Away" (Ann Miller)

"I Love a Piano" (Judy Garland)

"Ragtime Violin" (Judy Garland, Fred Astaire)

"Snooky Ookums" (Judy Garland, Fred Astaire)

"When the Midnight Choo Choo Leaves for Alabam' " (Judy Garland, Fred Astaire)

"It Only Happens When I Dance with You" (reprise) (Judy Garland)

"Steppin' Out with My Baby" (Fred Astaire)

"A Couple of Swells" (Judy Garland, Fred Astaire)

"The Girl on the Magazine Cover" (Richard Beavers)

"Better Luck Next Time" (Judy Garland)

"Easter Parade" (Judy Garland, Fred Astaire)

ADDENDA

★ Gene Kelly had originally been scheduled to play the Astaire part but broke his ankle on the eve of production. Fred Astaire came out of retirement to do *Easter Parade* but was worried that the public would not accept a romance between Judy Garland and himself due to more than twenty years difference in age.

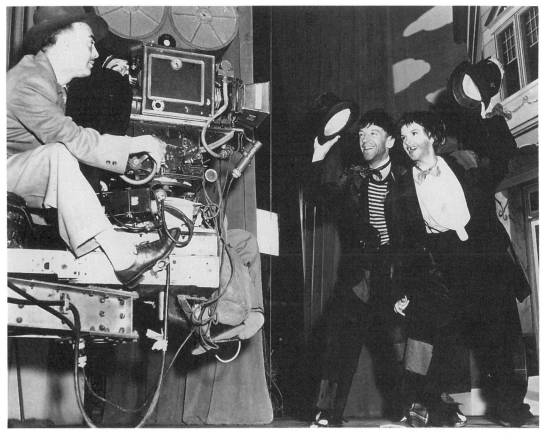

★ *Easter Parade* was one of the top moneymakers of the year.

★ "Mr. Monotony," sung by Judy Garland, was cut from the film prior to release.

AWARDS/NOMINATIONS

Roger Edens and Johnny Green won an Academy Award for Best Scoring of a Musical Picture.

RECORDINGS

"Easter Parade" and "A Fella with an Umbrella" (with Peter Lawford) were released in 1948 on MGM 30185 (78).

"A Couple of Swells" (with Fred Astaire) was released in 1948 on MGM 30186 (78).

"Better Luck Next Time" was released in 1948 on MGM 30187 (78).

Easter Parade is available on MGM E-502 (33⅓), selections on MGM E-3227 (33⅓), MGM 23530 (33⅓).

"I Wish I Were in Michigan" is available on *Born in a Trunk: 1945–1950,* AEI 2110 (33⅓).

"Mr. Monotony" is available on *Cut! Out-Takes from Hollywood's Greatest Musicals,* vol. 1, DRG SBL 12586 (33⅓).

CONTEMPORARY COMMENTS

The New York Times, July 1, 1948
Miss Garland is a competent trouper, nimble on her feet and professionally sound vocally, but somehow we feel that Miss Miller pairs better with Astaire.

—T.M.P.

Time, July 5, 1948
As in "The Pirate," Miss Garland does a comic tramp dance, with teeth blacked out. She is very cute at this but, after all, she has other talents; it will be a pity if she gets typed as a hobo.

34 Words and Music

Metro-Goldwyn-Mayer
Released: December 1948
Running time: 119 minutes
Produced by Arthur Freed
Directed by Norman Taurog
Screenplay by Fred Finklehoffe, story by Guy Bolton and Jean Halloway, based on the lives of Richard Rodgers and Lorenz Hart, adaptation by Ben Feiner
Musical direction: Lennie Hayton
Orchestration: Conrad Salinger
Vocal arrangements: Robert Tucker
Musical numbers staged and directed by Robert Alton
Photography: Charles Rosher, Harry Stradling
Editors: Albert Akst, Ferris Webster
Art direction: Cedric Gibbons, Jack Martin Smith

CAST

Lorenz Hart . . . . Mickey Rooney
Eddie Lorrison Anders . . . . Perry Como
Joyce Harmon . . . . Ann Sothern
Richard Rodgers . . . . Tom Drake
Peggy McNeil . . . . Betty Garrett
Dorothy Feiner . . . . Janet Leigh
Herbert Fields . . . . Marshall Thompson
Mrs. Hart . . . . Jeanette Nolan
Bob Feiner, Jr. . . . . Richard Quine
shoe clerk . . . . Clinton Sundberg
Dr. Rodgers . . . . Harry Antrim
Mrs. Rodgers . . . . Ilka Gruning

Guest Stars:

June Allyson	Judy Garland
Lena Horne	Gene Kelly
Cyd Charisse	Mel Tormé
Vera-Ellen	Dee Turnell
Emory Parnell	Helen Spring
Edward Earle	The Blackburn Twins

SYNOPSIS

A loosely based biography of the partnership of Richard Rodgers and Lorenz Hart.

SONGS

"Manhattan" (Mickey Rooney, Tom Drake, Marshall Thompson)

"There's a Small Hotel" (Betty Garrett)

"Mountain Greenery" (Perry Como, chorus)

"Way Out West" (Betty Garrett)

"Where's That Rainbow?" (Ann Sothern)

"On Your Toes" (Cyd Charisse, Dee Turnell)

"This Can't Be Love" (instrumental, danced by Cyd Charisse and Dee Turnell)

"The Girl Friend" (instrumental, danced by Cyd Charisse and Dee Turnell)

"Blue Room" (Perry Como, danced by Cyd Charisse)

"Thou Swell" (June Allyson, The Blackburn Twins)

"With a Song in My Heart" (Tom Drake)

"Where or When" (Lena Horne)

"The Lady Is a Tramp" (Lena Horne)

"I Wish I Were in Love Again" (Judy Garland, Mickey Rooney)

"Johnny One Note" (Judy Garland)

"Blue Moon" (Mel Tormé)

"Spring Is Here" (Mickey Rooney)

"Slaughter on Tenth Avenue" (danced by Gene Kelly and Vera-Ellen)

"With a Song in My Heart" (Perry Como)

ADDENDA

★ Judy Garland was not originally scheduled to appear in *Words and Music*. She was ill and on suspension when she was offered $50,000 to do a song for the film and, based on its effect, $50,000 to do a second number.

★ This was the last screen appearance of Judy Garland and Mickey Rooney together. It was also Rooney's last film at MGM.

RECORDINGS

Words and Music was released on MGM M 37 (78) and MGM E 505 (33⅓). It is available on MCA 25029 (33⅓).

"I Wish I Were in Love Again" was released on Decca 24469 (78) in 1946.

"Johnny One Note" is available on *The Judy Garland Story*, vol. 2: *The Hollywood Years*, MGM E 4005 (33⅓).

---

35 In the Good Old Summertime

Metro-Goldwyn-Mayer

Released: July 1949

Running time: 104 minutes

Produced by Joe Pasternak

Directed by Robert Z. Leonard

Written for the screen by Albert Hackett, Frances Goodrich, and Ivan Tors, based on a screenplay by Samson Raphaelson, based on a story by Miklos Laszlo

Musical sequences directed by Robert Alton

Musical direction: Georgie Stoll

Vocal orchestrations: Conrad Salinger

Song "In the Good Old Summertime" written by George Evans and Ben Shields

Photography: Harry Stradling

Editor: Adrienne Fazan

Art direction: Cedric Gibbons, Randall Duell

CAST

Veronica Fisher .... Judy Garland
Andrew Larkin .... Van Johnson
Otto Oberkugen .... S. Z. ("Cuddles") Sakall
Nellie Burke .... Spring Byington
Hickey...................... Buster Keaton
Louise Parkson .... Marcia Van Dyke
Rudy Hansen .... Clinton Sundberg
Aunt Addie .... Lillian Bronson
Policeman................. Ralph Sanford

S. Z. Sakall, Van Johnson, and Judy Garland.

SYNOPSIS

A romance between two pen pals who are unaware that they work together (antagonistically) in the same music shop.

SONGS

"Chicago" (title music) (orchestra)

"In the Good Old Summertime" (Van Johnson, Buster Keaton, Spring Byington, S. Z. Sakall, chorus)

"Meet Me Tonight in Dreamland" (Judy Garland)

"Put Your Arms Around Me, Honey" (Judy Garland)

"Wait Till the Sun Shines, Nelly" (barbershop quartet)

"Play That Barbershop Chord" (Judy Garland, barbershop quartet)

"I Don't Care" (Judy Garland)

"Merry Christmas" (Judy Garland)

ADDENDA

★ "Last Night When We Were Young," sung by Judy Garland, was cut from the film prior to release.

★ *In the Good Old Summertime* was one of the top moneymakers of the year.

★ This was Buster Keaton's last appearance for MGM.

RECORDINGS

"Put Your Arms Around Me, Honey" and "Meet Me Tonight in Dreamland" were released in 1949 on MGM 50025 (78).

"Play That Barbershop Chord" and "I Don't Care" were released in 1949 on MGM 50026 (78).

In the Good Old Summertime was released on MGM L 11 (78).

CONTEMPORARY COMMENTS

The New York Times, August 5, 1949
Miss Garland is fresh as a daisy and she sings a number of nostalgic songs in winning fashion. In fact, her slightly amusing and free wheeling interpretation of "I Don't Care" brought a burst of applause, which is not a common tribute in a movie house.

—T.M.P.

Time, July 18, 1949
Thanks to efficient research *Summertime* has a deceptively substantial appearance.... Its only other claim to style is Judy Garland. In several spots, she manages to give the show the look and pace of a bang-up musical.

Newsweek, August 22, 1949
But Miss Garland's voice—as appealing as ever—this time plays second fiddle to one of her best straight comedy performances.

---

36 **Summer Stock**

Metro-Goldwyn-Mayer
Released: August 1950
Running time: 110 minutes
Produced by Joe Pasternak
Directed by Charles Walters
Screenplay by George Wells and Sy Gomberg, based on a story by Sy Gomberg
Songs by Harry Warren and Mack Gordon, Saul Chaplin, Jack Brooks, Harold Arlen and Ted Koehler
Music direction: Johnny Green and Saul Chaplin
Dances staged by Nick Castle
Orchestration: Conrad Salinger and Skip Martin

Photography: Robert Planck
Editor: Albert Akst
Art direction: Cedric Gibbons, Jack Martin Smith

CAST

Jane Falbury	Judy Garland
Joe Ross	Gene Kelly
Orville Wingait	Eddie Bracken
Abigail Falbury	Gloria DeHaven
Esmé	Marjorie Main
Herb Blake	Phil Silvers
Jasper Wingait	Ray Collins
Sarah Higgins	Nita Bieber
Artie	Carleton Carpenter
Harrison Keath	Hans Conried

SYNOPSIS

A New England farm girl has her life disrupted when her irresponsible younger sister invites a group of impecunious New York actors to use her barn as a summer theater.

SONGS

"If You Feel Like Singing, Sing" (Judy Garland)

"Happy Harvest" (Judy Garland)

"Dig, Dig, Dig for Your Dinner" (Gene Kelly)

"Mem'ry Island" (Gloria DeHaven, Hans Conried)

"Blue Jean Polka" (danced by Judy Garland, Gene Kelly)

"You Wonderful You" (Gene Kelly, Judy Garland)

"Friendly Star" (Judy Garland)

"It's All for You" (Gene Kelly, Judy Garland, chorus)

"You Wonderful You" (reprise) (Judy Garland, Gene Kelly)

"Heavenly Music" (Gene Kelly, Phil Silvers)

"Get Happy" (Judy Garland)

"Happy Harvest" (reprise) (Judy Garland, Gene Kelly, Phil Silvers)

ADDENDA

★ This was Judy Garland's last film for MGM.

★ The British title is *If You Feel Like Singing*.

★ The "Get Happy" number, considered by many to be the highlight of the movie, was added as an afterthought, after production had been completed.

RECORDINGS

"Happy Harvest" and "If You Feel Like Singing, Sing" were released in 1950 on MGM 3025 (78).

"Friendly Star" and "Get Happy" were released in 1950 on MGM 3025 (78) and MGM 30254 (X-45).

Summer Stock was released on MGM M 54 (78) and MGM E 519 (33⅓).

CONTEMPORARY COMMENTS

Time, September 11, 1950

Summer Stock, no great shakes as a cinemusical, serves nonetheless as a welcome reminder of Judy Garland's unerring way with a song. Ill, and in and out of trouble with her studio, Actress Garland has been off the screen since last year's *In the Good Old Summertime.* . . . But none of it seems to have affected her ability as one of Hollywood's few triple threat girls. Thanks to Actress Garland's singing, dancing and acting. . . . the picture seems considerably better than it is . . . her voice and showmanlike delivery do wonders for the whole score.

Variety, August 9, 1950

Garland fans will cheer her "Get Happy" . . . Miss Garland is at her best in vocal delivery and looks, and sells the song with contagious rhythm. However, not far behind is "Happy Harvest" . . . She also clicks with "Friendly Star."

37 A Star Is Born

Warner Bros. Release
Transcona Enterprises Production
Released: September 1954
Running time: 181 minutes
Produced by Sidney Luft
Directed by George Cukor
"Born in a Trunk" sequence directed by Richard Barstow
Screenplay by Moss Hart, based on a screenplay by Dorothy Parker, Alan Campbell, and Robert Carson, based on a story by William A. Wellman and Robert Carson
Music: Harold Arlen

Lyrics: Ira Gershwin

"Born in a Trunk" number by Leonard Gershe

Musical direction: Ray Heindorf

Vocal arrangements: Jack Cathcart

Orchestration: Skip Martin

Dance direction: Richard Barstow

Set direction: George James Hopkins

Production design: Gene Allen

Associate producer: Vern Alves

Photography: Sam Leavitt

Photographed in CinemaScope and Technicolor

Editor: Folmar Blangsted

Art direction: Malcolm Bert

CAST

Esther Blodgett/
Vicki Lester .... Judy Garland
Norman Maine .... James Mason
Matt Libby .... Jack Carson
Oliver Niles .... Charles Bickford
Danny McGuire .... Tom Noonan
            with
Lucy Marlow   Amanda Blake
Irving Bacon   Hazel Shermet
Wilton Graff   Grady Sutton
James Brown   Lotus Robb

SYNOPSIS

An alcoholic film star discovers a young woman of extraordinary talent singing with a band. As he is fostering her discovery by the studio, they fall in love, and after her career is launched, they marry. While her career is moving from success to success, his is disintegrating due to his drinking. Her professional heights are paralleled by his personal degradation.

GARLAND SONGS

"Gotta Have Me Go with You"

"The Man That Got Away"

"Born in a Trunk" sequence includes
    "I'll Get By"
    "You Took Advantage of Me"
    "Black Bottom"
    "The Peanut Vendor"
    "Melancholy Baby"
    "Swanee"

"Here's What I'm Here For"

"It's a New World"

"Someone at Last"

"Lose That Long Face"

ADDENDA

★ Transcona Enterprises was owned by Judy Garland and her husband, Sidney Luft.

★ Originally, Garland and Luft had wanted Cary Grant to play the James Mason role. Grant, after much thought, decided against the part, fearing the tendency of audiences to find drunks comic.

★ It was decided to use the new CinemaScope process after principal photography had begun. The initial footage was scrapped and scenes re-filmed, greatly increasing the cost of the production.

★ "The Man That Got Away" sequence in the film was the third one photographed. George Cukor and production designer Gene Allen were dissatisfied with the visual effects of the first two versions. The number was redesigned and refilmed using the same track but different lighting, costuming, and staging.

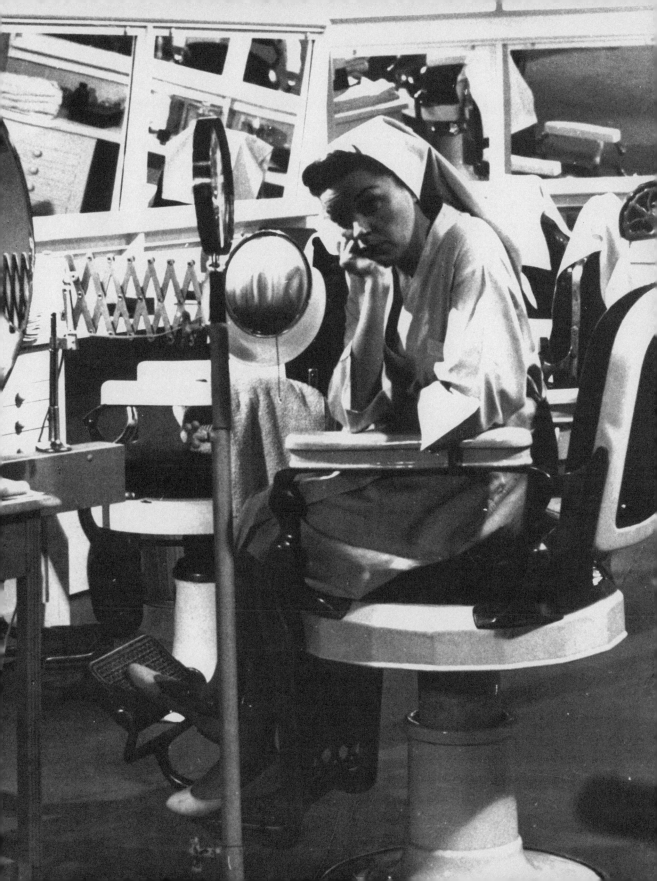

★ Garland sang all out with the playback while filming "The Man That Got Away" number. It took twenty-seven takes to get it in the can.

★ The "Born in a Trunk" sequence was not part of the original production plan. It was added as an afterthought after principal production was finished.

★ *A Star Is Born* had the first premiere to be televised nationally. The celebrity interviews and proceedings were so successful that the show was rebroadcast the following night.

★ *A Star Is Born* ran in its original release version for two months. Harry Warner then cut the film from 181 minutes to 154 minutes. It is generally agreed that he eviscerated a masterpiece. Fourteen minutes of character development material was cut from the first half, and the "Here's What I'm Here For" and "Lose That Long Face" numbers were taken out.

★ In 1983, a reconstructed version was released. Twenty-two minutes were restored and several segments reconstructed visually with stills against the original soundtrack. Pieces of the film are still missing.

★ *Life,* for the second time, used Garland for its cover on the September 13, 1954, issue reviewing *A Star Is Born.*

★ When Garland was nominated for Best Actress for *Star,* she received no studio

support. Warner Bros. did not place a single ad for their biggest release of the year.

★ After Judy lost the Oscar to Grace Kelly for *The Country Girl,* she received more than a thousand telegrams of regret and dismay. Groucho Marx wired "This is the biggest robbery since Brink's."

★ *A Star Is Born* was originally part of a multipicture deal for Transcona production and Warners release. Because of the expense of *Star,* the other films were never made.

★ *A Star Is Born* was one of the top moneymakers of the year.

AWARDS/NOMINATIONS

Judy Garland was nominated for Best Actress; she won a Golden Globe award for Best Actress (musical/comedy). James Mason was nominated for Best Actor. "The Man That Got Away" was nominated for Best Song. Ray Heindorf was nominated for Best Scoring of a Musical Picture. Malcolm Bert, Gene Allen, Irene Sharaff, and George James Hopkins were nominated for Best Art Direction (color).

RECORDINGS

"The Man That Got Away" and "Here's What I'm Here For" were released in 1954 on Columbia 40270 (78).

A Star Is Born was released in 1954 on Columbia CL 1101 (33⅓).

In 1988, a true (not remastered) stereo version of the original film soundtrack was released on CD (Columbia CK 34889) and cassette (CBS JST 44389).

"When My Sugar Walks Down the Street," an unused number from the "Born in a Trunk" sequence, and Roger Edens running through "Somewhere There's a Someone" are available on *Cut! Out-Takes from Hollywood's Greatest Musicals,* vol. 3, Out-Take Records OFT 3 (33⅓).

CONTEMPORARY COMMENTS

The New York Times, October 12, 1954
Those who have blissful recollections of David O. Selznick's "A Star Is Born" as probably the most affecting movie ever made about Hollywood may get themselves set for a new experience that should put the former one in the shade . . .

[George Cukor] . . . gets performances from Miss Garland and Mr. Mason that make the heart flutter and bleed.
—Bosley Crowther

Time, October 25, 1954
[Judy Garland] . . . gives what is just about the greatest one-woman show in modern movie history. . . . she has never sung better. . . . Her big, dark voice sobs, sighs, sulks and socks them out like a cross between Tara's harp and the late Bessie Smith. . . . Everybody's little sister, it would seem, has grown out of her braids and into a tiara.

Newsweek, November 1, 1954
A Star Is Born is best classified as a thrilling personal triumph for Judy Garland.

As an actress Miss Garland is more than adequate. As a mime and comedienne she is even better. But as a singer she can handle anything from torch songs and blues to ballads. In more ways than one, the picture is hers.

Life, September 13, 1954

A Star Is Born, the year's most worrisome movie, has turned out to be one of its best. In it one-time teenage star Judy Garland, now 32 and out of movies for four years, not only makes a film comeback almost without precedent but puts herself right in line for an Oscar.

. . . a brilliantly staged, scored and photographed film . . . principal credit for the success of *A Star Is Born* unquestionably goes to imaginative, tireless, talented Judy.

Variety, September 29, 1954

[*A Star Is Born*] will not only mop up as a commercial entry: this indie production for WB release set a number of artistic standards . . .

The casting is ideal; the direction sure; the basic ingredients honest and convincing all the way. Miss Garland glitters with that stardust which in the plot the wastrel James Mason recognizes.

---

38 Pepe

Columbia Pictures
Released: December 1960
Running time: 195 minutes
Produced and directed by George Sidney
Screenplay by Dorothy Kingsley and Claude Binyon, screen story by Leonard Spigelgass and Sonya Levien, based on a play by L. Bush-Fekete
Associate producer: Jacques Gelman
Music and lyrics by André Previn, Hans Wittstatt, Augustin Lara, Dore Langdon, and Maria Teresa Lara
Music supervision and background score: Johnny Green

Photography: Joe MacDonald
Editors: Viola Lawrence, Al Clark
Art direction: Ted Haworth

CAST

Cantinflas
Judy Garland
   (voice only)
Shirley Jones
Dan Dailey
Carlos Montalban

Edward G. Robinson
William Demarest
Ernie Kovacs
Matt Mattox
Vicki Trickett
Hank Henry

Guest Stars:
Maurice Chevalier
Michael Callan
Richard Conte
Ann B. Davis
Jimmy Durante
Greer Garson
Joey Bishop
Janet Leigh
Jay North
André Previn
Debbie Reynolds

Bing Crosby
Charles Coburn
Bobby Darin
Sammy Davis, Jr.
Zsa Zsa Gabor
Hedda Hopper
Peter Lawford
Jack Lemmon
Kim Novak
Donna Reed
Cesar Romero

SYNOPSIS

A Mexican peasant is brought north of the border by an alcoholic Hollywood director to serve as a groom for a horse purchased in Mexico.

SONGS

"Pepe" (Shirley Jones)
"Mimi" (Maurice Chevalier)
"September Song" (Maurice Chevalier)
"Hooray for Hollywood"
   (Sammy Davis, Jr.)
"The Rumble" (André Previn)
"That's How It Went, All Right" (Bobby Darin)
"Far Away Part of Town" (Judy Garland)
"Suzy's Theme" (Johnny Green)

"Pennies from Heaven" (Bing Crosby)
"Let's Fall in Love" (Bing Crosby)
"South of the Border" (Bing Crosby)
"Lovely Day" (Shirley Jones)

ADDENDA

★ *Pepe* was one of the top moneymakers of the year.

AWARDS/NOMINATIONS

Joe MacDonald was nominated for Best Color Cinematography; Ted Haworth and William Kiernan for Best Art Direction (color); Edith Head for Best Costume Design (color); Columbia Studio Sound Department, Charles Rice, director, for Best Sound; Viola Lawrence and Al Clark for Best Film Editing. "Far Away Part of Town," written by André Previn and Dore Langdon, was nominated for Best Song, and Johnny Green was nominated for Best Scoring of a Musical Picture.

RECORDINGS

The soundtrack for *Pepe* is available on Colpix CP/CPS 507 (33⅓) and Pye International NPL 28015 (33⅓).

---

39 Judgment at Nuremberg

United Artists Release
Roxlom Production
Released: October 1961
Running time: 190 minutes
Produced and directed by Stanley Kramer
Associate producer: Philip Langner
Screenplay by Abby Mann, based on a television script by Abby Mann
Music: Ernest Gold
Photography: Ernest Laszlo

Editor: Frederick Knudston
Production designer: Rudolph Sternad
Art direction: Rudolph Sternad, George Milo

CAST

Judge Dan Haywood .... Spencer Tracy
Ernst Janning .... Burt Lancaster
Colonel Tad Lawson ... Richard Widmark
Madame Bertholt .... Marlene Dietrich
Hans Rolfe .... Maximilian Schell
Irene Hoffman .... Judy Garland
Rudolph Peterson ...... Montgomery Clift
Captain Byers .... William Shatner
Senator Burkette .... Edward Binns
Judge Kenneth Norris .... Kenneth MacKenna
Emil Hahn .... Werner Klemperer
General Merrin .... Alan Baxter
Werner Lammpe .... Torben Meyer
with
Ray Teal   Martin Brandt
Virginia Christine   Ben Wright
Joseph Bernard   John Wengraf
Karl Swenson   Howard Caine
Otto Waldis   Olga Fabian
Sheila Bromley   Bernard Kates
Jana Taylor   Paul Busch

SYNOPSIS

An American judge at the Nuremberg war trials is faced with the issue of how much responsibility and guilt an individual must bear for crimes committed or condoned by him on the order of, and in the interest of, the State.

ADDENDA

★ When Garland reported to the set to start working on her first real part since *Star,* the crew gave her a standing ovation.

AWARDS/NOMINATIONS

Judgment in Nuremberg was cited by the New York Film Critics as one of the Ten Best Pictures of the Year.

The picture was nominated for the Academy Award for Best Picture of the Year. Maximilian Schell won for Best Actor. Montgomery Clift was nominated for Best Supporting Actor and Judy Garland for Best Supporting Actress. Stanley Kramer was nominated for Best Direction; Abby Mann for writing (Best Screenplay Based on Material from Another Medium); Ernest Laszlo for Cinematography (black and white); Rudolph Sternad and George Milo for Best Set Decoration Black and White; Frederick Knudston for Best Film Editing; and Jean Louis for Best Costume Design Black and White.

Judy Garland won the Golden Globe Cecil B. DeMille Award in 1962 for her "contribution to the entertainment industry throughout the years."

CONTEMPORARY COMMENTS

The New York Times, December 20, 1961
[Stanley Kramer and Abby Mann] ...have...a...young hausfrau whom Judy Garland makes amazingly real tell a horrifying tale of trumped-up charges of "racial contamination" against an elderly Jew.

—Bosley Crowther

Variety, October 18, 1961
Both Clift and Miss Garland bring great emotional force and conviction to their chores, he as a somewhat deranged victim of Nazi sterility measures, she as a German accused of relations with a Jew at a period when such an activity was forbidden and punishable by death for the Jew.

40 Gay Purr-ee

Warner Bros. Release
UPA Production
Released: November 1962
Running time: 86 minutes
Produced by Henry G. Saperstein
Associate producer: Lee Orgel
Directed by Abe Leviton
Screenplay by Dorothy and Chuck Jones
Music and lyrics by Harold Arlen and E. Y. Harburg
Music arranged and conducted by Mort Lindsey
Vocal arrangements by Joseph J. Lilley
Photography: Roy Hutchcroft, Dan Miller, Jack Stevens, Duane Keegan
Editor: Ted Baker
Art direction: Victor Haboush

CAST

(Voices only)

Judy Garland	Julie Bennett
Hermione Gingold	Red Buttons
Mel Blanc	Morey Amsterdam
Robert Goulet	Joan Gardner
Paul Frees	

SYNOPSIS

A country cat, a town cat, and their misadventures with some city slickers.

SONGS

"Gay Purr-ee Overture" (Judy Garland and chorus)
"Mewsette" (Robert Goulet)
"Little Drops of Rain" (Judy Garland)
"The Money Cat" (Paul Frees and The Mellow Men)
"Portraits of Mewsette" (Orchestra)

"Take My Hand, Paree" (Judy Garland)

"Paris Is a Lonely Town" (Judy Garland)

"Bubbles" (Robert Goulet, Red Buttons, and The Mellow Men)

"Roses Red, Violets Blue" (Judy Garland)

"Little Drops of Rain" (reprise) (Robert Goulet)

"Paris Is a Lonely Town" (Orchestra)

"The Horse Won't Talk" (Paul Frees)

"The Mewsette Finale" (Robert Goulet, Judy Garland, and chorus)

RECORDINGS

The soundtrack for *Gay Purr-ee* is available on Warner Bros. B/BS 1479 (33⅓) and Warner Bros. W/WS 802 (33⅓) (U.K.).

The Garland songs are also on *Judy Garland: More than a Memory*, Stanyan 1095 (33⅓).

CONTEMPORARY COMMENTS

The New York Times, December 6, 1962
Mewsette, a nice enough little lady cat, is most interesting when Miss Garland is warbling superbly.

—Howard Thompson

41 A Child Is Waiting

United Artists Release
Stanley Kramer Production
Released: January 1963
Running time: 104 minutes
Produced by Stanley Kramer
Associate producer: Philip Langner
Directed by John Cassavetes
Screenplay by Abby Mann, based on a television play by Abby Mann

Music by Ernest Gold
Photography: Joseph LaShelle
Editor: Gene Fowler, Jr., Robert C. Jones
Art direction: Rudolph Sternad
Set direction: Joseph Kish
Song "Snowflake" by Marjorie D. Kurtz
Poem "The Mist and I" by Dixie Wilson

CAST

Dr. Matthew Clark . . . . Burt Lancaster
Jean Hansen . . . . Judy Garland
Sophie Widdicombe . . . . . . Gena Rowlands
Ted Widdicombe . . . . Steven Hill
Reuben Widdicombe . . . . . . Bruce Ritchey
Mattie . . . . Gloria McGehee
Goodman . . . . Paul Stewart
Douglas Benham . . . . Lawrence Tierney
Miss Fogarty . . . . Elizabeth Wilson
Miss Brown . . . . Barbara Pepper
Holland . . . . John Morley
Mrs. McDonald . . . . June Walker
Dr. Lombardi . . . . Marlo Gallo
Dr. Sack . . . . Frederick Draper

SYNOPSIS

An unmarried woman joins the staff of a private school for mentally retarded children.

GARLAND SONGS

"Snowflake" (Judy Garland, with children)

CONTEMPORARY COMMENTS

The New York Times, February 14, 1963
Miss Garland's misty-eyed compassion and Mr. Lancaster's crisp authority . . . are of a standard dramatic order.

—Bosley Crowther

Variety, January 7, 1963
Skillfully executed and tastefully performed . . . Judy Garland gives a sympathetic portrayal of an overly involved teacher who comes to see the error of her obsession with the plight of one child.

---

42 I Could Go On Singing

United Artists Release
Barbican Production
Released: March 1963
Running time: 99 minutes
Produced by Stuart Millar and Lawrence Turman
Directed by Ronald Neame
Screenplay by Mayo Simon, based on a story by Robert Dozier
Title song by Harold Arlen and E. Y. Harburg
Music supervision: Saul Chaplin
Associate producer: Dennis Holt
Photography: Arthur Ibbetson
Editor: John Shirley
Art direction: Wilfred Shingleton

CAST

Jenny Bowman .... Judy Garland
David Donne .... Dirk Bogarde
George Kogan .... Jack Klugman
Matt .... Gregory Phillips
Ida .... Aline MacMahon
Miss Plimpton ....Pauline Jameson
Hospital surgeon .... Jeremy Burnham

Guests:
Russell Waters
Leon Cortez
Gerald Sim

SYNOPSIS

A famous American singer, while on a concert tour in Britain, looks up a former lover by whom she had a child.

GARLAND SONGS

"I Could Go On Singing"
"Hello, Bluebird"
"It Never Was You"
"I Am the Monarch of the Sea" (with boys chorus)
"By Myself"

ADDENDA

★ The British title is *The Lonely Crowd.*
★ This was Judy Garland's last film appearance.
★ *I Could Go On Singing* was the only film Judy Garland made abroad.

RECORDINGS

The soundtrack for *I Could Go On Singing* is available on Capitol ST 1861 (33⅓).

CONTEMPORARY COMMENTS

The New York Times, May 16, 1963
Considering what Judy Garland has done in movies over the years and how many of her fans still love her, no matter what she does, it is sad to have to say the little lady is not at the top of her form.
—Bosley Crowther

Time, April 19, 1963
Her acting . . . may be the best of her career. . . . If the Judy who once stole Andy Hardy's heart is gone somewhere over the rainbow of hard knocks and sleeping pills, Garland the actress seems here to stay.

Jack Klugman watches Judy get ready to perform in *I Could Go on Singing.*

Newsweek, April 22, 1963
The Magna Carta was signed in 1215. Shortly thereafter, Judy Garland sang "Somewhere Over the Rainbow," and ever since, she has had her special place in the hearts of millions. . . . She sings a number of songs . . . but singing isn't really what she does any more. Acting is not exactly what she does, either. . . .

But she's, well, Judy Garland. And we love her. . . . It's part of our way of life . . . And for people who like this kind of thing, this is the kind of thing they'll like.

Variety, March 13, 1963
A soulful performance is etched by Miss Garland, who gives more than she gets from the script.

Miscellaneous and Undated Shorts

1 Musical short, with Kay Kyser

Probably a Will Rogers Memorial Hospital promotional film, with money parts deleted.

2 General promotional short

For the Will Rogers Memorial Hospital.

3 "Screen Snapshots," series 15

Produced by Columbia Pictures, with Judy Garland, Bette Davis, and Ken Maynard credited.

RADIO APPEARANCES

———————— ★ ————————

"Radio generated a lot of publicity in those days, and the shows were treated like Broadway first nights. They had studio audiences, so you'd get all dolled up . . ."

Myrna Loy, *Being and Becoming*

———————— ★ ————————

"Judy is one of the greatest talents, male or female, in Hollywood. . . . we've done a great many radio shows together, and she's the perfect illustration of the 100% professional. You can't help being drawn by her magnetism. And it rubs off on you, too. Nobody can be professionally indifferent when Judy Garland's part of the act."

Bing Crosby, CBS interview in 1955

———————— ★ ————————

Judy Garland appeared on network radio from 1935 (almost simultaneously to her signing with Metro) through 1957, long after she had left the studio and established a new career in films, on the concert stage, and on television. Including the series on which she was a regular cast member for a season at a time, Judy made over two hundred appearances on the coast-to-coast ether. There are major performers who spent more time on radio. But there are few performers of her stature who have had so large and significant a part of their careers so generally ignored.

In the thirties and forties, radio was a vital and vibrant entertainment medium. It was a unique combination of the remnants of vaudeville, with its variety shows and standup comics; theater, with its translations of pictures and plays; and concerts, with their live music and popular singers. It was a medium, too, the studios used for testing new talent, showcasing stars, and publicizing new movies and music.

Radio, however, didn't take itself as seriously as either motion pictures or

Broadway. It was freer. There was room for improvisation and ad-libbing. And because it was live, usually in front of an audience as well as a microphone, there was no room for retakes or repetition. In many ways, radio assayed performers as the sound stage and recording sessions did not.

Judy Garland thrived on radio.

On radio, she tested her skills and experimented with style. She worked with a vast array of polished professionals—both within and outside the studio system. She performed in a range of vehicles beyond those MGM fashioned for her. She worked from scripts, and she departed from them with the best.

If Judy grew up in public view on the screen, it was on radio—with its more freewheeling approach and live audiences —that she honed the talents that only came to the fore during her concert years. And radio provided her professional life with important elements of continuity.

Radio and motion pictures had an intense, if little noted, symbiotic relationship. Most Hollywood personalities spent a significant amount of time on the air. Between pictures they made appearances to advertise their latest release, or their studio's. Actors introduced, emceed, or acted in radio dramas or on variety shows. Singers did all this and sang songs from their latest movies. Radio broadcasts were replete with references to the pictures and personalities on the screen.

When MGM set out to build a star, no resource was ignored. Publicists churned out press releases and fan magazine arti-

cles. Carefully crafted private lives were made selectively public to gossip columnists. Personal appearances were arranged. And radio exposure, exposure to the millions who went to the movies even if they did not read the fan literature or follow the columns, made movie unknowns vaguely familiar names and voices.

One gauge, then, of Metro's attitude toward Judy Garland early in her career can be charted on radio. Judy was signed by the studio in 1935, and in 1936 she was loaned out to Twentieth Century-Fox for *Pigskin Parade* and used in a test short, *Every Sunday*. Despite the increasing word of mouth in the community about Metro's "vocal find," no one knew quite what to do with her. In 1936, she was on only one major radio program and cut only two sides with Decca.

Then she sang her famous serenade to Clark Gable at the MGM commissary. The script for *Broadway Melody of 1938* was revised to include her and her "You Made Me Love You." In 1937, Judy made two dozen radio appearances, becoming a member of the cast of "Jack Oakie's College" after an initial appearance in January and a regular guest on the "Good News" programs in 1937 and 1938, programs MGM used to showcase talent and push its latest film releases.

From that point, until television replaced radio as a primary entertainment medium, Judy Garland was never off the air, or away from a live audience, for more than a few months at a time. In fact, between the personal-appearance tours MGM arranged to tout her films and her appearances on radio, Garland spent far more time singing in person than she did in recording sessions.

This continuity of audience contact is significant for Judy Garland's career. She was one of the very few child stars of the thirties and forties to make a successful transition to adult actress. In addition, she built an even greater career off the screen, as a vocalist and concert artist. She learned from the finest professionals at MGM, but her regular personal appearances and radio broadcasts gave her every opportunity to test skills and approaches for immediate audience feedback. Feedback that came not only from coaches, technicians, and producers but from the people who bought the tickets and records.

The immediacy is important. It is difficult to predict with assurance what will sell successfully in the entertainment marketplace. But if the audience is right in front of you, it's not difficult to know when it's with you or when you've lost its full attention. Talented and sensitive performers pick up on intangible, but perceptible, audience reactions. They attune their performances to those signals. Done often enough, their acuity becomes a virtual sixth sense and results in a dynamic and creative tension between the public and the performer.

Judy Garland was training in, and mastering, this dynamic for nearly fifteen years before her formal concert career began, a period that included her formative years as a professional entertainer. For nearly fifteen years—more than half her life by 1950 (not counting her early

years on the road or her performances as part of the Gumm Sisters act), Judy had regular and direct contact with the ticket-buying public. Not only did she see when and how she was most successful with them, she had the opportunity, too, to watch other polished professionals work their audiences.

Early in her radio career, for example, she was a season regular on the Bob Hope shows, and Hope encouraged ad-libbing and repartee; it was part of his act to be the object of humor as well as its initiator. She worked also with Edgar Bergen, Jack Benny, Fanny Brice, Danny Kaye, and other comedians, as well as dramatic actors ranging from Lionel Barrymore to Alan Ladd to Fredric March, particularly during the war years and after.

During these same years, she was also singing a far greater array of songs than would ever appear as formal recordings or as numbers in her films. On her early radio broadcasts, most of her songs were either from her movies or comedy versions of tunes designed to get the maximum mileage out of her youth.

But by the forties, when she was both an established star and out of her teens, she used and tested her Metro-defined vocal style. Particularly on Armed Forces Radio Service broadcasts, she played with swing and jazz rhythms and techniques that MGM had, by that time, virtually eliminated from her motion picture renditions. Listen, for example, to her rendition of "Dixieland Band" (1944).

Because radio performances were live, without retakes, existing transcriptions are enormously informative about the development of the Garland style. Not all her experiments were successful. Songs like "Abe Lincoln Had Just One Country" (1943), for example, or "We're Off to See Herr Hitler" (1943) will never make anyone's list of Top 10 favorites, although they suited the patriotic fervor of the moment. Her "operetta" sketch with Danny Kaye and Lauritz Melchior, in 1947, parody though it may have been, does not show Judy to her best advantage, nor does her ensemble rendition of "Tearbucket Jim," from a Bing Crosby show, also in 1947. The point, however, is not the occasional failure but the continual experimentation, both with the kind of material she sang and how she sang it. Judy may have been cast in a screen formula by MGM, but on radio she extended those parameters.

Radio, too, gave her an opportunity to sing with other professional singers, singers with polished styles and impressive skills. Her songs with Bing Crosby, for example, or Frank Sinatra, set in the relative informality of a radio studio, before live audiences, have an added element of excitement, humor, and ease that stems from the apparent pleasure of singing with well-matched partners.

When Garland sang with Crosby, for instance, she had no need to suppress her vocal power to accommodate him, as she did in duets with Fred Astaire or Gene Kelly. Indeed, part of the fun of their songs together (and one of the reasons collectors so avidly seek recordings of the two of them) is the obvious enjoyment with which they melded Garland's intensity and Crosby's low-keyed approach into unusually successful duets.

During Judy's Metro years, she made only one purely dramatic appearance on the screen, in *The Clock,* with Robert Walker, in 1945. Her performance was a sensitive and delicate one, showing a dramatic ability that MGM rarely exploited. While this role was an oddity for Garland on film, she had been testing the nonmusical medium on radio. By the time *The Clock* was released, Judy had made a half-dozen broadcast comedies and dramas, where any musical sequences were purely incidental to the plot.

In 1941, she starred in a radio production of "Merton of the Movies," opposite Mickey Rooney, and while Mickey played (overplayed, rather) a country bumpkin, Judy still chased Mickey. But by 1942, she graduated to meatier roles with dramatic, as opposed to musical comedy, costars. In 1942 and 1943, she re-created the Katharine Hepburn role in "Morning Glory" opposite John Payne, with Adolphe Menjou; the Janet Gaynor role in "A Star Is Born" opposite Walter Pidgeon (with Adolphe Menjou again); and played opposite Alan Ladd in "Ringside Table."

MGM never followed up on Garland's success in *The Clock;* its screen formula for her was set. But between that film and her tour de force 1954 remake of *A Star Is Born,* Judy Garland had been practicing her dramatic skills on radio. She starred in "Holiday" (1946) and "Alice Adams" (1950), two more Katharine Hepburn roles; "Drive In," a virtual one-woman show, in 1946; and "Cinderella" (1951) and "Lady in the Dark," with John Lund, in 1953. These were aside from broadcast re-creations of her screen roles.

Radio was a perfect medium for a vocalist/actress to develop her skills. For where there was a studio audience for immediate feedback, to the listeners at their radios the performers were invisible. Garland's increasing ability to create dramatic power, humor, and whimsy totally through tone of voice and vocal control is highlighted by these radio performances.

If you follow her from "Merton" or "Star" through "Drive In" to "Lady in the Dark," you find Judy Garland's expanding prowess in subtly imbuing her dialogue with an emotional dynamic of depth and texture that is missed on the screen. The dark intensity in her role as Liza Elliott in "Lady," for example, is significantly greater than that of her Esther/Vicki character in the 1942 "Star," but it presages the controlled tension of the 1954 film. Similarly, there is a bemused, wistful, and confused quality to her character in the 1951 "Cinderella" that gives her performance a delicate balance among comedy, drama, and fantasy; it is this balance that, in large part, makes the production so charming.

Garland's broadcasting career, then, narrows the divide between her Metro and post-Metro film performances. For if Judy's screen image came together for MGM in 1943 in *Girl Crazy,* her dramatic skills coalesced for her in the late forties and early fifties, on radio.

Radio, too, provided the bridge between the Gumm Sisters' assault on vaudeville and Judy Garland's revitalization of the "two-a-day." In some ways, she had never left the stage.

One of the more notable aspects of the mature Garland was her ability to give an acute professional appraisal of her own performances. This kind of skill can only be developed through a sure knowledge of limits as well as abilities, and limits are not determined by hewing to the boundaries of past successes. Metro-Goldwyn-Mayer had found formulas for Judy's success that made her a bankable commodity, and the studio wasn't about to risk much experimentation. Fortunately for her, when she was fired in 1950, Judy Garland had already taken both the risk and her own measure as an artist.

This chapter concentrates on network radio broadcasts and Armed Forces Radio Service (AFRS). It does not include the vast number of local radio appearances Judy Garland made during her career (although an occasional local broadcast of interest is included).

1935

1 "The Shell Chateau Hour" October 26, 1935

NBC: WEAF, Red Network
 (60 minutes)
Music: Victor Young and His Orchestra

STARRING

Wallace Beery (guest host for Al Jolson)
Guests:
Fanny Brice   Vance Breese
Judy Garland   Harry Stockwell

GARLAND SONGS

"Broadway Rhythm"

ADDENDA

★ This was Judy's network radio debut.
★ Judy recorded her classic version of "Over the Rainbow" with the Victor Young Orchestra for Decca release in 1939. Young also backed her on a number of other recordings from her early MGM years.

RECORDINGS

Judy Garland, 1935–1951, Star-Tone ST 201 (33⅓), and *Born in a Trunk: Discovery*, AEI 2108 (33⅓), have "Broadway Rhythm."

2 "The Shell Chateau Hour" November 16, 1935

NBC: WEAF, Red Network
 (60 minutes)
Music: Victor Young and His Orchestra

STARRING

Wallace Beery (substituting for Al Jolson)
Guests:
Bill Tilden   Judy Garland
Allan Jones   Patsy Kelly
Sigmund Spaeth   Fay Helen

GARLAND SONGS

"Zing! Went the Strings of My Heart"

ADDENDA

★ Judy was performing on this program the night her father died.

RECORDINGS

"Zing!" is on *The Judy Garland Musical Scrapbook*, Star-Tone ST 208 (33⅓).

1936

1 "The Shell Chateau Hour"
August 6, 1936

NBC: WEAF, Red Network
  (60 minutes)

S T A R R I N G

Wallace Beery (substituting for Al Jolson)

Guests:

Joe Cook   Judy Garland
Margaret Sullavan   Larry Crabbe

G A R L A N D   S O N G S

"After You've Gone"

1937

1 "Jack Oakie's College"
January through June, 1937

CBS: (60 minutes)
Producer: Bill Lawrence
Writers: Hugh Wedlock, Howard Snyder
Music: Georgie Stoll Orchestra, Benny
  Goodman Orchestra
Master of ceremonies: Rupert Hughes

C A S T

Jack Oakie   Al Shaw
Joe Penner   Sam Lee

Judy Garland was added to the cast on
February 23, 1937. She was described as
"a young blues singer."

She appeared on the program on:

January 5, with
John Boles   George Jessel
The Yale Glee Club

February 23, with
The Benny Goodman Quartet

Judy sang "Dear Mr. Gable" on the air for
the first time. (*Broadway Melody of 1938*
was in production, and she had just
joined the cast.)

March 2, with
Hugh Herbert
Mary Carr
The Alexander Swingtime Chorus
The Williams Glee Club

March 9, with
George Jessel
The Alexander Swingtime Chorus

From March 30 through June 22, 1937,
Judy Garland appeared every week.

A D D E N D A

★ This program, which premiered on
  June 30, 1936, was originally called
  "The Camel Caravan," with music by
  the Nat Shilkret and Benny Goodman
  bands. The name was changed to "Jack
  Oakie's College" on December 29,
  1936, and Georgie Stoll replaced Nat
  Shilkret.

★ Georgie Stoll was music director on
  many of Judy's films for MGM.

★ June 22, 1937, was the last show. It was
  replaced on the air by "Benny Goodman's Swing School."

RECORDINGS

A cut of Judy singing "Smiles" on this program is on *Judy Garland, 1935–1951*, Star-Tone ST 201 (33⅓).

---

2 "Ben Bernie and All the Lads" February 2, 1937

NBC: WJZ, Blue Network (30 minutes)

STARRING

Ben Bernie and His Orchestra

Guest: Judy Garland

GARLAND SONGS

"You Made Me Love You"
"Oh Say Can You Swing"

ADDENDA

★ Judy sang "You Made Me Love You" in *Broadway Melody of 1938,* which would be released in July of 1937.
★ The NBC Network "personality card" on Judy for the period describes her as "child singer and motion picture actress."

---

3 "Hollywood Hotel" July 16, 1937

CBS (60 minutes)
Episode: "Broadway Melody of 1938"

STARRING

Robert Taylor   Billy Gilbert
Buddy Ebsen   Sophie Tucker
Judy Garland   George Murphy
Eleanor Powell

ADDENDA

★ This broadcast was in the same month as the general release of the film of the same name.
★ In 1940, she costarred with George Murphy in her first adult screen role in *Little Nellie Kelly.* They costarred again, in 1942, in *For Me and My Gal.*

---

4 "Ben Bernie and All the Lads" October 12, 1937

NBC: WJZ, Blue Network (30 minutes)

STARRING

Ben Bernie and His Orchestra

Guest: Judy Garland

GARLAND SONGS

"They Can't Take That Away from Me"
"Got a Pair of New Shoes"

ADDENDA

★ "Got a Pair of New Shoes" was sung by Judy in her 1937 film *Thoroughbreds Don't Cry.*

5 **"Thirty Minutes in Hollywood"**
October 24, 1937

WOR   (30 minutes)
Music: Tommy Tucker and His
    Orchestra

STARRING

George Jessel

Guests:
Bert Wheeler
Norma Talmadge
Judy Garland

GARLAND SONGS

"Dear Mr. Gable (You Made Me Love
    You)"

6 **"New Faces of 1938"**
November 4, 1937

NBC: WEAF, Red Network
    (60 minutes)
Music director: Meredith Willson
Master of ceremonies: Robert Leonard

GUESTS

Eleanor Powell   Judy Garland
Igor Gorin   Buddy Ebsen
Ukulele Ike   Sophie Tucker
George Murphy

GARLAND SONGS

"Your Broadway and My Broadway"
"Broadway Rhythm"
"Everybody Sing" (with chorus)

ADDENDA

★ These songs were from Judy's first
feature-length MGM film, *Broadway
Melody of 1938* (1937), with the same
cast that guested on this show (with the
exception of Ukulele Ike). The program was dedicated to the film.

★ The name "New Faces of 1938" was
changed to "Good News" on subse-
quent broadcasts. This was the series
premiere. The series was produced in
association with MGM.

Publicity shot of Judy walking to the MGM studios.

RECORDINGS

"Broadway Rhythm" is available on *Born in a Trunk. Discovery,* AEI 2108 (33⅓), and *Judy Garland, 1935–1951,* Star-Tone ST 201 (33⅓).

7 **"Good News of 1938"**
November 18, 1937

NBC: WEAF, Red Network
   (60 minutes)
Music director: Meredith Willson

GARLAND SONGS
unidentified

8 **"Good News of 1938"**
November 25, 1937

NBC: WEAF, Red Network
   (60 minutes)
Music director: Meredith Willson

GUESTS
Allan Jones
Judy Garland
Fanny Brice

GARLAND SONGS
"Got a Pair of New Shoes"

ADDENDA
★ Judy costarred with Allan Jones and Fanny Brice in the film *Everybody Sing,* which would be released in February 1938.

1938

1 **"Good News of 1938"**
January 6, 1938

NBC: WEAF, Red Network
   (60 minutes)
Music director: Meredith Willson

GUESTS
Judy Garland
other guests unidentified

GARLAND SONGS
"The Sextette" from Donizetti's *Lucia di Lammermoor* (with chorus)
Interpolations:
   "Smiles"
   "Christopher Columbus"
"Suddenly" (with special lyrics)
Interpolations:
   "Two Hearts That Swing in ¾ Time"
   "While Strolling Through the Park One Day"

2 **"Good News of 1938"**
January 20, 1938

NBC: WEAF, Red network (60 minutes)
Music director: Meredith Willson
Master of ceremonies: Robert Taylor

GUESTS
Allan Jones
Judy Garland

Fanny Brice, Judy Garland, and Allan Jones in the film *Everybody Sing.*

GARLAND SONGS

"Smiles" (with special lyrics)

RECORDINGS

"Smiles" is on *Born in a Trunk. Discovery,* AEI 2108 (33⅓).

---

3 **"Good News of 1938"**
February 3, 1938

NBC: WEAF, Red Network
   (60 minutes)
Music director: Meredith Willson
Master of ceremonies: Robert Taylor

GUESTS

Allan Jones
Fanny Brice
Judy Garland

GARLAND SONGS

"Everybody Sing"
"Love's Old Sweet Song"
unidentified song—duet with Fanny Brice

ADDENDA

★ Judy sang "Everybody Sing" in *Broadway Melody of 1938,* which had been released the previous July.

**4 "Good News of 1938"
February 17, 1938**

NBC: WEAF, Red Network
    (60 minutes)
Music director: Meredith Willson
Master of ceremonies: Robert Taylor

GUESTS

Allan Jones
Judy Garland
Maureen O'Sullivan

GARLAND SONGS

"Always" (not certain)
"Down on Melody Farm"

ADDENDA

★ Garland sang "Down on Melody Farm"
  in *Everybody Sing,* in which she appeared with Allan Jones. The film was
  coming into release as this program
  was being aired.

**5 "Good News of 1938"
April 7, 1938**

NBC: WEAF, Red Network
    (60 minutes)
Music director: Meredith Willson
Master of ceremonies: Robert Taylor

GUESTS

Judy Garland   Fanny Brice
Frank Morgan   Sam Levene
Hanley Stafford

GARLAND SONGS

"Stompin' at the Savoy"
"Why? Because" (with Fanny Brice)

ADDENDA

★ Judy Garland appeared with Fanny
  Brice in the film *Everybody Sing,* which
  was released in February 1938. Garland
  and Brice sang "Why? Because" in the
  movie.
★ "Stompin' at the Savoy" was one of
  Judy's first two sides recorded for
  Decca and released in 1936. It is avail-
  able on *Collector's Items, 1936–1945,*
  MCA 2-4046 (33⅓).

**6 "Good News of 1938"
April 14, 1938**

NBC: WEAF, Red Network
    (60 minutes)
Music director: Meredith Willson
Master of ceremonies: Robert Taylor

GUESTS

Judy Garland   Freddie Bartholomew
Adrian (costume designer)   Fanny Brice
Frank Morgan   Hanley Stafford
Bernard McFadden

GARLAND SONGS

"Why? Because" (with Fanny Brice)
"College Swing" (special lyrics)
Interpolations:
    "Notre Dame Victory Song"
    "On Brave Old Army Team"
    "Fight for USC"
    "Anchors Aweigh"

7 **"Good News of 1938"**
April 21, 1938

NBC: WEAF, Red Network
(60 minutes)
Music director: Meredith Willson
Master of ceremonies: Robert Taylor
Announcer: Ted Parson

GUESTS

Frank Morgan	Clark Gable
Myrna Loy	Fanny Brice
Lionel Barrymore	Judy Garland
General H. H. "Hap" Arnold	

GARLAND SONGS

"There's a Gold Mine in the Sky"
"My Heart Is Taking Lessons"

8 **"Good News of 1938"**
April 28, 1938

NBC: WEAF, Red Network
(60 minutes)
Music director: Meredith Willson

GUESTS

Judy Garland	Douglas McPhail
Betty Jaynes	Fanny Brice
Maureen O'Sullivan	Frank Morgan
Max Baer	Robert Young

GARLAND SONGS

"Thanks for the Memory" (special lyrics)

RECORDINGS

"Thanks for the Memory" is available on *The Wit and Wonder of Judy Garland,* DRG 5179 (33⅓). It is also on *Born in a Trunk. Discovery,* AEI 2108 (33⅓).

9 **"Good News of 1938"**
May 5, 1938

NBC: WEAF, Red Network
(60 minutes)
Master of ceremonies: Robert Young
Announcer: Ted Parson

GUESTS

Judy Garland	Florence Rich
Amy Stafford	Clark Gable
Frank Morgan	

GARLAND SONGS

"How Deep Is the Ocean?"
"God's Country" (special lyrics)
"Serenade" (with chorus)

ADDENDA

★ Judy sang "God's Country" in *Babes in Arms,* which would be released in September 1939.

RECORDINGS

"How Deep Is the Ocean?" (recorded in 1945) is available on *Born in a Trunk. Superstar: 1945–1950,* AEI 2110 (33⅓). "God's Country" is on *Born in a Trunk. Stardom: 1940–1945,* AEI 2109 (33⅓).

10 Premiere of "Marie Antoinette" July 8, 1938

NBC: Blue Network (60 minutes), broadcast from the Cathay Circle Theatre, Hollywood
Interviewer: Don Wilson

GUESTS

Robert Young	Barbara Stanwyck
John Barrymore	Hedda Hopper
Tyrone Power	Judy Garland
Helen Hayes	Peter Lorre
Louella Parsons	Clark Gable
Freddie Bartholomew	Norma Shearer
Jeanette MacDonald	Basil Rathbone
James Stewart	Paul Muni
L. B. Mayer	

ADDENDA

★ Judy costarred with Freddie Bartholomew in *Listen, Darling,* which would be released in October 1938.

11 "The Rinso Program Starring Al Jolson" July 12, 1938

CBS (30 minutes)

ADDENDA

★ Judy Garland substituted for Martha Raye.
★ On January 26, 1964, Garland and Raye finally worked together when Raye was a guest on "The Judy Garland Show."

12 "Good News of 1939" September 8, 1938

NBC: WEAF, Red Network (60 minutes)
Music director: Meredith Willson
Master of ceremonies: Robert Young

GUESTS

Fanny Brice	Norma Shearer
Hanley Stafford	Judy Garland

GARLAND SONGS

"In Between"
"Could You Pass in Love?" (with Robert Young, Frank Morgan, Meredith Willson)
"My Lucky Star"
Interpolation:
  "Love Me and the World Is Mine"
"Alexander's Ragtime Band"
"I Love You"
"School Days"
"Love, Your Magic Spell Is Everywhere
"Mother" (special lyrics)
"A Tisket a Tasket"
"At Dawning" (a dramatization)

ADDENDA

★ Judy sang "In Between" in *Love Finds Andy Hardy,* released in July 1938.

RECORDINGS

"Could You Pass In Love?" is available on *Cut! Out-Takes from Hollywood's Greatest Musicals,* vol. 3, Out-Take Records OFT 3 (33⅓).
A studio version of "In Between" is available on *Judy Garland: Greatest Perfor-*

mances, Decca DL 8190 (33⅓), and *Judy at The Palace,* Decca ED 620 (45) and DL 6020 (33⅓).

---

13 **"Good News of 1939"**
October 20, 1938

NBC: WEAF, Red Network
(60 minutes)
Music director: Meredith Willson
Master of ceremonies: Robert Young
Announcer: Ted Parson

GUESTS

Judy Garland   Frank Morgan
Fanny Brice   Joan Crawford
Billie Burke   Hanley Stafford

GARLAND SONGS

"On the Bumpy Road to Love" (special lyrics)
"Zing! Went the Strings of My Heart"

ADDENDA

★ Both songs that Judy sang on this program she sang, as well, in the film *Listen, Darling,* which was released in the same month as this broadcast.

---

14 **"National Redemption**
Movement Program"
December 14, 1938

NBC: WJZ, Blue Network (30 minutes)
Music director: Meredith Willson
Masters of ceremonies: Truman Bradley (first half), Robert Taylor (second half)

GUESTS

Tony Martin   Donald Crisp
Judy Garland   Edward Arnold
Jackie Searl   Mickey Rooney
Wayne Morris   Jackie Cooper
James Cagney   Edward G. Robinson
Lewis Stone   Pat O'Brien
Jean Parker   Jeanette MacDonald
Edith Fallows

Judy Garland joined Mickey Rooney, Lewis Stone, and Jean Parker in a "Hardy Family sketch."

ADDENDA

★ Judy had made her first appearance in the Hardy family series in *Love Finds Andy Hardy,* released in July 1938.
★ NBC described the program as part of "a nationwide commemoration of the 147th anniversary of the American Bill of Rights."

1939

---

1 **"Hollywood Screen Guild Theater"**
January 8, 1939

CBS (30 minutes)
Variety show, with music and dialogue
Director: Mitchell Leisen
Consulting writer: Morrie Ryskind
Music: Oscar Bradley and His Orchestra
Master of ceremonies: George Murphy
Announcer: John Conte

GUESTS

Judy Garland   Joan Crawford
Reginald Gardiner   Ralph Morgan
Jack Benny

GARLAND SONGS

"Sweet or Swing?"

"Thanks for the Memory" (in "operatic" style)

ADDENDA

★ Judy was the first guest on the first show of the series.

★ Appearances on this series were donated by performers to the Motion Picture Relief Fund.

RECORDINGS

Judy Garland on Radio, Radiola MR 1040 (33⅓), has both songs from this broadcast. The two numbers are also on *Born in a Trunk. Discovery,* AEI 2108 (33⅓).

---

2 **"Council of Stars"**
January 22, 1939

CBS (60 minutes)

This program, hosted by Eddie Cantor for the March of Dimes, has been cited as a Judy Garland appearance. Despite CBS's listing of this program on her "personality card," she is not listed among the cast in CBS's records of the program itself. I can find no record of her appearance on this broadcast.

---

3 **"The Pepsodent Show**
Starring Bob Hope"
March 7, 1939

NBC: WEAF, Red Network (30 minutes)

Master of ceremonies: Bob Hope

Announcer: Bill Goodwin

REGULARS

Skinnay Ennis and His Orchestra
Patsy Kelly
Jerry Colonna

Guest: Judy Garland

GARLAND SONGS

"Franklin D. Roosevelt Jones" (special lyrics)

Interpolations:
"Yankee Doodle"
"Stars and Stripes Forever"
"Columbia the Gem of the Ocean"
"Go to Sleep, My Baby"

---

4 **"Tune Up Time"**
April 6, 1939

CBS (45 minutes)

Master of ceremonies: Walter O'Keefe

with

André Kostelanetz and His Orchestra
Kay Thompson and The Rhythm Singers
Judy Garland

GARLAND SONGS

"Sweet Sixteen"

ADDENDA

★ On July 1, 1943, Judy Garland gave her first concert with a symphony orchestra, the Philadelphia Orchestra, directed by André Kostelanetz.

★ There were only four broadcasts of "Tune Up Time" in 1939.

RECORDINGS

"Sweet Sixteen," from this broadcast, is on *Judy! Judy! Judy!,* Star-Tone ST 224 (33⅓).

5 "The Pepsodent Show Starring Bob Hope" May 9, 1939

NBC: WEAF, Red Network
  (30 minutes)
Master of ceremonies: Bob Hope
Announcer: Bill Goodwin

REGULARS

Skinnay Ennis and His Orchestra
Six Hits and A Miss
Patsy Kelly
Jerry Colonna

Guest: Judy Garland

GARLAND SONGS
unidentified

6 "Maxwell House Coffee Time" June 29, 1939

NBC: WEAF, Red Network
  (60 minutes)
Episode: "Behind the Scenes at the Making of *The Wizard of Oz*"
Host: Robert Young

GUESTS

Ray Bolger   E. Y. Harburg
Harold Arlen   Fred Stone
Hanley Stafford   Frank Morgan
Bert Lahr   Fanny Brice
Meredith Willson
  and the NBC Orchestra

GARLAND SONGS

"Over the Rainbow"

ADDENDA

★ This was the first time that Judy sang "Over the Rainbow" on the radio. The program was dedicated to *The Wizard of Oz*, which went into general release in August.

★ Judy had worked with Fanny Brice the previous year in *Everybody Sing*.

RECORDINGS

Behind the Scenes at the Making of "The Wizard of Oz, Jazz 17 (33⅓). "Over the Rainbow," from this broadcast, is also available on *Judy Garland on Radio*, Radiola MR 1040 (33⅓).

7 "The Fred Waring Show" August 1939

NBC (30 minutes)

GARLAND SONGS
"Over the Rainbow"

Judy and Mrs. L. Frank Baum "reading"
The Wizard of Oz.

ADDENDA

★ Garland was in New York for the New York premiere of *The Wizard of Oz.*
★ Waring dedicated this program to Garland and the film.
★ The contents of this program have not been personally verified.

8 **"Screen Guild Theatre"**
September 24, 1939

CBS (30 minutes)
Variety show
Director: Roger Pryor
Music: Oscar Bradley and His Orchestra
Master of ceremonies: Roger Pryor

GUESTS

Judy Garland   Ann Sothern
Mickey Rooney   Cary Grant

ADDENDA

★ Garland and Rooney had by this time been teamed by MGM; their first film was *Love Finds Andy Hardy,* released in July 1938. Their next joint venture, *Babes in Arms,* would be released in October 1939.

9 **"The Pepsodent Show**
Starring Bob Hope"
September 26, 1939

NBC: WEAF, Red Network
   (30 minutes)
Master of ceremonies: Bob Hope
Announcer: Bill Goodwin

REGULARS

Skinnay Ennis and His Orchestra
Six Hits and A Miss
Jerry Colonna

This was the premiere of a new season for the show. As of this date, for the season, Judy Garland became a regular member of the cast. She appeared on the show weekly, with the exception of the October 3, 1939, January 1, 1940, May 21, 1940, and May 28, 1940, shows. The May 21, 1940, show originated from Chicago, and Dolores Reade (Mrs. Bob Hope) substituted for Judy. The May 28, 1940, show originated from New York, and Cobina Wright, Jr., substituted.

10 **Opening of Arrowhead Spring Hotel**
December 16, 1939

CBS (25 minutes), broadcast from Palm Springs, California

CELEBRITIES

Al Jolson
Rudy Vallee
Judy Garland

1940

1 "Red Cross War Fund Program"
May 26, 1940

CBS/NBC: WJZ, Blue Network
   (60 minutes)
Master of ceremonies: Eddie Cantor

SPEAKERS

Norman H. Davis, Chairman of the
   American Red Cross
Eleanor Roosevelt
Wayne C. Taylor, Red Cross delegate to
   Europe

TALENT

Vivien Leigh and Laurence Olivier
Gertrude Lawrence
Jerry Colonna
Barry Wood and Lyn Murray's Chorus
Frank Black and orchestra
Bob Hope
Walter Huston
Jimmy Durante
Lynn Fontanne and Alfred Lunt (in a
   scene from Robert E. Sherwood's *There
   Shall Be No Night*)
Jack Benny and Don Wilson
Edgar Bergen and Charlie McCarthy
Judy Garland and David Brookman's
   Orchestra and Chorus

GARLAND SONGS

"Over the Rainbow"

ADDENDA

★ *The Wizard of Oz* had been released in
   August 1939.

2 "Lux Radio Theatre"
October 28, 1940

CBS (60 minutes)
Episode: "Strike Up the Band"
Musical director: John Scott Trotter

STARRING

Mickey Rooney
Judy Garland

3 "The Pepsodent Show
Starring Bob Hope"
December 24, 1940

NBC: WEAF, Red Network
   (30 minutes)
Master of ceremonies: Bob Hope
Announcer: Bill Goodwin

REGULARS

Skinnay Ennis and His Orchestra
Six Hits and A Miss
Jerry Colonna

GARLAND SONGS

"I'm Nobody's Baby"
"Franklin D. Roosevelt Jones"
"It's a Great Day for the Irish"

ADDENDA

★ "I'm Nobody's Baby" is from *Andy
   Hardy Meets Debutante*, released in July
   1940. "It's a Great Day for the Irish" is
   from *Little Nellie Kelly*, released in November 1940. "Franklin D. Roosevelt
   Jones" is a Garland song from *Babes
   on Broadway*, which would be released
   in 1941.

RECORDINGS

"I'm Nobody's Baby" and "Franklin D. Roosevelt Jones" are on *The Best of Judy Garland*, MCA 24003 (33⅓). "It's a Great Day for the Irish" is on *Collector's Items, 1936–1945*, MCA 2-4046 (33⅓).

1941

1 **"Bundles for Britain"**
January 1, 1941

NBC: WJZ, Blue Network (60 minutes)

STARRING

Claudette Colbert	The Merry Macs
Merle Oberon	Jack Benny
Adolphe Menjou	Mickey Rooney
Charles Boyer	Ronald Colman
Myrna Loy	Tony Martin
James Cagney	Judy Garland
Walter Brennan	Brian Donlevy

GARLAND SONGS

"I Hear a Rhapsody"

2 **"Silver Theatre"**
January 26, 1941

CBS (30 minutes)
Episode: "Love's New Sweet Song"
Director: Conrad Nagel
Master of ceremonies: Conrad Nagel

STARRING

Judy Garland
Warren McCollom
with Elliott Lewis

ADDENDA

★ This was written especially for radio by True Boardman.

3 **Motion Pictures Awards Program**
February 22, 1941

All networks, broadcast from Los Angeles with Bette Davis, Franklin Delano Roosevelt, and others

GARLAND SONGS

"America (My Country Tis of Thee)"

RECORDINGS

Judy Garland, 1935–1951, Star-Tone ST 201 (33⅓).

4 **"Islam Temple Shrine**
Saint Patrick's Day Program"
March 15, 1941

NBC: WEAF, Red Network (60 minutes) broadcast from Los Angeles
Speaker: Governor C. Olsen

STARRING

Dennis Morgan	Mickey Rooney
Louis B. Mayer	Judy Garland
Edward Arnold	

GARLAND SONGS

"Wearing of the Green"

RECORDINGS

"Wearing of the Green" is available on *Collector's Items, 1936–1945*, MCA 2-4046 (33⅓).

---

5 **"Millions for Defense" ("Treasury Hour")**
July 2, 1941

CBS (60 minutes)
Produced by Howard Dietz and Paul Monroe
Continuity by Herman Wouk and Don Johnson
Music: Al Goodman and His Orchestra, Ray Bloch Choir
Master of ceremonies: Fred Allen

STARRING

Judy Garland   Minerva Pious
Grace Moore   Charles Laughton
Mickey Rooney

Garland and Rooney did a skit that closed the first half of the program.

ADDENDA

★ This program replaced Fred Allen's show for the summer. It consisted of "star talent from New York's Broadway and Hollywood" for the purpose of fostering the sale of defense bonds.
★ This was the first show of the series.
★ Charles Laughton recited the Gettysburg Address.

Publicity shot for "Millions for Defense."

---

6 **"The Chase and Sanborn Hour"**
September 7, 1941

NBC: WEAF, Red Network
(60 minutes)
Music: Ray Noble and His Orchestra

STARRING

Edgar Bergen and Charlie McCarthy

Guests:
Judy Garland
Abbott and Costello

GARLAND SONGS

"All the Things I Love"
"Daddy" (special lyrics)

RECORDINGS

Both songs are on *Judy! Judy! Judy!*, Star-Tone ST 224 (33⅓).

---

7 **"Silver Theatre"**
October 12, 1941 (Episode 1)
October 19, 1941 (Episode 2)

CBS (30 minutes)
Episode: "Eternally Yours"
Director: Conrad Nagel
Music director: Felix Mills
Based on the story "Mr. Onion" by Dana Burnett
Adapted by Forrest Barnes

STARRING

Judy Garland
Edgar Barrier

Guests:
Elliott Lewis
Tommy Cook (in Episode 2)

ADDENDA

★ CBS described the play as "a story of faith which comes to a young couple through the unusual agency of a plaster doll and, later, a child."

---

8 **"Motion Picture Industry Community Chest Drive"**
November 3, 1941

KFWB

GARLAND SONGS

"Share a Little"

ADDENDA

★ The contents of this program have not been personally verified.

---

9 **"Lux Radio Theatre"**
November 9, 1941

CBS (60 minutes)
Episode: "Babes in Arms"
Director: Roger Pryor
Musical director: Oscar Bradley
Adapted by Harry Krouman and Charles Tazewell

STARRING

Mickey Rooney
Judy Garland

GARLAND SONGS

"Good Morning" (with Mickey Rooney)
"God's Country" (with Mickey Rooney)

RECORDINGS

"Good Morning" (with Mickey Rooney) is on *Hollywood on the Air,* Radiola 1718 3/4 (33⅓). "God's Country" is on *Born in a Trunk. Stardom: 1940–1945,* AEI 2109 (33⅓).

---

10 **"Lux Radio Theatre"**
November 17, 1941

CBS (60 minutes)
Episode: "Merton of the Movies"
Producer/Director: Cecil B. DeMille
Musical director: Louis Silvers

STARRING

Mickey Rooney
Judy Garland

ADDENDA

★ The CBS publicity release for "Merton of the Movies" read: "The comedy concerns the adventures of Merton Gill, a naive country lad who dreams of going to Hollywood and becoming a film star. When he is fired from Gashwiler's General Store he considers it his long-awaited opportunity, withdraws all his savings and leaves for the cinema Mecca. There he is befriended by Miss Montague, stand-in for a studio's leading lady—and through her Merton soon finds himself much more of a Hollywood figure than he had bargained for."

RECORDINGS

This performance is available on *Merton of the Movies*, Pelican 139 (33⅓).

---

11 **"The Chase and Sanborn Hour" December 7, 1941**

NBC: WEAF, Red Network
  (60 minutes)
Music: Ray Noble and His Orchestra

STARRING

Edgar Bergen and Charlie McCarthy

GARLAND SONGS

"Zing! Went the Strings of My Heart"

ADDENDA

★ Garland and her husband, David Rose, had flown to Fort Ord, near Monterey, California, so that she could entertain the troops with this broadcast. They did not get the news that the Japanese had attacked Pearl Harbor and that the United States was at war until about midday.

★ The script for the program was not changed; the program was, however, interrupted for frequent news bulletins.

---

12 **"Motion Picture Industry Community Chest Drive" December 15, 1941**

KFWB

GARLAND SONGS

"Abe Lincoln Had Just One Country"

ADDENDA

★ The contents of this program have not been personally verified.

---

13 **"Millions for Defense" ("Treasury Hour") December 23, 1941**

NBC: WJZ, Blue Network (60 minutes)
Master of ceremonies: Fredric March (in New York), Edward Arnold (in Hollywood)

STARRING

Fanny Brice   Judy Garland
Hanley Stafford   Alec Templeton
Marlene Dietrich

GARLAND SONGS

"Abe Lincoln Had Just One Country"

1942

1 "The Chase and Sanborn Hour"
June 21, 1942

NBC: WEAF, Red Network
   (60 minutes)
Music: Ray Noble and His Orchestra

STARRING

Edgar Bergen and Charlie McCarthy

Guests:
Judy Garland
Abbott and Costello

GARLAND SONGS

"I Never Knew I Could Love Anybody"

RECORDINGS

Her song is available on *Born in a Trunk.
Stardom: 1940–1945*, AEI 2109 (33⅓).

**2 "Lux Radio Theatre"
October 6, 1942**

CBS (60 minutes)
Episode: "Morning Glory"
Producer: Cecil B. DeMille
Adaptation by George Wells
Musical director: Louis Silvers
Announcer: Melville Ruick

STARRING

Judy Garland
John Payne
Adolphe Menjou

ADDENDA

★ This was a straight dramatic performance.
★ Judy Garland played Eva Lovelace, a young woman with an overwhelming ambition to be a great actress.

**3 Command Performance
December 24, 1942**

ADDENDA

★ Performance not personally verified.

**4 "Elgin Christmas Day Canteen"
December 25, 1942**

CBS (120 minutes)
Master of ceremonies: Don Ameche
Announcer: Bill Goodwin

GUESTS

Judy Garland   Abbott and Costello
Bob Hope   Gracie Fields
Bette Davis

Judy had a dramatic spot with Bob Hope that lasted 10 minutes, 48 seconds.

ADDENDA

★ CBS billed this as a Christmas Day salute to "America's fighting forces."

**5 "Lux Radio Theatre"
December 28, 1942**

CBS (60 minutes)
Episode: "A Star Is Born"
Producer: Cecil B. DeMille
Adaptation by George Wells
Musical director: Louis Silvers
Announcer: Melville Ruick

STARRING

Judy Garland
Walter Pidgeon
Adolphe Menjou

ADDENDA

★ This is the original, nonmusical version. Judy's role was a straight dramatic performance.

RECORDINGS

The entire performance is available on *Judy Garland in "A Star Is Born,"* Radiola MR 1155 (33⅓).

**6 "Command Performance" #35 (AFRS)
(exact date uncertain)**

Master of ceremonies: Bob Hope

STARRING

Judy Garland   Claudette Colbert
David Rose and   Lana Turner
    His Orchestra

GARLAND SONGS

"It's a Great Day for the Irish"
"On the Sunny Side of the Street"

ADDENDA

★ This was part of the War Department
Series H-18 (#35).

1943

**1 "Screen Guild Players"
March 22, 1943**

CBS (60 minutes)
Episode: "For Me and My Gal"
Musical director: Wilbur Hatch

STARRING

Judy Garland
Gene Kelly
Dick Powell

GARLAND SONGS

"Oh, You Beautiful Doll" (Dick Powell)
"For Me and My Gal" (Judy Garland and
    Gene Kelly)
"Till We Meet Again" (Judy Garland)
"Ballin' the Jack" (Judy Garland and Gene
    Kelly)

"How Ya Gonna Keep 'Em Down on the
    Farm" (Judy Garland)

ADDENDA

★ On March 10, 1943, CBS listed George
Murphy, not Powell, to be in the cast.

**2 "Free World Theater"
March 28, 1943**

NBC: WJZ, Blue Network (30 minutes)
Episode: "The Music of Freedom"
Music: Gordon Jenkins and His
    Orchestra

STARRING

Ronald Colman   Kenny Baker
    (Narrator)   Lee Sweetland
Judy Garland

GARLAND SONGS

"The Wings of Freedom (There'll Always
Be an England)"

3 "Command Performance" #61 (AFRS) April 6, 1943

STARRING

Bob Hope
Judy Garland
Lee Sweetland

GARLAND SONGS

"I Never Knew"
"Over the Rainbow"

ADDENDA

★ This was part of the War Department H-18 series.

4 "The Pause That Refreshes on the Air" July 4, 1943

CBS (30 minutes)
Music: André Kostelanetz
Master of ceremonies: David Rose

Judy Garland is guest soloist.

GARLAND SONGS

"That Old Black Magic"
"Over the Rainbow"
"I Left My Heart at the Stage Door Canteen"
"I'm Getting Tired So I Can Sleep"
"Russian Winter"
"This Is the Army, Mr. Jones"

ADDENDA

★ The last four songs are from Irving Berlin's *This Is the Army*.

★ Garland was in New York for this broadcast as part of a two-week tour to USO camps in Pennsylvania and New York. (On July 1, she had also given a concert at Robin Hood Dell outside of Philadelphia—see "Concerts.") The tour itself actually got started on July 8.

RECORDINGS

"This Is the Army, Mr. Jones" is on *The Judy Garland Scrapbook*, Star-Tone ST 208 (33⅓). "That Old Black Magic" (recorded in 1942) is available on *The Best of Judy Garland*, MCA 24003 (33⅓).

5 "Silver Theatre" December 12, 1943

CBS (30 minutes)
Episode: "Ringside Table"
Director: Conrad Nagel
Musical director: Felix Mills

STARRING

Judy Garland
Alan Ladd

ADDENDA

★ Judy had the role of a singing star in a New York nightclub. Ladd was an FBI agent impersonating a playboy while shadowing a nightclub manager suspected of being an enemy agent.

6 "Christmas Program"
December 25, 1943

CBS (120 minutes)
Master of ceremonies: Robert Young
Announcer: Ken Carpenter

STARRING

Judy Garland   Lena Horne
Bing Crosby   Cass Daley
Bob Hope   Adia Kuznetzoff
Jack Benny   The Revuers
Henry Busse and   The Charioteers
   His Orchestra   Butch & Buddy
Carmen Miranda

7 "Mail Call" #140 (date uncertain)

Music: AFRS Orchestra
Mistress of ceremonies: Judy Garland
Announcer: Don Wilson

STARRING

Carmen Cavallaro
The Merry Macs
Bob Hope

GARLAND SONGS

"Dear Mr. Gable (You Made Me Love
   You)"

1944

1 "Mail Call" (date uncertain)

GUESTS

Bing Crosby   Jimmy Durante
Judy Garland   Arthur Treacher

ADDENDA

★ This program has not been personally
   verified.

2 "Command Performance" #106
(AFRS)
March 5, 1944

Announcer: Ken Carpenter

STARRING

Judy Garland
Frank Sinatra
Bob Hope

GARLAND SONGS

"No Love, No Nothin' "
"Desert Island" sketch (with Sinatra,
   Hope)
"Embraceable You" (with Sinatra)

RECORDINGS

"No Love, No Nothin' " is on *Collector's
   Items, 1936–1945*, MCA 2-4046
   (33⅓).

3 "The Frank Sinatra Show"
May 24, 1944

CBS (30 minutes)
Host: Frank Sinatra
Announcer: Truman Bradley

Judy Garland is guest star.

CAST

Jerry Lester
The Vimms Vocalists
Axel Stordahl and His Orchestra

GARLAND SONGS

"Embraceable You" (with Sinatra)
"Zing! Went the Strings of My Heart"

4 "The Bakers of America Salute to the Armed Forces"
June 4, 1944

NBC: WEAF, Red Network
    (60 minutes)
Master of ceremonies: Bill Goodwin

STARRING

Judy Garland   Gracie Fields
Edgar Bergen   Bob Hope
Gracie Allen   George Burns
Bing Crosby

GARLAND SONGS

"The Way You Look Tonight" (with Bing
    Crosby)
"The Trolley Song"
"Long Ago and Far Away"

ADDENDA

★ "The Trolley Song" is from *Meet Me in St. Louis,* which would be released in December 1944.

5 "The Chase and Sanborn Hour"
June 25, 1944

NBC: WEAF, Red Network
    (60 minutes)

GUESTS

Judy Garland
Matt Crowley
Gracie Fields

GARLAND SONGS

"The Boy Next Door"
"Long Ago and Far Away"

RECORDINGS

"Long Ago and Far Away" is available on *The Wit and Wonder of Judy Garland* DRG SL 5179 (33⅓).

6 "Command Performance" #122 (AFRS)
June 25, 1944

CBS
Musical director: Meredith Willson
Announcer: Ken Carpenter

STARRING

Judy Garland   Bing Crosby
Bob Hope   Frank Sinatra

SONGS

Comedy monologue (Bob Hope)

"Dixieland Band" (Judy Garland)

Comedy sketch (Judy Garland, Bob Hope, Bing Crosby, Frank Sinatra)

"I Love You" (Bing Crosby)

"You Are" (Frank Sinatra)

Medley:

"You Are My Sunshine" (Bing Crosby, Frank Sinatra)

"Sonny Boy" (comedy version) (Frank Sinatra)

"You're the Top" (comedy version) (Bing Crosby)

"You're the Top" (reprise) (Frank Sinatra)

"I'm the Top" (Bob Hope, Bing Crosby, Frank Sinatra)

"Something to Remember You By" (Judy Garland, Bing Crosby)

ADDENDA

★ The premise of the show is that Judy Garland is auditioning Bing Crosby and Frank Sinatra to see who will costar with her in her next picture. Bob Hope is the "neutral" judge.

★ Command Performance #122 was part of the War Department H-18 series. It was later retranscribed and shipped as Command Performance #190.

RECORDINGS

Judy's "Dixieland Band," from this broadcast, is available on *The Wit and Wonder of Judy Garland,* DRG SL 5179 (33⅓), and *Born in a Trunk. Stardom: 1940–1945,* AEI 2109 (33⅓).

7 "Everything for the Boys" Program
July 11, 1944

NBC: WEAF, Red Network
(30 minutes)

Music: Gordon Jenkins and His Orchestra

Master of ceremonies: Dick Haymes (summer replacement for Ronald Colman)

The series format had the master of ceremonies and guest star have a two-way conversation with two service people from an overseas battle zone. Judy talked with servicemen stationed in Honolulu.

GUEST STAR

Judy Garland

ADDENDA

★ Garland and Haymes sang "There's a Tavern in the Town" (an Autolite singing commercial). It is on *The Judy Garland Musical Scrapbook,* Star-Tone ST 208 (33⅓).

8 "Your All-Time Hit Parade" #44
(AFRS)
August 13, 1944

Broadcast on NBC: WEAF, Red Network
(30 minutes)

Master of ceremonies: Harry Von Zell

GUESTS

Judy Garland

Tommy Dorsey and His Orchestra

SONGS

"What Is This Thing Called Love?"
(Tommy Dorsey, Bonnie Lou Williams,
orchestra)

"On the Sunny Side of the Street"
(Tommy Dorsey, The Sentimentalists
—vocal)

"I'll Be Seeing You" (Tommy Dorsey, Bob
Allen, orchestra)

"April in Paris" (Tommy Dorsey
Orchestra)

"Over the Rainbow" (Judy Garland,
Tommy Dorsey Orchestra)

"I May Be Wrong" (Judy Garland, Tommy
Dorsey Orchestra)

"The Song Is You" (Tommy Dorsey
Orchestra)

ADDENDA

★ Judy's songs, with Tommy Dorsey and
His Orchestra, were issued on V-Disc
335-A (Army) and Navy V-Disc 159-A
(both 78 rpm).

RECORDINGS

"I May Be Wrong," from this broadcast, is
available on *Judy Garland (1935–1951)*,
Star-Tone SL 201 (33⅓), and *Born in a
Trunk. Stardom: 1940–1945*, AEI 2109
(33⅓).

**9 "The Chase and Sanborn Hour"
September 3, 1944**

NBC: WEAF, Red Network
(60 minutes)
Music: Ray Noble and His Orchestra
Announcer: Bill Goodwin

GUEST

Judy Garland

GARLAND SONGS

(uncertain)
"I'm Glad There Is You"
"Swinging on a Star"

**10 Democratic National Committee
November 6, 1944**

CBS/NBC (60 minutes)
Narrator: Humphrey Bogart

GUESTS

Judy Garland   Claudette Colbert
James Cagney   Irving Berlin
Keenan Wynn   Joseph Cotten
Groucho Marx

GARLAND SONGS

"You Gotta Get Out and Vote"

SYNOPSIS

Stars, soldiers, and citizens urge the public to reelect Franklin Delano Roosevelt.

ADDENDA

★ Judy spoke on behalf of FDR.
★ This was called the "One Thousand
Club of America" on the NBC broad-
cast.

RECORDINGS

The Judy Garland Musical Scrapbook, Star-
Tone ST 208 (33⅓), contains "You
Gotta Get Out and Vote."

11 **"Everything for the Boys" Program
December 26, 1944**

NBC: WEAF, Red Network
    (30 minutes)
Master of ceremonies: Ronald Colman

GUEST

Judy Garland

Colman and Judy spoke with servicemen
    from the Pacific on a two-way hook-up.

1945

1 **"Esquire's Second Annual
All-American Jazz Concert"
January 1945**

NBC: WJZ, Blue Network (90 minutes)

GUESTS

Judy Garland	Jerome Kern
Jack Benny	Billie Holiday
Danny Kaye	Lena Horne
Duke Ellington	Anita O'Day
Benny Goodman	and others
Louis Armstrong	

ADDENDA

★ This concert was a benefit for the Vol-
  unteer Army Canteen Service. It was
  held at the Los Angeles Philharmonic
  Auditorium.
★ Judy Garland presented an award to
  Anita O'Day, who was in the "New
  Stars" division.

2 **"March of Dimes"
January 20, 1945**

CBS/NBC (70 minutes), from Hollywood
Master of ceremonies: Bing Crosby
Announcer: Ken Carpenter

GUESTS

Frank Sinatra	John Scott Trotter
Judy Garland	Axel Stordahl

ADDENDA

★ This program was the last segment on
  "The President's Birthday Ball," which
  on NBC was called "America Salutes
  the President's Birthday."
★ This program is variously dated. NBC
  includes it in its programming records
  for January 20. CBS has it listed for January 30. Since, in this instance, NBC's
  records are more complete, their dating
  is followed here.

3 **"Command Performance" #166
(AFRS)
April 29, 1945**

Episode: "Dick Tracy in B-Flat"

GUESTS

Judy Garland	Jimmy Durante
Harry Von Zell	Cass Daley
Frank Morgan	Dinah Shore
Frank Sinatra	Bob Hope
Bing Crosby	Andrews Sisters
Jerry Colonna	

Judy and Jimmy Durante reviewing the script for
"Dick Tracy in B-Flat."

GARLAND SONGS

"Whose Dream Are You" (Bing Crosby)

"Who's That Knocking at My Door" (Bing Crosby, Dinah Shore)

"I Had a Friend, and I Had a Phone" (Dinah Shore)

"I'm the Top" (Bob Hope)

"A Wandering Actor I" (Frank Morgan)

"The Music Goes Round and Round" (Jimmy Durante)

"Over the Rainbow" (Judy Garland)

"I'm Gonna Go for You" (Judy Garland, Bob Hope)

"Whose Dream Are You" (reprise) (Bing Crosby)

"Apple Blossom Time" (Andrews Sisters)

"All the Things You Are" (Frank Sinatra, Bing Crosby)

"Sunday, Monday, and Always" (Bing Crosby, Bob Hope, Frank Sinatra)

"The Trolley Song" (Cass Daley)

"Finale" (all)

ADDENDA

★ This was recorded in Hollywood on February 15, 1945, for later broadcast overseas.

RECORDINGS

"Dick Tracy in B-Flat" is on *Curtain Calls* 100/1 (33⅓). It is also available on Sandy Hook 2052 (33⅓) and Scarce Rarities 5504 (33⅓).

---

4 **"The Jerry Wayne Show"**
August 10, 1945

CBS (30 minutes)

GARLAND SONGS

"If I Had You"
"Love"

Comedy sketch (with Jerry Wayne)

ADDENDA

★ Garland was originally scheduled to appear on July 27, 1945. The appearance was postponed due to illness.
★ For the August 10 appearance, Garland was in New York for the opening of *The Harvey Girls*.

RECORDINGS

"If I Had You" is available on *Collector's Items, 1936–1945*, MCA 2-4046 (33⅓), and "Love" is on *The Best of Judy Garland*, MCA 24003 (33⅓).

---

5 **"The Danny Kaye Show"**
October 5, 1945

CBS (30 minutes)
Music: The Axel Stordahl Orchestra

STARRING

Judy Garland
Frank Sinatra

GARLAND SONGS

"How Deep Is the Ocean?"
"Gotta Be This or That" (with Sinatra)
Comedy sketch about 1995 (with Sinatra)
"My Romance" (with Sinatra)

ADDENDA

★ Garland and Sinatra substituted for Danny Kaye, who was on a USO tour.
★ This performance has been variously dated as June 14, 1945, and June 25, 1945. CBS archives record that this segment aired on October 5, 1945.
★ The performance went overseas on AFRS (Danny Kaye show #22).

RECORDINGS

"How Deep Is the Ocean?" is available on *Born in a Trunk. Superstar: 1945–1950*, AEI 2110 (33⅓). "Gotta Be This or That" and "My Romance," as well as "How Deep Is the Ocean?," are on *Frank Sinatra and Judy Garland*, ZA-FIRO ZV 892 (33⅓).

6 "Jerome Kern Memorial"
December 9, 1945

CBS (60 minutes)
Music: Al Goodman Orchestra, Robert Armbruster Orchestra

STARRING

Judy Garland   Jack Smith
Nelson Eddy   Frank Sinatra
Dinah Shore   Hildegarde
Bing Crosby   Earl Wrightson
Patrice Munsel

GARLAND SONGS

"Look for the Silver Lining"

ADDENDA

★ This program was presented by ASCAP.
★ Supervising this special program were Oscar Hammerstein II, Richard Rodgers, Irving Berlin, and Deems Taylor.

7 "Command Performance" (AFRS)
December 25, 1945

Announcer: Ken Carpenter

STARRING

Bob Hope   Johnny Mercer
Ginny Simms   Dinah Shore
The Pied Pipers   Judy Garland
Bing Crosby

GARLAND SONGS

"Have Yourself a Merry Little Christmas"

ADDENDA

★ I have not been able to verify an AFRS number for this program.

1946

1 "Lux Radio Theatre"
January 28, 1946

CBS (60 minutes)
Episode: "The Clock"
Producer: William Keighley
Musical director: Louis Silvers
Host: William Keighley

STARRING

Judy Garland
John Hodiak

ADDENDA

★ This program was later transcribed for AFRTS (Armed Forces Radio and Television Service) as "Radio Theater" #12 (RU: 25-0).

2 "The Bob Crosby Show"
July 17, 1946

CBS (30 minutes)

STARRING

Bob Crosby and His Orchestra

Guest: Judy Garland

GARLAND SONGS

"I Got the Sun in the Morning"
"If I Had You"

ADDENDA

★ Judy had cut her first two released sides for Decca with Bob Crosby in 1936. Crosby was also featured in her 1943 film, *Presenting Lily Mars*.

RECORDINGS

Decca released her recording of "If I Had You" in 1945. It is available on *Collector's Items*, MCA 2-4046 (33⅓). "I Got the Sun in the Morning" is available on *Judy Garland in "Annie Get Your Gun,"* SoundStage 2303 (33⅓).

---

3 "Hollywood Star Time" September 14, 1946

CBS (30 minutes)
Episode: "Holiday"

STARRING

Judy Garland
Reed Hadley

ADDENDA

★ This was a straight dramatic performance.

---

4 "Command Performance" #241 (AFRS) September 29, 1946

STARRING

Judy Garland
Frank Sinatra
Phil Silvers

GARLAND SONGS

"I Got the Sun in the Morning"
"Movie Star" sketch (with Sinatra and Silvers)

RECORDINGS

"I Got the Sun in the Morning" is on *Judy Garland in "Annie Get Your Gun,"* SoundStage 2302 (33⅓).

Judy Garland performing in "Drive-In" for "Suspense" (see page 116).

5 "Suspense"
November 21, 1946

CBS (30 minutes)
Episode: "Drive-In"
Producer: William Spier
Musical director: Lud Gluskin

STARRING

Judy Garland

ADDENDA

★ Judy played a waitress who accepts a stranger's offer of a drive home and discovers, when he takes her to an isolated spot, that he is an escaped madman who has committed one murder and is out to commit another.

★ This program was transcribed for AFRTS (RU: 28-4-5B, side two).

6 "Philco Radio Time"
November 27, 1946

ABC (30 minutes)

GUESTS

Judy Garland
Les Paul

ADDENDA

★ This was the Bing Crosby show sponsored by Philco.

7 "Lux Radio Theatre"
December 2, 1946

CBS (60 minutes)
Episode: "Meet Me in St. Louis"
Producer: William Keighley

Writer: Sally Benson
Music director: Louis Silvers
Host: William Keighley
Announcer: John Milton Kennedy

STARRING

Judy Garland   Tom Drake
Margaret O'Brien   Gale Gordon

GARLAND SONGS

"Meet Me in St. Louis, Louis"
"The Boy Next Door"
"The Trolley Song"
"Have Yourself a Merry Little Christmas"

ADDENDA

★ Sally Benson wrote the original stories in *The New Yorker* on which the movie was based.
★ This performance is part of the AFRTS "Radio Theater" series, #21.

RECORDINGS

This performance is available on *Meet Me in St. Louis,* Pelican 118 (33⅓).

1947

1 **"Command Performance" #143 (AFRS)**
May 29, 1947

Master of ceremonies: Lionel Barrymore

STARRING

Judy Garland   Bill Goodwin
Lena Romay   Ginny Simms
George Murphy   Greer Garson
Don Wilson   Lauritz Melchior

Peter Lind Hayes   Paul Lukas
Jack Benny   Frank Sinatra
Orson Welles   Harry Von Zell
Danny Kaye   Dinah Shore
Fred Allen   Jimmy Durante
Nelson Eddy   Ernst Lubitsch
Eddie ("Rochester") Anderson

GARLAND SONGS

"Operetta" sketch (with Danny Kaye and Lauritz Melchior)

ADDENDA

★ This performance celebrated the fifth anniversary of the AFRS. It was part of the H-9 series.

2 **"Philco Radio Time"**
February 19, 1947

ABC (30 minutes)
Producer: Bill Morrow
Music: John Scott Trotter and His Orchestra, Skitch Henderson
Host: Bing Crosby
Announcer: Ken Carpenter

GUESTS

Judy Garland
William Frawley
Leo McCarey

GARLAND SONGS

"Connecticut" (Judy Garland, Bing Crosby)
"Rosabelle MaGee" (Bing Crosby)
"I've Got You Under My Skin" (Judy Garland)
"Ida" (Bing Crosby, William Frawley)

Comedy sketch (Bing Crosby, Judy Garland, Leo McCarey, William Frawley)

"Tearbucket Jim" (Bing Crosby, Judy Garland, Leo McCarey, William Frawley)

"And So to Bed" (Bing Crosby)

RECORDINGS

"Tearbucket Jim" is on *The Judy Garland Musical Scrapbook,* Star-Tone ST 208 (33⅓). A complete performance is on *Philco Radio Time,* vol. 1, Totem 1002 (33⅓).

---

3 "ShowTime" #275 (AFRS)
August 12, 1947

Episode: "Meet Me in St. Louis"
Orchestra and chorus directed by Georgie Stoll

STARRING

Judy Garland

Guests:
The AFRS ShowTime Players

GARLAND SONGS

"Meet Me in St. Louis, Louis"
"The Boy Next Door"
"Skip to My Lou"
"The Trolley Song"

ADDENDA

★ The Garland songs were also transcribed for the "Music of the Theater" series, #43.

1948

---

1 "The Chesterfield Supper Club"
May 6, 1948

NBC: WEAF, Red Network
(15 minutes)

GUESTS

Judy Garland   Fred Astaire
Irving Berlin   Perry Como

GARLAND SONGS

"I Wish I Were in Michigan"
"Easter Parade" (with Fred Astaire)
"A Fella with an Umbrella" (with Perry Como)

ADDENDA

★ The film *Easter Parade,* from which these songs come, would be put into general release in July 1948.

RECORDINGS

Aside from the soundtrack albums, "Michigan" is available on *Born in a Trunk. Superstar: 1945–1950,* AEI 2110 (33⅓). "A Fella with an Umbrella" (with Peter Lawford) is on *Born to Sing,* MGM D 134 (33⅓).

Fred Astaire, Judy Garland, and Johnny Green rehearsing for a radio performance of *Easter Parade.*

2 "The Tex and Jinx Show"
June 30, 1948

WNBC (30 minutes)
Masters of ceremonies: Jinx Falkenburg,
   Tex McCrary
Guest Stars:
in New York:
   Irving Berlin
   Ann Miller
   Helen Carroll and Her Escorts
in Hollywood:
   Judy Garland
   Fred Astaire
   with Johnny Green, André Previn

GARLAND SONGS

"Blue Skies" (partial)
"How Deep Is the Ocean?" (partial)
"It Only Happens When I Dance with
   You" (with Fred Astaire)

ADDENDA

★ The program was a salute to Irving Berlin and the New York premiere of *Easter Parade,* opening that night.
★ Irving Berlin commented that "no one has ever sung my songs better than Judy Garland."

3 "Kraft Music Hall"
September 30, 1948

NBC: WEAF, Red Network
   (30 minutes)

STARRING

Al Jolson
Oscar Levant
Judy Garland (guest star)

GARLAND SONGS

"Over the Rainbow" (partial)
"Johnny One Note"
"Pretty Baby" (with Al Jolson)

ADDENDA

★ This program was transcribed for AFRS in series R-90, #2.

RECORDINGS

Judy Garland on Radio, Radiola MR 1040
   (33⅓).

4 "Philco Radio Time"
October 8, 1948

ABC (30 minutes)
Music: John Scott Trotter and His Orchestra, The Rhythmaires
Announcer: Ken Carpenter

STARRING

Bing Crosby

Guest Star: Judy Garland

SONGS

"Love Somebody" (Bing Crosby)

"Rambling Rose" (Bing Crosby)

"Over the Rainbow" (Judy Garland)

"For Me and My Gal" (Judy Garland, Bing Crosby)

"Embraceable You" (Judy Garland, Bing Crosby)

ADDENDA

★ This program was transcribed for AFRS in "The Golden Days of Radio" series, AFRS #596 (RU: 38-8 1B).

RECORDINGS

The "For Me and My Gal" and "Embraceable You" duets with Bing Crosby are on *Judy Garland (1935–1951)*, Star-Tone 201 (33⅓).

1949

"The Bing Crosby Show" October 5, 1949

CBS (30 minutes)

Producer: Bill Morrow

Writer: Bill Morrow

Music: John Scott Trotter

The Rhythmaires

Announcer: Ken Carpenter

Guest Star: Judy Garland

GARLAND SONGS

"I Don't Care"

"Ma, He's Making Eyes at Me" (with Bing Crosby)

"Maybe It's Because" (with Bing Crosby)

Comedy skit included tales of early radio days and the pros and cons of television and what Garland and Crosby can do to prepare for it.

ADDENDA

★ Judy Garland had been scheduled to appear on the series premiere on CBS on September 21, 1949, but had to cancel due to illness. Peggy Lee substituted. (On December 1, 1963, Peggy Lee guested on "The Judy Garland Show."

★ This program was transcribed for AFRS as #189 (series END-44).

★ Judy's "Maybe It's Because" (with Bing Crosby) was transcribed by the Voice of America for broadcast on its "Radio Varieties, USA" program, #22 (VOA Master #DS-1796).

RECORDINGS

Judy Garland on Radio, Radiola MR 1040 (33⅓), includes "I Don't Care" and "Ma, He's Making Eyes At Me." "Ma, He's Making Eyes At Me" is also on *The Judy Garland Musical Scrapbook,* Star-Tone ST 208 (33⅓). "Maybe It's Because" is on *Judy and Her Partners in Rhythm and Rhyme,* Star-Tone ST 213 (33⅓).

1950

Judy and Vincente Minnelli behind the scenes at a "Bing Crosby Show" broadcast.

---

1 **"The Bing Crosby Show"**
October 11, 1950

CBS (30 minutes)
Music: John Scott Trotter and His Orchestra, The Rhythmaires
Announcer: Ken Carpenter

Guest Star: Judy Garland

GARLAND SONGS

"Sam's Song" (with Bing Crosby and The Rhythmaires)

"Goodnight Irene" (comedy version) (ensemble)
"Get Happy"

ADDENDA

★ This was the second season premiere, originally scheduled for October 4, but postponed due to the death of Crosby's father.

★ This program was part two of AFRS #218 (series END-44).

2 **"The Bing Crosby Show"**
October 18, 1950

CBS (30 minutes)
Music: John Scott Trotter and His
  Orchestra, The Rhythmaires
Announcer: Ken Carpenter

GUESTS

Judy Garland
Bob Hope

GARLAND SONGS

"Tzena, Tzena, Tzena" (with Bing Crosby
  and The Rhythmaires)
"Friendly Star"

ADDENDA

★ This program was part one of AFRS
  #218 (series END-44).
★ "Tzena, Tzena, Tzena" was transcribed
  by the Voice of America for broadcast
  on "Radio Varieties, USA," #56 (VOA
  Master #DS-2495).

3 **"The Theatre Guild on the Air"**
November 5, 1950

NBC (60 minutes)
Episode: "Alice Adams"
Director: Lawrence Langner
Narrator: Roger Pryor

STARRING

Judy Garland as Alice Adams
Thomas Mitchell as Virgil Adams
Ann Shoemaker as Mrs. Adams

ADDENDA

★ This was a straight dramatic perfor-
  mance.
★ "Alice Adams" was written by Booth
  Tarkington and adapted for radio by
  S. Mark Smith.

4 **"The Bing Crosby Show"**
December 6, 1950

CBS (30 minutes)
Music: John Scott Trotter and His
  Orchestra, The Rhythmaires
Announcer: Ken Carpenter

GARLAND SONGS

"Rudolph, the Red-nosed Reindeer"
  (with Bing Crosby)
"Rock-a-Bye Your Baby with a Dixie
  Melody"

ADDENDA

★ Special lyrics for "Rudolph" were written by Bill Morrow. (This version, sung
  by Garland and Crosby, gives a whole
  new life to the song.)

RECORDINGS

Bing Crosby at the Music Hall, AJAZZ 523
  (33⅓), includes both cuts.

5 **"Lux Radio Theatre"**
December 25, 1950

CBS (60 minutes)
Episode: "The Wizard of Oz"
Producer: William Keighley
Music director: Rudy Schrager
Announcer: William Kennedy

S T A R R I N G

Judy Garland

G A R L A N D   S O N G S

"Over the Rainbow"
"We're Off to See the Wizard"
"Over the Rainbow" (reprise)

A D D E N D A

★ This version of "Over the Rainbow" is
interesting as a transition between
Judy's MGM version and the concert
version she would sing henceforth.
(See "Records: The Concert Years" for
a discussion of both interpretations.)

R E C O R D I N G S

This radio broadcast of *The Wizard of Oz*
is available on Sandy Hook MR 1109
(33⅓) and Radio Yesterday RadioBook
#2 (cassette).

6 **"The Bob Hope Show"**
(date uncertain)

NBC (30 minutes)

S T A R R I N G

Bob Hope

Guests:
Judy Garland
Bing Crosby

G A R L A N D   S O N G S

"The Third Man Theme" (comedy version) (with Bob Hope, Bing Crosby)

1951

1 **"Salute to Bing Crosby"**
January 9, 1951

CBS (30 minutes)

S T A R R I N G

George Jessel   Louis Armstrong
Judy Garland   Jack Teagarden
Amos 'n' Andy   William S. Paley
Bob Hope

G A R L A N D   S O N G S

"Rock-a-Bye Your Baby with a Dixie
Melody"

A D D E N D A

★ This was a broadcast commemorating
Bing Crosby's twentieth anniversary in
show business.

R E C O R D I N G S

Garland's "Rock-a-Bye Your Baby" from
this program is on *Judy Garland (1935–
1951)*, Star-Tone ST 201 (33⅓).

2 **"The Bing Crosby Show"**
January 10, 1951

CBS (30 minutes)

3 **"The Bob Hope Show"**
January 30, 1951

NBC (30 minutes)
Music conducted by Les Brown

STARRING

Bob Hope

Guests:

Judy Garland	Lois Singleton
Jane Morgan	Jack Kirkwood

GARLAND SONGS

"Wonderful Guy"

4 **"The Bing Crosby Show"**
February 7, 1951

CBS (30 minutes)
Music: John Scott Trotter and His Orchestra
Announcer: Ken Carpenter

GARLAND SONGS

"You Made Me Love You"
"Just the Way You Are" (with Bing
    Crosby)
Comedy skit with songs by Garland and
    Crosby:
        "In My Merry Oldsmobile"
        "Hello, My Baby"
        "Some Rainy Afternoon"
        "Walking My Baby Back Home"

ADDENDA

★ "Just the Way You Are" (with Bing
Crosby) was transcribed by the Voice
of America for broadcast on its "Radio
Varieties, USA," program #56 (VOA
Master #DS-2495).

RECORDINGS

All the above songs are on *Frances Ethel
Gumm and Harry Lillis Crosby: Judy and
Bing Together,* Legend 1973 (33⅓).

5 **"The Big Show"**
February 11, 1951

NBC (90 minutes)

GUESTS

Tallulah Bankhead	The Andrew Sisters
Judy Garland	Gordon MacRae
Groucho Marx	
Dean Martin and Jerry Lewis	

GARLAND SONGS

"Get Happy"
"You and I" (with chorus)
"Let Me Call You Sweetheart" (ensemble)

RECORDINGS

"Get Happy" is available on *Born in a
Trunk. Superstar: 1945–1950,* AEI 2110
(33⅓).

6 "The Hallmark Playhouse" February 15, 1951

CBS (30 minutes)
Episode: "Cinderella"
Producer/director: Bill Gay
Story by Jerome Lawrence and Robert
   E. Lee
Music composed and conducted by
   Lyn Murray
Host and narrator: James Hilton
Announcer: Frank Goss

STARRING

Judy Garland

Guests:
Witfield Connor   Sara Brenner
Verna Felton   Mary Jane Croft
Eleanor Audley

GARLAND SONGS

"Wishing Will Make It So"
"Wishing Has Made It True"

ADDENDA

★ This was an adaptation of the "Perrault's Fairy Tales" version of Cinderella.
★ Judy Garland played a writer whose short stories are regularly rejected because they sound "too much like Cinderella."
★ (It's a charming production.)

7 "The Bing Crosby Show" March 7, 1951

CBS (30 minutes)
Music: John Scott Trotter
Announcer: Ken Carpenter

GARLAND SONGS

"Just the Way You Are" (with Bing
   Crosby)
"Mean to Me"

RECORDINGS

Frances Ethel Gumm and Harry Lillis Crosby, Legend 1973 (33⅓).

8 "The Bing Crosby Show" March 14, 1951

CBS (30 minutes)
Music: John Scott Trotter
Announcer: Ken Carpenter

GARLAND SONGS

"Just the Way You Are" (comedy version)
   (with Bing Crosby)

ADDENDA

★ A contemporary CBS description of the show: "Judy Garland plays 'Bounce-Along' Garland, a gal who aims to bring law and order to the West, and [Bing] plays 'Sagalong' Crosby, a rough-and-ready varmint who knows little about the law and less about order." The climax of the skit is a parody of "Just the Way You Are" by Judy and Bing.

9 **"The Bing Crosby Show"**
March 21, 1951

CBS (30 minutes)
Music: John Scott Trotter
Announcer: Ken Carpenter

GUESTS

Judy Garland
Les Paul
Mary Ford

GARLAND SONGS

"How Could You Believe Me?" (with Bing
   Crosby)
"Carolina in the Morning"

RECORDINGS

"How Could You Believe Me?" is on
*Frances Ethel Gumm and Harry Lillis
Crosby,* Legend 1973 (33⅓), and *Judy
Garland in Holland,* vol. 3, Obligato
GIH 6100 (33⅓). "Carolina in the
Morning" is on *Judy Garland in Hol-
land,* vol. 3, and *Judy Garland (1935–
1954),* Star-Tone ST 201 (33⅓).

10 **"The Bing Crosby Show"**
March 28, 1951

CBS (30 minutes)
Announcer: Ken Carpenter

GUESTS

Judy Garland
Charles Durand
Guy Brion

GARLAND SONGS

"You Made Me Love You"
"Rock-a-Bye Your Baby with a Dixie
   Melody"
"April Showers"
"Limehouse Blues" (with Bing Crosby)
"April in Paris" (with Bing Crosby)
"Isle of Capri" (with Bing Crosby)
"The Story of Sorrento" (with Bing
   Crosby)

RECORDINGS

With the exception of "The Story of Sorrento," these tracks are available on
Judy Garland in Holland, vol. 3, Obligato GIH 6100 (33⅓), *Judy Garland
(1935–1951),* Star-Tone ST 201 (33⅓),
and *Frances Ethel Gumm and Harry Lillis Crosby,* Legend 1973 (33⅓).

11 **"United Red Feather Campaign of
America"**
September 30, 1951

WNBC (30 minutes)
Announcer: Don Wilson

GUESTS

Jane Wyman   Dinah Shore
Judy Garland   Bing Crosby
Richard Warfield   Jimmy Durante
Ray Milland   Mario Lanza
Tony Martin
With a special address by President Harry
   S. Truman

GARLAND SONGS

"You're Just in Love" (with Bing Crosby)

ADDENDA

★ The United Red Feather organization, according to President Truman, provided "special help and services for men and women in the armed forces."

RECORDINGS

"You're Just in Love" (with Bing Crosby) is on *Frances Ethel Gumm and Harry Lillis Crosby,* Legend 1973 (33⅓).

1952

1 "Guest Star" #277 (AFRS) (date uncertain)

(15 minutes)
Orchestra directed by Jack Cathcart
Announcer: Del Sharbutt

STARRING

Judy Garland

GARLAND SONGS

"You Made Me Love You"
"For Me and My Gal"
"The Boy Next Door"
"The Trolley Song"
"A Pretty Girl Milking Her Cow"

ADDENDA

★ This was a transcribed feature produced by the Treasury Department to foster the sale of Defense Bonds.

2 "The Bing Crosby Show" May 21, 1952

CBS (30 minutes)
Music: John Scott Trotter
Announcer: Ken Carpenter

GARLAND SONGS

"The Boy Next Door"
"When You're Smiling"
"Am I In Love" (with Bing Crosby)

ADDENDA

★ From a CBS publicity release on Judy's May 21 and 28 and June 4 "Bing Crosby Show" stints: "The three-broadcast engagement on 'The Bing Crosby Show' marks Miss Garland's first activity in radio since her recent sensational vaudeville engagement at the Palace Theatre in New York."

3 "The Bing Crosby Show" May 28, 1952

CBS (30 minutes)
Music: John Scott Trotter
Announcer: Ken Carpenter

GARLAND SONGS

"Rock-a-Bye Your Baby with a Dixie Melody"
"Carolina in the Morning"
"Noodlin' Rag" (with Bing Crosby)
"Isle of Capri" (with Bing Crosby)
"April in Paris" (with Bing Crosby)

RECORDINGS

With the exception of "Noodlin' Rag," these songs are available on *Judy Garland in Holland,* vol. 3, Obligato GIH 6100 (33⅓), and *Frances Ethel Gumm and Harry Lillis Crosby,* Legend 1973 (33⅓).

4 **"The Bing Crosby Show" June 4, 1952**

CBS (30 minutes)
Music: John Scott Trotter and His Orchestra, The Rhythmaires
Announcer: Ken Carpenter

STARRING

Bing Crosby

Guest Star: Judy Garland

SONGS

"Be My Life's Companion" (Bing Crosby)
"After You've Gone" (Bing Crosby)
"You Made Me Love You" (Judy Garland)
Duets: (Judy Garland, Bing Crosby)
　"Hello, My Baby"
　"In My Merry Oldsmobile"
　"Walking My Baby Back Home"
　"In My Merry Oldsmobile" (comedy version)
　"You're Just in Love"
"My Love Has Come Along" (Bing Crosby)
"Over the Rainbow" (Judy Garland)

ADDENDA

★ Garland and Crosby sing "Sound Off" as a singing commercial for Chesterfield cigarettes.

5 **"The General Electric Program" October 30, 1952**

CBS (30 minutes)
Music: John Scott Trotter Orchestra, Jud Conlon and the The Rhythmaires, Ziggy Elman
Announcer: Ken Carpenter

STARRING

Judy Garland

SONGS

"Alexander's Ragtime Band" (Judy Garland, with The Rhythmaires)
"Cuanto Le Gusta" (Jud Conlon and The Rhythmaires)
"Wish You Were Here" (Judy Garland)
"I Got Rhythm" (John Scott Trotter and His Orchestra)
"Stars Begin to Fall" (Jud Conlon and The Rhythmaires)
"A Pretty Girl Milking Her Cow" (Judy Garland)
"And the Angels Sing" (Ziggy Elman, orchestra)
"Carolina in the Morning" (Judy Garland)
"Manhattan Rag" (jazz band)
"You Belong to Me" (Judy Garland, with The Rhythmaires)

ADDENDA

★ Judy Garland stepped in to headline a special CBS Radio show in place of a scheduled "Bing Crosby Show" when Crosby's wife was dying and Bing could not appear.

RECORDINGS

Judy Garland on Radio, Radiola MR 1040 (33⅓). Side two contains the complete program, including commercials. "Wish You Were Here" is also on *The Big Band Era: The Passing of the 40s*, vol. IV, Vintage Records 4604 (33⅓).

1953

1 **"Lux Radio Theatre"**
February 16, 1953

CBS (60 minutes)
Episode: "Lady in the Dark"

STARRING

Judy Garland as Liza Elliott
John Lund as Charlie Johnson

GARLAND SONGS

"How Lovely to Be Me"
"This Is New"
"The Rights of Womankind"
"My Ship (Has Sails That Are Made of Silk)"

ADDENDA

★ This program was transcribed for the AFRTS "Radio Theater" series, #10.

RECORDINGS

Radio Yesteryear, *Voices of Hollywood #30* (cassette)

1954

1 **"Bing Crosby Twentieth Anniversary Tribute"**
September 24, 1954

NBC (90 minutes)
Host: Gary Crosby

GUESTS

Paul Whiteman   Irving Berlin
John Scott Trotter   Connie Boswell
Johnny Mercer   Bob Hope
Judy Garland   Les Paul
Perry Bodkin (Crosby's guitar
    accompanist)

GARLAND SONGS

"Swinging on a Star"

2 **"Best of All"**
October 11, 1954

NBC (60 minutes)
Music director: Skitch Henderson
Master of ceremonies: Kenneth Banghart

Judy was interviewed by Jinx Falkenburg at the East Coast premiere of *A Star Is Born* at the Paramount Theater in New York.
The program was devoted to music from Judy's movies. It also included Garland

James Mason and Judy Garland meet in *A Star Is Born*.

songs from the soundtrack of *A Star Is Born*:

"Gotta Have Me Go with You"
"The Man That Got Away"
"Born in a Trunk" sequence

1957

"Nightline"
April 30, 1957

NBC (60 minutes)
Master of ceremonies: Walter O'Keefe

GUESTS

(on tape, in order of appearance)

Charles Laughton	David Brinkley
Fibber McGee and Molly	Jack Benny
Leon Pearson	Eartha Kitt
Martin Agronsky	George Jessel
Frances Faye	Judy Garland
Fanny Brice	

GARLAND SONGS

"By Myself"

ADDENDA

★ This was the premiere of the show. Its format was taped interviews and recorded music.

RECORDINGS

Alone, Capitol T 835 (33⅓).

2 **"Nightline"**
August 30, 1957

NBC (60 minutes)
Judy sang a lullaby to her children as she prepared them for bed. Children's voices are also heard.

ADDENDA

★ This was a taped interview, from Garland's home in California.

Air Trailers

During the 1930s and 1940s, MGM produced special fifteen-minute recordings for radio. These were designed to advertise the studio's latest releases and to keep Metro's name and stars before the radio audience. The programs were introduced as "Leo on the air . . . ," and the movie trailers included both some dialogue and the film songs the studio expected to be most popular.

1 **"Broadway Melody of 1938"** (1937)

SONGS

"Everybody Sing" (Judy Garland)
"Feeling Like a Million" (George Murphy, Eleanor Powell)
"Dear Mr. Gable" (Judy Garland)
"Your Broadway and My Broadway" (Sophie Tucker, cast)

2 **"Everybody Sing"** (1938)

SONGS

"The Show Must Go On" (Allan Jones)
"Swing, Mr. Mendelssohn, Swing" (Judy Garland)
"The One I Love" (Allan Jones)
"Why? Because" (Judy Garland, Fanny Brice)

3 **"Listen, Darling"** (1938)

GARLAND SONGS

"Zing! Went the Strings of My Heart"
"Ten Pins in the Sky"
"On the Bumpy Road to Love"

4 **"The Wizard of Oz"** (1939)

SONGS

"Over the Rainbow" (Judy Garland)
"The Merry Old Land of Oz" (chorus)
"Follow the Yellow Brick Road" (Munchkins)

"If I Only Had a Brain, a Heart, the Nerve"
(Judy Garland, Ray Bolger, Jack Haley,
Bert Lahr)

"We're Off to See the Wizard" (Judy
Garland, Ray Bolger, Jack Haley, Bert
Lahr)

5 "Babes in Arms" (1939)

SONGS

"Good Morning" (Judy Garland, Mickey
Rooney)

"Where or When" (Douglas McPhail,
Betty Jaynes)

"Figaro" (Judy Garland)

"Minstrel" sequence (Judy Garland,
Mickey Rooney)

"I Cried For You" (Judy Garland)

"God's Country" (ensemble)

Judy sings "Silent Night."

6 Christmas Trailer (1939)

Episode: "Hardy Family Christmas
Greetings"

GARLAND SONGS
"Silent Night"

7 "Little Nellie Kelly" (1940)

GARLAND SONGS

"Nellie Kelly, I Love You" (with Douglas
McPhail, chorus)

"A Pretty Girl Milking Her Cow"

"Singin' in the Rain"

"It's a Great Day for the Irish" (with
Douglas McPhail, chorus)

8 Christmas Trailer (1940)

Judy Garland and Mickey Rooney talk to
people on Hollywood and Vine.

9 "Babes on Broadway" (1941)

GARLAND SONGS

"Babes on Broadway" (with cast)

"How About You?" (with Mickey Rooney)

"Hoe Down"

"Chin Up, Cheerio, Carry On"

"Minstrel" show (with Mickey Rooney,
chorus)

10 "For Me and My Gal" (1942)

SONGS

"Oh, You Beautiful Doll" (George Murphy)

"For Me and My Gal" (Judy Garland, Gene Kelly)

"When You Wore a Tulip" (Judy Garland, Gene Kelly)

"After You've Gone" (Judy Garland)

"It's a Long Way to Tipperary" (Judy Garland)

"Goodbye Broadway, Hello France" (Chorus)

"Smiles" (Judy Garland)

"Frenchy" (Gene Kelly, Ben Blue)

"Pack Up Your Troubles" (Judy Garland)

"When Johnny Comes Marching Home" (Judy Garland)

Judy Garland introduces Gene Kelly, "from the Broadway stage," to his "new audience" (moviegoers).

4

RECORDS: THE FILM YEARS

"Music is neither improbable nor unnatural. We may not go around talking to each other in song, but we often have a song in mind that expresses a mood, an unconscious thought, a dream. The musical takes the song from the back of the mind. . . . If it is done with taste and imagination, the audience will recognize their own dreams, their own moods reflected and magnified . . ."

John Kobal, *Gotta Sing, Gotta Dance*

★

"No one has ever sung my songs better than Judy Garland."

Irving Berlin, NBC interview in 1948

★

Judy Garland is generally thought of as a film star. She is associated in the public mind with some of the greatest of the Hollywood movie musicals, and, of course, much of her repertoire throughout her life was songs from those movies.

But first and foremost, Judy Garland was a singer.

She was signed by MGM in 1935, without a screen test, because of her voice, and the studio had her in recording sessions before it could figure out how to bring her to the screen.

She made her first professional record in 1936 with the Bob Crosby Orchestra, and, having just turned fourteen, she was one of the youngest recording artists ever. When she appeared on the "Shell Chateau" radio program in 1935, in a section of the show dedicated to new talent, Wallace Beery raved about her voice and predicted a glorious future based upon it. But she first achieved public and critical recognition in the movies for her rendition of "Dear Mr. Gable (You Made Me Love You)" in *Broadway Melody of 1938* (1937).

Garland, unlike other major movie singers of the forties, did not come to the screen with a Big Band career behind her. She was signed by Metro as a young teenager and developed professionally within its precincts. She became a skilled professional songstress in the movies rather than a songstress who came to the movies.

For a bright and ambitious youngster, MGM, in those years, was a working university of the popular performing arts. The studio prided itself not only on having "more stars than there are in heaven," but the best technicians, craftsmen, and support staff. Judy's career at Metro was guided by such talents as Roger Edens and Kay Thompson, and her primary producer was Arthur Freed, a successful lyricist in his own right.

It was an environment in which a musical talent of stamina and intelligence could prosper. It was also a business environment that aimed for dead center in the marketplace.

It is hard to separate Judy Garland's voice from her screen image during her Metro years. Her hit singles from that period— "Over the Rainbow," "The Trolley Song," "On the Atchison, Topeka and the Santa Fe," among others—all came from her movies. Vocally, she embodied a purity of voice and an innocence of artifice in delivery that imbued even the most banal lyrics with an emotional reality. This was united in the movies with characters whose primary traits always included honesty, vulnerability, and a sense of fun and good humor.

For an America leaving behind the Great Depression only to enter World War II, there was a yearning for simple verities that an apparently uncomplicated

acting and singing style matched. Judy's movie characters had sincere motivations and unselfish reactions. They sang of basic emotions in straightforward lyrics, if often with complex melodic lines. Judy conveyed hope and sadness, joyousness and despair—but never cynicism. And she united the vocal and the visual so expertly that part of the continuing allure of the early Garland recordings is nostalgia, nostalgia for a simpler time, enhanced by remembrances of the films that seemed to capture them.

But all this merely describes Judy Garland's effect; it does not explain how she achieved it. For her vocal performances grew in richness, breadth, depth, and technical sophistication parallel with her acting. She was charming in *Broadway Melody of 1938* or *Love Finds Andy Hardy*. But she was a comedienne of note in *In the Good Old Summertime* and a dramatic actress of sensitivity and skill in *The Clock*. Her "Swing, Mr. Charlie" and "Dear Mr. Gable" are fun, sung with enormous verve and talent. But her "Johnny One Note," "Better Luck Next Time," her 1949 "Last Night When We Were Young," and 1950 "Friendly Star" bear repeated listenings quite apart from any associated movies or visual images.

From her earliest recordings and radio broadcasts, Judy sang a lyric as if she were talking to someone specific, with an intent to convey a thought. She did not deviate from the music, but she controlled her breathing around the meaning of the words. Her pauses for breath are the pauses one would take in conversation. They punctuate the line. They never truncate it.

It was this instinctive, apparently visceral, respect for words and music, together and as a whole, that formed the basis for the effectiveness of the Garland style. When most of us hear a song, we hear it as a combination of words and music. Usually we can hum the tune, but it is the words, or the emotions evoked by the combination of the two, that make us remember the song.

During her film years, Garland developed the skills she needed to go well beyond singing a lyric. She learned to drive through the words to their essence. She used the music the way a musician uses an instrument, as a means of communication. And she used vocal techniques to flesh out the sensibilities behind the words.

Garland's voice always had a natural fluctuation of intensity when she sang. The vibrating loudness and softness of breath passing over her vocal cords, called a tremolo, created a tremulous quality that heightened any inherent sadness in a lyric.

Judy controlled her natural tremolo to precise emotional effect. Her sad songs show a pronounced vibrating quality in her voice, while in her upbeat numbers, she diminished the vocal fluctuations. Compare, for example, "But Not for Me" with "I Got Rhythm," both from the 1943 film *Girl Crazy,* both by George and Ira Gershwin. The first song is a lament over a lost and never-to-be-recovered love; the second is a celebration of joy. Garland's voice in "I Got Rhythm" appears stronger and surer, filled with happiness. In "But Not for Me," the more delicate quality of the voice, and by implication the vulnerability of the person behind it, comes in large part from the more apparent vocal trembling.

The widening and narrowing of her tremolo, the greater and lesser fluctuations of loudness and softness of breath over her vocal cords, became a critical, if seemingly artless, element in Garland's ability to plumb the emotions of a sad or tender song—without intruding on the joy of an upbeat one. The technique holds through any pairing of tender and high-spirited numbers. Listen to "Love of My Life" and "Mack the Black" from *The Pirate,* "Better Luck Next Time" and "Easter Parade" from *Easter Parade,* or "Have Yourself a Merry Little Christmas" and "The Trolley Song" from *Meet Me in St. Louis.*

Garland's famous quality of "vulnerability" stems from her controlled emphasis on vocal trembling when she wants to sell tender or sad.

Judy's earliest recordings are filled with a boisterous enthusiasm that leaps at the ear and matches impeccably the jazz rhythms of "Stompin' at the Savoy" or "All God's Chillun Got Rhythm." Jazz and swing were the initial categories into which Hollywood placed her; on screen, she was singing "Balboa" for Twentieth Century-Fox in *Pigskin Parade,* "Everybody Sing" in *Broadway Melody of 1938,* and "Swing, Mr. Mendelssohn" in *Everybody Sing* for MGM.

The form, of course, is perfect for a vocalist who wants to experiment with technique and effect, and experiment Garland did. In her first half dozen or so years with MGM, she mastered modulation, the transition from one key to another, and started to use it to influence mood, often employing it as a transition from a song's introductory verse into the heart of the lyric and beat. She learned, too, to modulate the volume of a tone, accentuating elements of the lyric by underscoring specific notes and measures. And she played with improvising around the melodic line. If you listen carefully to early Garland recordings such as "You Can't Have Everything," "Bei Mir Bist Du Schoen," "Buds Won't Bud," or "Blues in the Night," you find her talent coming increasingly under intelligent control.

In her early years at Metro-Goldwyn-Mayer, the studio had some difficulty finding the right screen image for Judy. MGM settled on her image as a singer much more quickly. The success of "Dear Mr. Gable" and "Over the Rainbow," coupled with the deepening and ripening of her voice and her growing technical skills and vocal polish, found her spending much of the early forties recording ballads and upbeat numbers with (always excepting Gershwin, of course) a diminished to nonexistent jazz inflection.

In addition, during what might be called her middle MGM period, the studio backed her up in recording sessions with lusher arrangements, employing more strings and fewer and more mellow horns. Gone was the swing band; enter the studio orchestra in full play. In blending with these arrangements, Garland never gave up her straightforward delivery. But she had to soften her voice, emphasizing delicacy to the virtual exclusion of vocal power in the ballads, resulting in the sweeter sound you hear in songs like "No Love, No Nothin' " and "A Journey to a

Star," both recorded in 1943, or "This Heart of Mine," recorded in 1945.

By the midforties, Judy Garland was an established box-office draw; as such, she developed some influence over the studio's direction of her career. Much against executive better judgment, she was allowed to make a purely dramatic, nonmusical film, *The Clock*, in 1945. It was a success. Shortly thereafter, her recordings show her returning to a more natural style, a style that allowed her to use the pure vocal power she possessed, singing from the chest with an open throat.

It was the style Garland would keep developing and perfecting until the end of her life. Her arrangements became cleaner and musically more sophisticated. In "Get Happy," for instance, a jazz inflection reappeared. And by the time she left Metro in 1950, she had acquired virtually all the basic techniques she would assemble and reassemble to such astonishing effect during the fifties and early sixties.

Compare, for example, "The Trolley Song," recorded in 1944, with "On the Atchison, Topeka and the Santa Fe," recorded in 1946 for the soundtrack of *The Harvey Girls*. Both are up-tempo numbers. But notice in "The Trolley Song," Judy never really lets go. At the climax of each chorus, she restrains the power behind her voice, and, at the end of the song, she is swallowed into the ensemble singing. In "On the Atchison, Topeka," however, she shows an increasing level of power with each chorus, and her voice dominates the ensemble, making the ending that much more dynamic.

"Johnny One Note" was meant to be

fun and was written to display virtuosity. It is a song that demands sustained force and, simultaneously, clarity and precision. Garland's rendition, recorded in 1948, rings out with sheer pleasure in performance. Not only does she hold her notes, but she amplifies their impact by sustaining them in true vibrato, a rapid fluctuation of pitch so that the ear hears the center of the tone. A vibrato creates a pulsating effect, one of strength and power. It is a musical exclamation point. And so Garland used it, to create a vibrancy that sharpens her emotional contact with the listener.

What makes Garland's later Metro recordings worth repeated listenings is the artful combination of such vocal techniques, wedded to a naturally powerful voice—in the hands of a singer who respects both the words and music of the songs she sings.

"Better Luck Next Time" (1948), for instance, is a straightforward Garland ballad. But notice how she varies her pacing so that when the lyric repeats that love is something that happens once, "not twice," her "not twice" is actually spoken, not sung. Yet when she sings "better luck next time / that could never be," she builds on "that could never be" by varying the volume of the tone under "never," while sustaining the note under "be" in the first refrain and sustaining it in vibrato in the second and third—giving the whole phrase added power. When the chorus states, "Made my mind up to make another start / I've made my mind up / But I can't make up my heart," Garland gives each successive phrase a wider tremolo, a greater vocal trembling that emphasizes the pain. And in the last two refrains of "that could never be," she modulates down—and goes from a vibrato into an almost spoken tremolo. Suddenly, a sad song is a song of despair.

Garland sang a song the way people hear it. She sang words and music together, as mutually reinforcing aspects of one whole. She had the talent, and developed the skill, to bridge the distance between composer/lyricist and audience, to convey to millions of individual listeners each song's unique emotional quality. She developed an artistry of such transparency that it has often been taken for being unwitting.

Just how "witting" it was can be seen even more clearly in the brilliance of Garland's musicianship during her concert years.

A. SINGLES

1 **"Swing Mr. Charlie"**
[J. Russell Robinson, Irving Taylor, Harry
Brooks (1936)]
"Stompin' at the Savoy"
[Andy Razaf, Benny Goodman, Chick Webb,
Edgar Sampson (1936)]

Label:
    Decca 848 (78)
    Brunswick 02267 (78)
Released: 1936

Judy singing with Bob Crosby and His Orchestra from
her 1943 film *Presenting Lily Mars.*

ADDENDA

★ Judy Garland was just fourteen (she
was born on June 10, 1922) when she
recorded these songs on June 12, 1936,
with the Bob Crosby Orchestra, making
her one of the youngest-ever recording
artists.

★ In 1943, Garland made *Presenting Lily
Mars,* in which Bob Crosby and His Orchestra had a featured role.

★ On November 27, 1935, she recorded
"No Other One" and "All's Well" with
the Victor Young Orchestra. Decca did
not release these sides.

ALBUMS

Albums with "Swing Mr. Charlie" and
  "Stompin' at the Savoy":
Collector's Items, 1936–1945
  (See section B, Albums, #11)
The Young Judy Garland
  (See section B, #32)

---

2 **"Everybody Sing"**
[Nacio Herb Brown, Arthur Freed (1937)]
**"When Two Love Each Other"—the Henry King
Orchestra—no vocal**

Label: Decca 1332 (78)
Released: 1937

ADDENDA

★ Judy Garland introduced "Everybody
  Sing" in *Broadway Melody of 1938*
  (1937).
★ This recording is with Georgie Stoll
  and His Orchestra. It was recorded on
  August 30, 1937.

ALBUMS

Albums with "Everybody Sing":
Collector's Items, 1936–1945
  (See section B, #11)
The Young Judy Garland
  (See section B, #32)

---

3 **"All God's Chillun Got Rhythm"**
[Gus Kahn, Bronislau Kaper, Walter Jurmann
(1937)]
"Everybody Sing"

Label: Decca 1432 (78)
Released: 1937

ADDENDA

★ "All God's Chillun Got Rhythm" comes
  from the film *A Day at the Races*. This
  recording is with Victor Young and His
  Orchestra, recorded on August 30,
  1937.

ALBUMS

Albums with "All God's Chillun Got
  Rhythm":
Collector's Items, 1936–1945
  (See section B, #11)
The Young Judy Garland
  (See section B, #32)

---

4 **"(Dear Mr. Gable) You
Made Me Love You"**
[Joseph McCarthy, James V. Monaco (written in
1913): interpolations by Roger Edens (1937)]
"You Can't Have Everything"
[Mack Gordon, Harry Revel (1937)]

Label:
  Decca 1463 (78)
  Decca 9-25493 (45)
Released: 1937

ADDENDA

★ Garland sang "(Dear Mr. Gable) You
  Made Me Love You" in *Broadway Melody of 1938* (1937).

★ Judy's rendition of "You Made Me Love You" had a significant impact on Harry James's style and career.

"On May 21, 1941, he recorded 'You Made Me Love You' . . . Despite our [friends and critics] warnings, the record proved to be a hit, and the James band was on the way to stardom.

"He recorded the tune for a very simple reason: he loved the way Judy Garland sang the song. I remember his raving about her . . ." (from George T. Simon, *The Big Bands,* 4th ed.).

★ "You Made Me Love You" was introduced by Al Jolson at the Winter Garden Theater in *Honeymoon Express* in 1913. Judy revitalized it, and Harry James turned out a million-selling record. As a result, *Variety* named it one of its "Golden 100 Tin Pan Alley Song" selections.

★ "You Can't Have Everything" is from the 1937 film of the same name, where it was sung by Alice Faye.

★ Judy Garland recorded both songs with Harry Sosnik and His Orchestra on September 24, 1937.

ALBUMS

Albums with "(Dear Mr. Gable)":
The Judy Garland Souvenir Album (See section B, #1)
Judy Garland—Greatest Performances (See section B, #5)
Judy at The Palace (See section B, #8)
The Best of Judy Garland (See section B, #9)
Judy Garland's Greatest Hits (See section B, #10)
The Judy Garland Story, vol. 2, *The Hollywood Years* (See section B, #19)

The Very Best of Judy Garland (See section B, #20)
Judy Garland in Song (See section B, #22)
Judy Garland [The Golden Archive Series] (See section B, #23)
Judy Garland—The Golden Years at MGM (See section B, #24)
Forever Judy (See section B, #25)
Judy Garland: From the MGM Classic Films (1938–1950) (See section B, #31)
Albums with "You Can't Have Everything":
The Judy Garland Souvenir Album (See section B, #1)
Collector's Items, 1936–1945 (See section B, #11)
The Young Judy Garland (See section B, #32)

---

5 "Cry, Baby, Cry"
[Jimmy Eaton, Terry Shand (1938)]
"Sleep, My Baby, Sleep"
[Eddie Pola, Franz Steininger]

Label: Decca 1796 (78)
Released: 1938

ADDENDA

★ Both songs were recorded with Harry Sosnik and His Orchestra on April 25, 1938.

★ "Cry, Baby, Cry" was on "Your Hit Parade" for nine weeks; it held the number one spot for one week.

ALBUMS

Albums with "Cry, Baby, Cry":
The Young Judy Garland
   (See section B, #32)
Albums with "Sleep, My Baby, Sleep":
Collector's Items, 1936–1945
   (See section B, #11)

---

6 **"It Never Rains But It Pours"**
[Mack Gordon, Harry Revel (1938)]
"Ten Pins in the Sky"
[Joseph McCarthy, Milton Ager (1938)]

Label:
   Decca 2017 (78)
   Brunswick 02656 (78)
Released: 1938

ADDENDA

★ Judy Garland sang "It Never Rains But It Pours" in *Love Finds Andy Hardy* (1938).
★ She sang "Ten Pins in the Sky" in *Listen, Darling* (1938).
★ Both cuts were recorded with Harry Sosnik and His Orchestra on August 21, 1938.

ALBUMS

Albums with "It Never Rains But It Pours" and "Ten Pins in the Sky":
Collector's Items, 1936–1945
   (See section B, #11)
The Young Judy Garland
   (See section B, #32)

---

7 **"Over the Rainbow"**
[E. Y. Harburg, Harold Arlen (1939)]
"The Jitterbug"
[E. Y. Harburg, Harold Arlen (1939)]

Label:
   Decca 2672 (78)
   Decca 23961 (78)
   Decca 9-23961 (45)
Released: 1939

ADDENDA

★ "Over the Rainbow" is the Judy Garland classic from *The Wizard of Oz* (1939).
★ The 1939 recording with Victor Young and His Orchestra is estimated to have sold several million copies over the years.
★ The song won Harburg and Arlen an Academy Award for Best Song.
★ This recording was on "Your Hit Parade" for fifteen weeks. It was number one for seven weeks. It is on the "ASCAP All-Time Hit Parade" and *Variety*'s "Fifty-Year Hit Parade."
★ "The Jitterbug," recorded with the Victor Young Orchestra, was originally to have been in *The Wizard of Oz*. It was cut before the film's release. It is worth listening to for the Arlen rhythms and Harburg wit as well as the Garland singing.

    The tune seems to have been a transitional one for Judy at MGM, lending itself to her swing inclinations as opposed to the more conventional approach of her middle MGM period.

★ Both songs were recorded July 28, 1939.

★ These recordings, on Decca 23961, are among Decca's list of "all-time best-selling standards." They are also on Decca DL 8387 (33⅓).

ALBUMS

Albums with "Over the Rainbow":
Judy Garland—Greatest Performances (See section B, #5)
Judy at The Palace (See section B, #8)
The Best of Judy Garland (See section B, #9)
Judy Garland's Greatest Hits (See section B, #10)
The Judy Garland Story, vol. 2, *The Holly-wood Years* (See section B, #19)
The Very Best of Judy Garland (See section B, #20)
Judy Garland in Song (See section B, #22)
Judy Garland [The Golden Archive Series] (See section B, #23)
Judy Garland—The Golden Years at MGM (See section B, #24)
Forever Judy (See section B, #25)
Judy Garland: From the MGM Classic Films (See section B, #31)

---

8 **"Over the Rainbow"**
"(Dear Mr. Gable) You Made Me Love You"

Label:
    MGM KCC 166 (45)
    Decca 2-3962 (78)
    Decca 9-23961 (45)
    Decca 25493 (78)
Released: 1939

---

9 **"(Dear Mr. Gable) You Made Me Love You"**
"Sleep, My Baby, Sleep"

Label: Decca 25393 (78)

---

10 **"In Between"**
[Roger Edens (1938)]
"Sweet Sixteen"
[Roger Edens (1939)]

Label:
    Decca 15045 (78)
    Decca 29233 (78)
    Decca 40219 (78)
    Decca 9-40219 (45)
Released: 1939

ADDENDA

★ Garland sang "In Between" in *Love Finds Andy Hardy* (1938).

★ Both songs were recorded with the Victor Young Orchestra on July 28, 1939.

ALBUMS

Albums with "In Between":
The Judy Garland Souvenir Album (See section B, #1)
Judy Garland—Greatest Performances (See section B, #5)
Judy at The Palace (See section B, #8)
Albums with "Sweet Sixteen":
The Judy Garland Souvenir Album (See section B, #1)
Judy at The Palace (See section B, #8)
The Best of Judy Garland (See section B, #9)

Judy recording for the soundtrack of *Broadway Melody of 1938*.

11 "Zing! Went the Strings of My Heart"
[James F. Hanley (1935)]
"Fascinating Rhythm"
[Ira and George Gershwin (1924)]

Label: Decca 18543 (78)
Released: 1939

ADDENDA

★ "Zing!" was sung by Judy Garland in *Listen, Darling* (1938). It is from the 1934 musical *Thumbs Up,* with Bobby Clark and Paul McCullough.
★ "Fascinating Rhythm" was introduced by Fred and Adele Astaire in 1924 in *Lady, Be Good.*
★ Judy Garland recorded both songs on July 29, 1939, with the Victor Young Orchestra.
★ On the same date, Judy recorded "Swanee." Decca did not release this cut.

ALBUMS

Albums with "Zing! Went the Strings of My Heart":
The Judy Garland Third Souvenir Album
   (See section B, #3)
The Magic of Judy Garland
   (See section B, #7)
The Best of Judy Garland
   (See section B, #9)
Albums with "Fascinating Rhythm":
The Judy Garland Third Souvenir Album
   (See section B, #3)
Miss Show Biz (See section B, #12)
The Young Judy Garland
   (See section B, #32)

12 "Embraceable You"
[Ira and George Gershwin (1930)]
"Swanee"
[Irving Caesar, George Gershwin (1919)]

Label: Decca 2881 (78)
Released: 1939

ADDENDA

★ Judy Garland sang "Embraceable You" four years later in *Girl Crazy* (1943).
★ Both songs were recorded with Victor Young and His Orchestra on October 16, 1939.
★ "Swanee" was George Gershwin's first hit. It comes from the 1919 musical production *Sinbad,* starring Al Jolson.
★ These songs are among Decca's list of "all-time best-selling standards."

ALBUMS

Albums with "Embraceable You" (1939) and "Swanee" (1939):
Collector's Items, 1936–1945
   (See section B, #11)

13 "Oceans Apart"
[Mickey Rooney, Sidney Miller]
"Figaro"
[Roger Edens (1939)]

Label:
   Decca 2873 (78)
   Brunswick 2873 (78) (U.K.)
Released: 1939

ADDENDA

★ Garland sang "Figaro" in *Babes in Arms* (1939).

★ Both songs were recorded with Victor Young and His Orchestra on October 16, 1939.

ALBUMS

Albums with "Oceans Apart":
The Judy Garland Souvenir Album
 (See section B, #1)
Collector's Items, 1936–1945
 (See section B, #11)
Albums with "Figaro":
The Judy Garland Souvenir Album
 (See section B, #1)

---

14 **"Friendship"** (with Johnny Mercer)
[Cole Porter (1939)]
"Wearing of the Green"
[Roger Edens (1940)]

Label: Decca 3165 (78)
Released: 1940

ADDENDA

★ "Wearing of the Green" was recorded on April 10, 1940, with the Bobby Sherwood Orchestra.
★ "Friendship" is from *DuBarry Was a Lady*. It was recorded on April 15, 1940, with the Victor Young Orchestra.

ALBUMS

Albums with "Friendship":
Miss Show Biz (See section B, #12)
The Young Judy Garland
 (See section B, #32)
From the Decca Vaults
 (See section B, #33)

Publicity shot of Judy recording at home, ca. 1941.

Judy Garland: The Beginning
 (See section B, #35)
Albums with "The Wearing of the Green":
Collector's Items, 1936–1945
 (See section B, #11)

---

15 **"Buds Won't Bud"**
[E. Y. Harburg, Harold Arlen (1937)]
"I'm Nobody's Baby"
[Benny Davis, Milton Ager, and Lester Santly (1921)]

Label: Decca 3174 (78)
Released: 1940

ADDENDA

★ Garland sang "I'm Nobody's Baby" in *Andy Hardy Meets Debutante* (1940).

★ Garland's recording of "I'm Nobody's Baby" was on "Your Hit Parade" for eleven weeks.

★ "Buds Won't Bud" was recorded for the film but cut before release. That was the second time the song had been cut. It was originally written for the 1937 Broadway musical "Hooray for What!" but didn't make it there either. It finally was sung on the screen by Ethel Waters in *Cairo* (1942).

★ Garland recorded both songs, with Bobby Sherwood conducting, on April 10, 1940.

ALBUMS

Albums with "Buds Won't Bud":
Collector's Items, 1936–1945
    (See section B, #11)
Albums with "I'm Nobody's Baby":
The Magic of Judy Garland
    (See section B, #7)
The Best of Judy Garland
    (See section B, #9)
Judy Garland's Greatest Hits
    (See section B, #10)
The Judy Garland Story, vol. 2, *The Hollywood Years* (See section B, #19)
Judy Garland (See section B, #21)
Judy Garland [The Golden Archive Series]
    (See section B, #23)
Judy Garland—The Golden Years at MGM
    (See section B, #24)
Forever Judy (See section B, #25)

16 **"The End of the Rainbow"**
[Sammy Cahn, Saul Chaplin]
"The End of the Rainbow"—the Woody Herman Orchestra—no vocal

Label: Decca 3231 (78)
Released: 1940

ADDENDA

★ This song was recorded with Bobby Sherwood conducting the orchestra on April 10, 1940.

ALBUMS

Albums with "The End of the Rainbow":
Collector's Items, 1936–1945
    (See section B, #11)

17 **"Our Love Affair"**
[Arthur Freed, Roger Edens (1940)]
"I'm Always Chasing Rainbows"
[Harry Carroll, Joseph McCarthy (1918)]

Label: Decca 3593 (78)
Released: 1940

ADDENDA

★ Garland sang "Our Love Affair" in *Strike Up the Band* (1940). The song was nominated for an Academy Award. (It lost to Ned Washington–Leigh Harline's "When You Wish Upon a Star," from *Pinocchio.*)

★ She sang "I'm Always Chasing Rainbows" in *Ziegfeld Girl* (1940).

★ Both songs were recorded on December 18, 1940, with the David Rose Orchestra.

ALBUMS

Albums with "Our Love Affair":
The Magic of Judy Garland
(See section B, #7)
The Best of Judy Garland
(See section B, #9)
Born in a Trunk. Stardom: 1940–1945
(See section B, #29)
Albums with "I'm Always Chasing
Rainbows":
Judy Garland, Volume II
(See section B, #6)
The Magic of Judy Garland
(See section B, #7)
The Best of Judy Garland
(See section B, #9)
Judy Garland's Greatest Hits
(See section B, #10)
*Judy Garland: From the MGM Classic
Films (1938–1950)*
(See section B, #31)
From the Decca Vaults
(See section B, #33)

---

18 **"It's a Great Day for the Irish"**
[Roger Edens (1940)]
"A Pretty Girl Milking Her Cow"
[Adaptation by Roger Edens (1940)]

Label:
Decca 3604 (78)
Decca 25043 (78)
Decca 9-25043 (45)
Released: 1940

ADDENDA

★ Both songs were sung by Judy Garland
in *Little Nellie Kelly* (1940). David Rose
conducted the orchestra at the record-

ing session on December 18, 1940, for
both songs.
★ These recordings, on Decca 25043, are
among Decca's list of "all-time best-selling standards."

ALBUMS

Albums with "It's a Great Day for the
Irish":
Collector's Items, 1936–1945
(See section B, #11)
Albums with "A Pretty Girl Milking Her
Cow":
The Magic of Judy Garland
(See section B, #7)
The Best of Judy Garland
(See section B, #9)
Judy Garland's Greatest Hits
(See section B, #10)

---

19 **"The Birthday of a King"**
[H. H. Neidlinger]
"The Star of the East"
[Amanda Kennedy, George Cooper]

Label:
Decca 4050 (78)
Decca 23658 (78)
Decca 9-2368 (45)
Released: 1940

ADDENDA

★ Both songs were recorded on July 20,
1941, with the David Rose Orchestra.

ALBUMS

Albums with "The Birthday of a King" and
"The Star of the East"
Judy Garland: The Beginning
(See section B, #35)

20 "How About You?"
[Ralph Freed, Burton Lane (1941)]
"Franklin D. Roosevelt Jones"
[Harold Rome (1938)]

Label: Decca 4072 (78)
Released: 1941

ADDENDA

★ Garland sang both songs in *Babes on Broadway* (1941).
★ They were recorded on October 24, 1941, with the David Rose Orchestra.
★ "How About You?" is a rare instance of one songwriter praising another in his lyrics. ("I like a Gershwin tune . . .") The song was nominated for an Academy Award for "best song" in 1942. (It lost to Irving Berlin's "White Christmas," from *Holiday Inn.*)
★ "Franklin D. Roosevelt Jones" comes from the revue *Sing Out the News.* The song won an ASCAP award as one of the best songs of 1938.

ALBUMS

Albums with "How About You?":
Judy Garland—Greatest Performances
   (See section B, #5)
The Young Judy Garland
   (See section B, #32)
Albums with "Franklin D. Roosevelt Jones":
The Magic of Judy Garland
   (See section B, #7)
The Best of Judy Garland
   (See section B, #9)

21 "Blues in the Night"
[Johnny Mercer, Harold Arlen (1941)]
"The End of the Rainbow"

Label: Decca 4081 (78)
Released: 1941

ADDENDA

★ "Blues in the Night" was recorded on October 24, 1941, with the David Rose Orchestra.
★ This song is from the 1941 movie *Blues in the Night.* The picture was originally titled *Hot Nocturne,* but the number was impressive enough that the film name was changed. It was nominated for an Academy Award in 1941. It lost to Oscar Hammerstein II and Jerome Kern's "The Last Time I Saw Paris," from *Lady, Be Good.* (In 1943, John Garfield did a comic gangster variation in the film *Thank Your Lucky Stars.*)
★ "The End of the Rainbow" was recorded on April 10, 1940, with the Bobby Sherwood Orchestra.

ALBUMS

Albums with "Blues in the Night":
Collector's Items, 1936–1945
   (See section B, #11)

22 "Poor You"
[Burton Lane, E. Y. Harburg (1942)]
"Last Call for Love"
[Burton Lane, E. Y. Harburg, Margery Cummings (1942)]

Label: Decca 18320 (78)
Released: 1942

ADDENDA

★ Both songs come from the 1942 film *Ship Ahoy*. They were recorded on April 3, 1942, with the David Rose Orchestra.

Judy Garland and fiancé David Rose.

ALBUMS

Albums with "Poor You":
Collector's Items, 1936–1945
   (See section B, #11)
Judy Garland: The Beginning
   (See section B, #35)
Albums with "Last Call for Love":
Collector's Items, 1936–1945
   (See section B, #11)
From the Decca Vaults
   (See section B, #33)

23 "For Me and My Gal"
(with Gene Kelly)
[Edgar Leslie and E. Ray Goetz, George W. Meyer (1917)]
"When You Wore a Tulip" (with Gene Kelly)
[Jack Mahoney, Percy Wenrich (1914)]

Label:
   Decca 18480 (78)
   Decca 9-25115 (45)
   Decca 25115 (78)
Released: 1942

ADDENDA

★ Both songs were sung by Judy Garland and Gene Kelly in *For Me and My Gal* (1942). They were recorded on July 26, 1942 with the David Rose Orchestra.

★ These recordings, on Decca 25115, are among Decca's select group of "all-time best-selling standards."

★ In the film *For Me and My Gal*, the setting for the title song was 1916; that was a year before it was actually written.

ALBUMS

Albums with "For Me and My Gal":
Judy Garland Sings (See section B, #4)
Judy Garland—Greatest Performances
    (See section B, #5)
Judy at The Palace (See section B, #8)
The Best of Judy Garland
    (See section B, #9)
Judy Garland's Greatest Hits
    (See section B, #10)
Albums with "When You Wore a Tulip":
The Judy Garland Second Souvenir Album
    (See section B, #1)
Judy Garland Sings (See section B, #41)
Judy Garland—Greatest Performances
    (See section B, #5)
Judy at The Palace (See section B, #8)
The Best of Judy Garland
    (See section B, #9)
Judy Garland's Greatest Hits
    (See section B, #10)

ALBUMS

Albums with "I Never Knew":
The Judy Garland Third Souvenir Album
    (See section B, #3)
The Magic of Judy Garland
    (See section B, #7)
The Best of Judy Garland
    (See section B, #9)
The Judy Garland Musical Scrapbook
    (1935–1949) (See section B, #27)
Born in a Trunk. Stardom: 1940–1945
    (See section B, #29)
Albums with "On the Sunny Side of the
    Street":
The Judy Garland Second Souvenir Album
    (See section B, #2)
The Judy Garland Third Souvenir Album
    (See section B, #3)
The Best of Judy Garland
    (See section B, #9)

---

24 "I Never Knew"
[Tom Pitts, Ray Egan, Roy Marsh (1920)]
**"On the Sunny Side
of the Street"**
[Dorothy Fields, Jimmy McHugh (1930)]

Label: Decca 18524 (78)
Released: 1942

ADDENDA

★ "I Never Knew" was recorded on July
   26, 1942, with the David Rose Orchestra. The arrangement is by Paul Whiteman.
★ "On the Sunny Side of the Street" was
   recorded on April 3, 1942, with the
   David Rose Orchestra. It comes from
   the 1930 Broadway show *The International Revue.*

---

25 "That Old Black Magic"
[Johnny Mercer, Harold Arlen (1942)]
"Poor Little Rich Girl"
[Noel Coward (1925)]

Label: Decca 18540 (78)
Released: 1942

ADDENDA

★ "That Old Black Magic" was recorded
   by Judy Garland on July 26, 1942. The
   song was first used in the 1942 film
   Star Spangled Rhythm. It was nomi-
   nated for the Academy Award for best
   song. (It lost to Mack Gordon–Harry
   Warren's "You'll Never Know," from
   Hello, Frisco, Hello.)
★ "Poor Little Rich Girl" was recorded on
   April 3, 1942. The orchestra was under

the direction of David Rose. The song comes from the Broadway show *Charlot's Revue,* imported from London.

ALBUMS

Albums with "That Old Black Magic":
The Judy Garland Second Souvenir Album
    (See section B, #2)
The Judy Garland Third Souvenir Album
    (See section B, #3)
The Magic of Judy Garland
    (See section B, #7)
The Best of Judy Garland
    (See section B, #9)
Albums with "Poor Little Rich Girl":
The Judy Garland Second Souvenir Album
    (See section B, #2)
The Judy Garland Third Souvenir Album
    (See section B, #3)
Judy Garland—Greatest Performances
    (See section B, #5)
The Best of Judy Garland
    (See section B, #9)
Miss Show Biz (See section B, #12)
The Young Judy Garland
    (See section B, #32)

---

26 "Embraceable You"
"Could You Use Me?"
(with Mickey Rooney)
[Ira and George Gershwin (1930)]

Label: Decca 23308 (78)
Released: 1943

ADDENDA

★ This version of "Embraceable You," which Garland sang in *Girl Crazy* (1943), has a noticeably different voice and more mature quality than her 1939 release on Decca 2881 (78).

★ Garland also sang "Could You Use Me?" in *Girl Crazy.*
★ Both songs were recorded on November 4, 1943, with the Georgie Stoll Orchestra.

ALBUMS

Albums with "Embraceable You":
The Magic of Judy Garland
    (See section B, #7)

---

27 "But Not for Me"
[Ira and George Gershwin (1930)]
"Treat Me Rough"—Mickey Rooney

Label: Decca 23309 (78)
Released: 1943

ADDENDA

★ Judy Garland sang "But Not for Me" in *Girl Crazy* (1943). This cut was recorded on November 4, 1943, with the Georgie Stoll Orchestra.
★ For those not old enough to remember, the Beatrice Fairfax referred to in the song was the Hearst papers' personal advice columnist—the "Dear Abby" of the twenties.

ALBUMS

Albums with "But Not for Me":
The Magic of Judy Garland
    (See section B, #7)
The Best of Judy Garland
    (See section B, #9)
The Judy Garland Story, vol. 2, *The Hollywood Years* (See section B, #19)
The Very Best of Judy Garland
    (See section B, #20)
Judy Garland in Song (See section B, #22)

"Bidin' My Time" scene from 1943 film *Girl Crazy*.

28 **"Bidin' My Time"**
(with the Leo Diamond Harmonica
Quintet)
[Ira and George Gershwin (1930)]
"I Got Rhythm"
[Ira and George Gershwin (1930)]

Label: Decca 23310 (78)
Released: 1943

ADDENDA

★ Both songs were sung by Judy Garland
  in *Girl Crazy* (1943).
★ "I Got Rhythm" was recorded on November 2, 1943.

★ "Bidin' My Time" was recorded on No-
  vember 4, 1943.
★ Both songs were recorded with the
  Georgie Stoll Orchestra.

ALBUMS

Albums with "Bidin' My Time":
Miss Show Biz (See section B, #12)
The Young Judy Garland
  (See section B, #32)
Albums with "I've Got Rhythm":
Collector's Items, 1936–1945
  (See section B, #11)

29 **"No Love, No Nothin' "**
[Leo Robin, Harry Warren (1943)]
"A Journey to a Star"
[Leo Robin, Harry Warren (1943)]

Label:
Decca 18584 (78)
Brunswick 03515 (78)
Released: 1943

ADDENDA

★ Both songs are from the 1943 film *The Gang's All Here*. Garland recorded them with Georgie Stoll conducting on December 22, 1943.

ALBUMS

Albums with "No Love, No Nothin' " and "A Journey to a Star":
Collector's Items, 1936–1945
(See section B, #11)

30 **"Meet Me in St. Louis, Louis"**
[Andrew B. Sterling, Kerry Mills (1904)]
"Skip to My Lou"
[Ralph Blane, Hugh Martin (1944)]

Label: Decca 23360 (78)
Released: 1944

ADDENDA

★ Both songs were sung by Judy Garland in *Meet Me in St. Louis* (1944). They were recorded for Decca on April 21, 1944, with the Georgie Stoll Orchestra.
★ *Meet Me in St. Louis* was the first time Ralph Blane and Hugh Martin wrote the complete score for a film.

ALBUMS

Albums with "Meet Me in St. Louis, Louis":
Judy Garland—Greatest Performances
(See section B, #5)
Judy at The Palace (See section B, #8)
The Best of Judy Garland
(See section B, #9)
Judy Garland's Greatest Hits
(See section B, #10)

31 **"The Trolley Song"**
[Ralph Blane, Hugh Martin (1944)]
"Boys and Girls Like You and Me"
[Oscar Hammerstein II, Richard Rodgers (1943)]

Label: Decca 23361 (78)
Released: 1944

ADDENDA

★ Judy Garland sang "The Trolley Song" in *Meet Me in St. Louis* (1944). It was recorded on April 21, 1944, with Georgie Stoll conducting the orchestra. It was on "Your Hit Parade" for fourteen weeks and held first place for five weeks.
★ The song received an Academy Award nomination for Best Song. (It lost to Johnny Burke–James Van Heusen's "Swinging on a Star," from *Going My Way*.) *Variety* picked "The Trolley Song" for its "Fifty-Year Hit Parade."
★ Judy recorded "Boys and Girls Like You and Me" on April 20, 1944, for the same movie, but it was cut before release. The song was originally written for *Oklahoma!* but was dropped from the New York production.

★ Both songs were recorded with the Georgie Stoll Orchestra.

★ Ralph Blane came across the inspiration for "The Trolley Song" in a public library, where he found a picture of a 1903 double decker trolley in a book about old St. Louis. The photo's caption was "Clang, Clang, Clang Went the Trolley."

ALBUMS

Albums with "The Trolley Song":
Judy Garland—Greatest Performances"
(See section B, #5)
Judy at The Palace (See section B, #8)
The Best of Judy Garland
(See section B, #9)
Judy Garland's Greatest Hits
(See section B, #10)
The Judy Garland Story, vol. 2, *The Hollywood Years* (See section B, #19)
The Very Best of Judy Garland
(See section B, #20)
Judy Garland (See section B, #21)
Judy Garland [The Golden Archive Series]
(See section B, #23)
Judy Garland—The Golden Years at MGM
(See section B, #24)
Forever Judy (See section B, #25)
Judy Garland: From the MGM Classic Films (1938–1950)
(See section B, #31)

32 **"Have Yourself a Merry Little Christmas"**
[Ralph Blane, Hugh Martin (1944)]
"The Boy Next Door"
[Ralph Blane, Hugh Martin (1944)]

Label: Decca 23362 (78)
Released: 1944

ADDENDA

★ Both songs were sung by Judy Garland in *Meet Me in St. Louis* (1944). They were recorded on April 20, 1944, with the Georgie Stoll Orchestra. "The Boy Next Door" was also released on Decca 29296 (78).

ALBUMS

Albums with "Have Yourself a Merry Little Christmas":
The Best of Judy Garland
(See section B, #9)
Judy Garland's Greatest Hits
(See section B, #10)
Albums with "The Boy Next Door":
Judy Garland, Volume II
(See section B, #6)
Judy Garland's Greatest Hits
(See section B, #10)
The Judy Garland Story, vol. 2, *The Hollywood Years* (See section B, #19)
The Very Best of Judy Garland
(See section B, #20)
Judy Garland (See section B, #21)
Judy Garland [The Golden Archive Series]
(See section B, #23)
Judy Garland—The Golden Years at MGM
(See section B, #24)
Forever Judy (See section B, #25)

33 "The Trolley Song"
"Meet Me in St. Louis, Louis"

Label:
    Decca 25494 (78)
    Decca 9-25494 (45)
Released: 1944

ADDENDA

★ Both songs were recorded on April 21, 1944.
★ These recordings, on Decca 25494, are among Decca's list of "all-time best-selling standards."

34 "The Boy Next Door"
"The Trolley Song"

Label: Brunswick 03558 (78)

35 "Over the Rainbow"
"I May Be Wrong (But I Think You're Wonderful)"
[Harry Ruskin, Henry Sullivan (1929)]

Label:
    V Disc 335-A (78)
    Navy V Disc 159-A (78)
Released: 1944

ADDENDA

★ Both songs were recorded with the Tommy Dorsey Orchestra in August 1944. They were broadcast on Armed Forces Radio Service (AFRS), "Your All-Time Hit Parade," #44 on August 13, 1944. (Tommy Dorsey filled in for Harry James, who had been hurt in a baseball game.)
★ "I May Be Wrong" was introduced in the 1929 revue *Murray Anderson's Almanac*, where it was sung by Jimmy Savo.

ALBUMS

Albums with "I May Be Wrong":
Born in a Trunk. Stardom: 1940–1945
    (See section B, #30)

36 "Yah-ta-ta, Yah-ta-ta"
(with Bing Crosby)
[Johnny Burke, Jimmy Van Heusen (1945)]
"You've Got Me Where You Want Me"
(with Bing Crosby)
[Harry Warren, Johnny Mercer]

Label: Decca 23410 (78)
Released: 1945

ADDENDA

★ "Yah-ta-ta, Yah-ta-ta" was recorded on March 9, 1945, with the Joseph Lilley Orchestra.

ALBUMS

Albums with "Yah-ta-ta, Yah-ta-ta":
From the Decca Vaults
    (See section B, #33)

37 **"Connecticut"** (with Bing Crosby)
[Ralph Blane, Hugh Martin (1945)]
"Mine" (with Bing Crosby)
[Ira and George Gershwin (1933)]

Label: Decca 23804 (78)
Released: 1945

ADDENDA

★ Both songs were recorded with the Joseph Lilley Orchestra.
★ "Connecticut" was recorded on March 9, 1945.
★ "Mine" is from the 1933 Ryskind-Kaufman–Gershwin stage musical *Let 'Em Eat Cake.*

38 **"Mine"** (with Bing Crosby)
"You've Got Me Where You Want Me" (with Bing Crosby)

Label: Decca 28210 (78)
Released: 1945

39 **"If I Had You"**
(with The Merry Macs)
[Ted Shapiro, Jimmy Campbell, Reginald Connelly (1928)]
"On the Atchison, Topeka and the Santa Fe" (with The Merry Macs)
[Johnny Mercer, Harry Warren (1945)]

Label: Decca 23436 (78)
Released: 1945

ADDENDA

★ "If I Had You" was the background music to Garland film *The Clock* (1945).
★ Judy Garland sang "On the Atchison, Topeka and the Santa Fe" in *The Harvey Girls* (1946). This recording was on "Your Hit Parade" for fourteen weeks.
★ "On the Atchison" was the Academy Award winner for Best Song and is on *Variety*'s "Fifty-Year Hit Parade."
★ Harry Warren apparently liked trains. He also wrote the music for "Shuffle Off to Buffalo" (with Al Dubin, for *42nd Street*—1933) and "Chattanooga Choo-Choo" (with Mack Gordon, for *Sun Valley Serenade*—1941).

ALBUMS

Albums with "If I Had You":
Judy Garland Sings (See section B, #4)
Collector's Items, 1936–1945 (See section B, #11)
Miss Show Biz (See section B, #12)
From the Decca Vaults (See section B, #33)
Albums with "On the Atchison, Topeka and the Santa Fe":
Judy Garland Sings (See section B, #4)
The Best of Judy Garland (See section B, #9)
Judy Garland's Greatest Hits (See section B, #10)
Miss Show Biz (See section B, #12)
Judy Garland: From the MGM Classic Films (1938–1950) (See section B, #31)
From the Decca Vaults (See section B, #33)

40 "Have Yourself a Merry Little Christmas" "You'll Never Walk Alone"
[Oscar Hammerstein II, Richard Rodgers (1943)]

Label:
  Decca 9-29295 (45)
  Decca 29295 (78)
Released: 1945

ADDENDA

★ "You'll Never Walk Alone" was recorded on July 10, 1945. It comes from the 1945 musical *Carousel*.

★ "Have Yourself a Merry Little Christmas" was originally written with a hopeless tone to the lyrics. Judy Garland felt that adding her ability to sell a sad song to the unhappiness of the words would make the number too depressing. It was rewritten to express more optimism.

ALBUMS

Albums with "You'll Never Walk Alone":
Judy Garland—Greatest Performances
  (See section B, #5)
Judy Garland, Volume II
  (See section B, #6)
The Best of Judy Garland
  (See section B, #9)

41 "The Boy Next Door" "Smilin' Through"
[Arthur Penn (1919)]

Label:
  Decca 9-29296 (45)
  Decca 29296 (78)
Released: 1945

ADDENDA

★ Judy Garland sang "The Boy Next Door" in *Meet Me in St. Louis* (1944). It was recorded on April 20, 1944.

★ "Smilin' Through" was recorded on July 10, 1945, with the Lyn Murray Orchestra.

ALBUMS

Albums with "Smilin' Through":
Collector's Items, 1936–1945
  (See section B, #11)

42 "This Heart of Mine"
[Arthur Freed, Harry Warren (1943)]
"Love"
[Ralph Blane, Hugh Martin (1945)]

Label:
  Decca 18660 (78)
  Brunswick 03623 (78)
Released: 1945

ADDENDA

★ Both songs were recorded on January 26, 1945, with the Victor Young Orchestra.

★ "Love" was also released on Decca 23688 (78).

★ Both songs were introduced in *Ziegfeld Follies of 1946*. Garland sang neither of them in the movie.

ALBUMS

Albums with "This Heart of Mine":
The Judy Garland Third Souvenir Album
 (See section B, #3)
Collector's Items, 1936–1945
 (See section B, #11)
Albums with "Love":
The Best of Judy Garland
 (See section B, #9)
Miss Show Biz (See section B, #12)
Born in a Trunk. Stardom: 1940–1945
 (See section B, #29)

43 "Smilin' Through"
"You'll Never Walk Alone"

Label:
 Decca 23539 (78)
Decca 9-23539 (45)
Released: 1945

ADDENDA

★ Both songs were recorded on July 10, 1945, with Lyn Murray directing the chorus and orchestra.

44 "In the Valley"
[Johnny Mercer, Harry Warren (1945)]
"On the Atchison, Topeka and the Santa Fe"

Label: Decca 23458 (78)
Released: 1945

ADDENDA

★ "In the Valley" was Garland's opening song in *The Harvey Girls* (1946). It was recorded October 7, 1945, with the Lennie Hayton Orchestra. "On the Atchison" was also released on Decca 23436 (78).

45 "Round and Round"
[Johnny Mercer, Harry Warren (1945)]
"Wait and See"—Kenny Baker

Label: Decca 23459 (78)
Released: 1945

ADDENDA

★ In *The Harvey Girls* (1946), Judy Garland sings "Round and Round" as part of an ensemble. It was recorded on May 14, 1945, with Kay Thompson, chorus, and the Lennie Hayton Orchestra.

46 **"It's a Great Big World"**
(with Virginia O'Brien, Betty Russell)
[Johnny Mercer, Harry Warren (1945)]
"The Wild, Wild West"—Virginia O'Brien

Label: Decca 23460 (78)
Released: 1945

ADDENDA

★ This number was sung by Judy Garland, Virginia O'Brien, and Cyd Charisse (dubbed by Betty Russell) in *The Harvey Girls* (1946). It was recorded on October 7, 1945, with the Lennie Hayton Orchestra.

47 **"For You, For Me, For Evermore"**
(with Dick Haymes)
[Ira and George Gershwin (1946)]
"Aren't You Kind of Glad We Did?"
(with Dick Haymes)
[Ira and George Gershwin (1946)]

Label: Decca 23687 (78)
Released: 1946

ADDENDA

★ Both songs were recorded on September 11, 1946, with the Gordon Jenkins Orchestra.
★ For both songs, Ira Gershwin worked with melodies and notes his brother had left behind after his death in 1937.

ALBUMS

Albums with "For You, For Me, For Evermore" and "Aren't You Kind of Glad We Did?":
Judy Garland Sings (See section B, #4)
Judy Garland: The Beginning
   (See section B, #35)

48 **"Changing My Tune"**
[Ira and George Gershwin (1946)]
"Love"
[Ralph Blane, Hugh Martin (1945)]

Label: Decca 23688 (78)
Released: 1946

ADDENDA

★ "Changing My Tune" was recorded on September 11, 1946, with the Gordon Jenkins Orchestra. The song was assembled from manuscripts found after George Gershwin's death.

ALBUMS

Albums with "Changing My Tune"
Judy Garland: The Beginning
   (See section B, #35)

49 **"There Is No Breeze"**
[Dorothy Dick, Alstone]
"Don't Tell Me That Story"
[Joseph Lilley]

Label: Decca 23746 (78)
Released: 1946

ADDENDA

★ Both songs were recorded on October 1, 1946, with the Gordon Jenkins Orchestra.

ALBUMS

Albums with "There Is No Breeze":
Judy Garland Sings (See section B, #4)
Judy Garland: The Beginning
　(See section B, #35)
Albums with "Don't Tell Me That Story":
From the Decca Vaults
　(See section B, #33)

50 **"Look for the Silver Lining"**
[Buddy DeSylva, Jerome Kern (1920)]
"Life Upon the Wicked Stage"—Virginia O'Brien

Label:　MGM 30002 (78)
Released:　1946

ADDENDA

★ Garland sang "Look for the Silver Lin-
　ing" in *Till the Clouds Roll By* (1946). It
　was recorded with the Lennie Hayton
　Orchestra.

ALBUMS

Albums with "Look for the Silver Lining":
Judy Garland Sings (See section B, #13)
Look for the Silver Lining
　(See section B, #15)
Judy Garland (with the MGM Orchestra)
　(See section B, #17)
The Judy Garland Story, vol. 1, *The Star
　Years* (See section B, #18)
The Very Best of Judy Garland
　(See section B, #20)
Judy Garland [The Golden Archive Series]
　(See section B, #23)
Judy Garland—The Golden Years at MGM
　(See section B, #24)
Forever Judy (See section B, #25)

51 **"Who?"**
[Otto Harbach, Oscar Hammerstein II, Jerome
Kern (1925)]
"Can't Help Lovin' Dat Man"—Lena Horne

Label:　MGM 30003 (78)
Released:　1946

ADDENDA

★ Garland sang "Who?" in *Till the Clouds
　Roll By* (1946). It was recorded with
　the Lennie Hayton Orchestra.

ALBUMS

Albums with "Who?":
Judy Garland Sings (See section B, #13)
Get Happy (See section B, #14)
Judy Garland (with the MGM Orchestra)
　(See section B, #17)
The Judy Garland Story, vol. 1, *The Star
　Years* (See section B, #18)
Judy Garland—The Golden Years at MGM
　(See section B, #24)
*Judy Garland: From the MGM Classic
　Films (1938–1950)*
　(See section B, #31)

52 **"Look for the Silver Lining"**
"Who?"

Label:
　MGM 30431 (78)
　MGM 30212 (X-45)
Released:　1946

53 **"I Wish I Were in Love Again"**
[Lorenz Hart, Richard Rodgers (1937)]
"Nothing but You"
[Lorenz Hart, Richard Rodgers (1940)]

Label: Decca 24469 (78)
Released: 1947

ADDENDA

★ In 1948, in *Words and Music,* Judy Garland sang "I Wish I Were in Love
Again" in a duet with Mickey Rooney.
★ The song had originally been introduced in the stage production of *Babes
in Arms,* but MGM did not use the
number in the movie of the same name,
starring Judy Garland and Mickey Rooney.
★ "Nothing but You" is from the 1940
Broadway show *Higher and Higher.*
★ Both songs were recorded on January
15, 1947.

ALBUMS

Albums with "I Wish I Were in Love
    Again":
Born to Sing (See section B, #26)
Judy Garland: The Beginning
    (See section B, #35)
Albums with "Nothing but You"
Judy Garland: The Beginning
    (See section B, #35)

54 **"Be a Clown"** (with Gene Kelly)
[Cole Porter (1948)]
"The Pirate Ballet"—no vocal

Label: MGM 30097 (78)
Released: 1948

ADDENDA

★ "Be a Clown" was a Judy Garland/Gene
Kelly duet in *The Pirate* (1948). It was
recorded with the Lennie Hayton Orchestra.
★ Gene Kelly persuaded Cole Porter to
add a rousing comic number to the
score after it had been completed, and
"Be a Clown" was the result. The song
is a direct antecedent to the "Make 'Em
Laugh" number in *Singin' in the Rain.*
(Try humming the two of them to
yourself.)

55 **"Love of My Life"**
[Cole Porter (1948)]
"You Can Do No Wrong"
[Cole Porter (1948)]

Label: MGM 30098 (78)
Released: 1948

ADDENDA

★ Judy Garland sang both songs in *The
Pirate* (1948). They were recorded with
the Lennie Hayton Orchestra. "Love of
My Life" was also released on MGM
30202 (78).

ALBUMS

Albums with "Love of My Life":
Judy Garland Sings (See section B, #13)
Get Happy (See section B, #14)
Judy Garland (with the MGM Orchestra) (See section B, #17)
The Judy Garland Story, vol. 1, *The Star Years* (See section B, #18)
Judy Garland—The Golden Years at MGM (See section B, #24)
Born to Sing (See section B, #26)

56 "Mack the Black"
[Cole Porter (1948)]
"Nina"—Gene Kelly

Label: MGM 30099 (78)
Released: 1948

ADDENDA

★ Judy Garland sang "Mack the Black" in *The Pirate* (1948). It was recorded with the Lennie Hayton Orchestra.

★ In the original nonmusical stage production of *The Pirate,* the pirate's name is Estramundo. Porter suggested changing it to Macoco and calling him "Mack the Black." It was a private joke. A friend's nickname was "Mack the Black."

57 "Johnny One Note"
[Lorenz Hart, Richard Rodgers (1937)]
"I Wish I Were in Love Again"
(with Mickey Rooney)

Label: MGM 30172 (78)
Released: 1948

ADDENDA

★ Garland sang both songs in *Words and Music* (1948). "I Wish I Were in Love Again" was a duet with Mickey Rooney. Both were recorded with the Lennie Hayton Orchestra.

★ "Johnny One Note" had originally been written for, and part of, the 1937 Broadway production of *Babes in Arms.* MGM cut the number from the 1939 film starring Judy Garland and Mickey Rooney.

ALBUMS

Albums with "Johnny One Note":
Judy Garland Sings (See section B, #13)
Get Happy (See section B, #14)
Judy Garland (with the MGM Orchestra) (See section B, #17)
The Judy Garland Story, vol. 1, *The Star Years* (See section B, #18)
The Very Best of Judy Garland (See section B, #20)
Judy Garland [The Golden Archive Series] (See section B, #23)
Judy Garland—The Golden Years at MGM (See section B, #24)
Born to Sing (See section B, #26)
Born in a Trunk. Superstar: 1945–1950 (See section B, #30)
Judy Garland: From the MGM Classic Films (See section B, #31)

58 "Easter Parade"
[Irving Berlin (1933)]
"A Fella with an Umbrella"
(with Peter Lawford)
[Irving Berlin (1948)]

Label: MGM 30185 (78)
Released: 1948

ADDENDA

★ Garland sang both songs in *Easter Parade* (1948). They were recorded with Johnny Green and the MGM Orchestra.

★ Berlin first used the melody for "Easter Parade" in 1917 in a song called "Smile and Show Your Dimple." It went nowhere.

ALBUMS

Albums with "Easter Parade" and "A Fella with an Umbrella":
Born to Sing (See section B, #26)

"I Love a Piano" scene from 1948 film *Easter Parade*.

59 **"A Couple of Swells"**
(with Fred Astaire)
[Irving Berlin (1948)]
Medley:
"I Love a Piano"
[Irving Berlin (1915)]
"Snooky Ookums" (with Fred Astaire)
[Irving Berlin (1913)]
"When the Midnight Choo-Choo Leaves for Alabam' "
(with Fred Astaire)
[Irving Berlin (1912)]

Label: MGM 30186 (78)
Released: 1948

ADDENDA

★ Both "A Couple of Swells" and the side-two medley were sung by Judy Garland and Fred Astaire in *Easter Parade* (1948). They were recorded with Johnny Green and the MGM Orchestra.
★ The "A Couple of Swells" routine came about when Irving Berlin walked into the studio and suggested doing a "tramps" number. There were no objections, and, thus, one of Astaire and Garland's more famous songs was born.

ALBUMS

Albums with "A Couple of Swells" and Medley:
Born to Sing (See section B, #26)

60 **"Better Luck Next Time"**
[Irving Berlin (1948)]
"It Only Happens When I Dance with You"—Fred Astaire

Label: MGM 30187 (78)
Released: 1948

ADDENDA

★ Garland sang "Better Luck Next Time" in *Easter Parade* (1948). It was recorded with Johnny Green conducting the MGM Orchestra.

ALBUMS

Albums with "Better Luck Next Time":
Judy Garland (with the MGM Orchestra) (See section B, #17)
The Judy Garland Story, vol. 1, *The Star Years* (See section B, #18)
Judy Garland in Song (See section B, #22)
Judy Garland—The Golden Years at MGM (See section B, #24)

61 **"Put Your Arms Around Me, Honey"**
[Junie McCree, Albert Von Tilzer (1910)]
"Meet Me Tonight in Dreamland"
[Beth Slater Whitson, Leo Friedman (1909)]

Label:
MGM 50025 (78)
MGM 30205 (78)
Released: 1949

ADDENDA

★ Both songs were Garland numbers in *In the Good Old Summertime* (1949). They were recorded with the Georgie Stoll Orchestra.

ALBUMS

Albums with "Put Your Arms Around Me, Honey":

Judy Garland Sings (See section B, #13)

Look for the Silver Lining
(See section B, #15)

Judy Garland (with the MGM Orchestra)
(See section B, #17)

Judy Garland (See section B, #21)

Forever Judy (See section B, #25)

Born to Sing (See section B, #26)

Judy Garland: From the MGM Classic Films (1938–1950)
(See section B, #31)

Albums with "Meet Me Tonight in Dreamland":

Judy Garland (with the MGM Orchestra)
(See section B, #17)

The Judy Garland Story, vol. 1, *The Star Years* (See section B, #18)

Judy Garland (See section B, #21)

Judy Garland: From the MGM Classic Films (1938–1950)
(See section B, #31)

ALBUMS

Albums with "Play That Barbershop Chord":

Judy Garland Sings (See section B, #13)

Look for the Silver Lining
(See section B, #15)

Judy Garland (with the MGM Orchestra)
(See section B, #17)

The Judy Garland Story, vol. 1, *The Star Years* (See section B, #18)

Judy Garland (See section B, #21)

Albums with "I Don't Care":

Judy Garland (with the MGM Orchestra)
(See section B, #17)

The Judy Garland Story, vol. 1, *The Star Years* (See section B, #18)

The Very Best of Judy Garland
(See section B, #20)

Judy Garland in Song (See section B, #22)

Judy Garland—The Golden Years at MGM
(See section B, #24)

Born to Sing (See section B, #26)

Born in a Trunk. Superstar: 1945–1950
(See section B, #30)

---

62 "Play That Barbershop Chord"
(with The King's Men)
[William Tracy, Lewis F. Muir (1910)]
"I Don't Care"
[Jean Lennox, Harry O. Sutton (1905)]

Label:
  MGM 50026 (78)
  MGM 30206 (78)
Released: 1949

ADDENDA

★ Both songs were Garland numbers in *In the Good Old Summertime* (1949). They were recorded with the Georgie Stoll Orchestra.

---

63 "Merry Christmas"
[Spielman, Torre]
"Look for the Silver Lining"

Label: MGM 30212 (78)
Released: 1949

ADDENDA

★ Judy Garland sang "Merry Christmas" in *In the Good Old Summertime* (1949). It was recorded with the Georgie Stoll Orchestra.

64 **"Happy Harvest"**
[Mack Gordon, Harry Warren (1950)]
"If You Feel Like Singing, Sing"
[Mack Gordon, Harry Warren (1950)]

Label: MGM 30251 (78)
Released: 1950

ADDENDA

★ Judy Garland sang both songs in *Summer Stock* (1950). They were recorded with Johnny Green and the MGM Orchestra.

ALBUMS

Albums with "If You Feel Like Singing, Sing":
Judy Garland (with the MGM Orchestra) (See section B, #17)
The Judy Garland Story, vol. 1, *The Star Years* (See section B, #18)
The Very Best of Judy Garland (See section B, #20)
Judy Garland in Song (See section B, #22)

65 **"Friendly Star"**
[Mack Gordon, Harry Warren (1950)]
"Get Happy"
[Ted Koehler, Harold Arlen (1930)]

Label: MGM 30254 (78)
Released: 1950

ADDENDA

★ Judy Garland sang both songs in *Summer Stock* (1950). They were recorded with Johnny Green and the MGM Orchestra.

★ "Get Happy" was originally sung by Ruth Etting in the 1930 Broadway show *9:15 Revue,* but Garland's version of it is generally credited with turning it into a classic.

ALBUMS

Albums with "Friendly Star":
Judy Garland (See section B, #21)
Judy Garland—The Golden Years at MGM (See section B, #24)
Born in a Trunk. Superstar: 1945–1950 (See section B, #30)
Albums with "Get Happy":
The Very Best of Judy Garland (See section B, #20)
Judy Garland in Song (See section B, #22)
Judy Garland [The Golden Archive Series] (See section B, #23)
Judy Garland—The Golden Years at MGM (See section B, #24)
Born in a Trunk. Superstar: 1945–1950 (See section B, #30)
Judy Garland: From the MGM Classic Films (1938–1950) (See section B, #31)

66 **"Get Happy"**
"Johnny One Note"

Label: MGM 30429 (78)

"Get Happy" number from *Summer Stock*.

---

67 "Put Your Arms Around Me, Honey"
"Love of My Life"

Label: MGM 30430 (78)

---

68 "Last Night When We Were Young"
[Harold Arlen, E. Y. Harburg (1936)]
"Play That Barbershop Chord"

Label: MGM 30432 (78)

---

69 "The Trolley Song"
"Cocktails for Two"—Tommy Dorsey

Label: Vogue Picture Records (no
   release number) (78)
Released: 1946 (uncertain)

ADDENDA

★ Vogue issued its picture disks for approximately a two-year period between 1945 and 1947. Since this disk was issued with no number, it is difficult to obtain a precise release date.

B. ALBUMS

1 The Judy Garland Souvenir Album

Label: Decca A-76 (33⅓)

SIDE ONE

"(Dear Mr. Gable) You Made Me Love
   You"
   [Joseph McCarthy, James V. Monaco
      (1913); interpolations by Roger
      Edens (1937)].
   From *Broadway Melody of 1938*—1937
"You Can't Have Everything"
   [Mack Gordon, Harry Revel (1937)]
   Recorded 1937
"Figaro"
   [Roger Edens (1939)]
   From *Babes in Arms*—1939

SIDE TWO

"Oceans Apart"
   [Mickey Rooney, Sidney Miller]
   Recorded 1939
"In Between"
   [Roger Edens (1938)]
   From *Love Finds Andy Hardy*—1938
"Sweet Sixteen"
   [Roger Edens (1939)]
   Recorded 1939

ADDENDA

★ This album is composed of Decca releases 1463, 2878, and 15045.

2 The Judy Garland Second Souvenir Album

Label: Decca A-349 (33⅓)

SIDE ONE

"For Me and My Gal" (with Gene Kelly)
   [Edgar Leslie, E. Ray Goetz, George W.
      Meyer (1917)]
   From *For Me and My Gal*—1942
"When You Wore a Tulip" (with Gene
   Kelly)
   [Jack Mahoney, Percy Wenrich (1914)]
   From *For Me and My Gal*—1942
"That Old Black Magic"
   [Johnny Mercer and Harold Arlen
      (1942)]
   Recorded 1942
"Poor Little Rich Girl"
   [Noel Coward (1925)]
   Recorded 1942

SIDE TWO

"Zing! Went the Strings of My Heart"
   [James F. Hanley (1935)]
   From *Listen, Darling*—1938
"Fascinating Rhythm"
   [Ira and George Gershwin (1924)]
   Recorded 1939
"On the Sunny Side of the Street"
   [Dorothy Fields, Jimmy McHugh
      (1930)]
   Recorded 1942
"I Never Knew"
   [Tom Pitts, Ray Egan, Roy Marsh
      (1920)]
   Recorded 1942

ADDENDA

★ This album is composed of previous Decca releases: 18480, 18540, 18543, and 18524.

3 **The Judy Garland Third Souvenir Album**

Label: Decca A-671 (33⅓)

SIDE ONE

"On the Sunny Side of the Street"
Recorded 1942
"I Never Knew"
Recorded 1942
"That Old Black Magic"
Recorded 1942
"Poor Little Rich Girl"
Recorded 1942

SIDE TWO

"Zing! Went the Strings of My Heart"
From *Listen, Darling*—1938
"Fascinating Rhythm"
Recorded 1939
"This Heart of Mine"
[Arthur Freed, Harry Warren (1943)]
Recorded 1945
"Love"
[Ralph Blane, Hugh Martin (1945)]

ADDENDA

★ This album consists of material previously released on Decca 18524, 18540, 18543, and 18660.

4 **Judy Garland Sings**
(with Dick Haymes, Gene Kelly, The Merry Macs, and the Gordon Jenkins Orchestra)

Label: Decca A 6825 (33⅓)

SIDE ONE

"If I Had You" (with The Merry Macs)
[Ted Shapiro, Jimmy Campbell, Reginald Connelly (1928)]
Background music to *The Clock*—1945
"On the Atchison, Topeka and the Santa Fe" (with The Merry Macs)
[Johnny Mercer, Harry Warren (1946)]
From *The Harvey Girls*—1946
"Aren't You Kind of Glad We Did?" (with Dick Haymes)
[Ira and George Gershwin (1946)]
Recorded 1946
"For You, For Me, For Evermore" (with Dick Haymes)
[Ira and George Gershwin (1946)]
Recorded 1946

SIDE TWO

"Don't Tell Me That Story" (with Gordon Jenkins Orchestra)
[Joseph Lilley]
Recorded 1946
"There Is No Breeze" (with Gordon Jenkins Orchestra)
[Dorothy Dick, Alstone]
Recorded 1946
"For Me and My Gal" (with Gene Kelly)
From *For Me and My Gal*—1942
"When You Wore a Tulip" (with Gene Kelly)
From *For Me and My Gal*—1942

ADDENDA

★ The songs in this album were previously released on Decca 23436, 23687, 23746, and 25115.

5 Judy Garland—Greatest Performances

Label:
Decca DL 8190 (33⅓)
Brunswick AH 11 (33⅓) (U.K.)

SIDE ONE

"(Dear Mr. Gable) You Made Me Love You"
From *Broadway Melody of 1938*—1937
"Over the Rainbow"
[E. Y. Harburg, Harold Arlen (1939)]
From *The Wizard of Oz*—1939
"How About You?"
[Ralph Freed, Burton Lane (1941)]
From *Babes on Broadway*—1941
"In Between"
From *Love Finds Andy Hardy*—1938
"For Me and My Gal" (with Gene Kelly)
From *For Me and My Gal*—1942
"Love"
[Ralph Blane, Hugh Martin (1945)]
Recorded 1945

SIDE TWO

"The Trolley Song"
[Ralph Blane, Hugh Martin (1944)]
From *Meet Me in St. Louis*—1944
"Meet Me in St. Louis, Louis"
[Andrew B. Sterling, Kerry Mills (1904)]
From *Meet Me in St. Louis*—1944
"Poor Little Rich Girl"
Recorded 1942

"Sweet Sixteen"
Recorded 1939
"When You Wore a Tulip" (with Gene Kelly)
From *For Me and My Gal*—1942
"You'll Never Walk Alone"
[Oscar Hammerstein II, Richard Rodgers (1943)]
Recorded 1945

ADDENDA

★ Brunswick AH 11 is an abridged version. It does not contain "Love" and "Sweet Sixteen."

6 Judy Garland, Volume II

Label: Decca ED 2050 (X-45)

SIDE ONE

"Smilin' Through"
[Arthur Penn (1919)]
Recorded 1945
"You'll Never Walk Alone"
Recorded 1945

SIDE TWO

"The Boy Next Door"
[Ralph Blane, Hugh Martin (1944)]
From *Meet Me in St. Louis*—1944
"I'm Always Chasing Rainbows"
[Harry Carroll, Joseph McCarthy (1918)]
From *Ziegfeld Girl*—1941

Judy Garland, Gene Kelly rehearsing for 1942 film *For Me and My Gal.*

7 The Magic of Judy Garland

Label:
    Decca DL 4199 (33⅓)
    Ace of Hearts AH 128 (33⅓) (U.K.)

SIDE ONE

"I Never Knew"
    Recorded 1942
"On the Sunny Side of the Street"
    Recorded 1942
"Franklin D. Roosevelt Jones"
    [Harold Rome (1938)]
    From *Babes on Broadway*—1941
"But Not for Me"
    [Ira and George Gershwin (1930)]
    From *Girl Crazy*—1943
"I'm Always Chasing Rainbows"
    From *Ziegfeld Girl*—1941
"Our Love Affair"
    [Arthur Freed, Roger Edens (1940)]
    From *Strike Up the Band*—1940

SIDE TWO

"That Old Black Magic"
    Recorded 1942
"A Pretty Girl Milking Her Cow"
    [Adaptation by Roger Edens (1940)]
    From *Little Nellie Kelly*—1940
"On the Atchison, Topeka and the Santa Fe"
    From *The Harvey Girls*—1946
"Embraceable You"
    [Ira and George Gershwin (1930)]
    From *Girl Crazy*—1943
"Zing! Went the Strings of My Heart"
    From *Listen, Darling*—1939
"I'm Nobody's Baby"
    [Benny Davis, Milton Ager, Lester Santly (1921)]
    From *Andy Hardy Meets Debutante*—1940

8 Judy at The Palace

Label:
    Decca ED 620 (X-45)
    Decca DL 6020 (33⅓) [10″]

SIDE ONE

"(Dear Mr. Gable) You Made Me Love You"
    From *Broadway Melody of 1938*—1937
"Over the Rainbow"
    From *The Wizard of Oz*—1939

SIDE TWO

"The Trolley Song"
    From *Meet Me in St. Louis*—1944
"Meet Me in St. Louis, Louis"
    From *Meet Me in St. Louis*; side recorded in 1944, not the film version

SIDE THREE

"In Between"
    From *Love Finds Andy Hardy*—1938
"Sweet Sixteen"
    Recorded in 1939

SIDE FOUR

"For Me and My Gal" (with Gene Kelly)
    From *For Me and My Gal*—1942
"When You Wore a Tulip" (with Gene Kelly)
    From *For Me and My Gal*—1942

ADDENDA

★ Do not be fooled by the album title or the jacket blurb. All eight cuts come from Garland's MGM period. The tracks were recorded between 1939 and 1944.

★ The album contains selections from *Judy Garland—Greatest Performances*, Decca DL 8190 (33⅓).

9 The Best of Judy Garland

Label:
Decca DXB 172 (33⅓)
Decca DXSB 7172 (33⅓)
MCA 24003 (33⅓)
MCAC 24003 (cassette)

SIDE ONE

"(Dear Mr. Gable) You Made Me Love
    You"
    From *Broadway Melody of 1938*—1937
"Over the Rainbow"
    From *The Wizard of Oz*—1939
"Franklin D. Roosevelt Jones"
    From *Babes on Broadway*—1941
"For Me and My Gal" (with Gene Kelly)
    From *For Me and My Gal*—1942
"Love"
    Recorded 1945

SIDE TWO

"The Trolley Song"
    From *Meet Me in St. Louis*—1944
"Meet Me in St. Louis, Louis"
    From *Meet Me in St. Louis*; side
    recorded in 1944
"Poor Little Rich Girl"
    Recorded 1942
"Sweet Sixteen"
    Recorded 1939
"When You Wore a Tulip" (with Gene
    Kelly)
    From *For Me and My Gal*—1942
"You'll Never Walk Alone"
    Recorded 1945

SIDE THREE

"I Never Knew"
    Recorded 1942
"On the Sunny Side of the Street"
    Recorded 1942

"The Boy Next Door"
    From *Meet Me in St. Louis*—1944
"But Not for Me"
    From *Girl Crazy*—1943
"I'm Always Chasing Rainbows"
    Recorded 1940
"Our Love Affair"
    From *Strike Up the Band*—1940

SIDE FOUR

"A Pretty Girl Milking Her Cow"
    From *Little Nellie Kelly*—1940
"That Old Black Magic"
    Recorded 1942
"On the Atchison, Topeka and the Santa
    Fe" (with The Merry Macs)
    From *The Harvey Girls*—1946; side
    recorded in 1945
"Have Yourself a Merry Little Christmas"
    From *Meet Me in St. Louis*—1944
"I'm Nobody's Baby"
    From *Andy Hardy Meets Debutante*—
    1940
"Zing! Went the Strings of My Heart"
    From *Listen, Darling*—1939

10 Judy Garland's Greatest Hits

Label: Decca 75150 (33⅓)

SIDE ONE

"You Made Me Love You"
    From *Broadway Melody of 1938*—1937
"Over the Rainbow"
    From *The Wizard of Oz*—1939
"I'm Nobody's Baby"
    From *Andy Hardy Meets Debutante*—
    1940
"I'm Always Chasing Rainbows"
    From *Ziegfeld Girl*—1941
"A Pretty Girl Milking Her Cow"
    From *Little Nellie Kelly*—1940

"For Me and My Gal"
From *For Me and My Gal*—1942

SIDE TWO

"When You Wore a Tulip" (with Gene Kelly)
From *For Me and My Gal*—1942
"Meet Me in St. Louis, Louis"
From *Meet Me in St. Louis*—1944
"The Boy Next Door"
From *Meet Me in St. Louis*—1944
"The Trolley Song"
From *Meet Me in St. Louis*—1944
"Have Yourself a Merry Little Christmas"
From *Meet Me in St. Louis*
"On the Atchison, Topeka and the Santa Fe"
From *The Harvey Girls*—1946

---

11 **Collector's Items, 1936–1945**

Label:
Decca DEA 75 (33⅓)
Coral CP-53 and CP-54 (33⅓) (U.K.)
MCA 2-4046 (33⅓)
MCAC 2-24046 (cassette)

SIDE ONE

"Stompin' at the Savoy"
[Andy Razaf, Benny Goodman, Chick Webb, Edgar Sampson (1936)]
Recorded 1936
"Swing Mr. Charlie"
[J. Russell Robinson, Irving Taylor, Harry Brooks]
Recorded 1936
"Everybody Sing"
[Nacio Herb Brown, Arthur Freed (1937)]
From *Broadway Melody of 1938*—1937

"All God's Chillun Got Rhythm"
[Gus Kahn, Bronislau Kaper, Walter Jurmann (1937)]
Recorded 1937
"You Can't Have Everything"
[Mack Gordon, Harry Revel (1937)]
Recorded 1937
"Sleep, My Baby, Sleep"
[Eddie Pola, Franz Steininger]
Recorded 1938

SIDE TWO

"Blues in the Night"
[Johnny Mercer, Harold Arlen (1941)]
Recorded 1941
"No Love, No Nothin' "
[Leo Robin, Harry Warren (1943)]
Recorded 1943
"A Journey to a Star"
[Leo Robin, Harry Warren (1943)]
Recorded 1943
"This Heart of Mine"
[Arthur Freed, Harry Warren (1943)]
Recorded 1943
"If I Had You" (with The Merry Macs)
[Ted Shapiro, Johnny Campbell, Reginald Connelly (1928)]
Background to *The Clock*—1945
Recorded 1945
"Smilin' Through"
[Arthur Penn (1919)]
Recorded 1945

SIDE THREE

"Cry, Baby, Cry"
[Jimmy Eaton, Terry Shand (1938)]
Recorded 1938
"Ten Pins in the Sky"
[Joseph McCarthy, Milton Ager (1938)]
From *Listen, Darling*—1938

"It Never Rains but It Pours"
[Mack Gordon, Harry Revel (1938)]
From *Love Finds Andy Hardy*—1938
"Oceans Apart"
Recorded 1939
"(Can This Be) The End of the Rainbow"
[Sammy Cahn, Saul Chaplin]
Recorded 1940
"Buds Won't Bud"
[E. Y. Harburg, Harold Arlen (1937)]
Cut from *Andy Hardy Meets Debutante*
—1940

SIDE FOUR

"Swanee"
[Irving Caesar, George Gershwin
(1919)]
Recorded 1939
"Embraceable You"
[Ira and George Gershwin (1930)]
1939 version
"I Got Rhythm"
[Ira and George Gershwin (1930)]
From *Girl Crazy*—1943
"Wearing of the Green"
[Roger Edens (1940)]
Recorded 1940
"It's a Great Day for the Irish"
[Roger Edens (1940)]
From *Little Nellie Kelly*—1940
"How About You?"
From *Babes on Broadway*—1941

ADDENDA

★ Coral CP-53 contains sides one and
three. Coral CP-54 contains sides two
and four.

12 **Miss Show Biz**

Label: Brunswick AH 48 (33⅓) (U.K.)

SIDE ONE

"Friendship" (with Johnny Mercer)
[Cole Porter (1939)]
Recorded 1940
"It's a Great Big World" (with Virginia
O'Brien and Betty Russell)
[Johnny Mercer, Harry Warren (1945)]
From *The Harvey Girls*—1946
"On the Atchison, Topeka and the Santa
Fe"
From *The Harvey Girls*—1946
"If I Had You"
Recorded 1945
"Love"
[Ralph Blane, Hugh Martin (1945)]
Recorded 1945

SIDE TWO

"Changing My Tune"
[Ira and George Gershwin]
Recorded 1946
"Bidin' My Time"
[Ira and George Gershwin (1930)]
From *Girl Crazy*—1943
"Fascinating Rhythm"
Recorded 1939
"Poor Little Rich Girl"
Recorded 1942
"Nothing But You"
[Lorenz Hart and Richard Rodgers
(1940)]
Recorded 1946

13 Judy Garland Sings

Label: MGM E 82 (33⅓) [10″]

SIDE ONE

"Who?"
[Oscar Hammerstein II, Jerome Kern (1925)]
From *Till the Clouds Roll By*—1946
"Get Happy"
[Ted Koehler, Harold Arlen (1930)]
From *Summer Stock*—1950
"Love of My Life"
[Cole Porter (1948)]
From *The Pirate*—1948
"Johnny One Note"
[Lorenz Hart, Richard Rodgers (1937)]
From *Words and Music*—1948

SIDE TWO

"Look for the Silver Lining"
[Buddy DeSylva, Jerome Kern (1920)]
From *Till the Clouds Roll By*—1946
"Play That Barbershop Chord" (with the King's Men)
[William Tracy, Lewis F. Muir (1910)]
From *In the Good Old Summertime*—1949
"Last Night When We Were Young"
[E. Y. Harburg, Harold Arlen (1936)]
Recorded in 1949 for *In the Good Old Summertime* but cut before the film's release
"Put Your Arms Around Me, Honey"
[Junie McCree and Albert Von Tilzer (1910)]
From *In the Good Old Summertime*—1949

ADDENDA

★ Garland's 1949 version of "Last Night When We Were Young" is considered by some to be one of its finest renditions. Roy Hemming, in *The Melody Lingers On* (p. 19), says: "Few singers have ever been able to project the quiet ache of Harburg's lyrics about love's 'morning after' and arch their way through Arlen's unusual melody as unforgettably as Judy Garland, especially in her soundtrack recording of the song for *In the Good Old Summertime*."

Compare this version with her 1956 rendition on *Judy* (Capitol T-734) and see if you don't agree that the later one is better still.

14 Get Happy

Label: MGM X-1038 (X-45)

SIDE ONE

"Get Happy"
From *Summer Stock*—1950
"Love of My Life"
From *The Pirate*—1948

SIDE TWO

"Johnny One Note"
From *Words and Music*—1948
"Who?"
From *Till the Clouds Roll By*—1946

"Play That Barbershop Chord" number from *In the Good Old Summertime*.

15 Look for the Silver Lining

Label: MGM X-1116 (X-45)

SIDE ONE

"Put Your Arms Around Me, Honey"
From *In the Good Old Summertime*—
1949
"Look for the Silver Lining"
From *Till the Clouds Roll By*—1946

SIDE TWO

"Play That Barbershop Chord"
From *In the Good Old Summertime*—
1949
"Last Night When We Were Young"
Recorded in 1949 for *In the Good Old Summertime* but cut before the film's release

ADDENDA

★ The contents of this album have not been personally verified.

16 If You Feel Like Singing, Sing

Label: MGM X-268 (33⅓) [10″]

SIDE ONE

"Last Night When We Were Young"
Recorded in 1949 for *In the Good Old Summertime* but cut before the film's release
"Play That Barbershop Chord"
From *In the Good Old Summertime*—
1949
"Who?"
From *Till the Clouds Roll By*—1946
"Look for the Silver Lining"
From *Till the Clouds Roll By*—1946

SIDE TWO

"Put Your Arms Around Me, Honey"
From *In the Good Old Summertime*—
1949
"Love of My Life"
From *The Pirate*—1948
"Get Happy"
From *Summer Stock*—1950
"Johnny One Note"
From *Words and Music*—1948

17 Judy Garland
(with the MGM Orchestra)

Label: MGM E3140 (33⅓)

SIDE ONE

"Last Night When We Were Young"
Recorded for *In the Good Old Summertime* but cut before the film's release, 1949
"Play That Barbershop Chord"
From *In the Good Old Summertime*—
1949
"Who?"
From *Till the Clouds Roll By*—1946
"Look for the Silver Lining"
From *Till the Clouds Roll By*—1946
"Put Your Arms Around Me, Honey"
From *In the Good Old Summertime*—
1949
"Love of My Life"
From *The Pirate*—1948

SIDE TWO

"Get Happy"
From *Summer Stock*—1950
"Johnny One Note"
From *Words and Music*—1948

Gene Kelly and Judy Garland in *The Pirate*.

"Better Luck Next Time"
   [Irving Berlin (1948)]
   From *Easter Parade*—1948
"If You Feel Like Singing, Sing"
   [Mack Gordon, Harry Warren (1950)]
   From *Summer Stock*—1950
"I Don't Care"
   [Jean Lennox, Harry O. Sutton (1905)]
   From *In the Good Old Summertime*—
   1949
"Meet Me Tonight in Dreamland"
   [Beth Slater Whitson, Leo Friedman
   (1909)]
   From *In the Good Old Summertime*—
   1949

ADDENDA

★ This album is an extended version of *If
   You Feel Like Singing, Sing* (MGM X-
   268 [33⅓]).

18 **The Judy Garland Story,
vol. 1, The Star Years**

Label:
   MGM 3989-P (33⅓)
   MGM C-886 (33⅓) (U.K.)

SIDE ONE

"Last Night When We Were Young"
   Recorded for *In the Good Old Summer-
   time* but cut before the film's release,
   1949
"Play That Barbershop Chord"
   From *In the Good Old Summertime*—
   1949
"Who?"
   From *Till the Clouds Roll By*—1946
"Look for the Silver Lining"
   From *Till the Clouds Roll By*—1946
"Love of My Life"
   From *The Pirate*—1948

SIDE TWO

"Get Happy"
   From *Summer Stock*—1950
"Johnny One Note"
   From *Words and Music*—1948
"Better Luck Next Time"
   From *Easter Parade*—1948
"If You Feel Like Singing, Sing"
   From *Summer Stock*—1950
"I Don't Care"
   From *In the Good Old Summertime*—
   1949
"Meet Me Tonight in Dreamland"
   From *In the Good Old Summertime*—
   1949

19 The Judy Garland Story, vol. 2, The Hollywood Years

Label:
MGM E 4005-P (33⅓)
MGM C-887 (33⅓)

SIDE ONE

"(Dear Mr. Gable) You Made Me Love You"
From *Broadway Melody of 1938*—1937
"Bei Mir Bist Du Schoen"
[Sammy Cahn and Saul Chaplin, Sholom Secunda (1937)]
Recorded in 1938 for *Love Finds Andy Hardy* but cut before the film's release
"I'm Nobody's Baby"
From *Andy Hardy Meets Debutante*—1940
"I Cried For You"
[Arthur Freed, Gus Arnheim, Abe Lyman (1923)]
From *Babes in Arms*—1939
"Singin' in the Rain"
[Nacio Herb Brown, Arthur Freed (1929)]
Recorded for *Little Nellie Kelly*—1940
"Danny Boy"
[F. E. Weatherly (1913)]
Recorded in 1940 for *Little Nellie Kelly* but cut before the film's release

SIDE TWO

"The Trolley Song"
From *Meet Me in St. Louis*—1944
"But Not for Me"
From *Girl Crazy*—1943
"Johnny One Note"
From *Words and Music*—1948
"The Boy Next Door"
From *Meet Me in St. Louis*—1944

"You Can't Get a Man with a Gun"
[Irving Berlin (1946)]
From *Annie Get Your Gun*—1950
"Over the Rainbow"
From *The Wizard of Oz*—1939

ADDENDA

★ "You Can't Get a Man with a Gun" was recorded by Judy Garland in 1949 during the shooting of *Annie Get Your Gun*. Garland was fired from MGM during the film's production, and the footage already shot was scrapped. This recording is from the unused soundtrack.

★ The out-takes of "Bei Mir Bist Du Schoen," "Singin' in the Rain," "Danny Boy," and "You Can't Get a Man with a Gun" had not previously been released.

★ "Bei Mir Bist Du Schoen" was Sammy Cahn's first hit song. Cahn actually only wrote the English lyrics for the original, Yiddish version. As Cahn tells the story, he became interested in the song when he and Saul Chaplin were at the Apollo Theater in Harlem one night when two black singers brought the house down with "Bei Mir Bist Du Schoen," sung in Yiddish. The Andrews Sisters saw the sheet music for the number at Cahn's apartment and started to record it for Decca—in Yiddish. Jack Kapp, of Decca, stopped the recording session and prevailed upon Cahn to write the English lyrics. It became one of the best-selling songs of 1938.

★ This album was released in England as MGM 2683005 (33⅓).

CONTEMPORARY COMMENTS

The American Record Guide, April 1962
Although I do not belong to the "Judy"

cult . . . , I deeply admire her as one of the three finest popular singers of—I'll say it —all time. . . . This is another fine souvenir album for collectors of fine songs and, of course, Judy Garland.

---

20 The Very Best of Judy Garland

Label: MGM E/SE 4204 (33⅓)

SIDE ONE

"Over the Rainbow"
    From *The Wizard of Oz*—1939
"(Dear Mr. Gable) You Made Me Love You"
    From *Broadway Melody of 1938*—1937
"The Trolley Song"
    From *Meet Me in St. Louis*—1944
"Johnny One Note"
    From *Words and Music*—1948
"Look for the Silver Lining"
    From *Till the Clouds Roll By*—1946
"The Boy Next Door"
    From *Meet Me in St. Louis*—1944

SIDE TWO

"I Cried for You"
    From *Babes in Arms*—1939
"Get Happy"
    From *Summer Stock*—1950
"If You Feel Like Singing, Sing"
    From *Summer Stock*—1950
"I Don't Care"
    From *In the Good Old Summertime*— 1949
"Singin' in the Rain"
    From *Little Nellie Kelly*—1940
"But Not for Me"
    From *Girl Crazy*—1943

---

21 Judy Garland

Label: Metro M/MS 505 (33⅓)

SIDE ONE

"Danny Boy"
    Recorded in 1940 for *Little Nellie Kelly* but cut before the film's release
"Meet Me Tonight in Dreamland"
    From *In the Good Old Summertime*— 1949
"Friendly Star"
    [Mack Gordon, Harry Warren (1950)]
    From *Summer Stock*—1950
"I'm Nobody's Baby"
    From *Andy Hardy Meets Debutante*— 1940
"I Cried for You"
    From *Babes in Arms*—1939

SIDE TWO

"The Boy Next Door"
    From *Meet Me in St. Louis*—1944
"Singin' in the Rain"
    From *Little Nellie Kelly*—1940
"The Trolley Song"
    From *Meet Me in St. Louis*—1944
"Put Your Arms Around Me, Honey"
    From *In the Good Old Summertime*— 1949
"Play That Barbershop Chord"
    From *In the Good Old Summertime*— 1949

ADDENDA

★ This album contains recordings previously released on MGM albums: *The Judy Garland Story,* vol. 1, *The Star Years,* MGM E 3989-P (33⅓), and *The Judy Garland Story,* vol. 2, *The Hollywood Years,* MGM E 4005-P (33⅓).

22 Judy Garland in Song

Label: Metro M/MS 581 (33⅓)

SIDE ONE

"Over the Rainbow"
   From *The Wizard of Oz*—1939
"Get Happy"
   From *Summer Stock*—1950
"If You Feel Like Singing, Sing"
   From *Summer Stock*—1950
"But Not for Me"
   From *Girl Crazy*—1943
"You Can't Get a Man with a Gun"
   From *Annie Get Your Gun*—1950

SIDE TWO

"Last Night When We Were Young"
   Recorded in 1949 for *In the Good Old Summertime* but cut before the film's release
"(Dear Mr. Gable) You Made Me Love You"
   From *Broadway Melody of 1938*—1937
"Bei Mir Bist Du Schoen"
   Recorded in 1939 for *Love Finds Andy Hardy* but cut before the film's release
"Better Luck Next Time"
   From *Easter Parade*—1948
"I Don't Care"
   From *In the Good Old Summertime*—1949

23 Judy Garland (The Golden Archive Series)

Label: MGM GAS (Golden Archive Series) 113 (33⅓)

SIDE ONE

"The Trolley Song"
   From *Meet Me in St. Louis*—1944
"Look for the Silver Lining"
   From *Till the Clouds Roll By*—1946
"Last Night When We Were Young"
   Recorded in 1949 for *In the Good Old Summertime* but cut before the film's release
"Danny Boy"
   Recorded in 1940 for *Little Nellie Kelly* but cut before the film's release
"Johnny One Note"
   From *Words and Music*—1948

SIDE TWO

"Over the Rainbow"
   From *The Wizard of Oz*—1939
"The Boy Next Door"
   From *Meet Me in St. Louis*—1944
"Get Happy"
   From *Summer Stock*—1950
"I Cried for You"
   From *Babes in Arms*—1939
"(Dear Mr. Gable) You Made Me Love You"
   From *Broadway Melody of 1938*—1937

24 Judy Garland— The Golden Years at MGM

Label: MGM SDP 1-2 (33⅓)

SIDE ONE

"You Made Me Love You"
   From *Broadway Melody of 1938*—1937
"Bei Mir Bist Du Schoen"
   Recorded in 1938 for *Love Finds Andy Hardy* but cut before the film's release

"Over the Rainbow"
From *The Wizard of Oz*—1939
"I'm Nobody's Baby"
From *Andy Hardy Meets Debutante*—
1940
"I Cried For You"
From *Babes in Arms*—1939

SIDE TWO

"Danny Boy"
Recorded in 1940 for *Little Nellie Kelly*
but cut before the film's release
"Singin' in the Rain"
From *Little Nellie Kelly*—1940
"But Not for Me"
From *Girl Crazy*—1943
"The Trolley Song"
From *Meet Me in St. Louis*—1944
"The Boy Next Door"
From *Meet Me in St. Louis*—1944

SIDE THREE

"Who?"
From *Till the Clouds Roll By*—1946
"Look for the Silver Lining"
From *Till the Clouds Roll By*—1946
"You Can't Get a Man with a Gun"
From *Annie Get Your Gun*—1950
"Love of My Life"
From *The Pirate*—1948
"Johnny One Note"
From *Words and Music*—1948

SIDE FOUR

"Better Luck Next Time"
From *Easter Parade*—1948
"I Don't Care"
From *In the Good Old Summertime*—
1949
"Last Night When We Were Young"
Recorded in 1949 for *In the Good Old
Summertime* but cut before the film's
release

"Friendly Star"
From *Summer Stock*—1950
"Get Happy"
From *Summer Stock*—1950

ADDENDA

★ This two-record set contains the same
tracks as *The Judy Garland Story*, vols.
1 and 2, *The Star Years* and *The Hollywood Years*—with the addition of
"Friendly Star."

25 **Forever Judy**

Label: MGM PX 102 (33⅓)

SIDE ONE

"Over the Rainbow"
From *The Wizard of Oz*—1939
"The Trolley Song"
From *Meet Me in St. Louis*—1944
"You Made Me Love You"
From *Broadway Melody of 1938*—1937
"Singin' in the Rain"
From *Little Nellie Kelly*—1940
"Look for the Silver Lining"
From *Till the Clouds Roll By*—1946

SIDE TWO

"Put Your Arms Around Me, Honey"
From *In the Good Old Summertime*—
1949
"I Cried for You"
From *Babes in Arms*—1939
"You Can't Get a Man with a Gun"
From *Annie Get Your Gun*—1950
"The Boy Next Door"
From *Meet Me in St. Louis*—1944
"I'm Nobody's Baby"
From *Andy Hardy Meets Debutante*—
1940

ADDENDA

★ These selections were previously released on *The Judy Garland Story,* vols. 1, MGM E 3980-P (33⅓), and 2, MGM E 4005-P (33⅓), and on *The Very Best of Judy Garland,* MGM E/SE 4204 (33⅓).

26 Born to Sing

Label: MGM D 134 (33⅓) [10″] (U.K.)

SIDE ONE

"A Couple of Swells" (with Fred Astaire)
[Irving Berlin (1948)]
From *Easter Parade*—1948
Medley:
"I Love a Piano"
[Irving Berlin (1915)]
"Snooky Ookums" (with Fred Astaire)
[Irving Berlin (1913)]
"When the Midnight Choo-Choo
Leaves for Alabam' " (with Fred
Astaire)
[Irving Berlin (1912)]
From *Easter Parade*—1948
"Put Your Arms Around Me, Honey"
From *In the Good Old Summertime*—
1949
"Johnny One Note"
From *Words and Music*—1948
"Get Happy"
From *Summer Stock*—1950

SIDE TWO

"A Fella with an Umbrella" (with Peter
Lawford)
[Irving Berlin (1948)]
From *Easter Parade*—1948

"I Don't Care"
From *In the Good Old Summertime*—
1949
"I Wish I Were in Love Again" (with
Mickey Rooney)
[Lorenz Hart, Richard Rodgers
(1937)]
From *Words and Music*—1948
"Love of My Life"
From *The Pirate*—1948
"Easter Parade" (with Fred Astaire)
[Irving Berlin (1933)]
From *Easter Parade*—1948

ADDENDA

★ The contents of this album have not been personally verified.

27 The Judy Garland Musical Scrapbook (1935–1949)

Label: Star-Tone ST 208 (33⅓)

SIDE ONE

"Zing! Went the Strings of My Heart"
Radio: "Shell Chateau"—November 16,
1935
"The Texas Tornado"
From *Pigskin Parade*—1936
"It's Love I'm After"
From *Pigskin Parade*—1936
"Balboa"
From *Pigskin Parade*—1936
"I Never Knew"
Recorded 1942
"That Old Black Magic"
Recorded 1942
"This Is the Army, Mr. Jones"
[Irving Berlin (1918)]
Radio: "Pause That Refreshes on the
Air"—July 4, 1938

"Gotta Get Out and Vote"
  Radio: Democratic National Committee program—November 6, 1944
"There's a Tavern in the Town" (with Dick Haymes)
  Radio: "Everything for the Boys" program—July 11, 1944
"Somebody Loves Me"
  [Buddy DeSylva, Ballard MacDonald, George Gershwin (1924)]
"Can't Help Lovin' That Man"
  [Oscar Hammerstein II, Jerome Kern (1927)]

SIDE TWO

"Love"
  [Ralph Blame, Hugh Martin (1945)]
"Liza"
  [Ira Gershwin, Gus Kahn, George Gershwin (1929)]
"Wait Till the Sun Shines, Nellie" (with Bing Crosby)
  [Andrew B. Sterling, Harry Von Tilzer (1905)]
  Radio
"I've Got You Under My Skin"
  [Cole Porter (1936)]
  Radio: "Philco Radio Time"—February 20, 1947
"Tearbucket Jim" (with Bing Crosby, William Frawley, Leo McCarey)
  Radio: "Philco Radio Time"—February 20, 1947
"Ma, He's Makin' Eyes at Me" (with Bing Crosby)
  [Sidney Clare, Con Conrad (1921)]
  Radio: "The Bing Crosby Show"—October 5, 1949
"Why Was I Born?"
  [Oscar Hammerstein II, Jerome Kern (1929)]

ADDENDA

★ The liner notes on this album are not notably accurate.

28 **Born in a Trunk: Discovery, 1935–1940**

Label: AEI 2008 (33⅓)

SIDE ONE

"Broadway Rhythm"
  Radio: "Shell Chateau"—October 26, 1935
"Zing! Went the Strings of My Heart"
  Radio: "Shell Chateau"—November 16, 1935
"Balboa"
  From *Pigskin Parade*—1936
"It's Love I'm After"
  From *Pigskin Parade*—1936
"The Texas Tornado"
  From *Pigskin Parade*—1936
"Smiles"
  Radio: "Jack Oakie's College"—1937

SIDE TWO

"Sweet Sixteen"
  Radio: "Tune Up Time"—April 6, 1939
"Sweet or Swing"
  Radio: Screen Guild Theatre—January 8, 1939
"Thanks for the Memory"
  Radio: Screen Guild Theatre—January 8, 1939
"Over the Rainbow"
  From *The Wizard of Oz*—1939
"Nobody"
  From *Strike Up the Band*—1940
"The Drummer Boy"
  From *Strike Up the Band*—1940

29 Born in a Trunk: Stardom, 1940–1945

Label: AEI 2109 (33⅓)

SIDE ONE

"Our Love Affair"
   Recorded 1940, from *Strike Up the Band*—1940
"The Peanut Vendor"
   [A. Wolfe Gilbert and Marion Sunshine, Moises Simons (1931)]
   Recorded 1941
"I Cried for You"
   Recorded 1941, from *Babes in Arms*—1939
"God's Country"
   [E. Y. Harburg, Roger Edens, Harold Arlen (1939)]
   Recorded 1941, from *Babes in Arms*—1939
"I Never Knew"
   Recorded 1942
"The Things I Love"
   [Harold Barlow, Lew Harris (1941)]
   Recorded 1942

SIDE TWO

"After You've Gone"
   [Henry Creamer, Turner Layton (1918)]
   Recorded 1943, from *For Me and My Gal*—1942
"How You Gonna Keep 'Em Down on the Farm"
   [Sam M. Lewis and Joe Young, Walter Donaldson (1919)]
   Recorded 1943, from *For Me and My Gal*—1942
"Speak Low"
   [Ogden Nash, Kurt Weill (1943)]
   Recorded in 1944

"I May Be Wrong"
   [Harry Ruskin, Henry Sullivan (1929)]
   Recorded 1944
"Love"
   [Ralph Blane, Hugh Martin (1945)]
   Recorded 1945
"The Dixieland Band"
   [Johnny Mercer, Bernard Hanighen (1935)]
   Recorded 1945

ADDENDA

★ "The Peanut Vendor," "God's Country," "The Things I Love," "How You Gonna Keep 'Em Down on the Farm," and "The Dixieland Band" had not previously been released.
★ "Speak Low" was introduced by Mary Martin in her first starring role on Broadway, in *One Touch of Venus,* in 1943.

30 Born in a Trunk: Superstar, 1945–1950

Label: AEI 2110 (33⅓)

SIDE ONE

"How Deep Is the Ocean?"
   [Irving Berlin (1932)]
   Recorded 1945
"I Don't Care"
   Recorded 1946
"The Right Romance"
   Recorded 1946
"Liza"
   Recorded 1946
"I've Got You Under My Skin"
   [Cole Porter (1936)]
   Recorded 1947
"Johnny One Note"
   Recorded 1948, from *Words and Music*—1948

SIDE TWO

"Michigan"
[Irving Berlin (1948)]
Recorded 1948, from *Easter Parade*—1948

"Why Was I Born?"
Recorded 1949

"You Made Me Love You"
Recorded 1949, from *Broadway Melody of 1938*—1937

"Rock-a-Bye Your Baby with a Dixie Melody"
[Sam M. Lewis and Joe Young, Jean Schwartz (1918)]
Recorded 1950

"Get Happy"
Recorded 1950, from *Summer Stock*—1950

"Friendly Star"
Recorded 1950, from *Summer Stock*—1950

ADDENDA

★ "How Deep Is the Ocean?," "The Right Romance," "Liza," "I've Got You Under My Skin," "Why Was I Born?," and "Rock-a-Bye Your Baby with a Dixie Melody" were previously unreleased recording session tracks.

---

31 Judy Garland: From MGM Classic Films (1938–1950)

Label:
MCA 25165 (33⅓)
MCAC 25165 (cassette)
MCAD 31176 (CD)

SIDE ONE

"Get Happy"
From *Summer Stock*—1950

"(Dear Mr. Gable) You Made Me Love You"
From *Broadway Melody of 1938*—1937

"Put Your Arms Around Me, Honey"
From *In the Good Old Summertime*—1949

"The Trolley Song"
From *Meet Me in St. Louis*—1944

"Meet Me Tonight in Dreamland"
From *In the Good Old Summertime*—1949

SIDE TWO

"Who?"
From *Till the Clouds Roll By*—1946

"On the Atchison, Topeka and the Santa Fe"
From *The Harvey Girls*—1946

"I'm Always Chasing Rainbows"
From *Ziegfeld Girl*—1941

"Johnny One Note"
From *Words and Music*—1948

"Over the Rainbow"
From *The Wizard of Oz*—1939

---

32 The Young Judy Garland

Label: MCA MCL 1731 (33⅓)

SIDE ONE

"Stompin' at the Savoy"
Recorded 1936

"Swing Mr. Charlie"
Recorded 1936

"All God's Chillun Got Rhythm"
Recorded 1937

"Everybody Sing"
Recorded 1937

"You Can't Have Everything"
Recorded 1938

"Cry, Baby, Cry"
Recorded 1938

"It Never Rains but It Pours"
Recorded 1938
"Ten Pins in the Sky"
Recorded 1938

SIDE TWO

"Swanee"
Recorded 1939
"How About You?"
Recorded 1941
"Bidin' My Time"
Recorded 1943
"Poor Little Rich Girl"
Recorded 1942
"Fascinating Rhythm"
Recorded 1939
"Friendship" (with Johnny Mercer)
Recorded 1940
"Buds Won't Bud"
Recorded 1940

33 From the Decca Vaults

Label:
MCA 907 (33⅓)
MCAC 907 (cassette)

SIDE ONE

"If I Had You" (with The Merry Macs)
Alternate take—recorded July 7, 1945
"Yah-ta-ta, Yah-ta-ta" (with Bing Crosby)
[Johnny Burke, Jimmy Van Heusen
(1945)]
Alternate take—recorded March 3,
1945
"Don't Tell Me That Story"
Alternate version—recorded October
1, 1946
"On the Atchison, Topeka and the Santa
Fe"

Third alternate version—recorded September 10, 1945
"March of the Doagies"
[Johnny Mercer, Harry Warren]
Recorded May 5, 1945, for *The Harvey
Girls* but cut before the film's release

SIDE TWO

"Friendship" (with Johnny Mercer)
Alternate take—recorded April 15,
1940
"I'm Always Chasing Rainbows"
Alternate take from *Ziegfeld Girl*—
1941, recorded December 18, 1940
"Poor You"
[Burton Lane, E. Y. Harburg (1942)]
Alternate take—recorded April 3, 1942
"The Last Call for Love"
[E. Y. Harburg, Margery Cummings,
Burton Lane (1942)]
Alternate take—recorded April 3, 1942
"I'm Just Wild About Harry"
[Noble Sissle, Eubie Blake (1921)]
Alternate take from *Babes in Arms*—
1939, recorded July 29, 1939. This
version was released in England.

34 Judy Garland: More Than a Memory

Label:
Stanyan SR 10095 (33⅓)
Stanyan POW 3001 (33⅓)

SIDE ONE

"Fascinating Rhythm"
Recorded 1939
"Figaro"
From *Babes in Arms*—1939
"Last Call for Love"
Recorded 1946

"Don't Tell Me That Story"
   Recorded 1946
"Heartbroken"
"Go Home, Joe"

SIDE TWO

"Without a Memory"
"Send My Baby Back to Me"
"Roses Red, Violets Blue"
"Take My Hand, Paree"
"Paris Is a Lonely Town"
"Little Drops of Rain"

ADDENDA

★ Only the first four cuts of this album are from Judy's MGM years.
★ "Heartbroken," "Go Home, Joe," "Without a Memory," and "Send My Baby Back to Me" were recorded on April 3, 1953, as singles for Columbia Records, with Paul Weston arranging and conducting.
★ "Roses Red, Violets Blue," "Take My Hand, Paree," "Paris Is a Lonely Town," and "Little Drops of Rain" are from the film *Gay Purr-ee* (1962). They were recorded in November 1961, with Mort Lindsey arranging and conducting.
★ This record is also informally known as *The Uncollected Judy Garland*.

---

35 **Judy Garland: The Beginning**

Label: DRG SL 5187 (33⅓)

SIDE ONE

"Friendship" (with Johnny Mercer)
   Recorded April 15, 1940
"The Birth of a King"
   Recorded July 20, 1941

"Poor You"
   Recorded April 3, 1942
"The Star of the East"
   Recorded July 20, 1941
"There Is No Breeze"
   Recorded October 1, 1946
"Nothing but You"
   Recorded January 15, 1947
"I Wish I Were in Love Again"
   Recorded January 15, 1947

SIDE TWO

"Embraceable You"
"Could You Use Me?" (with Mickey Rooney)
"But Not for Me"
"Treat Me Rough"—Mickey Rooney
"Bidin' My Time"
   These songs were recorded November 2 and 4, 1943.
"Aren't You Kind of Glad We Did?" (with Dick Haymes)
   Recorded September 11, 1946
"For You, For Me, For Evermore" (with Dick Haymes)
   Recorded September 11, 1946
"Changing My Tune"
   Recorded September 11, 1946

ADDENDA

★ This album contains some rare cuts, not readily available elsewhere.

---

36 **Judy! Judy! Judy!**

Label: Star-Tone ST 224 (33⅓)

SIDE ONE

"Daddy"
   Radio: "The Chase and Sanborn Hour"
   —September 7, 1941

"The Right Romance"
"All the Things I Love"
  Radio: "The Chase and Sanborn Hour"
    —September 7, 1941
Medley:
  "We're Off to See Herr Hitler"
  "I've Got Sixpence"
  "Bless Them All"
    Radio "Command Performance"—
    1943 (uncertain)
"Speak Low"
  Comedy skit (with Walter O'Keefe)
    includes: "Sweet Sixteen"
  Radio: "Tune Up Time"—April 6, 1939

ADDENDA

★ The information in the liner notes on this album is notably inaccurate.
★ Side two contains cuts from Garland's concert years:
  Cole Porter Medley
  "What the World Needs Now"
  "Give My Regards to Broadway"
  "It's All for You"
  "Till After the Holidays"
  "I'd Like to Hate Myself in the Morning"

C. SOUNDTRACKS AND SOUNDTRACK SELECTIONS

1 **Pigskin Parade** (1936)

Label: Pilgrim 4000 (33⅓)

2 **Broadway Melody of 1938** (1937)

Label: Motion Picture Tracks International MPT 3 (33⅓)

ADDENDA

★ This album includes "I'm Feeling Like a Million," which was recorded by Judy but not used in the film.

3 **Everybody Sing** (1937)

Label: Pilgrim 4000 (33⅓)

4 **The Wizard of Oz** (1939)

Label:
  Decca A-74 (78)
  Decca ED 561 (X-45) (2 records)
  Decca DL 8387 (33⅓)
  MGM X-3464 ST (45)
  MGM E-3464 ST (33⅓)
  MGM ST-3464 (33⅓)
  MGM E-3996 (33⅓)
  MGM PX-104 (33⅓)
  MGM 2353044 (33⅓) (U.K.)
  MCA 30046 (33⅓)
  AH 121 (33⅓)
  CBS AK 45356 (CD)

ADDENDA

★ Decca ED 561 and DL 3337 include "The Jitterbug," which was cut from the release print of the film. Victor Young conducts the orchestra and The Ken Darby Singers.
★ CBS AK 45356 (CD) also contains "The Jitterbug."
★ Decca ED 561 is side one of DL 3387.

5 **Babes in Arms** (1939)

Label: Curtain Calls CC 100/6-7 (33⅓)

6 Strike Up the Band (1940)

Label: Hollywood Soundstage 5009
   (33⅓)

7 Little Nellie Kelly (1940)

Label: Cheerio 5000 (33⅓)

8 Ziegfeld Girl (1941)

Label: Classic International Filmusicals
   3006 (33⅓)

9 Babes on Broadway (1941)

Label: Curtain Calls CC 100/6-7 (33⅓)

10 For Me and My Gal (1942)

Label: Soundtrak STK 107 (33⅓)

11 Presenting Lily Mars (1943)

Label: Soundtrak STK 117 (33⅓)
(This is a two-record set, with complete
   dialogue starting with the lion's roar.)

12 Girl Crazy (1943)

Label:
   Decca A-362 (78) (with Mickey
   Rooney)

Decca DL 5413 (33⅓) (selections, with
   Mickey Rooney)
Decca ED 2022 (X-45)
Hollywood SoundStage HS 5008 (33⅓)

ADDENDA
★ Selections included in Decca ED 2022:
   "Embraceable You"
   "Bidin' My Time"
   "But Not for Me"
   "I Got Rhythm"

13 Thousands Cheer (1943)

Label:
   Hollywood SoundStage No. 409 (33⅓)
   Cheerio 5000 (33⅓)

14 Meet Me in St. Louis (1944)

Label:
   Decca A-380 (78)
   Decca DL 8498 (33⅓)
   AEI 3101 (33⅓)

15 The Harvey Girls (1946)

Label:
   Decca A-388 (78)
   Decca DL 8498 (33⅓)
   AEI 3101 (33⅓)
   Hollywood SoundStage 5002 (33⅓)

16 Ziegfeld Follies of 1946 (1946)

Label: Curtain Calls CC 100/15-16

17 Till the Clouds Roll By (1946)

Label:
MGM M-1 (78)
MGM X-1 (45)
MGM E-501 (33⅓) [10″]
MGM E-3231 (33⅓)
MGM E-3779 (33⅓)
Sandy Hook SH 2080 (33⅓)

18 The Pirate (1948)

Label:
MGM M-21 (78)
MGM X-21 (45)
MGM E-21 (33⅓)
MGM E-3234 (33⅓)
MGM C-763 (33⅓) [U.K.]
MGM 2-SES-43 (33⅓)
MGM 23530 (33⅓) [U.K.]
MCA MCAD 5950 (CD)

19 Easter Parade (1948)

Label:
MGM M-40 (78)
MGM X-40 (45)
MGM E-502 (33⅓) [10″]
MGM 2-SES-40 (33⅓)
MGM E-3227 (33⅓)
MGM 23530 (33⅓) [U.K.]
MCA 1459 (33⅓)
MCA MCAD 6179 (CD)

20 Words and Music (1948)

Label:
MGM M-37 (78)
MGM X-37 (45)
MGM E-505 (33⅓) [10″]
MGM E-3232 (33⅓)
MGM E-3771 (33⅓)
MCA 25029 (33⅓)
MCA MCAD 5949 (CD)

21 In the Good Old Summertime (1949)

Label:
MGM L-11 (78)
MGM E-3232 (33⅓)
MGM ST-3232 (33⅓)
MCA 39083 (33⅓)

22 Summer Stock (1950)

Label:
MGM M-54 (78)
MGM X-56 (45)
MGM E-519 (33⅓) [10″]
MGM E3234 (33⅓)
MCA MCAD 5948 (CD)

23 Judy Garland in "Annie Get Your Gun"

Label:
Hollywood SoundStage 2302 (33⅓)
Sandy Hook SH 2053 (33⅓)
OurFed ACYC 100 (33⅓)

ADDENDA

★ SoundStage 2302 includes the song "Let's Go West Again," which was written especially for Judy by Irving Berlin and was dropped when she was no longer in the film.

Wardrobe test for *Annie Get Your Gun*.

D. RADIO PERFORMANCE RECORDINGS

1 Behind the Scenes at the Making of "The Wizard of Oz"

Maxwell House "Good News"—June 29, 1939
Label: Jass 17 (33⅓)

Guests:

Ray Bolger	E. Y. Harburg
Harold Arlen	Fred Stone
Hanley Stafford	Frank Morgan
Bert Lahr	Fanny Brice
	Robert Young

Meredith Willson and the NBC Orchestra

SONGS

"Over the Rainbow" (with Harold Arlen and E. Y. Harburg)
traditional version
extended version
"If I Only Had A . . ." (with Ray Bolger, Bert Lahr, Robert Young)
"The House Began to Pitch" (with chorus)
"If I Were King" (with Bert Lahr, Ray Bolger)

ADDENDA

★ This is an MGM transcription of the broadcast made for Harold Arlen's personal collection.
★ The NBC official title of the program was "Maxwell House Coffee Time."

2 Merton of the Movies

"Lux Radio Theater"—November 17, 1941
Label: Pelican 139 (33⅓)

Guest: Mickey Rooney

3 Drive-In

Drama starring Judy Garland
"Suspense"—November 21, 1946
Label: Command Performance Record (78)

4 Judy Garland in "A Star Is Born"

"Lux Radio Theater"—December 28, 1942
Label: Radiola MR 1155 (33⅓)

Guest: Walter Pidgeon

ADDENDA

★ This is the original, nonmusical version.

5 Lady in the Dark

"Lux Radio Theater"—February 16, 1953
Label:
   Command Performance Record (78)
   Radio Yesteryear Voices of Hollywood #30 (cassette)
Guest: John Lund

SONGS

"How Lovely to Be Me"
"This Is New"
"The Rights of Womankind"
"My Ship"

6 Dick Tracy in B-Flat

"Command Performance" [AFRS]—April 29, 1945
Label:
   Curtain Calls 100/1 (33⅓)
   Sandy Hook 2052 (33⅓)
   Scarce Rarities 5504 (33⅓)

Guests:

Bing Crosby	Frank Morgan
Jerry Colonna	Jimmy Durante
Dinah Shore	Cass Caley
Bob Hope	The Andrew Sisters
Harry Von Zell	Frank Sinatra

SONGS

"Over the Rainbow" (comedy version)
"I'm Gonna Go for You" (with Bob Hope)

ADDENDA

★ See chapter 3, Radio Appearances, for a full listing of tracks.

7 Meet Me in St. Louis

"Lux Radio Theater"—December 7, 1946
Label: Pelican 118 (33⅓)

Guests:
Margaret O'Brien
Tom Drake

8 The Wizard of Oz

"Lux Radio Theater"—December 25, 1950
Label:
Sandy Hook MR 1109 (33⅓)
Radio Yesterday RadioBook #2 (cassette)

9 Hollywood on the Air

Label: Radiola 1718¾ (33⅓)

SONGS

"Good Morning" (with Mickey Rooney)
From *Babes in Arms* on "Lux Radio Theater"—November 9, 1941
"It's Love I'm After"
From *Pigskin Parade*—1936
"The Texas Tornado"
From *Pigskin Parade*—1936
"Balboa"
From *Pigskin Parade*—1936
"For Me and My Gal" (with Gene Kelly)
From *For Me and My Gal*—1942
World War I Medley (with Gene Kelly)
From *For Me and My Gal*—1942
"Singin' in the Rain"
From *Little Nellie Kelly*—1940

ADDENDA

★ The contents of this album have not been personally verified.

10 Judy Garland on Radio

"Gulf Screen Guild Theatre"—January 8, 1939
Label: Radiola MR 1040 (33⅓)

SONGS

"Sweet or Swing?"
"Thanks for the Memory" (in "operatic" style)
From "The Gulf Screen Show"—January 8, 1939
"I Don't Care"
"Ma, He's Making Eyes at Me" (with Bing Crosby)
From "The Bing Crosby Show"—October 5, 1949
"Over the Rainbow" (partial)
"Johnny One Note"
"Pretty Baby" (with Al Jolson)
From "Kraft Music Hall"—September 30, 1948
"Over the Rainbow"
From "Maxwell House Coffee Time"—September 10, 1939
"Alexander's Ragtime Band" (with The Rhythmaires)
"Wish You Were Here"
"A Pretty Girl Milking Her Cow"
"You Belong to Me" (with the Rhythmaires)
From "The General Electric Program"—October 30, 1952

ADDENDA

★ This album contains a rare cut of a Judy Garland/Al Jolson duet. Side two is the complete "GE Program" broadcast.

11 Bing, Bob, and Judy

Label: Totem 1000 (33⅓)
Guests:
Bing Crosby
Bob Hope

12 Frances Ethel Gumm and Harry Lillis Crosby: Judy and Bing Together

Label: Legend 1973 (33⅓)

SONGS

"Just the Way You Are"
Comedy sketch:
    "Hello, My Baby, Hello, My Honey"
    "Merry Oldsmobile"
    "Some Rainy Afternoon"
    "Walking My Baby Back Home"
    "Merry Oldsmobile (reprise)"
"You Made Me Love You"
"How Could You Believe Me?"
"You're Just in Love"
Comedy sketch:
    "Tortured"
    "Boise, Idaho"
    "My Blue Blue Boy"
"Mean to Me"
"Limehouse Blues"
"April in Paris"
"Isle of Capri"

ADDENDA

★ These tracks are from "Bing Crosby Show" appearances on February 7, March 7, March 21, and March 28, 1951.

13 Judy Garland (1935–1951)

Label: Star-Tone ST 201 (33⅓)

SIDE ONE

"Broadway Rhythm"
    From "Shell Chateau"—October 26, 1935
"Smiles"
    From "Jack Oakie's College"—1937
"Over the Rainbow"
    From "Maxwell House Coffee Time"—June 20, 1939
"Nobody"
    From Strike Up the Band—1940
"America"
    From "Motion Picture Awards Program"—February 22, 1941
"I May Be Wrong"
    From "Your All-Time Hit Parade"—August 13, 1944
"I Don't Care"
    From "The Bing Crosby Show"—October 5, 1949

SIDE TWO

"Pretty Baby" (with Al Jolson)
    From "Kraft Music Hall"—September 30, 1948
"For Me and My Gal" (with Bing Crosby)
    From "The Bing Crosby Show"—October 8, 1948
"Who?" (with Bing Crosby)
"Embraceable You" (with Bing Crosby)
"The Bing Crosby Show"—October 8, 1948
"Alexander's Ragtime Band"
"Wish You Were Here"
"A Pretty Girl"

202 ★ THE COMPLETE JUDY GARLAND

"Carolina in the Morning"
"You Belong to Me"
"Rock-a-Bye Your Baby with a Dixie
Melody"
From "Salute to Bing Crosby"—January 9, 1951

ADDENDA

★ "Alexander's Ragtime Band," "Wish
You Were Here," "A Pretty Girl," "Carolina in the Morning," and "You Belong
to Me" are from "The General Electric
Program" (radio)—October 30, 1952.
★ The dating of some of these tracks on
the album cover is inaccurate.

14 **The Judy Garland Musical Scrapbook
(1935–1949)**

Label: Star-Tone ST 208 (33⅓)

ADDENDA

★ See Section B, #27.

15 **Philco Radio Time, vol. 1**

Label: Totem 1002 (33⅓)
Side two contains the complete February
19, 1947 broadcast, with Bing Crosby,
Judy Garland, William Frawley, and
Leo McCarey. (See Radio Appearances,
chapter 3.)

16 **The Wit and Wonder of Judy Garland**

Label: DRG SL 5179 (33⅓)

SONGS

"Thanks for the Memory"
From "Good News of 1938" (radio)—
April 28, 1938
"People Will Say We're in Love" (with
Bing Crosby)
Live broadcast of AFRS "Command
Performance"
"Dixieland Band"
Live broadcast of AFRS "Command
Performance" #122—June 25, 1944
"Long Ago and Far Away"
Live broadcast of AFRS "Command
Performance"

ADDENDA

★ Side one of the album is an exceptionally good compendium of selections for
hearing the development of Garland's
voice.
★ The album also includes:
"Dardanella"
[Fred Fisher, Felix Bernard, Johnny
Black (1919)]
Recorded live at Loew's State, New
York—1938
"Americana"
Unused rehearsal recording for
Every Sunday—1936
"Why Was I Born?"
Recorded in London—1960
"Lorna"
[Johnny Mercer, Mort Lindsey
(1964)]
From TV's "The Judy Garland Show"
—1964

17 20 Hits of a Legend

Label: Nostalgia 22004/42004 (33⅓)

SIDE ONE

Side one radio tracks consist of selections
    from "The Bing Crosby Show" in 1951
    and "Your All-Time Hit Parade" in
    1944:
"Over the Rainbow"
"Rock-a-Bye Your Baby with a Dixie Mel-
    ody"
"Limehouse Blues" (with Bing Crosby)
"Isle of Capri" (with Bing Crosby)
"How Could You Believe Me?" (with Bing
    Crosby)
"Swanee"
"It's a Great Day for the Irish"
"The Party's Over"
"Some People"

SIDE TWO

Selections from Garland's concert years,
    including:
"San Francisco"
"I Can't Give You Anything but Love"
"Come Rain or Come Shine"
"I'm Always Chasing Rainbows"
"A Foggy Day"
"Zing! Went the Strings of My Heart"
"Smile"
"If Love Were All"
"You're Nearer"
"Joey, Joey, Joey"

18 Judy Garland in Holland, vol. 3

Label: Obligato GIH 6100 (33⅓)

SONGS

Side two is from 1951 Bing Crosby radio
    programs on March 21 and March 28,
    1951:
"Rock-a-Bye Your Baby with a Dixie
    Melody"
"Limehouse Blues" (with Bing Crosby)
"April in Paris"
"Isle of Capri" (with Bing Crosby)
"Any Town Is Paris When You're Young"
    (Bing Crosby)
"Carolina in the Morning"
"How Could You Believe Me?" (with Bing
    Crosby)

19 Frank Sinatra and Judy Garland

Label: ZAFIRO ZV 892 (33⅓)

SIDE ONE

Garland Medley (instrumental)
    From TV: "The Judy Garland Show"—
    February 25, 1962
"You're Nobody Till Somebody Loves
    You" (Judy Garland, Frank Sinatra,
    Dean Martin)
    From TV: "The Judy Garland Show"—
    February 25, 1962
"I Can't Give You Anything but Love"
    (Judy Garland)
    From TV: "The Judy Garland Show"—
    February 25, 1962
"The One I Love" (Frank Sinatra, Dean
    Martin)
    From TV: "The Judy Garland Show"—
    February 25, 1962

"Gotta Be This or That" (Judy Garland, Frank Sinatra)
From Radio: "The Danny Kaye Show" —October 5, 1945

SIDE TWO

"Get Me to the Church on Time" (Frank Sinatra)

"That's Judy" (Frank Sinatra)

"My Romance" (Judy Garland, Frank Sinatra)
From Radio: "The Danny Kaye Show" —October 5, 1945

"Just in Time (Judy Garland)
From TV: "The Judy Garland Show"— February 25, 1962

"How Deep Is the Ocean?" (Judy Garland)
From Radio: "The Danny Kaye Show" —October 5, 1945

20 Judy Garland: Rare Early Radio Broadcasts

Label: Accessor Pro 1001 (33⅓)

SONGS

"Broadway Rhythm" (1935)
"Smiles" (1935)
"Over the Rainbow" (1939)
"Nobody" (1940)
"America" (1941)
"I May Be Wrong" (1944)
"I Don't Care" (1946)
"Alexander's Ragtime Band" (1952)
"Pretty Baby" (1946)
"For Me and My Gal" (with Bing Crosby) (1948)
"Who?" (with Bing Crosby) (1948)
"Embraceable You" (with Bing Crosby) (1948)

21 Judy and Her Partners in Rhythm and Rhyme

Label: Star-Tone ST 213 (33⅓)

SONGS

"Maybe It's Because" (with Bing Crosby)
From "The Bing Crosby Show"—October 5, 1940

"The Day After Forever" (with Dick Haymes)

"All Thru the Day" (with Gene Kelly)
From Rehearsal check

ADDENDA

★ The rest of the album contains duets from TV's "The Judy Garland Show."

E. MISCELLANEOUS ALBUMS WITH GARLAND SELECTIONS

1 Magnificent Moments from MGM Movies

Label: MGM E-4017 (33⅓)

SONGS

"Over the Rainbow"
From *The Wizard of Oz*—1939

"Johnny One Note"
From *Words and Music*—1948

2 The Very Best Motion Picture Musicals

Label:
MGM E-4171 (33⅓)
MGM SE-4171 (33⅓)

S O N G S

"Over the Rainbow"
From *The Wizard of Oz"*—1939
"Johnny One Note"
From *Words and Music*—1948

3 The MGM Thirtieth Anniversary Album

Label: MGM E3118 (33⅓)

S O N G S

"Easter Parade" (with Fred Astaire)
From *Easter Parade*—1948

4 The Original Hit Performances of the Late Thirties

Label: Decca DL 4000 (33⅓)

S O N G S

"(Dear Mr. Gable) You Made Me Love You"
From *Broadway Melody of 1938*—1937

5 The Original Hit Performances! Into the Forties

Label: Decca DL 4001 (33⅓)

S O N G S

"Over the Rainbow"
From *The Wizard of Oz*—1939
"For Me and My Gal" (with Gene Kelly)
From *For Me and My Gal*—1942

6 Open House

Label: Decca DL 4205 (33⅓)

S O N G S

"Meet Me in St. Louis, Louis"
From *Meet Me in St. Louis*—1944

7 House Party

Label: Decca DL 4206 (33⅓)

S O N G S

"Wearing of the Green"

8 Bing

Label: Decca DX 151 (33⅓)

S O N G S

"Yah-ta-ta, Yah-ta-ta" (with Bing Crosby)
Recorded 1945

9 Bing Sings: 96 of His Greatest Hits

Label: Reader's Digest—Collector's Edition (33⅓)

SONGS

"Mine" (Garland/Crosby duet recorded in 1945)

10 Around the Christmas Tree

Label: Decca DL 9056 (33⅓)

SONGS

"Have Yourself a Merry Little Christmas"
From *Meet Me in St. Louis*—1944

11 Bing: A Musical Autobiography, 1944–1947

Label:
Decca DL 9077 (33⅓)
Decca ED 1700 (33⅓)

SONGS

"Yah-ta-ta, Yah-ta-ta"
Recorded 1945

12 Both Sides of Bing Crosby

Label: Curtain Calls 100/2 (33⅓)

SONGS

"Your All-Time Flop Parade" (with Bing Crosby, The Andrews Sisters)

13 Girls . . . and More Girls

Label: Lion 70118 (33⅓)

SONGS

"Love of My Life"
From *The Pirate*—1948

14 Great Duets from MGM Musicals

Label: MGM 2353.116 (33⅓) (U.K.)

15 Hollywood Sings, vol. 3: The Boys and Girls

Label: Ace of Hearts 69 (33⅓) (U.K.)

SONGS

"Could You Use Me?" (with Mickey Rooney)
From *Girl Crazy*—1943
"Aren't You Kind of Glad We Did?" (with Dick Haymes)
Recorded 1946

16 Hollywood's Singing Stars

Label: MCA 9260-64 (33⅓) (U.K.)

17 The MGM Years

Label: Columbia Special Products P6S-5878 (33⅓)

Publicity photo from the thirties.

18 Music of the 1920s and 1930s

Label: Decca DL 734712 (33⅓)

19 Original Hit Performances! The Forties

Label: Decca DL 4007 (33⅓)

S O N G S

"The Trolley Song"
From *Meet Me in St. Louis*—1944

A D D E N D A

★ This album was released in the United Kingdom on Brunswick LAT 8369 (33⅓)

20 The Stars of the Silver Screen

Label: MCA 628344 DT (33⅓) (U.K.)

21 Those Wonderful Thirties, vol. 1

Label: Decca DEA 7-1 (33⅓)

S O N G S

"Over the Rainbow"
From *The Wizard of Oz*—1939

22 Twenty-Four-Karat Gold from the Sound Stage

Label: MGM S-242 (33⅓)

23 The Very Best of George Gershwin

Label: MGM E/SE 4242 (33⅓)

S O N G S

"But Not for Me"
From *Girl Crazy*—1943

24 The Very Best of Irving Berlin

Label: MGM E/SE 4240 (33⅓)

S O N G S

"Better Luck Next Time"
From *Easter Parade*—1948
"You Can't Get a Man with a Gun"
From *Annie Get Your Gun*—recorded 1950

25 The Very Best of Jerome Kern

Label: MGM E/SE 4241 (33⅓)

S O N G S

"Look for the Silver Lining"
From *Till the Clouds Roll By*—1946

26 The Very Best of Rodgers and Hart

Label: MGM E/SE 4238 (33⅓)

S O N G S

"Johnny One Note"
From *Words and Music*—1948

27 The Best of Dick Haymes

Label:
MCA MCL 1651 (33⅓)
MCA MCLC 1651 (cassette)
MCA MCFM 2720 (33⅓) (U.K.)

S O N G S

"Aren't You Kind of Glad We Did?"
(Garland/Haymes duet recorded in 1946)
"For You, For Me, For Evermore"
(Garland/Haymes duet recorded in 1946)

**28 Cut! Out-Takes from
Hollywood's Greatest Musicals**

Label: DRG SBL 12586 (33⅓)

S O N G S

"We Must Have Music" (with Tony
Martin)
From *Ziegfeld Girl*—1940
"Easy to Love"
From *Love Finds Andy Hardy*—1938
"Mr. Monotony"
From *Easter Parade*—1948
"D'Ye Love Me?"
From *Till the Clouds Roll By*—1946
"Hayride" (with Ray Bolger)
From *The Harvey Girls*—1946
"My Intuition" (with John Hodiak)
From *The Harvey Girls*
"March of the Doagies"
From *The Harvey Girls*
"Voodoo"
From *The Pirate*—1948
"I'll Plant My Own Tree"
From *Valley of the Dolls*—1968

**29 Cut! Out-Takes from
Hollywood's Greatest Musicals, vol. 2**

Label: DRG 12587 (33⅓)

S O N G S

"Bronco Busters" (with Mickey Rooney,
Nancy Walker)
Cut from *Girl Crazy*—1943
"Where There's Music"
"St. Louis Blues"
"It's a Long Way to Tipperary"
"In the Shade of the Old Apple Tree"
"Don't Sit Under the Apple Tree"
"It's Three O'Clock in the Morning"
"Broadway Rhythm"

A D D E N D A

★ All but the first track are from *Presenting Lily Mars* (1943). "St. Louis Blues,"
"It's a Long Way to Tipperary," "In the
Shade of the Old Apple Tree," and
"Don't Sit Under the Apple Tree" were
cut from the release print.

**30 Cut! Out-Takes from
Hollywood's Greatest Musicals, vol. 3**

Label: Out-Take Records OFT 3 (33⅓)

S O N G S

"Meet the Beat of My Heart"
From *Love Finds Andy Hardy*—1938
"Could You Pass in Love?"
From Radio: "Good News of 1938"—
September 8, 1938
Finale for *For Me and My Gal* (with Gene
Kelly, George Murphy)—1942

"I'm Feeling Like a Million"
  From Rehearsal cut for *Broadway Melody of 1938*—1937
  Judy's rendition was not used in the film.
"When My Sugar Walks Down the Street"
  Cut from *A Star Is Born*—1954
"Somewhere There's a Someone" ("Someone at Last")
  From Rehearsal cut for *A Star Is Born*—1954

31 Bing Crosby: The Radio Years, vol. 1

Label: GNP/Crescendo R 114761 (33⅓)

SONGS

"For Me and My Gal" (Garland/Crosby duet, October 8, 1948)

32 A Stanyan Christmas

Label: Stanyan SR 1076 (33⅓)

SONGS

"The Star of the East"
"The Birthday of a King"

ADDENDA

★ Both songs were recorded in 1940.

33 Nostalgia Goes Bananas

Label: Stanyan SR 1096 (33⅓)

SONGS

"Poor You" (1942)

34 Christmas Command Performances, 1944

Label: Nostalgia Enterprises 003-04 (33⅓)

35 Bing Crosby at the Music Hall

Label: AJAZZ 523 (33⅓)

SONGS

"Rudolph the Red-nosed Reindeer" (with Bing Crosby)
"Rock-a-Bye Your Baby with a Dixie Melody"
"Tortured" (with Bing Crosby)
"Boise, Idaho" (with Bing Crosby)
"My Blue, Blue Boy" (with Bing Crosby)
"These Lush Moments" (with Bing Crosby)

36 The Big Band Era: The Passing of the '40s, vol. IV

Label: Vintage Records 4604 (33⅓)

SONGS

"Wish You Were Here"
  From Radio: "The General Electric Program"—October 30, 1952

**37 Best of Fred Astaire:
From MGM Classic Films**

Label: MCA MCAD 31175 (CD)

SONGS

"A Couple of Swells" (with Fred Astaire)
Medley (with Fred Astaire):
  "I Love a Piano"
  "Snooky Ookums"
  "When the Midnight Choo-Choo
    Leaves for Alabam' "

ADDENDA

★ These songs are from the 1948 film
  Easter Parade.

**38 Best of Gene Kelly:
From MGM Classic Films**

Label: MCA MCAD 31177 (CD)

SONGS

"For Me and My Gal"
  From *For Me and My Gal*—1942

**39 Great Songs from MGM
Classic Films**

Label:
  MCA MCAD 31056 (CD)
  MCA MCAD 31130 (CD)
  MCA MCAD 31131 (CD)

SONGS

Volume 1:
  "Over the Rainbow"
    From *The Wizard of Oz*—1939

Volume 2:
  "The Trolley Song"
    From *Meet Me in St. Louis*—1944
  "Easter Parade" (with Fred Astaire)
    From *Easter Parade*—1948
Volume 3:
  "Johnny One Note"
    From *Words and Music*—1948
  "Put Your Arms Around Me, Honey"
    From *In the Good Old Summertime*—
    1949

40 The Frank Sinatra Duets

Label: PJ 001 (33⅓)

SONGS

"Gotta Be This or That" (with Frank
  Sinatra)
"My Romance" (with Frank Sinatra)

ADDENDA

★ Both songs are from "The Danny Kaye
  Show," broadcast October 5, 1945.

F. ARMED FORCES RADIO SERVICE BASIC MUSIC LIBRARY

During World War II, performers donated their services and performed for servicemen at home and overseas. The USO shows are most commonly known. However, during the war an extensive radio network—including American armed service stations, foreign leased stations, and shortwave stations—was developed to transmit live and canned performances. Part of what came to be a sophisticated radio network was the development of a basic music library from which the stations could choose recordings. The original "P" series of recordings, which were shipped during the war (beginning in 1943), were 16″ (33⅓ rpm). Armed Forces Radio Service (AFRS) continued after World War II, becoming Armed Forces Radio and Television Service (AFRTS) in May 1955.

What follows is a list of Judy Garland tracks, transcribed both during and after the war, listed by "P" disk, that are part of the AFRS/AFRTS's Basic Music Library.

1 **P-36 includes:**

"I Never Knew"
"Over the Rainbow"
"Zing! Went the Strings of My Heart"

2 **P-66 includes:**

"Embraceable You"
"The Man I Love"
"People Will Say We're in Love"
   (with Bing Crosby)

3 **P-226 includes:**

"The Trolley Song"
"The Boy Next Door"
"I May Be Wrong"
"Somebody Loves Me"

4 **P-704 includes:**

"Aren't You Kind of Glad We Did?"
   (with Dick Haymes)

5 **P-766 includes:**

"Connecticut" (with Bing Crosby)
"Changing My Tune" (with Gordon Jenkins)

6 **P-1661 includes:**

"Get Happy"
"Friendly Star"

7 **P-2204 includes:**

"You Made Me Love You"
"Over the Rainbow"
"The Trolley Song"
"Meet Me in St. Louis, Louis"
"In Between"
"Sweet Sixteen"

8 **P-2399 includes:**

"You've Got Me Where You Want Me"
   (with Bing Crosby)
"Mine" (with Bing Crosby)

9 **P-2453 includes:**

"Look for the Silver Lining"
"Johnny One Note"
"Love of My Life"
"Who?"

Following page: From the World War I Medley sequence in *For Me and My Gal.*

"Last Night When We Were Young"
"Put Your Arms Around Me, Honey"

---

10 P-3036 includes:

"Without a Memory"
"Send My Baby Back to Me"
"Go Home, Joe"
"Heartbroken"

---

11 P-3833 includes:

"Here's What I'm Here For"
"It's a New World"
"Someone at Last"

---

12 P-3834 includes:

"Lose That Long Face"
"Gotta Have Me Go with You"
"The Man That Got Away"

---

13 P-3835 includes:

"Born in a Trunk" Medley
    From *A Star Is Born*—1954

---

14 P-8049 includes:

"Paris Is a Lonely Town"
"Little Drops of Rain"

---

15 P-8055 includes:

"This Is My Lucky Day"
"I Happen to Like New York"
Palace Medley
    From *The Garland Touch*, Capitol SW
    1701 (33⅓)

---

16 P-8056 includes:

"Happiness Is Just a Thing Called Joe"
"You'll Never Walk Alone"
"Do I Love You?"
"More Than You Know"
"It's a Great Day for the Irish"
    From *The Garland Touch*

---

17 P-8083 includes:

"Gay Purr-ee Overture"
"Little Drops of Rain"
"Take My Hand, Paree"

18 P-8084 includes:

"Paris Is a Lonely Town"
"Roses Red, Violets Blue"
"Mewsette Finale" (with Robert Goulet, chorus)

19 P-8273 includes:

"I Could Go On Singing"
"Hello, Bluebird"

20 P-8837 includes:

"It's a Good Day"
"That's All"
"Some People"
"More"
"Island in the West Indies"
    From *Just for Openers,* Capitol W 2062 (33⅓)

21 P-8838 includes:

"Get Me to the Church on Time"
"Fly Me to the Moon"
"I Wish You Love"
"Jamboree Jones"
"Battle Hymn of the Republic"
"Maybe I'll Come Back"
    From *Just for Openers*

22 P-14018 includes:

Selections from *Live at The London Palladium* (with Liza Minnelli)
"Together"
Medley:
    "Swanee"
    "When the Saints Go Marching In"
    "He's Got the Whole World in His Hands"

23 P-14342 includes:

"A Fella with an Umbrella" (with Peter Lawford)
"Easter Parade" (with Fred Astaire)

24 P-14343 includes:

"A Couple of Swells" (with Fred Astaire)
"Better Luck Next Time"

25 P-14346 includes:

"Be a Clown" (with Gene Kelly)
"You Can Do No Wrong"
"Love of My Life"

26 P-14668 includes:

"You Made Me Love You"

27 P-14669 includes:

"Wizard of Oz" medley (with Lahr,
Bolger, Haley)
"Babes in Arms" medley (with Mickey
Rooney)
"Babes on Broadway" medley (with
Mickey Rooney)
"Under the Bamboo Tree" (with Margaret
O'Brien)
"Get Happy"

28 P-14670 includes:

"On the Atchison, Topeka and the Santa
Fe"

29 P-16091 includes:

"That's Entertainment"
"For Me and My Gal"
From *That's Entertainment,* Capitol
T-1467 (33⅓)

5

CONCERTS

★

*"The free spontaneous communication between the big bands and their fans
was a natural culmination of the music itself.
The approach of most outfits was so honest and direct that their fans
could recognize instinctively whether the bands were really trying
or merely coasting. When a musician played an especially exciting solo,
they'd cheer him for it, and when the band as a whole reached especially high
musical or emotional heights, it would be rewarded with enthusiastic,
honest, heartfelt yelling and cheering . . . real approval for a job well done."*

George T. Simon, *The Big Bands*

★

*"When the voice pours out, as rich and pleading as ever, we know where,
and how moved, we are—in the presence of a star, and embarrassed by tears."*

Kenneth Tynan, *The New Yorker*, May 23, 1959 (review of Garland concert)

★

Judy Garland, after leaving Metro-Goldwyn-Mayer, gave her first formal concert at the London Palladium in the beginning of April 1951. She gave her last concert at the end of March 1969, in Denmark. During the intervening eighteen years, she made more than a hundred major appearances, ranging from multiweek engagements to one-night stands, in theaters, arenas and auditoriums, and cabarets throughout the United States, Canada, Australia, and much of Europe.

Garland's concert career has both amazed and bemused critics. Amazed them because of the virtuosity of her performances and the skill with which she moved audiences, often beyond her singing, with sheer personality and bits of stage business they could not reduce to words in reviews. Bemused them because of the intensity of devotion she evoked, even when her voice was past its prime and total reliability was no longer assured.

Judy Garland overcame language barriers abroad, age barriers in the era of the "generation gap" and "never trust anyone over thirty," and occasionally vigorous hostile publicity to become internationally renowned as one of the greatest musical variety and concert performers of the twentieth century. The Garland legend begins with Judy's concert career.

Much of the apparent mystery of Judy Garland's concert appeal is not particularly mysterious, if often subtle and idiosyncratic to her. Garland was a great singer and a performer who exhibited a warmly appealing and approachable personality to her public. She never came across as a "star" making an appearance and impressed with her own status and abilities. She was an entertainer who earnestly wanted to entertain her audience. She carried to the concert stage the traits with which she had imbued her film characters, a general good-naturedness and a self-deprecating sense of humor which could be sharp but was never cynical.

From the first, audiences were with her.

The publicity Judy's emotional problems received during the late forties and her abrupt firing from Metro-Goldwyn-Mayer in 1950 were commonly supposed to have been devastating to her career. This was still the period of Hollywood glamour, after all, when stars had carefully crafted images, and private lives not matching those images were kept from view. (This was one of the sources of power for gossip columnists. Their scribblings either reinforced an actor's public personality or destroyed it.) Garland's problems were on full display; and, in theory at least, they didn't jibe with the girl-next-door picture that MGM had so carefully nurtured.

The conventional wisdom didn't hold true in Judy's instance. From her earliest performances, both her vocal and film characterizations had a gentleness, warmth, and openness that went beyond scripted dialogue or lyrics. It's part of what made her noticeable during her early years at MGM and a box-office attraction later. On screen or vinyl, she seemed "nice" and had a down-to-earth quality and sense of humor that resonated with the public. Nice people have problems, and nice people get fired; it happens in every neighborhood and most families. And you root for them to recover.

Having liked her on screen and records in the forties, people were both curious about her new stage act and willing to ignore rumors of her professional demise. They found the same warmth and openness they had always found attractive. But they also found a singer and performer freed of the restraints imposed by her movie roles, a formidable vocalist with a quite different style.

Most of the great popular singers whose careers had started in the thirties and forties started with the Big Bands. Early in their careers, they had supported the musicians, who were the real stars. Later, the musicians supported them. The instrumentalists provided the emotional substructure, the vocalist the phrasing and approach to convey the lyrical interpretation, but the singer maintained a certain emotional distance from the song, a certain aloofness.

Garland's concert style went beyond that partnership. She fused the words and music, enhancing the content of both. She created a vocal electricity that vaulted the footlights and reverberated through the hall, igniting personal recognition to each song's particular emotional dynamic.

Garland's mature vocal style commanded attention and evoked response. Part of the uniqueness of a Garland concert was the bond this created between Judy and those for whom she sang. The audience was denied, and renounced, the usual passivity of the entertained.

So also with the personality she displayed onstage. Throughout her concert years, reviewers noted that Judy would open her act appearing nervous and then warmed to audience response. Nervousness on the part of a performer who positions herself as a "star" lends itself to derision. Judy, however, never distanced herself from the people sitting before her. She created a unity.

She took to theaters, clubs, and huge arenas as if they were large living rooms. She conveyed the feeling that she was thrilled to be entertaining people whose opinions she valued. She both disarmed and delighted her audience with her down-to-earth anecdotes and improvisational wit. This, in itself, is enough to bring an audience to a performer's side. But Garland went further. She mastered the delicate art of developing a dialogue between stage and auditorium, and she had the skill and sensitivity to control overly enthusiastic fans whose exuberance might be distracting, without personally denigrating them. At the same time, she integrated spontaneous audience comments into her performance.

Judy Garland made the audience an integral part of the act. She involved her listeners in the success of each perfor-

mance by responding to them, by making them feel a personal importance to her and a need for their approval. Her nervousness, while real, served a precise emotional effect. So did her skilled performer's public, but intimate, byplay. They put into a more manageable perspective, a more human dimension, the power of her vocal performances. They wedded the famous Garland image of "vulnerability" to the intensity of her style, creating a complex and irresistible mix of sensibilities.

That is one reason Garland concerts varied in subtleties each night. Not only did Judy sing songs with slightly different nuances each time, she modulated her stage bits to the differences of character and chemistry each separate audience brings to a performance. The act itself may have remained the same throughout an engagement, but the audience dynamic expressed itself with different shadings. Thus, ardent fans would return to her concerts again and again, always finding something fresh. And, critics to the side, they were seeing something real. Even such experienced professionals as Gordon Jenkins could discover an excitement in watching what he called "little joyful bits of business that makes every night seem new" as he worked with her on concert tours.

Garland is generally credited with reviving the old vaudeville two-a-day. In vaudeville, shows were composed of a series of entertainers preceding the star attraction who would come on late in the program, the star position being next to closing. In smaller theaters, the shows were put on as often as five or six times a day (an early equivalent of continuous-performance movies). The more prestigious the house, the fewer the number of shows. In its heyday, the Palace (and other important houses such as the Winter Garden in New York) would have two performances, hence, the "two-a-day." As movies became more popular, the "two-a-days" declined. Garland's Palace show, developed along the lines of a "two-a-day," was so successful that the Palace theater management revised its policy and started booking in this format once again. Seven theatrical unions gave Judy lifetime membership for the work this new policy would bring its members.

What is more significant than what Judy Garland revitalized from the past, however, is how she helped create the American concert format of the future.

In France, the one-performer concert through the early sixties was generally composed of songs written specifically by and for that performer, as Edith Piaf's songs, for example, were designed especially for her. Because they were written with a particular person in mind, to be sung by that person alone, they had a strong dramatic power. Each was a brief essay, a chapter, within the context of the concert. Together, they created a story around the singer that gave the performance a unifying motif stemming from and supporting his or her public personality. This was a recognized format, sometimes called a "tour de chant."

The Judy/audience interplay created an American version of this. Garland concerts developed a conceptual framework in two ways. On the more obvious level were the Garland standards audiences demanded and Judy sang. The repeated renditions of songs associated with her movie career—from "You Made Me Love You" (*Broadway Melody of 1938*) through "The Man That Got Away" (*A Star Is Born*)—allowed the audience to indulge in nostalgia. But they also provided a bracketing of Judy's career, a context in which to see the singer/actress, and they fostered a deepened sense of intimate familiarity for those who had watched her grow up on the screen.

That sense of familiarity was strengthened by Judy's biographical anecdotes and quipping, which also provided a sense of mutual communication to her performances. The polished subtlety of her mature vocal style created new standards throughout the fifties and sixties and created new memories for her fans. In addition, the power of her style's impact on the listener promoted the illusion that she was not merely singing, but emoting, that she was revealing herself in each song. Thus, Judy Garland supplied the material, while the audience wrote the story line for Garland concerts.

This combination of entertainer/entertained interactions, with a musical and verbal dialogue and an unwritten subtext, has now become standard fare for concert performers. Yet only later did the responsibility for a concert theme become an almost mutual one. For Garland audiences, the approach was new, and as the story line developed over the years, enhanced by publicity and reviews, it became as much a part of the performances as the orchestrations behind the music. By the late fifties, when Judy Garland got up on a stage to sing, the audience populated that stage with their images of her and her history.

Garland concerts have been described as love fests between Judy and her fans. She provided the audience with consummate showmanship and an extraordinary range of magnificent singing. And because people could believe she was singing not merely with artistry but with deeply felt emotion, an emotion expressing a personal history, it was acceptable to feel, and reveal, the emotions her renditions evoked. It is far less embarrassing to be visibly moved by someone who is also moved and who so clearly wants to please than by a remote performer. It is also easier to show your feelings when those around you are showing theirs.

The concerts and audience reactions that have so bemused critics operated on a series of levels. Judy displayed extraordinary technical virtuosity. She conveyed a song's meaning directly, with its inherent emotion unfiltered. And she performed with an intrinsic gladness of talent and apparent joy in sharing it. And the audience responded to her singing. It empathized with the human being onstage. But further, stimulated by the context that Garland's vocal style and interaction developed, individuals in the crowd enjoyed, at once, a cathartic and unifying experience with both the performer and other members of the audience.

By the late sixties, reviewers noted time and again that Judy's voice and control were not what they had once been. She would, throughout this period, occasionally produce a rendition that was prime Garland, in top form. More important, she compensated for the loss of vocal purity through her showmanship, in part shifting the audience's focus from the vocal to the visual. This is one reason that the critics who concentrated their attention and reviews solely on her singing were confused, and in some cases clearly enraged, that the audiences continued to enjoy her performances.

An anonymous *Time* magazine scribe suggested that people came to the later Garland concerts to see her fail. This infuriated Judy, and rightly so. One wonders how she could so consistently attract hundreds, often thousands, of people at a time, who all had the extra money, the free evenings, and the sadism to travel to a concert and hope for failure. Then have other critics note how warmly audiences responded to her. *Time* got it backward. The public wanted her to succeed.

Garland fans went to Garland concerts because her showmanship, singing, and audience interaction created a performance where the whole was more important than any particular aspect of it.

Judy Garland presented her audiences with a talent that awed them, and she presented it in a very human guise that drew them close. She did not simply entertain them. She touched them. She created an experience of such power that many people still carry it with them today. For just as Garland artfully blended words and music to add unimagined dimensions to her songs, she melded the individuals in the audience and joined them to the words and music, creating a depth of excitement few people can either explain or forget.

This chapter focuses on Judy Garland's concert, cabaret, and "two-a-day" performances, where Garland was the primary headliner. It does not include such events as World War II war bond drives and personal appearance tours arranged by MGM.

1943

1 Robin Hood Dell, Philadelphia

July 1, 1943
With The Philadelphia Orchestra, under the direction of André Kostelanetz

SONGS

Gershwin numbers
Favorites from her films

CONTEMPORARY COMMENTS
The New York Times, July 2, 1943
Judy Garland, screen actress, drew a record breaking crowd of more than 30,000 persons to Robin Hood Dell . . . for her first appearance with a symphony orchestra.

More than 15,000 men, women and young devotees of swing jammed their way into the dell proper while another 15,000 sat on the grass and in vacant parking lots adjoining the outdoor bowl. The police estimated at least 5,000 persons left when unable to get within hearing distance. The previous Dell record was 14,250.

1951

1 The Palladium, London

Opening: April 9, 1951

Guests:
El Granadas and Peter
Tony Fayne and David Evans
Bedini Troupe
Max Bygraves
The Debonairs
Frances Duncan
Medlock and Marlowe

SONGS

"Limehouse Blues"
"Embraceable You"
"Just One of Those Things"
"The Trolley Song"
"Easter Parade"
"Get Happy"
"Rock-a-Bye Your Baby with a Dixie Melody"
"Over the Rainbow"

ADDENDA

★ This was a four-week engagement.
★ Garland followed this engagement with a tour of the British Isles that took her to Liverpool, Dublin, Glasgow, and Edinburgh. The tour ended in Birmingham, where the audience sang "Auld Lang Syne" to Judy.

CONTEMPORARY COMMENTS
London *Times,* April 10, 1951
Miss Judy Garland not only tops the bill at the Palladium this week, she also runs

away with the show. . . . She does every-thing with a complete good humour that quickly spreads through the audience, which she roused last night, to much en-thusiasm. The only criticism to be made is that she seems at times to be over straining her voice, and she might allow herself rather more of that quiet singing which suits her so well.

Sight and Sound, June 1951
The trick is an extraordinary mixture of humor, vitality and sincerity of feeling—which makes the most indifferent songs sound as if they meant something—and an intriguing, expressive face.

PALACE TWO-A-DAY

RKO PALACE THEATRE

2 The Palace Theater, New York

Opening: October 16, 1951
Staged by Charles Walters
Conductor: Don Albert (with the RKO Palace Orchestra)
Special lyrics and arrangements by Roger Edens
Musical director: Jack Cathcart
Garland's accompanist: Hugh Martin

Guests:

Smith and Dale	The Christianis
Max Bygraves	The Nicholas Brothers
Senor Wences	
Giselle and François Szoney	

SONGS

"Tonight's the Night"
Palace Medley:
    "Shine on Harvest Moon"
    "Some of These Days"
    "My Man"
    "I Don't Care"
"Rock-a-Bye Your Baby with a Dixie Melody"
Medley:
    "You Made Me Love You"
    "For Me and My Gal"
    "The Boy Next Door"
    "The Trolley Song"
"Get Happy"
"A Couple of Swells" (with Jack McClendon)
"Over the Rainbow"
"Love"
"A Pretty Girl Milking Her Cow"
"Liza"

ADDENDA

★ The engagement was extended into a record-breaking nineteen-week run.

★ Garland collapsed onstage from exhaustion on November 12. Performances were suspended until the sixteenth, when she resumed her evening and matinee schedule.

★ Due to the extraordinary success of her engagement, the Palace revised its policy and restored vaudeville to its booking schedule.

★ Seven AFL theatrical unions made Judy a lifetime member at a ceremony at the Hotel Astor because of the additional work the new policy would provide their members.

★ The songs listed above are from her closing night's performance.

★ The Christianis were described on the bill as "Europe's greatest acrobats"; the Nicholas Brothers were described as "international dancers of stage and screen" (the Nicholas Brothers were featured in a 1948 Garland film, *The Pirate*); and Senor Wences was described as a "famous international star"; Smith and Dale did "the variety classic 'Dr. Kronkhite' " with Geene Courtney; the Szoneys were described as "famous continental dancing stars"; Jack McClendon was one of Judy's "eight boyfriends." The other seven were Hal Bell, Jack Boyle, William Lundy, Bert May (dance specialty), Hamil Petrof, Jack Regas, and Ricky Ricardi.

Not all these performers were with the show through the entire engagement.

RECORDINGS

Judy Garland "Live" at The Palace, Classic International Theatremusic C.I.T. 2001 (33⅓)

This album was recorded on closing night.

CONTEMPORARY COMMENTS

The New York Times, October 17, 1951

Understandably enough, Miss Garland was extremely nervous despite the constant reassurance from a wildly applauding audience throughout the act. She managed, however, to convey a pleasant informality on stage. Full of zip and electric excitement, she gave plenty of evidence that she knows her way over the boards.

Variety, February 20, 1952

The Palace is back to a two-a-day vaudeville rebirth and if it ever takes hold permanently Judy Garland gets credit . . . and rates all of it . . . for berthing it there . . . Hers was a tour-de-force of no small caliber. The hep and sentimentality attuned firstnighters left the Palace in a burst of reflected stardust, for there is no disputing at any time, that the ex-Metro songstress is simonpure stellar quality.

Following page: Judy Garland and Joan Crawford at a party following the L.A. Philharmonic Auditorium concert.

1952

1 Philharmonic Auditorium, Los Angeles

Opening: April 21, 1952
The Palace show

ADDENDA

★ This was the beginning of a four-week engagement.
★ It was the evident and overwhelming success of this event, on Hollywood's own turf, that battered down the solid wall of resistance Judy Garland and her husband, Sid Luft, had been encountering in their efforts to return Garland to the screen and to produce *A Star Is Born.*

CONTEMPORARY COMMENTS

The New York Times, April 23, 1952
The actress opened the Civic Light Opera season with her vaudeville show, which set records at the Palace in New York. The throng of motion picture personalities packed the Philharmonic Auditorium for the sentimental occasion. There was scarcely a dry eye when Miss Garland, in a tramp costume, sat on the rim of the stage and wistfully sang "Over the Rainbow."

When the show was over, the audience applauded wildly and Judy received twenty large bouquets.

Billboard, May 3, 1952
It attracted the cream of the film colony's glitter and drew heavily from the social register. Metropolitan dailies gave the event dual coverage, a procedure saved for opening night of the opera, with extravagant space in the society pages as well as the theatrical section.

Judy sang as this reporter has never heard her sing before.

—Lee Zhito

2 The Curran, San Francisco

Opening: May 26, 1952
The Palace show

ADDENDA

★ This was a four-week engagement.

CONTEMPORARY COMMENTS

San Francisco Chronicle, May 28, 1952
Judy Garland brought a touch of the Palace and a touch of the Palladium to the Curran stage . . .

The headline act is warm and gay, and Judy's songs may bring legitimate lumps to an audience's throat. It is just that the legend of Judy Garland's comeback gets in the way of the act.

—William Hogan

1955

1 San Diego, California

July 8 and 9, 1955
Director/choreographer: Roger Edens
Special material: Leonard Gershe
Music director: Jack Cathcart
Staged by Paul Gorkin

Garland's accompanist: Eddie O'Neal
A Transcona Production

Guests:
The Wiler Brothers
Jerry Gray Orchestra
Frank Fontaine
The Hi-Lo's

SONGS

"The Man That Got Away"
"Carolina in the Morning"
"While We're Young" (with the Hi-Lo's)
"You Made Me Love You"
"For Me and My Gal"
"The Boy Next Door"
"The Trolley Song"
"Rock-a-Bye Your Baby with a Dixie
   Melody"
"A Couple of Swells"
"A Pretty Girl Milking Her Cow"
"Over the Rainbow"

ADDENDA

★ This engagement was a break-in a
  seven-city West Coast tour.
★ The show was staged as a legitimate
  revue. *Variety* reports that Roger Edens
  and Leonard Gershe "authored the special material, which has her working
  three specialties in each hour. They
  also did four original songs for her."
★ This tour was planned to be a prelimi-
  nary for Judy to work with Harry James
  cofeatured, starting September 8.
★ Sid Luft, Garland's husband, was setting up the tour, under MCA booking,
  in arenas and auditoriums. He wanted
  a $10,000 nightly guarantee for the
  show against 50 percent of the gross.
  Arena operators were leery of guaran-

tees, however, since Dean Martin and
Jerry Lewis and Ed Sullivan had had
abortive tours.

CONTEMPORARY COMMENTS

Variety, July 13, 1955
Judy Garland puts on a dazzling performance. . . . She has added a magnetic maturity to the old gamin quality and the
voice is as bewitching as ever. So long as
Miss Garland is onstage, it's a throwback
to the giants of oldtime vaude and, especially to a generation reared on TV, unforgettable "live" theatre.

2 Municipal Auditorium, Long Beach, California

July 11, 1955
The San Diego show

ADDENDA

★ The net proceeds of the performance
  went to the Exceptional Children's
  Foundation.
★ The rest of the tour included:
  Eugene, Oregon (July 14)
  Portland, Oregon (July 15 and 16)
  Seattle, Washington (July 17 and 18)
  Vancouver, British Columbia (July 19)
  Spokane, Washington (July 21)

1956

1 New Frontier, Las Vegas

Opening: July 16, 1956
Staged by Robert Alton
Conductor: Jack Cathcart

Guests:
The Amin Brothers
Judy's Boy Friends
The Risley Acrobatic Team
This was, basically, the Palace show.

SONGS

"Come Rain or Come Shine"
"Rock-a-Bye Your Baby with a Dixie
  Melody"
"Happiness Is Just a Thing Called Joe"
"A Pretty Girl Milking Her Cow"
"Liza"
"Over the Rainbow"

ADDENDA

★ This was Garland's club debut. It was
a four-week engagement, with two
shows nightly. Of the sixty-eight-min-
ute program, Judy sang for forty minutes.

CONTEMPORARY COMMENTS

Variety, July 18, 1956
One of the greatest modern day singers
caught fire last night . . . in the first nitery
engagement of her career. Late in making
her start on the saloon belt, Judy Garland
nevertheless belted across an unmistakable message that not only is she tops in
her field, but also the likely champ entertainer as long and as often as she desires
to play the bistro circuit.

2 Palace Theater, New York
(second appearance)

Opening: September 26, 1956
First half of the bill:
The Amin Brothers
Bob Williams
Pompoff, Thedy, and Family
Kora Kovach and Istvan Rabovsky
Alan King
Second half:
    Judy Garland (and her "Boy Friends")
Staged by Robert Alton
Supervised by Sid Luft

Special lyrics and arrangements by Roger
Edens and Kay Thompson
Special conductor: Jack Cathcart
House conductor: Myron Roman

Judy's "Boy Friends":

Lance Avant	Burnell Dietsch
Pat Gorman	Erme Preston
Gene Reed	Jerry Stabler
Meurisse Durree	Don Torrillo
John Lewis	Frank Davis
Bert May (featured)	

SONGS

"You Made Me Love You"
"For Me and My Gal"
"The Trolley Song"
"Over the Rainbow"
"This Is My Lucky Day"

ADDENDA

★ The engagement was originally scheduled for four weeks. After the reviews
came out, tickets went on sale for another four weeks.

CONTEMPORARY COMMENTS

The New York Times, September 27, 1956
But the songs begin so informally and
gather such vocal warmth and volume as
she puts her heart into them that you
would swear she is improvising them. A
song has not really been sung until Judy
pulls herself together and belts it through
the theatre.

—Brooks Atkinson

Variety, October 3, 1956
Miss Garland . . . makes a Brill Bldg. lyric
sound like a Shakespeare sonnet. She
could sing Toots Shor's menu and have

'em hungry for more. She takes command
of the rostrum as none does.

Her second half stint is a tour-de-force.

Dance Magazine, November 1956
Judy Garland's prowess is definitely in the
field of song, and yet in those moments
that she dances a bit or joins The Boy
Friends, the skilled dancers who work
with her, she does very well, blending
some of the slightly awkward, earnest appeal of her personality with the rhythmic
steps.

1957

1 **Flamingo, Las Vegas**

Opening: May 1, 1957
Staged by Robert Alton
Produced by Hal Belfer
Special material by Roger Edens
Conductor: Jack Cathcart

Guests:
Sid Kroft
The Alton Dancers
The Flamingoettes
Louis Basil Orchestra

SONGS

"This Is My Lucky Day"
"Rock-a-Bye Your Baby with a Dixie
Melody"
"The Man That Got Away"
"Come Rain or Come Shine"
"A Couple of Swells"
"A Pretty Girl Milking Her Cow"
"Over the Rainbow"

ADDENDA

★ This ninety-minute show was scheduled through May 22.

CONTEMPORARY COMMENTS

Variety, May 8, 1957

The Strip headliners and the local VIPs were there, and they gave Miss Garland a standing ovation for her efforts. Her act is dramatic yet punctuated with down to earth casualness; it is nostalgic yet holds its own in the freshness department; it is fulfilling in that it warmly presents with intimacy a living legend.

2 Riviera, Detroit, Michigan

Opening: May 30, 1957

Guests:
Alan King
Sid Kroft
The Amin Brothers
The Szoneys
Judy's Boy Friends

ADDENDA

★ This was a seven-day engagement.
★ Judy injured her ankle in her dressing room early in the run. For June 1 show, she was carried out for the second half of the show with her feet dangling over the edge of the stage.

CONTEMPORARY COMMENTS

Detroit News, May 31, 1957

In less time than it took to finish the first musical number, the near capacity crowd was won over. When she left, a couple of dozen songs and 90 minutes later, most everyone was on their feet; not to leave, but to ask for more.

Always, too, the Garland charm dominated the scene, together with the slight giggle and warm friendliness.

—Robert E. Lubeck

3 Dallas (Texas) Fair ("State Fair Musicals")

Opening: June 10, 1957
The Detroit show

ADDENDA

★ This was a two-week engagement.

CONTEMPORARY COMMENTS

Variety, June 26, 1957

Garland show drew the largest (2,451) season opening . . . in Musicals' history.

4 Loew's Capitol, Washington, D.C.

Opening: September 16, 1957
The Detroit show

ADDENDA

★ This was a one-week engagement.

CONTEMPORARY COMMENTS

Variety, September 25, 1957

Illness compelled Judy Garland to cancel her final performance . . . First half of the bill was virtually ended before the doctor clamped down on Miss Garland and prevented her from going on. She had a fever of 103 and Asian flu.

5 Mastbaum Theater, Philadelphia

Opening: September 26, 1957

Guests:
Alan King
Kovach & Rabovsky
Manuel and Marita Viera

SONGS

"Having a Party"
"By Myself"
"Mean to Me"
"After You've Gone"
"You Made Me Love You"
"For Me and My Gal"
"The Trolley Song"
"The Man That Got Away"
"How About Me?"
"This Is My Lucky Day"
"Rock-a-Bye Your Baby with a Dixie
    Melody"
"A Couple of Swells"
"Over the Rainbow"

ADDENDA

★ This was a one-week engagement.
★ The Mastbaum had been the largest
    theater in the country until Radio City
    Music Hall opened.

CONTEMPORARY COMMENTS

Philadelphia Inquirer, September 27, 1957
If the audience had had its way, Judy
would probably still be singing.

—Mildred Martin

6 Dominion Theatre, London

Opening: October 16, 1957

SONGS

"It's Lovely to Be Back in London"
"I Feel a Song Coming On"
"For Me and My Gal"
"The Trolley Song"
"The Man That Got Away"
"Rock-a-Bye Your Baby with a Dixie
    Melody"
"This Is My Lucky Day"
"A Couple of Swells"
"Over the Rainbow"
Encores:
    "Me and My Shadow"
    "Swanee"

ADDENDA

★ This engagement ran through November 16, 1957.
★ On opening night, the 3,000-seat theater was filled to capacity.
★ The opening song, "It's Lovely to Be Back in London," was written for Judy for this engagement by Roger Edens.

CONTEMPORARY COMMENTS

London Times, October 17, 1957
Her performance satisfies because from
the very first moment it gains her a
friendly intimacy with a huge audience
which is never lost again. Miss Garland's
superficial appeal is as a film heroine of
her youth; her real appeal is that of a
music hall personality who can hold a big
house doing very little that is worth discussing on paper.

Programme

1 OVERTURE
   The Dominion Theatre Orchestra
   Conductor ... **BOBBY HOWELL**

2 WARREN, DEVINE & SPARKES
   Comedy Acrobats

3 ALBERT and LES WARD
   Television and Radio Personalities

4 NINO, THE WONDER DOG
   A tail worth the telling

5 HOLGER & DOLORES
   American Dance Stylists

6 ALAN KING
   Warner Bros. New Comedy Star

7 *15 MINUTES INTERMISSION*

8 OVERTURE
   Judy Garland Medley
   GORDON JENKINS
   conducting the Dominion Theatre Orchestra

9 JUDY'S TEN BOY FRIENDS

LANCE AVANT	BURNELL DIETSCH
ERMIE PRESTON	JERRY STABLER
JIMMY BROOKS	BERT MAY
BILL LUNDY	MEURISSE DUREE
RICCI RICCARDI	RONNIE MARTINSEN

FEATURING—
BERT MAY   MEURISSE DUREE
and JIMMY BROOKS
ASSISTING MISS GARLAND IN
"WE'RE A COUPLE OF SWELLS"

10 **JUDY GARLAND**

Miss Garland's act staged and directed by ROBERT ALTON
and RICHARD BARSTOW

Special lyrics and musical arrangements by ROGER EDENS
(by courtesy of M.G.M. Studios)

Musical Director for Miss Garland ... **GORDON JENKINS**   Production Manager ... **GORDON WYNNE**
Entire production under the supervision of **SIDNEY LUFT**

The Management reserve the right to change, vary or omit without previous notice any item of the Programme.
The Press and Public Relations for the Judy Garland Show have been handled by the LESLIE FREWEN ORGANISATION Ltd.   Grosvenor 7671.
THE TAKING OF PHOTOGRAPHS IS NOT ALLOWED.

Variety, October 23, 1957
Judy Garland . . . has returned [to London] in devastating triumph . . . She fills the second half of the bill with a brilliantly staged, irresistible production which lasts nearly an hour and leaves the audience screaming eagerly for more.

Miss Garland again reveals herself as a performer of terrific versatility.

Melody Maker, October 10, 1957
Such was the appeal of her performance that in the very upper circles it will surely be social damnation to admit that one just hasn't been to see her.

—Tony Brown

Melody Maker, November 16, 1957
The most exciting thing about her performance is that it is completely different every night.

There is never any fluctuation in quality or effort or presentation, but she seldom conquers a song in exactly the same way and is constantly inserting little joyful bits of business that makes every night seem new.

—Gordon Jenkins

7 Palladium Theatre, London: "Royal Variety Performance"

November 18, 1957

Guests:

Gracie Fields   Tommy Steele
Max Bygraves   Herschel Henlere
Bob Monkhouse

CONTEMPORARY COMMENTS

Variety, November 20, 1957

The Royal Command Performance . . . had Judy Garland getting the top mitt of the occasion with Count Basie a close second and Mario Lanza a distant third. The layout is generally regarded as one of the best all around shows in years.

. . . Miss Garland, Basie and Lanza were among those presented to Her Majesty.

London *Times,* November 10, 1957

But even those who lament the fading away of old style variety would have to admit the streamlined brilliance of last night. . . . This was the average level: above it were performers who possess a special affinity with variety. . . . and Miss Judy Garland can be raffishly gay and sentimental.

8 Flamingo, Las Vegas

Opening: December 26, 1957
Special material: Roger Edens, Jack Cathcart
Produced by Sid Luft

Guests:
Bobby Van
Don Kirk
The Flamingoettes
Jack Cathcart Orchestra

SONGS

"I Feel a Song Coming On"
My Fair Lady Medley
Palace Medley:
    "When You Wore a Tulip"
    "How About Me?"
    "You're Just in Love" (with Bobby Van)
    "A Couple of Swells" (with Bobby Van)
    "Over the Rainbow"

CONTEMPORARY COMMENTS

Variety, January 1, 1958

Judy Garland returns to the Flamingo Room . . . this time without the dancing boys to back her. The emphasis is on song . . . Miss Garland's preem audience found her in excellent voice and with a pleasing air of informality.

1958

1 Town and Country Club, Brooklyn, New York

Opening: March 20, 1958

Guests:
Bobby Van
Buster Burnell Dancers
Ned Harvey Orchestra

SONGS

"Life Is Just a Bowl of Cherries"
"You Made Me Love You"
"When You Wore a Tulip" (with Bobby Van)
"By Myself"
"Mean to Me"
"After You've Gone"
"Rock-a-Bye Your Baby with a Dixie Melody"
"Swanee"

ADDENDA

★ This was scheduled to be a three-and-a-half-week engagement.

CONTEMPORARY COMMENTS

Variety, March 26, 1958
Judy Garland does not have to prove that she is a top attraction. She is, has been, and it's a well known fact; however, her opening . . . in the midst of a 24 hour snowstorm coupled with impossible driving conditions should dispel any and all doubts about Miss Garland's pulling power.

Variety, April 2, 1958
One of the stormiest nitery engagements ever to take place in any cafe in the country ended Sunday in Brooklyn when Judy Garland announced from the mike after two songs . . . to a full house of 1,700, that she had laryngitis and wouldn't be able to sing. The mike was cut off and Miss Garland, moving offstage said, "It doesn't matter, I've just been fired anyway."

2 Cocoanut Grove, Los Angeles

Opening: July 23, 1958
Conductor: Freddy Martin
Arrangements by Nelson Riddle, Gordon Jenkins, and Buddy Bregman
Staged by Charles Walters
Special material by Roger Edens

SONGS

"When You're Smiling"
"Zing! Went the Strings of My Heart"
"Purple People Eater"
Garland Medley:
    "You Made Me Love You"
    "For Me and My Gal"
    "The Trolley Song"
"When the Sun Comes Out"
"Rock-a-Bye Your Baby with a Dixie Melody"
"After You've Gone"
"A Pretty Girl Milking Her Cow"
"Swanee"
"I Can't Give You Anything but Love"
"Liza"
"Me and My Shadow"
"Over the Rainbow"

ADDENDA

★ This was a four-week engagement.

CONTEMPORARY COMMENTS

Variety, July 30, 1958
Her voice has never been better.... A pulsing emotional as well as musical instrument.

On some notes she opened pianissimo and swelled to fortissimo, a dramatic performance that few singers can match.

RECORDINGS

Garland at the Grove [Capitol ST/T 1118 (33⅓)]. The live recording of this album was done on August 6, 1958. It does not contain all the songs she sang.

3 **Orchestra Hall, Chicago**

Opening: September 4, 1958
Producer: Sid Luft
Garland material staged by Charles Walters
Special material and arrangements by Roger Edens
Music director: Nelson Riddle

PROGRAM

Act one:
Nelson Riddle and Orchestra:
   "Let's Face the Music"
   "You Are My Lucky Star"
   "You and the Night and the Music"
   "Younger Than Springtime"
   "Then I'll Be Happy"
   "Let Yourself Go"
Alan King

Act two:
Judy Garland
Nelson Riddle and Orchestra:
   "Lisbon Antigua"
   "Blue on Blue"
   "Brother John"
Judy Garland, Alan King:
   "A Couple of Swells"

GARLAND SONGS

"When You're Smiling"
"I Can't Give You Anything but Love"
"The Trolley Song"
"Purple People Eater"
"Over the Rainbow"
"Chicago"

ADDENDA

★ This engagement lasted through September 9.
★ The first night was a benefit performance for the Chicago Home for Girls.

CONTEMPORARY COMMENTS

Chicago Tribune, September 8, 1958
It is only the cheezy performer who widens the trench between the audience and the entertainer. Comes a Judy Garland to the stage and the gap narrows to a fine line, not so much of distinction as of balance.

Even songs that weren't written especially for her become hers by right of interpretation. She is an "original."

—Seymour Raven

4 The Sands, Las Vegas

Opening: October 1, 1958

Guests:
The Kings IV
The Texas Copa Girls
Antonio Morelli Orchestra
Produced by Jack Entratter

SONGS

"When You're Smiling"
"Come Rain or Come Shine"
"I Can't Give You Anything but Love"
"Zing! Went the Strings of My Heart"
"Purple People Eater"
"You Made Me Love You"
"For Me and My Gal"
"The Trolley Song"
"Do It Again"
"The Man That Got Away"
"Rock-a-Bye Your Baby with a Dixie
   Melody"
"Over the Rainbow"

CONTEMPORARY COMMENTS

Variety, October 8, 1958
. . . the act is pure Judy Garland, and on
opening night it was Judy Garland at her
best.

1959

1 Fontainebleau, Miami Beach, Florida

February 1959
Conductor: Neal Hefti

Guests:
Sid Kroft
Murray Schlamm
Sacasas Orchestra

ADDENDA

★ The opening night was a sellout, with a
   crowd of 800.

CONTEMPORARY COMMENTS

Variety, February 25, 1959
This was a tough, word passing collection
of jaded firstnighters who can make or
break an act in this town. To her warming, and obviously loosening up delight,
they built to constant mitt receptivity.

It takes a performer of stature to over-
come the sort of initial resistance the
Miami Beach cosmopolites present . . .
Miss Garland broke that up in short order.

2 Baltimore, Maryland

Opening: April 27, 1959

Guests:
Alan King
John Bubbles
The production personnel were the same
   as for the Metropolitan Opera concert,
   May 11, 1959.

GARLAND SONGS

"I Happen to Like New York"
"It's Almost Like Being in Love"
"This Can't Be Love"
"The Trolley Song"
"For Me and My Gal"
"Wonderful Guy"
"California, Here I Come"
"You Made Me Love You"
"Rock-a-Bye Your Baby with a Dixie
    Melody"
"Melancholy Baby"
"Swanee"
"Over the Rainbow"
Excerpts from "The Letter"

ADDENDA

★ The Baltimore audience and critics were not overjoyed with Garland's choice of "I Happen to Like New York." She joked with the audience and was forgiven on the basis of this being a tryout for the Metropolitan Opera appearance.

★ "The Letter" was written and composed by Gordon Jenkins. Garland recorded a full version of this [Capitol S/TAO 1188 (33⅓) and ST 1941 (33⅓)].

★ The specialty dancing was done by Carolyn Morris and Jack Leigh.

CONTEMPORARY COMMENTS

Baltimore Sun, April 28, 1959
It may be that Roger Edens, who put together most of the scenes, is depending too much on Miss Garland to make a show sorely lacking in originality seem fresh and new.

It is a rich and exciting voice, capable —when its owner really lets loose—of shooting prickles up the spine of even the most prosaic reviewer.

—R. H. Gardner

Evening Sun (Baltimore), April 28, 1959
Nobody, but nobody, can belt out a song like Judy Garland. At its best her voice is piercing, trumpet like and packed with amplified emotion that can fairly tear your heart out of its sockets.

—Hope Pantell

3 **Metropolitan Opera House, New York**

Opening: May 11, 1959
Producer: Sid Luft
Musical direction: Gordon Jenkins
Staged and choreographed by Richard Barstow
Special music and lyrics by Roger Edens
Orchestrations by Skip Martin
Scenery and costumes by Irene Sharaff
Choral direction by Robert Lenin
Associate to the producer: Herman Shapiro
Lighting by Jean Rosenthal

PROGRAM

Act one:
"At the Opera"
"I Happen to Like New York" (Judy Garland)
John Bubbles
Alan King

Act two:
"The Letter"
Bubbles and King
"Born in a Trunk" (Judy Garland, sequence from *A Star Is Born*)

CITY OF NEW YORK

KNOW ALL MEN BY THESE PRESENTS THAT I

ROBERT F. WAGNER

MAYOR OF THE CITY OF NEW YORK

DO HEREBY CITE FOR DISTINGUISHED AND EXCEPTIONAL SERVICE

JUDY GARLAND

ARTIST WHOSE UNIQUE TALENT HAS DELIGHTED MILLIONS OF MUSIC LOVERS
THROUGHOUT THE WORLD WITH THE CHARM AND VITALITY OF AMERICAN
POPULAR SONGS; ENTERTAINER WHO GIVES OF HERSELF AND HER ART
TO BRING CHEER AND HOPE TO MANY, PARTICULARLY BY HER DEVOTION
TO THE MYRIAD AFFLICTED YOUNGSTERS WHO BENEFIT FROM THE CHILDREN'S
ASTHMA RESEARCH INSTITUTE AND HOSPITAL; DEDICATED SINGER AND
ACTRESS WHO EVOKES THE WARMEST RESPONSE FROM HER MILLIONS
OF ADMIRERS.

In witness whereof, I have hereunto
set my hand and caused the Seal of
the City of New York to be affixed
this ELEVENTH day of MAY 19 59

Robert F. Wagner

"Quick Change" (Bubbles, singers, dancers)
"A Couple of Swells" (Judy Garland, Alan King)
"Judy's Olio" (Judy Garland)

OTHER SONGS

"Me and My Shadow" (with John Bubbles)

ADDENDA

★ This was a seven-day engagement.
★ The last number is "Judy's Olio." "Olio" is a vaudeville term for an act "in one" (a solo) performed in front of the first curtain, or close to the front of the stage.
★ The run was a benefit for the Children's Asthma Research Institute and Hospital in Denver.
★ On May 11, Judy Garland was cited by Mayor Robert Wagner of New York "for distinguished and exceptional service" in behalf of the Children's Hospital.
★ The gross for this engagement was estimated at $190,000, which *Variety* called "one of the alltime one-week takes in any theatre."

RECORDINGS

"The Letter" is available on Capitol ST 1941 (33⅓)

CONTEMPORARY COMMENTS

The New York Times, May 12, 1959
From the roars and the bravos that echoed through the house it was evident that long hair or short the Metropolitan still was the haven of good company.

That magnetism that she always had managed to exert upon an audience is as powerful as ever. The smooth voice that comes from deep down continues to stir the emotions and set an audience on the edge of its seat.

—Lewis Funke

The New Yorker, May 23, 1959
Backed by a well-drilled revue company, Judy Garland sang in New York last week. The engagement, which is now over, was limited; the pleasure it gave was not.

When the voice pours out, as rich and pleading as ever, we know where, and how moved, we are—in the presence of a star, and embarrassed by tears.

—Kenneth Tynan

4 Chicago Opera House

Opening: June 1, 1959
The program, cast, and production personnel were the same as for the Metropolitan Opera engagement.

ADDENDA

★ This was a one-week engagement. The first night was held as a benefit.
★ Note that Baltimore had made its point: Judy sang "I Happen to Like This Town," not "I Happen to Like New York."

CONTEMPORARY COMMENTS

Chicago Sun Times, June 3, 1959
Judy Garland, the minstrel gal with the voice that bubbles and beats, is still riding high on her rainbow.

She may look like a Wagnerian soprano, but she still sings like Andy Hardy's sweetheart. Her voice has that wonderful catch, a soar, and a solid friendship with the beat . . .

The rainbow dims when Judy isn't on stage, although there are a lot of laughs with . . . Alan King. . . . John W. Bubbles has all the polish of an old pro. . . . But the rest of the show should have stayed in the trunk.

—Glenna Syse

5 San Francisco War Memorial Opera House

Opening: July 1, 1959
This was the Metropolitan show.

ADDENDA

★ The engagement was for ten days.

CONTEMPORARY COMMENTS

San Francisco Chronicle, July 2, 1959
Judy Garland opened . . . to a deliriously happy audience who clapped and shouted

Judy Garland and her third husband, Sid Luft.

in approval throughout her performance, and finally ended by giving her a standing ovation.

—Paine Knickerbocker

1960

1 The Palladium, London

August 28, 1960
Conductor: Norrie Paramor

Guest: Quintette choir

SONGS

"I Happen to Like This Town"
"It's Almost Like Being in Love"
"This Can't Be Love"
"Do It Again"
"You Go to My Head"
"Puttin' on The Ritz"
"How Long Has This Been Going On?"
"Just You, Just Me"
"San Francisco"
A vocal tribute to Oscar Hammerstein II
"I Can't Give You Anything but Love"
"One for My Baby"
"It Never Was You"
"The Man That Got Away"
"Over the Rainbow"
"Swanee"

ADDENDA

★ Garland sang thirty-two songs in her two-hour show.

★ This performance, before a standing-room-only crowd, pulled in $12,000. A second appearance was scheduled for September 4, 1960.

CONTEMPORARY COMMENTS

The Associated Press, August 29, 1960
Judy Garland came back to the London Palladium tonight to thunderous acclaim.

Miss Garland had the audience cheering for five minutes before she even appeared on stage. And when she did appear, the audience yelled, cheered and applauded and cried, "Welcome back."

Variety, September 7, 1960
There aren't many artists who can get away without help at the London Palladium. Miss Garland did so triumphantly.

—Dick Richards

2 Palais de Chaillot, Paris

October 5 and 7, 1960
This was the 1960 Palladium show, with the addition of special-material opener for Paris and a Paris song medley.
Orchestra conducted by Norrie Paramor
Piano accompaniment by Dave Lee

CONTEMPORARY COMMENTS

Variety, October 12, 1960
Judy Garland . . . killed them by sheer talent. One of the first standing ovations since the war was handed to her by a wildly applauding audience.

Daily paper notices ran from raves to excellent. Scribes all noted her great voice, poise and ability to overcome the bad acoustics and barnlike aspects of the immense hall.

Judy and Maurice Chevalier at a Paris museum.

3 Olympia Music Hall, Paris

Opening: October 26, 1960

ADDENDA

★ The engagement ran through November 3.

★ This booking was made on the basis of Garland's success at the Palais de Chaillot. The original was to have a vaudeville type show, with acts preceding her. Judy changed her mind and did a one-woman show.

★ Following this engagement, Judy returned to England, where she played Birmingham (November 23) and De Montford Hall in Leicester (November 27th) before appearing at a gala at the Palladium on December 1. (The dates of the two British appearances have not been personally verified.)

CONTEMPORARY COMMENTS

Variety, November 2, 1960
Musical pix and her disks are known mainly to specialists so her success was strictly on her boff talents which overcame lingo differences.

4 The Palladium, London

December 1, 1960

ADDENDA

★ Judy Garland headlined the show, organized by the Variety Artists Benevolent Fund as a show-business tribute to the Saint John Ambulance Brigade. The rest of the lineup came primarily from the then running Palladium revue.
★ In a three-hour show, Garland was on for twenty-five minutes.
★ The Queen Mother was in attendance.

5 Amsterdam, Holland

December 10, 1960
Orchestra conducted by Norrie Paramor

SONGS

"When You're Smiling"
"Sail Away"
"It's Almost Like Being in Love"
"This Can't Be Love"
"You Go to My Head"
"Alone Together"
"Who Cares?"
"Just You, Just Me"
"Just in Time"
"The Man That Got Away"
"San Francisco"
"That's Entertainment"
"I Can't Give You Anything but Love"
"Come Rain or Come Shine"
"If Love Were All"
"Joey, Joey, Joey"
"You Made Me Love You"
"Stormy Weather"

"Rock-a-Bye Your Baby with a Dixie Melody"
"Over the Rainbow"

ADDENDA

★ The audience wouldn't let Garland go. She ended up repeating songs she had already sung for encores.

CONTEMPORARY COMMENTS
Billboard, November 28, 1960
The personal appearance of Judy Garland here . . . is getting much publicity . . .

One of the radio stations will present the show live, and will sign off some two hours later than usual. A special permit from the government will be necessary to accomplish this. The only other time that this has happened previously was on the occasion of a Louis Armstrong night concert.

RECORDINGS
Long-Lost Holland Concert, Obligato GIH 60 (33⅓); *Judy Garland in Holland,* vol. 2, Obligato GIH 610 (33⅓); *Judy Garland in Holland,* vol. 3, Obligato 610 (33⅓).

1961

1 Copenhagen, Denmark

January 19, 20, and 23, 1961

ADDENDA

★ Garland had to turn down an invitation to Pres. Kennedy's pre–Inaugural Ball in Washington on January 19 due to these concert commitments.

2 Oslo, Norway

January 27 and 28, 1961

3 Paris

February 2, 1961

4 Carnegie Hall, New York

April 23, 1961
Music director: Mort Lindsey

SONGS

"When You're Smiling"
Medley:
    "It's Almost Like Being in Love"
    "This Can't Be Love"
"Do It Again"
"You Go to My Head"
"Alone Together"
"Who Cares?"
"Puttin' on the Ritz"
"How Long Has This Been Going On?"
"Just You, Just Me"
"The Man That Got Away"
"San Francisco"
"I Can't Give You Anything but Love"
"That's Entertainment"
"Come Rain Or Come Shine"
"You're Nearer"
"A Foggy Day"
"If Love Were All"
"Zing! Went the Strings of My Heart"
"Stormy Weather"

Garland Medley:
    "You Made Me Love You"
    "For Me and My Gal"
    "The Trolley Song"
"Rock-a-Bye Your Baby with a Dixie
    Melody"
"Over the Rainbow"
"Swanee"
"After You've Gone"
"Chicago"

RECORDINGS

Judy At Carnegie Hall [Capitol S/WBO
    1569 (33⅓)]

ADDENDA

★ This justly famous Carnegie Hall concert was part of a multicity tour. Included in Garland's itinerary were
    Buffalo, New York; Miami Beach,
    Florida; Dallas, Texas; Houston,
    Texas; Birmingham, Alabama; At-
    lanta, Georgia; Charlotte, North
    Carolina; Greensboro, North Caro-
    lina; Philadelphia, Pennsylvania;
    Newark, New Jersey; Chicago, Illi-
    nois; Detroit, Michigan; Cleveland,
    Ohio; Forest Hills, New York; New-
    port, Rhode Island; Atlantic City,
    New Jersey; San Francisco, Califor-
    nia; Los Angeles, California; Denver,
    Colorado; White Plains, New York;
    Hartford, Connecticut; Rochester,
    New York; Pittsburgh, Pennsylvania;
    Boston, Massachusetts; Montreal,
    Canada; Toronto, Canada.

★ The tour started in Houston on February 9 and ended in Washington, D.C.,
on December 9, 1961. She played some
cities more than once.

JUDY

WORLD'S GREATEST ENTERTAINER

JUDY

IN PERSON

JUDY
GARLAND

ONLY NEW YORK CONCERT APPEARANCE

CARNEGIE HALL

SUNDAY APRIL 23 at 8:30 P. M.

ALL SEATS RESERVED: $9.90, 8.80, 7.70, 5.50, 3.30, 2.50 Tax Incl.

TICKETS NOW ON SALE — CARNEGIE HALL BOX OFFICE

CONTEMPORARY COMMENTS

Time, May 5, 1961

There are not many good girl singers these days, although there are plenty of echo chamber yowlers, and there is no one who can come within miles, or ERGs, of Judy. She has, in addition to lungs, clarity, drive and rhythm, an incredible amount of nostalgic pizzaz, a quality in bad repute because it is so unpleasant when it is faked.

. . . the best belter in the business.

Variety, April 26, 1961

It's virtually impossible to remain casual and uninvolved when she's at work. She demands as much from the audience as she does herself but everyone seems to enjoy participating . . . In fact, the aud couldn't resist anything she did.

Variety, October 25, 1961

(reviewing the Pittsburgh and Rochester shows)

Judy Garland had half the audience pressing against the stage begging for more at the end of her two and a half hour show. Rochester theatrical audiences traditionally are reserved.

(She pulled an audience of 4,600 in Rochester and 12,500 in Pittsburgh.)

Variety, November 1, 1961

(reviewing the Boston performance on October 27)

Judy Garland made history in Boston as the first femme performer solo to pack Boston Garden with its absolute 13,909 seat capacity, including seats behind the stage and obstructed perches.

Good Housekeeping, January, 1962

(reviewing the Forest Hills performance of July 1961, before 13,000)

She sat beside the piano and gave poignant new meaning to long forgotten show tunes. Her voice smoothed the stadium like a gentle hand on a silken coverlet, while she crooned intimate love lyrics. When she . . . belted out torch songs, her . . . ringing tones overpowered the sound of the thirty piece orchestra behind her. Between songs she told stories on herself, kidded with the musicians and stagehands, . . . and bantered with the anonymous voices in the crowd. She was like a middle-aged imp cavorting in front of a mirror, unaware that she was being watched.

—Rowland Barber

1962

1 Sahara, Las Vegas

Opening: September 17, 1962
Conductor: Mort Lindsey

SONGS

"Little Drops of Rain"
"Paris Is a Lonely Town"
"Hello, Bluebird"
"Sail Away"
"Joey, Joey, Joey"
"Zing! Went the Strings of My Heart"
"By Myself"
"Just in Time"
"The Man That Got Away"
"San Francisco"
"Chicago"

ADDENDA

★ This was originally a four-week engagement. It was extended two weeks.
★ Garland's act did not include "Over the Rainbow." Its absence was noticed.

CONTEMPORARY COMMENTS

Variety, September 26, 1962
Miss Garland . . . is more dramatically electric than ever, giving her stylized tones a virtual tour-de-force as she sobs, shouts, and caresses.

---

2 **Arie Crown Theatre, Chicago**

November 7, 1962

SONGS

"Hello, Bluebird"
"Do It Again"
"Rock-a-Bye Your Baby with a Dixie Melody"
"Swanee"

ADDENDA

★ 5,000 people attended this performance.
★ Judy was in Chicago for the world premiere of *Gay Purr-ee* at the State Lake. On November 8 and 9, she appeared on stage at the theater.

CONTEMPORARY COMMENTS

Chicago Tribune, November 8, 1962
Miss Garland . . . was having an offnight, plus a bad case of laryngitis.

Thru it all, the high voltage personality operated full force. Songs which wouldn't come out on their own were driven home with clenched fist or her own brand of seemingly infallible timing. It was, to put it rather indelicately, a triumph of moxie —with a capital G.

—Thomas Willis

Time, November 16, 1962
Singing "Swanee," she pointed to an imaginary note in the air, raised her sights, and shot a clean hole through the middle.

. . . she had turned near disasters into comedy skits and had brought off a remarkable performance despite a condition known locally as Chicago throat.

1963

---

1 **Harrah's, Lake Tahoe, Nevada**

Opening: February 7, 1963
Conductor: Leighton Noble
Produced by Art Barkow

SONGS

"Hello, Bluebird"
"The Trolley Song"
"Rock-a-Bye Your Baby with a Dixie Melody"
"Do It Again"
"As Long as He Needs Me"
"San Francisco"

ADDENDA

★ This engagement was scheduled to last three weeks. Judy missed the February 11 show due to a virus. By February 14, she was forced to cancel because of what doctors described as "complete physical exhaustion." Mickey Rooney was called in to substitute.

CONTEMPORARY COMMENTS

Variety, February 20, 1963
She galvanizes her audience as few entertainers have done since this . . . room opened in late '59. And she keeps 'em in a state of frenzy for her full 45 minute turn. The only lulls come with the prolonged applause, the standing ovations (three on opening night), and the cries for "More!"

Her phrasing is perfection, and she interprets the lyrics as if the song were written for her alone.

1964

1 Sydney Stadium, Sydney, Australia

May 11, 1964
Garland sang more than twenty songs in a two-hour show before an audience of 10,000.

2 Festival Hall, Melbourne, Australia

May 20, 1964
Conductor: Mort Lindsey

SONGS

"When You're Smiling"
"The Trolley Song"
"Love of My Life"
"The Man That Got Away"
"San Francisco"
"Puttin' on the Ritz"
"Rock-a-Bye Your Baby with a Dixie Melody"

CONTEMPORARY COMMENTS

Variety, May 27, 1964
The legend of Judy Garland was sadly and brutally shattered . . . last Wednesday before a 7,000 strong audience.

Sixty-seven minutes late in appearing, she talked and aimlessly wandered about the stage and the last thing she seemed to want to do was sing. Her total time on stage was 65 minutes, and she refused to take any bows or encores.

Apart from her fans, the musicians who accompanied Miss Garland were also outraged.

—Raymond Stanley

3 The Palladium, London: "Night of 100 Stars"

July 23, 1964

GARLAND SONGS

"Over the Rainbow"
"Swanee"

ADDENDA

★ This was an annual midnight charity performance in aid of the Actors Orphanage.

CONTEMPORARY COMMENTS

United Press International, July 24, 1964
Three hours out of a London nursing home, Judy Garland stepped into a spotlight at the Palladium Theater today and stopped the biggest charity show of the season. She did it against her doctors' advice.

The Beatles and a host of entertainers faded into the wings as Miss Garland brought the house down . . . The audience cheered so long that the show was forced to close. The final act . . . was cancelled.

Variety, July 29, 1964
It was Judy's Jamboree . . . The mothballed old phrase "show stopping" was for real when an ebullient Judy Garland stepped on stage.

---

4 The Palladium, London (with Liza Minnelli)

November 9, 1964

SONGS

"Once in a Lifetime"
"Just in Time"
"The Man That Got Away"
"Hello, Dolly!" (with Minnelli)
"Together" (with Minnelli)
Medley:
   "Bob White"
   "We Could Make Such Beautiful Music Together" (with Minnelli)
Medley (with Minnelli):
   "Hooray for Love"
   "After You've Gone"
   "By Myself"
   " 'S Wonderful"
   "How About You?"
   "Lover, Come Back to Me"
   "You and the Night and the Music"
   "It All Depends on You"
   "What Now My Love?"
"Who's Sorry Now?" (Minnelli)
"Smile"

"Make Someone Happy"
"The Music That Makes Me Dance"
Medley (with Minnelli):
   "He's Got the Whole World in His Hands"
   "When the Saints Go Marching In"
"Never Will I Marry"
"Swanee"
"Chicago"
"Over the Rainbow"
"San Francisco"

ADDENDA

★ This was originally to have been a one-night engagement. Tickets sold out so quickly that a second night was booked for the overflow. The second performance sold out as well.

RECORDINGS

Judy Garland and Liza Minnelli: Live at the Palladium [Capitol S/WBO 2295 (33⅓)], *The Judy Garland/Liza Minnelli Concert at The London Palladium* [Capitol EM 1249 (33⅓)], and *Judy Garland/Liza Minnelli "Live" at The London Palladium* [Capitol ST 1191 (33⅓)]

CONTEMPORARY COMMENTS

The New York Times, November 10, 1964
Judy Garland and her daughter Liza Minnelli gave their first concert together last night and they captured the audience in an emotional performance at the Palladium.

The audience, including the standees lining the back and side walls, enjoyed the mother and daughter act, but it was Miss Garland who turned cheers into ovations.

1965

1 O'Keefe Centre, Toronto, Canada

Opening: February 8, 1965
Orchestra conducted by Mort Lindsey
Production supervised by Mark Herron

Guests:
Nipsey Russell
The Allen Brothers

SONGS

"Swing Low, Sweet Chariot"
"This Can't Be Love"
"The Trolley Song"
"Rock-a-Bye Your Baby with a Dixie Melody"
"The Man That Got Away"
"Chicago"
"Smile"
"By Myself"

ADDENDA

★ This was a one-week engagement.

CONTEMPORARY COMMENTS

Variety, February 17, 1965
To her audience . . . , she still had a touch of the old alchemy to draw a standing, cheering ovation . . .

But, in truth, Miss Garland's voice was like sandpaper grinding, often missing the notes completely.

2 Fontainebleau, Miami Beach, Florida

Opening: March 11, 1965
Guests: The Allen Brothers

SONGS

"He's Got the Whole World in His Hands"
"When You're Smiling"
"Smile"
"Just in Time"
"Make Someone Happy"
"By Myself"
"The Music That Makes Me Dance"
"What Now, My Love?"

ADDENDA

★ This appearance was through March 20.
★ The local critics were pointedly bemused by the reviews Garland had gotten for the Toronto concert. Those reports clearly did not jibe with the performance they saw in Miami.

CONTEMPORARY COMMENTS

Miami Herald, March 13, 1965
She sang a full hour of tunes—some with her own trademark—others as new as today's hit parade. And she delivered each as though there was only today and tomorrow. . . . her voice danced.

—George Bourke

4 Cincinnati Gardens, Cincinnati, Ohio

May 29, 1965

CONTEMPORARY COMMENTS

Billboard, June 12, 1965
Miss Garland, in the first half of her concert, did six songs in a 20 minute period. A 10 minute intermission was stretched to nearly an hour, after which Miss Garland returned to the stage, supported by two local physicians who announced that she had a virus and temperature and would be unable to continue.

5 Thunderbird, Las Vegas

Opening: June 15, 1965
Conductor: Nick Perito, leading the Nat Brandwynne Orchestra
Choreography: René DeHaven
Produced by Jerry Schafer

Guests:
The Allen Brothers
Nelson Sardelli
The Thunderbird Dancers

SONGS

"He's Got the Whole World in His Hands"
"It's Almost Like Being in Love"
"This Can't Be Love"
"Smile"
"Just in Time"
"Over the Rainbow"

ADDENDA

★ This engagement was for two weeks.

CONTEMPORARY COMMENTS

Variety, June 23, 1965
With an air of confidence with which she seemed to want to reassure her fans, she grabbed the mike and in the distinctive Garland tones hoped for, socked across a memorable "He's Got the Whole World in His Hands."

6 Forest Hills Stadium, New York

July 17, 1965
Music director: Mort Lindsey

SONGS

"He's Got the Whole World in His Hands"
"It's Almost Like Being in Love"
"This Can't Be Love"
"Do It Again"
"As Long as He Needs Me"
"Just in Time"
"That's Entertainment"
"What Now, My Love?"
"When You're Smiling"
"Zing! Went the Strings of My Heart"
"The Man That Got Away"
"You Made Me Love You"
"For Me and My Gal"
"The Trolley Song"
"By Myself"
"Rock-a-Bye Your Baby with a Dixie Melody"
"San Francisco"
"Chicago"
"Over the Rainbow"

ADDENDA

★ Judy performed before an audience of 10,000.

CONTEMPORARY COMMENTS

The New York Times, July 19, 1965
That fascinating phenomenon of modern show business, the long and widely publicized love affair between Judy Garland and her following, was on full display Saturday night . . .

It [the audience] was extremely knowledgeable, well aware that Miss Garland's voice is just a memory; that she is often off pitch and that she frequently forgets lyrics.

It was also quick to respond to that potent fervor that Miss Garland packs into her delivery, even when her voice quavers and cracks. This audience also appreciated her wondrous sense of showmanship, with calculated pause, imitation dance steps and hand gestures that were not merely the nervous mannerisms of many television performers.

—Murray Schumach

Billboard, July 31, 1965
Judy Garland gave an energetic, frenetic and peripatetic 90 minute performance that was pure magic. . . . It was indeed difficult to judge on her voice alone, although for the most part it had power, control, and stayed on key. She simply is one of the rare artists who can transfix an audience by sheer personal magnetism.

—Robert Sobel

7 San Carlos, Puerto Rico

Opening: August 31, 1965

ADDENDA

★ This engagement lasted until September 5, 1965. (This engagement has not been personally verified.)

8 Greek Theatre, Los Angeles

Opening: September 13, 1965

ADDENDA

★ Garland broke her arm the day after her opening. She went on the next day with Mickey Rooney, Martha Raye, and Johnny Mathis helping out.

9 Sahara, Las Vegas

Opening: November 30, 1965

Guests:
Dave Barry
The Paul Steffen Dancers
Louis Basil's Sahara Orchestra

SONGS

"Just in Time"
"As Long as He Needs Me"
"What Now, My Love?"
"Joey, Joey, Joey"
"Stormy Weather"
"Do It Again"
"Rock-a-Bye Your Baby with a Dixie
   Melody"
"Chicago"
"You Made Me Love You"
"For Me and My Gal"
"The Trolley Song"
"Over the Rainbow"

ADDENDA

★ The engagement lasted until December
   15, 1965.

CONTEMPORARY COMMENTS

Variety, December 8, 1965
When she's through there's hardly a dry
eye in the audience. Miss Garland may
one day become the reason for the five
cornered handkerchief. The standard
hanky just isn't big enough to handle the
tears she wrings from the audience.

10 Astrodome, Houston, Texas

December 17, 1965
Conductor: Mort Lindsey

Guest: The Supremes

ADDENDA

★ The Astrodome had opened in April
   1965. It was a 60,000-seat auditorium,
   which Judy did not fill.

1966

1 Diplomat Hotel, Hollywood, Florida

Opening: February 2, 1966
Conductor: Nick Perito, leading the Van
   Smith Orchestra

Guest: Pat Henry

ADDENDA

★ This was a one-week engagement.

CONTEMPORARY COMMENTS

Variety, February 9, 1966
. . . Miss Garland in basically the same
show she did at the Fontainebleau last
season . . .

Voice shows even more tremolo than
usual, and early nervousness and mike
problems may be the reason her pipes
cracked occasionally. She also had a tendency to lose both key and rhythm, but
neither factor is deterrent to fans.

2 El Patio Club, Mexico City

Opening: August 17, 1966

ADDENDA

★ This was scheduled to be a two-week engagement. Judy performed for three evenings; the rest of the schedule was canceled due to illness.

1967

1 Westbury Music Fair, New York

Opening: June 13, 1967
Conductor: Colin Romoff

Guests:
Rip Taylor
John Bubbles

SONGS

"That's Entertainment"
"San Francisco"
"The Trolley Song"
"Just in Time"
"Old Man River"
"Swanee"
"Over the Rainbow"

ADDENDA

★ This was a six-day engagement.

CONTEMPORARY COMMENTS

Variety, June 21, 1967
Her once magnificent voice is virtually shattered. There are times when she summons those notes which made her fa-

mous. She was applauded midsong for these.

The age level [of the fans] mattered little. . . . The youngsters cheered as lustily and hung on every note . . . with as much zeal as their elders.

Billboard, July 1, 1967
But even hoarse, Miss Garland gives a song more meaning, more vitality than many a healthy performer.

—Robert Sobel

2 Camden Music Fair, New Jersey

Opening: July 10, 1967

ADDENDA

★ This was a one-week engagement.

3 The Palace Theater, New York (third appearance)

Opening: July 31, 1967
A Group V Ltd. Production
Music director: Bobby Cole
Staged by Richard Barstow
Costumes by Bill Smith Travilla

Guests:
John Bubbles   Lorna Luft
Jackie Vernon   Joe Luft
Francis Brunn

SONGS

"I Feel a Song Coming On"
Medley:
  "It's Almost Like Being in Love"
  "This Can't Be Love"

Garland Medley:
   "You Made Me Love You"
   "For Me and My Gal"
   "The Trolley Song"
"What Now, My Love?"
"Bob White" (with Lorna Luft)
"Jamboree Jones" (with Lorna Luft)
"Together" (with Lorna Luft, Joe Luft)
"Over the Rainbow"
"Old Man River"
"That's Entertainment"
"I Loved Him, but He Didn't Love Me"
"Rock-a-Bye Your Baby with a Dixie
   Melody"

ADDENDA

★ This was a month-long engagement.
★ Francis Brunn was a former circus star.

CONTEMPORARY COMMENTS

Variety, August 2, 1967
With the authority in stance, style and singing born of experience and authentic stardom through two generations, Miss Garland worked in "one" to full-stage.

. . . with the star most of all in command of every nuance whether it was a miscue, the recalcitrant mikes, the overly exuberant talkers from the audience, or fluffed lyrics.

—Abel Green

RECORDINGS

Judy Garland: At Home at The Palace, Opening Night. [ABC/S 620 (33⅓)]

4 Boston Common

August 31, 1967
Orchestra conducted by Bobby Cole

SONGS

"I Feel a Song Coming On"
"It's Almost Like Being in Love"
"Just in Time"
"Old Man River"
"The Trolley Song"
"Rock-a-Bye Your Baby with a Dixie
   Melody"
"Over the Rainbow"

ADDENDA

★ At the end of the performance, Mayor John Collins presented Judy with a silver bowl "on behalf of the 100,000 people who are here and the two and a half million who wish they could be here."
★ Following this engagement, Judy went to Cincinnati. (I have not been able to verify the Cincinnati booking.)

CONTEMPORARY COMMENTS

Boston Herald Examiner, September 1, 1967
Singer Judy Garland captivated an audience estimated at 100,000 persons . . . with more than an hour of the music that has made her a legend.

At one point, after an impromptu suggestion from a male admirer in the audience, the crowd serenaded Judy with several choruses of "Hello, Judy," sung to the melody of "Hello, Dolly."

—Bruce McCabe

Following page: Joe and Lorna Luft, Judy Garland, and John Bubbles at The Palace, 1967.

5 Post Pavilion of Music, Washington, D.C.

September 8 and 9, 1967

ADDENDA

★ The Post Pavilion is actually in Columbia, Maryland.
★ David Frye came on unannounced.

CONTEMPORARY COMMENTS

Washington Post, September 9, 1967
. . . her voice is ragged, but it's been ragged for years. Her rhythm is catching even when she throws it around. Her diction is a marvel of clarity.

In all this, its [*sic*] timing, the choice of informalities and the apparent improvisation, more is conveyed than said. It assumes a link between you out there and me up here. The assumptions are wholly valid and the evening wound up a love affair between a public personality and her public.

6 Chicago Opera House

September 14 through 16, 1967

Guests:

Francis Brunn	Lorna Luft
The Dunhills	Joe Luft
David Frye	

CONTEMPORARY COMMENTS

Chicago Tribune, September 15, 1967
The low notes, always husky, are brittle now. The top notes are an amplified howl. But they applaud. They start applauding at the first note, and stand to applaud some more at the last. Never has such a mutual admiration society convened in the Civic Opera House.

—William Leonard

7 Kiel Auditorium, St. Louis, Missouri

September 27, 1967

8 Cobo Arena, Detroit, Michigan

September 29, 1967

CONTEMPORARY COMMENTS

Detroit News, September 30, 1967
What is left is nostalgia—with enough of the special magic to make an evening with Judy Garland an unbelievable experience.

It would be easy to say the magic was all in the minds of the beholders. But even the most hardened cynic might wonder if he hadn't caught a twinkle of it himself from this capricious leprechaun on stage.

—Bob Carr

9 Clowes Memorial Hall, Indianapolis, Indiana

Two nights: October 1 and 2, 1967

ADDENDA

★ Following this engagement, Garland played Columbus, Ohio. (The Columbus booking has not been personally verified.)

CONTEMPORARY COMMENTS

Variety, October 11, 1967
Judy Garland chalked up a local victory in her current "comeback." She grossed $33,940 against a possible $36,000. Attendance was 4,050 out of a potential 4,400.

10 Bushnell Memorial, Hartford, Connecticut

October 20 and 21, 1967
A Concert Guild Production

Guests:
Hines, Hines, and Dad
Francis Brunn
Lorna Luft
Joe Luft

SONGS

"I Feel a Song Coming On"
"Old Man River"
"I Loved Him"
"Over the Rainbow"

ADDENDA

★ One of the Hines, Hines, and Dad was Gregory.

CONTEMPORARY COMMENTS

Hartford Courant, October 21, 1967
What other tiny, feminine woman, who never toted a barge or lifted a bale, could . . . make it sound as though she knew what it meant? None but Judy.

People have tried to explain her mystique but it could only be reported that as the program closed old men and women and young people flocked to the stage to reach out and touch her hand.

And when, in a husky voice, she sang her last song, "Over the Rainbow"—what else?—it was something that sent shivers down the spine.

—Barbara Carlson

11 Caesar's Palace, Las Vegas

Opening: November 29, 1967
Produced by Dave Victorson

Guests:
Lou Rawls (alternate shows with Garland)
Checkmates Ltd.
The Malmo Girls
Nat Brandwynne Orchestra

SONGS

"I Feel a Song Coming On"
"Just in Time"
"It's Almost Like Being in Love"
"How Insensitive"
"That's Entertainment"
"What Now, My Love?"
"Old Man River"
"Rock-a-Bye Your Baby with a Dixie Melody"
"Swanee"
"Over the Rainbow"

★ Garland appeared only at the midnight shows.

CONTEMPORARY COMMENTS

Variety, December 6, 1967

There is the magic of the Garland presence wedded to the almost elusive vocal quality that makes her 45 minute set a curiously unsettling experience. Whether in voice or not, there is always a super-charged authority present in sometimes awkward, often disturbing, yet never dull or lackadaisical delivery of any song, ballad or uptempo.

12 Felt Forum, New York

Opening: December 25, 1967

Guests:
The Dick Williams Singers
Mort Lindsey Orchestra

SONGS

"What Now, My Love?"
"The Battle Hymn of the Republic"
"Swanee"
"Over the Rainbow"

ADDENDA

★ Tony Bennett came up from the audience to sing a Christmas song to Judy.

CONTEMPORARY COMMENTS

Variety, December 27, 1967

Here is the Garland myth and magic at work. Personal theatre for many, vicarious nostalgia for the rest, there is a deep, or masochistic sense of participation in almost every number: Will Our Judy Make It Over the Rainbow?

—Leonard Levinson

1968

1 Civic Center, Baltimore, Maryland

February 1968

Guests:
Tony Bennett
Woody Allen

2 Back Bay Theatre, Boston

May 24 and 25, 1968

Guests:
Lorna Luft
Joe Luft

CONTEMPORARY COMMENTS

Variety, May 29, 1968

Judy Garland pulled a no show the second night of her two night concert . . .

The cancellation was not anticipated because Miss Garland had come to town the day before her first performance . . . and made several p.a.'s. One was at the Chelsea Naval Hospital, where she sang "Over the Rainbow" for wounded vets.

3 Garden State Arts Center, Holmdel, New Jersey

Opening: June 25, 1968

ADDENDA

★ The engagement lasted through June 29, 1968.

CONTEMPORARY COMMENTS

New York Times, June 30, 1968
Judy Garland fell down a short flight of stairs at stagefront tonight [June 29] during her performance . . . The singer was moved by ambulance . . .

Miss Garland stumbled several times in the first 20 minutes of her performance and tripped once on a microphone cord. Her voice seemed unsteady and off key and patrons were streaming out before the accident.

4 John F. Kennedy Stadium: Philadelphia Music Festival

July 20, 1968

OTHER ACTS

Count Basie Band
Jackie Wilson Trio
New York Electric String Ensemble

SONGS

"Once in a Lifetime"
"It's Almost Like Being in Love"
"Zing! Went the Strings of My Heart"
"The Sweetest Sounds"
"Over the Rainbow"

ADDENDA

★ The local review was titled "Garland Sings to 20,000 in Stadium." Count Basie and the other acts received two paragraphs at the end of the article.
★ Basie sat in with the orchestra to accompany Judy.

CONTEMPORARY COMMENTS

Philadelphia Inquirer, July 21, 1968
A warmly affectionate Judy Garland was her old self . . . , which means that she held the audience in the palm of her hand from her first entrance.

It was a love affair from first to last between Judy and her audience, with whom she chatted amiably between numbers.

This was not the longest show of the Philadelphia Music Festival series but was probably the best.

—Samuel L. Singer

5 "Talk of the Town," London

Opening: December 30, 1968
Conductor: Burt Rhodes

SONGS

"I Belong to London"
"It's Gonna Be a Great Day"
"The Man That Got Away"
"Just in Time"
"You Made Me Love You"
"For Me and My Gal"
"The Trolley Song"
"Over the Rainbow"

ADDENDA

★ This was a five-week engagement.
★ A pirate tape was made of this performance. It was the cause of litigation between Burt Rhodes and Garland. It later appeared as the album *Judy. London. 1969* [Juno S 1000 (33⅓)].

CONTEMPORARY COMMENTS

Variety, January 15, 1969
Those looking to Judy Garland for an impeccable, stopwatch timed, disciplined act clearly don't know what the gal is all about.

But those who are not abashed by genuine nostalgia and who can recognize and rise to the peculiar alchemy that makes a woman a personality as well as a performer will have a very good time.

1969

1 Stockholm, Sweden

March 19, 1969

ADDENDA

★ These Scandinavian performances were a double bill with Judy Garland and Johnny Ray.

2 Malmö, Sweden

March 23, 1969

3 Falkoner Center, Copenhagen, Denmark

March 25, 1969

ADDENDA

★ This was Judy Garland's last concert.

6

TELEVISION APPEARANCES

———————— ★ ————————

*"We all reacted like abandoned children. Musicals were over.
A lot of people could have gone straight into television except we had been taught
never to go on television. Some people went home and shook.
Others waited by their telephone."*

Debbie Reynolds, *Debbie: My Life*

———————— ★ ————————

"Judy Garland held television in the palm of her hand last night."

Jack Gould, *The New York Times* February 26, 1962

———————— ★ ————————

Judy Garland appeared on television sporadically between 1951 and 1969. Those appearances covered virtually the entire span of her concert-years career. Leaving aside for the moment her ill-fated twenty-six-week series, she made half a dozen major TV specials, was a special guest star on musical variety and late-night talk shows, was a guest host on "The Merv Griffin Show," a mystery guest on "What's My Line?," and was interviewed with some regularity throughout the years.

This, in addition to the taping for television of her 1964 London Palladium concert and her British TV appearances, makes it all the more disconcerting that the record of Judy Garland's small-screen career is virtually inaccessible to the average viewer. Indeed, it is far easier to view out-takes of *Annie Get Your Gun* than it is to see her 1955 *Ford Star Jubilee* special or her appearances on the Andy Williams, Perry Como, or Sammy Davis, Jr., shows.

Television, particularly in the 1950s and early 1960s, was a peculiarly evanescent medium. Programming was largely owned by the sponsors, not the networks or the producers. Despite the filming or taping of performances, many of the older shows have disappeared due to lack of interest on the part of the sponsor/owner or disputed ownership rights. In addition, television only discovered an economic resource in its history with the development of the syndicated rerun market, and this was largely dominated by situation comedies until after Garland's time.

Thus, what is in effect the only visual record of the mature artist at the height of her powers, and the record of how she later compensated for declining vocal prowess with superior showmanship and anecdotal skills, is substantially lost from public view. For television captured Judy Garland's ability to dominate a stage and captivate an audience. But it captured, too, the delicacy of that talent and how easily it could be hampered—and the communication between the performer and audience disrupted—by poor direction or insensitive stage values.

By 1955, Judy Garland had confounded the professional Cassandras in Hollywood and made an indelible mark on the history of show business, beyond anything she might have achieved at MGM. Against all the odds, she had returned to the screen, giving what even her detractors conceded was a brilliant performance in *A Star Is Born*. She had cut a swath on the concert stage, single-handedly revitalizing both the old vaudeville "two-a-day" and the Palace Theater (where Danny Kaye and others followed). And she had proven that —critics, studio politics, and dire prophecies to the side—the ticket-buying public was enthralled by her.

It was a unique performer and public personality that CBS signed to inaugurate its "Ford Star Jubilee" series of specials, and she was treated accordingly. The network fully intended to capitalize on a much publicized "phoenixlike" rise, issuing regular publicity releases before the broadcast, using still novel color cameras, and, in general, designing the sets and production around her. Judy Garland was treated as a "star," and the "special" was meant to be just that.

The program was a success. It incorporated elements of her well-honed concert revue; the songs were primarily Garland standards guaranteed to please, and Judy's voice was magnificent. It attracted the largest audience of any television special up to that time, and CBS quickly opened negotiations to sign Garland for the small screen. On December 25, 1955, Judy signed a five-year contract to make one special a year for the next five years, beginning January 1, 1956.

Trouble erupted immediately. CBS, much like MGM before it, had found a formula for Garland that worked. The network wanted the next special to be a linear descendant of the first: Judy would do her established routines and sing the songs the public already associated with her. The problem with the formula for the performer, however, was that it gulped down half a lifetime of material in each sixty- or ninety-minute bite. Garland had other ideas. She wanted to husband her standards and expand her material.

The resulting special, which aired in

April 1956, is, perhaps, some of the most anomalous thirty minutes in Judy Garland's highly eventful career. Staged by Richard Avedon, with Nelson Riddle as music director, the program was a peculiar combination of visual oddities and aural excellence. It was dismissed as a complete failure, ultimately leading to an acrimonious divorce between Garland and CBS and the dissolution of the five-year contract. Yet the *Judy* album, which was derived from this show, is considered by many to be her finest and was in the Top 40 for five weeks.

Compare this special to the British TV broadcast of part of the Judy Garland/Liza Minnelli concert at the London Palladium in 1964.

By the end of 1964, Judy's voice was past its peak, and she didn't have her previous ability to make it do exactly as she wanted, as she obliquely, and ruefully, admitted during the performance. But the staging was simple: orchestra at the back of the stage, the performers in simple attire, singing and talking to the audience. The camera merely focused on them, alternating closeups, long shots, and medium shots. And by doing so, it caught Judy mugging, interacting with the audience, and thoroughly enjoying Liza's performance. It also captured the obvious affection, admiration, and sense of fun between the two women onstage.

The result was an unusually enjoyable hour of television. Yet the recordings from the Palladium concert are certainly not among the best for Judy's voice or for her range and control. (Although, perversely, Capitol cut some of Garland's best vocals from its Palladium releases.)

The dichotomies are significant. People sit down in front of a TV prepared to have the eye take precedence over the ear, and they remember TV performances visually. But, in fact, there is a tension between the two senses, with the viewer's attention shifting, depending upon the programming. In a dramatic performance, for example, the musical message is subliminal as the eye focuses on the action. If what the audience hears doesn't support what it sees, the result is disengagement and a general sense of dramatic letdown.

But in a musical format, the balance of power reverses. The viewers more or less consciously register the sets, costuming, and physical movements as either supporting the singing and music or not. If what they see is distracting or discordant, the effect of what they hear is diminished or disrupted. There's a sense of musical failure, and this can be devastating to a singer. Conversely, if what they see sustains and backs the vocalist and musicians, it illuminates and amplifies what they hear. This transforms a performance into an event.

When the vocal and visual are united in both quality and purpose, the results can be stunning, as they were in Garland's 1962 special with Frank Sinatra and Dean Martin. Judy's voice was in its prime, as was Sinatra's. The easy and happy melding of the three styles created a heady mix of casual elegance, intensity, and informality. The program centered on singing, with no attempt to bring in unnecessarily ornate choreography, set design, or forced humor. This was unusual, and unusually successful, television. It acknowledged the vocal magic of Garland and Sinatra as the center, and the reason, for the show.

The most elaborately staged number was Judy's "The Man That Got Away." The camera came at Garland sitting alone at a table in a small room. It moved from an overhead shot to a medium shot, as Judy took the song out of its opening measures, and became a long shot as she slowly left the set and walked into the darkness, trailing the last bars of "the man that got away." The simplicity of the setting, restrained camera work, and vivid use of light and shadows both framed and illuminated her singing. The result was glorious, simultaneously visually and vocally arresting.

The program was a resounding success.

The point is not that Judy Garland was always superb and that an unsuccessful program was always someone else's fault. But her talent was an extraordinarily delicate one for the small screen.

Garland's concert persona, which television translated into the musical-variety format, relied on a dynamic balance between the richness of her singing and her unusual ability to communicate with her audience on a profoundly human level. The last third of her 1962 special, for example, was pure concert format: Judy was in slacks on the stage and runway, singing and doing her stage bits before a live audience. (This segment, by the way, is often used as a stand-in for her 1961 Carnegie Hall concert.) It is quintessential Garland, and the excitement of the audience is transmitted to the viewer, becoming part of the performance, building its power. Anything that distracted from the

sense of immediacy and human-to-human contact Garland could create disrupted her impact. On TV, it was easy to inadvertently come between Judy and the person on the other side of the box.

Talk shows were a natural medium for her, for not only would she sing, unencumbered by overdirection, but she could engage in unscripted conversation. Judy Garland was widely known in Hollywood as a wit and raconteur; her late-night appearances on television revealed to the public at large the engagingly impish and self-deprecating sense of humor with which she had been entrancing her concert and nightclub audiences. Her reminiscences on the Jack Paar programs, for instance, brought to life some of Hollywood's most glamorous stars—as teenagers sneaking cigarettes outside MGM's one-room schoolhouse or as somewhat eccentric house guests—and her stories about the traveling Gumm Sisters and vaudeville revived a world most of the audience never knew or remembered only dimly.

The general public (as opposed to fans) remembers the adult Judy Garland most vividly from these television appearances. They remember a woman who talked brightly on late-night TV and whose mature vocal style is framed for them by the greater or lesser success of her television specials and guest spots. A woman far removed from Dorothy on the yellow brick road. A woman who seemed to fit the mythology developed about her in the press. For talk-show interviewers almost inevitably referred to Garland's saga of trials and tribulations. Indeed, in many cases, their introductions set this as the explicit context in which she would perform.

Judy Garland's regularly reported show-business demises and phoenixlike rises covered enough column inches to make the original mythical bird flush in envy. Where other performers would have career ups and downs, Garland's were inevitably reported as the final trip "over the rainbow" or as "Judy's new rainbow." These obvious turns of phrase eventually became mandatory clichés with lives of their own.

Judy Garland's television appearances, particularly her later ones, are usually passed over quietly or considered a less-than-glorious aspect of her career, an obviously unfair judgment given some exceptionally good shows. But while other performers might have a good program, or a mediocre one, and go on with their careers, Judy's performances were fitted into an established mythology. She was too difficult and unreliable to build a show around. Or she was a living "legend," making another comeback.

The problem with myths, however, is that while they start as a way of explaining apparently inexplicable phenomena, they end up obscuring reality. The reality of Judy Garland on television is that a full range of exceptional, and exceptionally dynamic yet delicate, talents were displayed by a complex and vital performer. On television, at least, Judy Garland would have been far better served to have been seen, not as a "legend," but simply as a singer.

The listing below SONGS INCLUDED refers only to songs performed by Judy Garland. Any additional performers will be noted.

1 "Red Cross Fund Program"

February 27, 1951
CBS (30 minutes)
Master of ceremonies: Ed Sullivan

GUESTS

President Harry Truman
Secretary of Defense George C. Marshall
E. Roland Harriman
General David Sarnoff
Bob Hope
Bing Crosby
Kate Smith
Judy Garland

ADDENDA

★ This Garland appearance was taped, not live.

2 *A Star Is Born* World Premiere

September 29, 1954
From the Pantages Theater, Los Angeles
Celebrity interviews and the proceedings surrounding the world premiere of the picture *A Star Is Born*.

ADDENDA

★ This was the first nationally televised premiere of a motion picture.
★ The show was successful enough that it was rebroadcast the following night.

3 "Tonight"

September 29, 1954
NBC (90 minutes)
Announcer: Gene Rayburn
Judy Garland and her husband, Sid Luft, were broadcast by mobile hookup at the premiere of *A Star Is Born*. The appearance consisted of a few moments of conversation with Hollywood emcee Jack Carson, who was also in the film.

STARRING

Steve Allen

ADDENDA

★ The segment devoted to the premiere ran from 11:45 to 11:59 (E.T.).
★ The celebrities who were greeted on the way to see the picture were (in order of appearance): Debbie Reynolds, Dennis Morgan, Susan Ball, Kim Novak, Peggy Lee, Ray Bolger, Gordon Scott, Danny Thomas, Andy Devine, William Bendix, Natalie Wood, Sophie Tucker, George Jessel, Joan Crawford, Cesar Romero, Marie Wilson, Gloria Nelson, Cameron Mitchell, Jack Palance, Doris Day, June Haver, Fred MacMurray.

4 Academy Awards Nominations Show

NBC
February 12, 1955
Judy was nominated for Best Actress for *A Star Is Born*.

5 "The Ford Star Jubilee"

"The Judy Garland Show" (Special)
September 24, 1955
CBS (90 minutes) (color)
Producer: Sid Luft
Production adviser: Ralph Levy
Associate producers:
    Bernie Gold
    Paul Harrison
Director: Paul Harrison
Music: Jack Cathcart
Writers:
    Carroll Carroll
    John Tackaberry

Choreographer: Miriam Wilson
Origination: Hollywood ("live")
Hostess: Judy Garland
Emcee: David Wayne

GUESTS

Mitsuko Sawamura	The Goofers
The Escorts	Robert Lamouret

SONGS INCLUDED

"This Is the Time of the Evening"
"While We're Young"
"You Made Me Love You"
"Swanee"
"It's de-Lovely"
"But Not for Me"

Garland Medley:
    "For Me and My Gal"
    "The Boy Next Door"
    "The Trolley Song"
"Rock-a-Bye Your Baby with a Dixie
    Melody"
Palace Medley:
    "Shine On, Harvest Moon"
    "Some of These Days"
    "My Man"
    "I Don't Care"
"Get Happy"
"The Man That Got Away"
"A Couple of Swells" (with David Wayne)
"Over the Rainbow"

ADDENDA

★ This program is usually cited as Judy's television debut. It was, in the sense that this was the first time she appeared on TV in a variety-show format.

★ A portable dressing room was built by "Ford Star Jubilee" so that Garland would lose no time in costume changes and could spend most of the ninety-minute show before the cameras. Her costumes were especially designed for the still novel color cameras.

★ This was the introduction of "This Is the Time of the Evening," written for Judy's television debut by Roger Edens.

★ The Garland Medley was included in the show at the request of fans who wrote in advance asking that she sing songs from her movies.

★ This was the premiere program of the "Ford Star Jubilee" series.

David Wayne and Judy Garland on "Ford Star Jubilee." Following page: From Judy's 1956 CBS special.

★ On November 3, 1956, "Ford Star Jubilee" presented the first television showing of the movie *The Wizard of Oz*.

★ Mitsuko Sawamura was a twelve-year-old Japanese singer of American popular songs (she learned them phonetically); The Goofers were a comedy quintet; Robert Lamouret was a ventriloquist; and The Escorts were a dancing chorus.

CONTEMPORARY COMMENTS

The New York Times, September 26, 1955
Always exciting to watch and hear.

Perhaps there are other singers who can deliver a version of "Over the Rainbow" with more technical skill than Miss Garland. But no one has yet been heard who can sing this song with the poignant appeal Judy gives it.

—J. P. Shanley

6 **"Tonight"**

December 26, 1955
NBC
Judy was interviewed briefly through a mobile hookup from Hollywood at the premiere of *The Man with the Golden Arm*.

7 **"The Judy Garland Show"** (Special)

April 8, 1956
CBS (30 minutes)
Producer: Sid Luft
Director: Richard Avedon

Music director: Nelson Riddle
Hostess: Judy Garland

GUESTS

Peter Gennaro
Leonard Pennario

SONGS INCLUDED

"Last Night When We Were Young"
"I Feel a Song Comin' On"
"April Showers"
"Life Is Just a Bowl of Cherries"
"Dirty Hands, Dirty Face"
"Maybe I'll Come Back"

ADDENDA

★ This special was the basis for the *Judy* album (1956), Capitol T/DT-734, music arranged and conducted by Nelson Riddle. It is widely thought to be one of the finest of her recording studio albums. [See section H, #2]

★ Leonard Pennario was, in addition to being a guest, also Judy's accompanist on the piano.

★ The program preempted the regularly scheduled "General Electric Theater" that night and is occasionally miscited as a "G.E. Theater" production. It was a CBS special.

★ On December 25, 1955, Garland signed a contract with CBS for one program a year for five years, beginning January 1, 1956. This special was to have been the first of the five. It was the only one produced under the agreement. In March 1957, Garland filed suit against CBS for breach of contract and libel.

8 "Golden Globe Awards" Presentation

March 16, 1960
Judy appeared with other previous winners. She had won for *A Star Is Born*.

9 "Here's Hollywood"

June 23, 1961
NBC (30 minutes)
Producer: William Kayden
Directors:
Van Fox
Gene Law
Writers:
Martin Wark
Liz Murphy
Bill Walker

STARRING

Helen O'Connell
Dean Miller
Helen O'Connell interviewed Judy, who was filming *Judgment at Nuremberg*.

10 "Here's Hollywood"

January 23, 1962
NBC (30 minutes)
Producer: William Kayden
Directors:
Van Fox
Gene Law
Writers:
Martin Wark
Liz Murphy
Bill Walker

STARRING

Helen O'Connell
Jack Linkletter
Judy was interviewed in West Berlin by
Jack Linkletter.

---

11 **"The Judy Garland Show" (Special)**

February 25, 1962
CBS (60 minutes) (black & white)
Executive producers:
Freddie Fields
David Begelman
Producer: Norman Jewison
Associate producer: Chiz Schultz
Director: Norman Jewison
Music director: Mort Lindsey
Creative consultant: Kay Thompson
Art director: Gary Smith
Special material:
Frank Peppiat
John Aylesworth

GUESTS

Frank Sinatra
Dean Martin

SONGS INCLUDED

"Just in Time"
"When You're Smiling"
"You Do Something to Me" (with Frank
Sinatra)
"Too Marvelous for Words" (Frank
Sinatra)
"You Do Something to Me" (reprise)
(with Frank Sinatra)
"You Must Have Been a Beautiful Baby"
(Dean Martin)
"You Do Something to Me" (reprise)
(with Frank Sinatra, Dean Martin)

"I See Your Face Before Me" (Frank
Sinatra)
"The Man That Got Away"
"The One I Love Belongs to Somebody
Else" (Frank Sinatra, Dean Martin)
"I Can't Give You Anything but Love"
Garland Medley (with Frank Sinatra,
Dean Martin):
"Let There Be Love"
"You're Nobody Till Somebody Loves
You"
"You Made Me Love You"
"The Trolley Song"
"Rock-a-Bye Your Baby with a Dixie
Melody"
"Swanee"
"San Francisco"

ADDENDA

★ Both the vocal and visual effect of "The
Man That Got Away" number in this
special are, unusually, comparable to
the original in *A Star Is Born*.
★ This show was taped over a period of
three nights before audiences that
started lining up as much as two hours
before the studio doors opened.

RECORDINGS

"I Can't Give You Anything but Love,"
"Just in Time," and "The One I Love
Belongs to Somebody Else" (with
Frank Sinatra and Dean Martin) from
this special are on *Frank Sinatra and
Judy Garland* [ZAFIRO ZV 892 (33⅓)].
"Let There Be Love"/"You're Nobody
Till Somebody Loves You" is on *Judy
Garland: The Great Duets* [Paragon
1001 (33⅓)].

CONTEMPORARY COMMENTS

The New York Times, February 26, 1962
The pairing of Miss Garland and Mr. Sinatra early in the program was an inspiration in itself. Before the viewer's eyes were two of popular music's most gifted artists in extracting maximum meaning from the lyrics of familiar standards and in so doing make the numbers come alive all over again.

Miss Garland's total involvement and passionate sincerity were contagious . . . It was the spell the occasional performer can weave in his or her own way and everyone, without knowing precisely why, is glad to savor. Miss Garland is to be numbered among the theatre's chosen few.

—Jack Gould

12 Fourteenth Annual Emmy Awards

May 22, 1962
NBC (110 minutes)
Executive producer: Fred Coe
Producer: Claude Traverse
Director: Dick Schneiber
Music director: Harry Sosnik
Written by Robert Goldman
Hosts:
   Johnny Carson, in New York
   David Brinkley, in Washington, D.C.
   Bob Newhart, in Hollywood
The show included a taped scene from Garland's 1962 special and a tape of her singing "When You're Smiling."

Dean Martin, Judy, and Frank Sinatra rehearsing for Judy's 1962 special.

13 "The Jack Paar Show"

December 7, 1962
NBC (60 minutes)
Producer: Jack Paar
Associate producer: Tom Cochran
Director: Hal Gurnee
Writers:
   Paul Keyes
   Bob Howard
   Robert Orbin
Announcer: Jim Lucas
Starring: Jack Paar

GUESTS

Judy Garland
Robert Goulet
José Melis

SONGS INCLUDED

"Paris Is a Lonely Town"
"Little Drops of Rain"
"Mewsette" (with Robert Goulet)

ADDENDA

★ Judy reminisced about her early days in Hollywood, her vaudeville touring days, Deanna Durbin, and the amusing things that happened when she toured in the act with her family.

RECORDINGS

Part of Garland's conversation with Paar is on *The Wit and Wonder of Judy Garland* [DRG SL 5179 (33⅓)]. (The dating on the album jacket is incorrect.)

14 "Judy And Her Guests, Phil Silvers and Robert Goulet" (Special)

March 19, 1963
CBS (60 minutes)
Producer: Burt Shevelove
Director: Charles S. Dubin
Musical producer: Saul Chaplin
Musical director: Mort Lindsey
Writer: Larry Gelbart
Choreographers:
   Marc Breaux
   Dee Dee Wood
Garland's gowns by Edith Head
Origination: New York (tape)

STARRING

Judy Garland

Guests:
Phil Silvers
Robert Goulet

SONGS INCLUDED

"Hello, Bluebird"
"Hello, Bluebird" (reprise) (with Phil
   Silvers, Robert Goulet)
"I Happen to Like New York"
"Manhattan" (comedy song) (with Phil
   Silvers)
"Love Walked In" (Robert Goulet)
"Here I'll Stay" (with Robert Goulet)
"Through the Years"
"If Ever I Would Leave You" (Robert
   Goulet)
"Love Is a Lovely Thing" (with Robert
   Goulet)
"Get Happy"
Medley:
   "It's Almost Like Being in Love"
   "This Can't Be Love"
"By Myself"
"I'm Following You" (comedy song) (with
   Phil Silvers, Robert Goulet)
"I Could Go On Singing"

ADDENDA

★ Judy had appeared with Robert Goulet
on "The Jack Paar Show" in 1962, the
same year both lent their voices to the
soundtrack of *Gay Purr-ee*. She had costarred with Phil Silvers in *Summer
Stock* in 1950.

CONTEMPORARY COMMENTS

The New York Times, March 20, 1963
Miss Garland and Robert Goulet indulged
in a protracted duet of standard tunes that
were distressingly overarranged and ov-
ersung. And the meaning of the lyrics was
made subordinate to the awkward direction which required the two principals to
look into each other's eyes for an inter-
minable period.

—Jack Gould

15 **"Sunday Night At
The London Palladium"**

March 1963
British television

SONGS INCLUDED

"It's Almost Like Being in Love"
"Comes Once in a Lifetime"
"I Could Go On Singing"
"Smile"

ADDENDA

★ Parts of this show were televised in the
United States on "The Ed Sullivan
Show" later in March 1963.

★ The contents of this program have not
been personally verified.

16 **"The Ed Sullivan Show"**

April 14, 1963
CBS (60 minutes)
Host: Ed Sullivan

GUESTS

Judy Garland   Margo Henderson
Frank Ifield   The Pusztati Troupe
The Schaller Brothers   The Dior Sisters
Mac Ronay   Cliff Richard
Peter O'Toole   The Del Reys
The Rastellis   Ruppert's Bears
Topo Gigio ("The Italian Mouse")

SONGS INCLUDED

"Smile"
"I Could Go On Singing"

ADDENDA

★ This program was produced in London.
Garland's segment is from a taping at
the London Palladium in March before
an audience of over 2,000. The show
also included footage shot at the world
premiere of *I Could Go On Singing*,
Judy's last film, at London's Plaza Theatre.

17 **Series: "The Judy Garland Show"**

Weekly
September 29, 1963, through March 29,
1964

18 **"The Jack Paar Show"**

December 11, 1964
NBC (60 minutes)
Producer: Jack Paar
Associate producer: Tom Cochran
Director: Hal Gurnee
Writers:
    Paul Keyes
    Bob Howard
    Robert Orbin
Announcer: Jim Lucas

STARRING

Jack Paar

Guests:
Judy Garland
Robert Morley
Randolph Churchill

SONGS INCLUDED

"Never Will I Marry"
"What Now, My Love?"

ADDENDA

★ This show was taped in London, at the Prince Charles Theatre.

RECORDINGS

The Wit and Wonder of Judy Garland [DRG SL 5179 (33⅓)] contains Garland's reminiscences about Marlene Dietrich from this show.

---

19 "Judy and Liza. Live. At The London Palladium"

December 1964
British television
Produced and staged by Mark Herron
Orchestra conducted by Harry Robinson
Pianist: Laurie Holloway
Directed for television by Colin Clews
Stage décor: Sean Kenny

SONGS INCLUDED

"Once in a Lifetime"
"Just in Time"
"Gypsy in My Soul" (Liza Minnelli)
"Hello, Dolly" (with Liza Minnelli)
"Together" (with Liza Minnelli)
"Hooray for Love" (with Liza Minnelli)
"The Man That Got Away"
"After You've Gone"
"By Myself" (Liza Minnelli)
" 'S Wonderful"
"How About You?" (with Liza Minnelli)
"Lover, Come Back to Me" (Liza Minnelli)
"You and the Night and the Music"

"It All Depends on You" (with Liza Minnelli)
"The Music That Makes Me Dance"
"It's Just a Matter of Time" (Liza Minnelli)
Duet:
   "Get Happy"
   "Happy Days Are Here Again" (Liza Minnelli)
"He's Got the Whole World in His Hands" (with Liza Minnelli)
"Who's Sorry Now?" (Liza Minnelli)
"San Francisco"
"Over the Rainbow"
"Chicago" (with Liza Minnelli)

---

20 "On Broadway Tonight"

February 5, 1965
CBS (60 minutes)
Producer: Irving Mansfield
Director: Dave Geisel
Musical director: Harry Sosnik
Writers:
   David Greggory
   Saul Turtletaub
Origination: New York (tape)
Host: Rudy Vallee

GUEST STAR

Judy Garland

Guests:
Peter and Christopher Allen
Dick Roman
Pete Barbutti
The Spaghetti Minstrels
Augie and Margo

Judy and Liza on stage together.

SONGS INCLUDED

"When You're Smiling"
Medley:
    "It's Almost Like Being in Love"
    "This Can't Be Love"
    "I Wish You Love" (with the Allen
       Brothers)
"The Music That Makes Me Dance"
"Rock-a-Bye Your Baby with a Dixie
   Melody"
"Don't Rain on My Parade" (The Allen
   "Brothers)
"Wherever We Go" (The Allen Brothers)
"Somewhere" (Dick Roman)
"I Left My Heart in San Francisco"
   (Dick Roman)

ADDENDA

★ Many of Judy's early recordings, in-
  cluding "(Dear Mr. Gable) You Made
  Me Love You" (1937), were made with
  Harry Sosnik directing the orchestra.

★ Judy Garland met the Allen Brothers on
  her Australian tour. She was instrumental in having them signed for this
  program, their first American television
  exposure. (She also introduced Peter
  Allen to her daughter Liza, whose first
  husband he became.)

21 The Academy Awards Show

April 1965
ABC
Judy Garland sang a special tribute to
   Cole Porter.

SONGS INCLUDED

Medley:
    "Night and Day"
    "I Get a Kick Out of You"
    "You're the Top"
    "Let's Do It"
    "Don't Fence Me In"
"You'd Be So Nice to Come Home To"
"It's de-Lovely"
"My Heart Belongs to Daddy"
"So in Love"
"I Love You"
"From This Moment On"
"Night and Day" (reprise)

RECORDINGS

Judy! Judy! Judy! [Star-Tone ST 224
   (33⅓)]

22 "The Andy Williams Show"

("Kraft Music Hall" Special)
September 20, 1965
NBC (60 minutes) (color)
Producer: Bob Finkel
Director: Bob Henry
Writers:
   Harry Crane
   Don Hinkley
Music director: Jack Elliott
Choreographer: Nick Castle

STARRING

Andy Williams

Guests:
Judy Garland
David McCallum
Cliff Arquette

SONGS INCLUDED

"On a Wonderful Day Like Today" (Andy Williams)

(David McCallum lip-synchs to Judy's "The Man That Got Away")

"The Trolley Song" (Judy Garland, Andy Williams, cast)

"Get Happy" (Judy Garland)

"Over the Rainbow" (partial) (Judy Garland)

"Rock-a-Bye Your Baby with a Dixie Melody" (Judy Garland, Andy Williams)

"You Made Me Love You" (Judy Garland, Andy Williams)

"On the Atchison, Topeka and the Santa Fe" (Judy Garland, Andy Williams)

"Why Don't We Do This More Often?" (Judy Garland, Andy Williams)

"I've Got That Feeling" (Andy Williams)

"All Through the Night" (Andy Williams)

"They're Draining Snyders Swamp in the Morning" (Andy Williams, Cliff Arquette)

Theme from "The Pawnbroker" (Andy Williams)

---

23 "The Ed Sullivan Show"

October 3, 1965
CBS (60 minutes) (color)
Producer: Bob Precht
Host: Ed Sullivan

GUESTS

Judy Garland	Topo Gigio
Tom Jones	Jackie Vernon
The Swinging Lads	Sophie Tucker
The Marquis Chimps	

SONGS INCLUDED

"Come Rain or Come Shine"
"By Myself"
"Rock-a-Bye Your Baby with a Dixie Melody"

---

24 "Perry Como's Kraft Music Hall" (Special)

February 28, 1966
NBC (60 minutes) (color)
Producer: Ray Charles
Director: Clark Jones
Writers:
   Goodman Ace
   Bill Angelos
   Buz Kohan
Choreographer: Danny Daniels
Music director: Nick Perito
Host: Perry Como
Announcer: Frank Gallop

Regulars:
Nick Perito Orchestra
The Ray Charles Singers

GUESTS

Judy Garland	Bill Cosby

(As the show opens, Perry Como and Judy Garland are deciding that the program would be more entertaining if it had a plot as well as singing and conversation. They hatch up a rumor that Judy's $100,000 Maltese diamond ring has been stolen. Como asks Bill Cosby to do a little spying around to find the ring. Cosby's efforts and reports are shown during the program.)

SONGS

Production number (Judy Garland, Perry Como, singers, dancers):
"If You Feel Like Singing, Sing"
"It's a Grand Night for Singing"
"This Is All I Ask" (Perry Como)
"What Now, My Love?" (Judy Garland)
"Just in Time" (Judy Garland)
(Cosby returns to question Judy, who answers by singing parts of her well-known songs.)
Where did you lose the ring?—"Somewhere over the rainbow . . ."
How do I get there?—"Clang, clang, clang went the trolley . . ."
A man in the case . . . Is he still around?—"Good riddance, goodbye . . ."
Do you suspect anybody else?—"How can I ignore the boy next door . . ."
How can I find him now?—"Swanee . . ."
Don't worry. You can sleep easy.—"Rock-a-Bye Your Baby with a Dixie Melody"
Judy Garland and Perry Como Medley:
"Bye, Bye Blues"
"My Honey's Lovin' Arms"
"For Me and My Gal"
(Cosby gives a telephone report on his progress and a monologue on his childhood in Philadelphia.)
"Big Noise from Winnetka" (instrumental) (Bobby Haggart, Bobby Rosengarden)
Perry Como Medley:
"But Beautiful"
"Make Someone Happy"
"Cu-Cu-Ru-Cu-Cu"
"Side by Side" (Judy Garland, Perry Como, Bill Cosby)

Perry Como, Judy, and Bill Cosby rehearse.

ADDENDA

★ This show was one of seven "Perry Como Kraft Music Hall" specials that preempted regular segments of "The Andy Williams Show."
★ This show was taped February 20, 1966.

25 **"The Sammy Davis, Jr., Show"**

March 18, 1966
NBC (60 minutes)
Executive producer: Sammy Davis, Jr.
Producer: Joe Hamilton
Director: Clark Jones
Writers:
   Buz Kohan
   Bill Angelos
Musical director: George Rhodes
Choreographer: Lester Wilson
Host: Sammy Davis, Jr.
Announcer: William B. Williams

GUESTS

Judy Garland
Nipsey Russell
Tom Jones
Lada Edmund, Jr. ("Hullabaloo" dancer)
Lester Wilson

SONGS INCLUDED

"My Mother, the Car" (Sammy Davis, Jr.)
"Climb Every Mountain" (Sammy Davis, Jr.)
(Nipsey Russell comedy monologue)
"Promise Her Anything" (Tom Jones)
"Scarlet Ribbons" (Sammy Davis, Jr., Tom Jones)
"What's New, Pussycat?" (Sammy Davis, Jr., Tom Jones in lip synch)

(At the half-hour, Davis introduced Garland.)

"When You're Smiling" (Judy Garland)

Medley (Judy Garland):

   "The Man That Got Away"

   "Give My Regards to Broadway"

Judy Garland, Sammy Davis, Jr., Medley:

   "A Couple of Swells"

   "How About You?"

   "Bidin' My Time"

   "For Me and My Gal"

   "Ding, Dong, the Witch Is Dead"

   "Meet Me in St. Louis, Louis"

   "It's a New World" (Judy Garland)

   "Johnny One Note" (Judy Garland)

   "I Got Rhythm" (Sammy Davis)

   "Get Happy"

   "On the Atchison, Topeka and the Santa Fe"

   "I Wish I Were in Love Again"

   "Treat Me Rough" (Sammy Davis, Jr.)

   "If I Only Had a Brain . . ."

   "A Couple of Swells" (reprise)

ADDENDA

★ This show was taped on February 27, 1966, in Brooklyn, New York.

---

26 "The Sammy Davis, Jr., Show"

March 25, 1966

NBC (60 minutes)

Host: Sammy Davis, Jr.

Announcer: William B. Williams

GUESTS

Judy Garland

Frank Gorshin

Teri Thornton (substituting for Sarah Vaughan)

The Lettermen

SONGS INCLUDED

"Once in a Lifetime" (Sammy Davis, Jr.)

"With a Song in My Heart" (Sammy Davis, Jr.)

The Lettermen Medley:

   "Days of Wine and Roses"

   "Charade"

   "Dear Heart"

   "Pink Panther"

   "Moon River"

   "Mr. Lucky"

(Gorshin impressions of Marlon Brando, Rod Steiger, Richard Burton, Peter Falk, Burt Lancaster, Kirk Douglas—if they had been cast as Batman.)

"You" (Teri Thornton)

"This Is All I Ask" (Teri Thornton)

At twelve minutes into the hour, Judy joins the show.

Garland Medley:

   "It's Almost Like Being in Love"

   "This Can't Be Love"

   "If Love Were All"

   "Love"

Judy Garland, Sammy Davis, Jr., Medley:

   "Let Me Entertain You" (Judy Garland, Sammy Davis, Jr.)

   "Alexander's Ragtime Band" (Judy Garland, Sammy Davis, Jr.)

   "April Showers" (Sammy Davis)

   "Look for the Silver Lining" (Judy Garland)

   "Keep Your Sunny Side Up" (Sammy Davis, Jr.)

   "Life Upon the Wicked Stage" (Judy Garland)

   "Rock-a-Bye Your Baby with a Dixie Melody" (Sammy Davis, Jr.)

   "When You're Smiling" (Judy Garland)

"You're a Grand Old Flag" (Judy Garland, Sammy Davis, Jr.)

Judy breaks up Sammy Davis, Jr., on "The Sammy
Davis, Jr., Show."

Simultaneously:

"Ma, He's Making Eyes At Me" (Judy Garland)

"Toot, Toot, Tootsie" (Sammy Davis, Jr.)

"Carolina in the Morning" (Judy Garland, Sammy Davis, Jr.)

"California, Here I Come" (Judy Garland, Sammy Davis, Jr.)

"Swanee" (Judy Garland, Sammy Davis, Jr.)

"Born in a Trunk" (Judy Garland, Sammy Davis, Jr.)

ADDENDA

★ This show was taped March 6, 1966, in Brooklyn, New York.

27 "The Ed Sullivan Show"

August 7, 1966
CBS (60 minutes) (color)
Host: Ed Sullivan

GUESTS

Judy Garland	Peter Sellers
Tom Jones	The Swingle Singers
Jackie Vernon	Hendra and Ullett
The Marquis Chimps	
The Leyte Philippine Dancers	

SONGS INCLUDED

"Come Rain or Come Shine"
"By Myself"
"Rock-a-Bye Your Baby with a Dixie Melody"

ADDENDA

★ Garland's segment, along with those of Jackie Vernon and Tom Jones, was a rebroadcast from the October 3, 1965, "Ed Sullivan Show."

28 "The Hollywood Palace"

September 3, 1966
ABC (60 minutes) (color)
Executive producer: Nick Vanoff
Producer: William O. Harbach
Director: Grey Lockwood
Musical director: Mitchell Ayres
Writers:
  Joe Bigelow
  Jay Burten
Choreographers:
  Marc Breaux
  Dee Dee Wood
  Hollywood Palace Orchestra
Hostess: Judy Garland

GUESTS

Gene Baylos
Vic Damone
The Lyons Family
Chita Rivera
Jack Burns and Avery Schreiber
The Three Bragazzis

SONGS INCLUDED

"Once in a Lifetime"
"Blue Is the Color" (Chita Rivera)
"A Couple of Swells"
"I Loved Him"
"Quiet Nights of Loving You" (Vic Damone)
West Side Story Medley:
  "Maria" (Vic Damone)
  "Something's Coming"
  "Maria" (reprise) (Vic Damone)

"Somewhere" (with Vic Damone)
"Tonight" (with Vic Damone)
Palace Medley:
    "Shine On, Harvest Moon"
    "Some of These Days"
    "My Man"
    "I Don't Care"

ADDENDA

★ This program was originally scheduled to appear on November 13, 1965, and is often miscited in listings of Garland's television appearances.

---

29 "What's My Line?"

March 5, 1967
CBS (30 minutes)
Executive producer: Gil Fates
Director: Franklin Heller
Origination: New York ("live")
Host: John Daly
Panelists:
    Arlene Francis
    Bennett Cerf
Guest panelists:
    Polly Bergen
    Tony Randall

Judy Garland was the "mystery guest."

---

30 "Today"

March 16, 1967
NBC (120 minutes) (color)
Garland was interviewed by Barbara Walters. She talked about singing in vaudeville when she was thirty months old,

about having "a stage mother who wouldn't quit" (NBC program note), about her enduring friendships with Mickey Rooney and Donald O'Connor. She also said that she had fasted for thirty days a couple of years before and hadn't had a problem with her weight since then.

ADDENDA

★ Judy's interview with Barbara Walters was aired as two segments of the program, from 7:41 to 7:59 A.M. (E.T.) and from 8:16 to 8:24 A.M.
★ Joe and Lorna Luft, her children, appeared and participated in the interview. (They loved *The Wizard of Oz.*)
★ The interview was filmed in Judy's hotel suite in New York City. She was in town to attend Liza's wedding and to meet the press regarding the announcement that she would star in *Valley of the Dolls.*

---

31 "A Funny Thing Happened on the Way to Hollywood . . . with Jack Paar"

May 16, 1967
NBC (60 minutes)
Judy swapped stories with Jack and talked about her career.
Producer: Jack Haley, Jr.
Director: Hal Gurnee
Writers:
    Jack Paar
    Bob Howard
    David Lloyd
Musical director: Pat Williams

STARRING

Jack Paar

Guests:
Judy Garland
Bob Newhart

RECORDINGS

Part of the conversation between Garland
and Paar is on *The Wit and Wonder of
Judy Garland* [DRG SL 5179 (33⅓)].
(The dating in the liner notes is incorrect.)

32 "The Tonight Show Starring Johnny Carson"

June 24, 1968
NBC (90 minutes)
Regulars:
    Doc Severinsen
    Jack Haskell (substituting for Ed
    McMahon)

STARRING

Johnny Carson

Guests:
Judy Garland
Bennett Cerf
Monti Rock III (rock 'n' roll singer)
The Philadelphia Mummers Band

ADDENDA

★ Judy sang one line of "Brother, Can You
  Spare a Dime?"

33 "The Mike Douglas Show"

July 1968
Syndicated
Host: Mike Douglas

GUESTS

Judy Garland
Peter Lawford

SONGS INCLUDED

"For Once in My Life"
"How Insensitive"
"Blue Skies" (with Peter Lawford)
"Over the Rainbow"

ADDENDA

★ The contents of this program have not been personally verified.

---

34 **"The Dick Cavett Show"**

December 1968
ABC (90 minutes)
Producer: Tony Converse
Director: David Barnhizer
Announcer: Fred Foy
Music director: Bobby Rosengarden
Host: Dick Cavett

SONGS INCLUDED

"Till After the Holidays"

ADDENDA

★ The contents of this program have not been personally verified.

RECORDINGS

Judy! Judy! Judy! [Star-Tone ST 224 (33⅓)]

---

35 **"The Tonight Show Starring Johnny Carson"**

December 17, 1968
NBC (90 minutes)
Regulars:
Doc Severinsen
Ed McMahon

STARRING

Johnny Carson

Guests:
Judy Garland
Shari Lewis
Jerry Kramer (Green Bay Packers)
Slappy White (comedian)

SONGS INCLUDED

"It's All for You"
"Till After the Holidays"

ADDENDA

★ Judy also sang one line of "Dinah" and "Brother, Can You Spare a Dime?"

RECORDINGS

Judy! Judy! Judy! [Star-Tone ST 224 (33⅓)]

---

36 **"The Merv Griffin Show"**

December 1968
Syndicated (90 minutes)
Host: Merv Griffin
Announcer: Arthur Treacher
Music director: Mort Lindsey

SONGS INCLUDED

"Have Yourself a Merry Little Christmas"
"The Trolley Song"
"I'd Like to Hate Myself in the Morning"

ADDENDA

★ The contents of this and the following two programs have not been personally verified.

RECORDINGS

Judy! Judy! Judy! [Star-Tone ST 224 (33⅓)] contains "I'd Like to Hate My-self in the Morning." The song is also on *Judy. London. 1969* [Juno S 1000 (33⅓)].

---

37 "The Merv Griffin Show"

December 1968
Syndicated (90 minutes)
Guest Host: Judy Garland

SONGS   INCLUDED

"Just in Time"
"If You Were the Only Boy in the World"
   (with Arthur Treacher)

---

38 "Sunday Night at the London Palladium"

February 1969
British television

SONGS   INCLUDED

"Get Happy"
"For Once in My Life"
"I Belong to London"

7

"THE JUDY GARLAND SHOW"

———————— ★ ————————

"The musical is not a medium for directors or writers . . .
The musical is a performer's medium . . ."

Ethan Mordden, *The Hollywood Studios*

———————— ★ ————————

"It was indeed difficult to judge her on voice alone . . .
She simply is one of the rare artists who can transfix an audience
by sheer personal magneticism."

Robert Sobel, *Billboard* July 31, 1965 (review of Garland concert)

———————— ★ ————————

The Judy Garland Show" ran on CBS from September 29, 1963, through March 29, 1964. The network touted it as the answer to the devastation wrought on its Sunday evening schedule by NBC's popular series "Bonanza," a program that had already consigned Jack Benny's CBS show to history. Garland fared no better than Benny; but in Judy's case, the program's demise was credited to personal failure.

It was an expensive failure for the network, which spared no expense on pro-duction. It was a more expensive failure for Garland, who had hoped to achieve some financial stability and security through the series but who, instead, found her flaws denounced as the source of all the program's problems and her strengths dismissed as largely irrelevant to a television series.

CBS was once described as trying to turn Judy Garland into "the superstar next door." Perhaps more profoundly unfortunate is the fact that Garland had already achieved that extraordinary balancing act in her concert appearances, but network executives didn't understand it—or believe it would play on the tube. And, as Mike Dann, a CBS "decision-maker," said in an early interview, "She's far too insecure about TV to exercise her own judgment. She knows we know what's good for her."

"The Judy Garland Show" lasted twenty-six weeks. In that time, Judy performed with several dozen guests, including some of the finest show-business talent and some thoroughly forgettable "stars" of the moment. She endured abrupt changes in production personnel and watched her professional persona systematically shredded in an attempt by the network to "humanize" her. In those twenty-six weeks, she also sang several hundred songs, including some of her most stirring renditions.

In retrospect, "The Judy Garland Show" was an extraordinary exercise.

Part of Judy Garland's concert allure was the warm friendliness of her personality. The audience sensed it and responded to it. It was, in fact, one of the critical components of her personal magnetism, a magnetism reviewers noted time and again. On television, this warmth was revealed, in part, in the obvious delight Judy had in a talented guest's excellence. She was not only the star of the series, she was a one-woman cheering section and, most significantly, one of the entertained.

Television, like radio before it, showed Judy Garland not only as a singer and clown but as an irrepressibly enthusiastic audience. Judy was probably second only to Jack Benny in the ease with which other performers could send her into giggles and laughter. Her ability to be genuinely amused, indeed occasionally broken up, not merely by ad-libs but by material that had obviously been rehearsed, added an extra dimension of spontaneity and informality to her performances. Given her infectious laugh, moreover, her amusement spread to the other performers and to the audience at large; it is impossible to laugh and not enjoy yourself.

Garland's ease with other performers and her ability to project an aura of personal warmth were a critical aspect of her success. CBS executives, however, soon decided that one element of this intangible equation—her physical contact with her guests (unscripted touching, as it were)—was simply unacceptable on national television.

They had decided even earlier, from the beginning in fact, that any performer of Judy Garland's stature and reputation must, by definition, be a remote figure to the television audience. Thus, they would "deglamorize" her. Judy on television must be "humanized." (This came as a shock to Garland, who had never thought of herself as particularly glamorous or inhuman.)

Cheerfully disregarding all evidence that people responded to Judy on a quite personal and human level, and clearly believing that only idiots watched the "idiot box," they would reshape her image to their image of the lowest common denominator. They would transform "Miss Show Business" with a running gag of which Garland was the butt; she was straight woman to Jerry Van Dyke's attempts to teach the "little old lady" (who used to be fat) about television. And to further insure that no viewer might see her as above him, guests were given dialogue that included disparaging remarks—in the guise of humor. To Garland fans, this was a grotesque joke. To the average viewing public, it was disjunctive with their image of her and, ultimately, as boring as any one-liner used too often.

Musical variety is a particularly difficult format. Unlike musical comedy, it has no book, no story line, to sustain it or carry the performers. As a series, its success depends on a subtle mix of the attractiveness or likability of the primary performer, the overall quality of entertainment offered week after week, and a fit between what the viewers expect of the show and its star and what the show delivers.

With the sure knowledge of viewers' tastes that had made CBS programming such a precise science, the network executives systematically undermined each of these essential elements for "The Judy Garland Show," simultaneously confusing the public and demoralizing Garland.

By 1963, the general public recognized Judy Garland as a world-class singer and musical-variety entertainer (albeit one most of them had never seen personally). That is what they expected to see on television. Instead, they were presented week after week with a woman whose talents and extraordinary showmanship were verbally diminished and progressively enchained. They were presented, too, with a woman whose joy in performance was being leached away and who was increasingly tense. Compare, for example, the fun Judy registered physically when performing with Mickey Rooney, on the first show taped, or with Donald O'Connor, on

the first show aired, with the tightness and obvious restraint with which she held herself by the February 9 performance, the first in full-concert format.

Despite some extraordinary singing—her rendition of "The Battle Hymn of the Republic" comes immediately to mind—the viewing public was denied an unfettered performing Garland, the Garland who, flaws and all, created a bond with her audiences. Even glorious singing will not carry a television performance if the visual and contextual signals are off.

The program's running gag and conceptual underpinnings missed on two counts: The less pleasant aspects of the Judy Garland legend were unconsciously emphasized without the public's feeling the full force of her talent and personality, those very qualities which had made her a legend to begin with. And without a "living legend" as a target, the attempts to "humanize" Judy were not only tasteless, they were pointless. A very significant divide was created between viewer expectations and what the show delivered.

The program tried to provide week-to-week continuity by establishing two recurring spots: Garland's "Born in a Trunk" segment, in which Judy sang alone on a largely unencumbered stage, produced many of the vocals which have appeared as recordings. The second running segment was the "Tea for Two" spot, which was designed to allow her to display her ready wit and skills as a conversationalist. (This brought down the executive edict of "no touching.")

But the overall quality of guest entertainment offered each week varied dramatically and disrupted continuity of audience anticipation. For the most part, Garland's guests were artists of significant talent, but this was not consistently so. Aiming for "relevance" and attempting to capture the younger viewing audience, ephemeral personalities were periodically showcased. As early as on the fourth-show broadcast, the world was given the opportunity to hear George Maharis sing; the sixth show, on November 3, produced Judy performing with Zina Bethune.

If the public wasn't confused about Garland's image within the first two months of airing, viewers were certainly unsure whether she would be onstage with Ethel Merman or Barbra Streisand, or with entertainers of slightly less impressive talent.

Judy has been criticized for losing interest in rehearsals as the series progressed and only putting forth her best efforts with guests who challenged her. Perhaps rightly so; she was, after all, the star of the program. It is not difficult to understand, however, why an entertainer of her experience and expertise, and with a photographic memory for scripted dialogue, would feel a less than compelling need to practice for appearances with some of these visiting performers. Yet her duets with, for example, Diahann Carroll, Bobby Darin, Jack Jones, Peggy Lee, Barbra Streisand, Martha Raye, Liza Minnelli, and her singing with the Count Basie Band show no evidence of disinterest. Indeed, these represent some of the highlights of the series, and Garland's enjoyment rings clear.

It cannot be emphasized too strongly how visual a medium television is or how critical, if subtle, the interplay between the vocals and their context in a musical variety format. The recordings derived from the series soundtrack contain singing that rewards repeated listenings. "I'll Show Them All," for example, from the January 5 show, "I Wish You Love," from the October 20 show, "Supper Time," from the March 29 show, and "Joey," from the March 22 show, compare favorably with any of Judy's concert renditions.

But as the series progressed, the songs lost their impact visually, as the looseness and freedom that contributed to what reviewers repeatedly described as an indescribable essence that dominated a concert stage was drained from Garland's performances on national television. Put simply, the star wasn't having fun, and while this did not diminish her vocal artistry, it didn't make for enthralling viewing either.

If one could watch the February 9, 1964, broadcast, for instance, followed immediately by the December 1964 televised Palladium program, the essence of musical variety on television would become immediately apparent. Both shows were in concert format, with the orchestra onstage behind Garland. The focus of both was singing, not production numbers. And Judy was in better voice for the former than for the latter. Yet on the Palladium program, she was having a good time performing, obviously feeling no particular restrictions on her physical movements or on letting her personality flow. A spark, and Garland sparkle, is transmitted from the set to the viewer.

Television transmits the essence of a performance, its wholeness, as much as it transmits visual images and sounds. On "The Judy Garland Show," Judy's unique performing electricity was dampened.

It is, of course, possible that Garland, even unfettered and at her best, could not have sustained a series. Week after week vocal brilliance and personal performing enthusiasm is difficult to maintain, although she maintained it for nineteen weeks doing two-a-days at the Palace.

What is sure, however, is that neither Judy nor the viewing public ever got the opportunity to find out whether her concert appeal would transfer to the small screen on a continuing basis. The network was so determined to present her as a Betty Crocker with a voice, an average person rather than a unique talent, that the audiences only caught fleeting glimpses of Judy Garland on "The Judy Garland Show."

The following albums are from chapter 8, Records: The Concert Years, section K ("The Judy Garland Show") and section L (Anthology Albums).

Weekly Series
September 29, 1963, to March 29, 1964

CBS (60 minutes)
Sundays, 9:00–10:00 P.M. E.T.
Executive producer: Norman Jewison
Producers:
   Gary Smith
   William Colleran
   Bill Hobin
   George Schlatter
   John Bradford
Director:
   Bill Hobin
   Dean Whitmore
Music director: Mort Lindsey
Special musical material: Mel Tormé
Head writers:
   Arnie Sultan
   Marvin Worth
   John Bradford
Writers:
   William Nichols
   Bernard Rothman
   Tom Waldman
   Frank Waldman
   Frank Peppiat
   John Aylesworth
Choreography:
   Ernest Flatt
   Nick Castle
   Marc Breaux
   Dee Dee Wood
   Peter Gennaro
   Danny Daniels
   Wally Siebert

Dance arrangements: Jack Elliott
Choral director: Jud Conlon
Art director: Robert Kelly
Costume designer: Ray Aghayan
Origination: Hollywood (tape)

S T A R R I N G

Judy Garland
Regulars: Jerry Van Dyke

A D D E N D A

★ The contents of the shows are based upon viewing; where viewing was not possible, I am indebted to CBS Television, Music Clearance Division, for providing musical compositions performed.

---

1 **September 29, 1963**

Series premiere
Producer: Gary Smith
Director: Bill Hobin
Writers:
   Arnie Sultan
   Marvin Worth
   William Nichols
   Bernard Rothman

Guest: Donald O'Connor

S O N G S

Opening production number (Judy Garland, dancers):
   "Call Me Irresponsible"
   "The Sky Is My Ceilin' "
   "Keep Your Sunny Side Up"
Jerry Van Dyke lip-synchs to Judy's voice:
   "The Man That Got Away"
Judy Garland, Donald O'Connor Medley:
   "Be My Guest"

"We're Undecided"
"Inka Dinka Doo" (Donald O'Connor)
"If You Knew Susie" (Judy Garland)
"My Mammy"
"Ah, Sweet Mystery of Life"
"Rose Marie"
"Sweetheart"
"Stout-hearted Men"
"Italian Street Song"
"Indian Love Call"
Production number (Donald O'Connor, dancers, singers):
"Sing, You Sinners"
"Sinner Man"
Judy Garland:
"Fly Me to the Moon"
Donald O'Connor lip-synchs to Judy's voice:
"The Man That Got Away"
Production number (full cast):
"The World Is Your Balloon"
Vaudeville Medley (Judy Garland, Donald O'Connor):
"Good Old Days of Vaudeville"
"Nagasaki"
"Yaaka Hula Hickey Dula"
"I Can Always Find a Little Sunshine at the YMCA"
"At the Moving Picture Ball"
"Old Soft Shoe"
Trunk sequence: Judy Garland
"Born in a Trunk"
"Chicago"
Closing: Judy Garland
"Maybe I'll Come Back"

ADDENDA

★ O'Connor and Garland had been friends since vaudeville days, when they both had bookings in San Francisco. They attended the Lawler school for professional children together.

★ This show, the first to be aired, was the seventh in order of production and taping.

ALBUMS

The Garland/O'Connor numbers are on *Judy Garland: The Greatest Duets* [Broadcast Tributes BTRIB 0002 (33⅓)]
Albums with "Chicago":
Judy—The Legend (See section K, #4)
Judy Garland Concert (See section K, #11)
Judy Garland. Live! From Hollywood, vol. 1 (See section K, #13)
Judy Garland. The Collection. Live! (See section K, #17)
Unforgettable Judy Garland (See section K, #18)
The Hits of Judy Garland (See section L, #1)
The Judy Garland Deluxe Set (See section L, #2)
The Magic of Judy Garland (See section L, #8)
The Immortal Judy Garland (See section L, #11)
Judy Garland—20 Hits (See section L, #13)
Albums with "Fly Me to the Moon":
Just for Openers (See section K, #1)
Judy (See section K, #2)
All of Judy (See section K, #10)
Judy Garland. The Collection. Live! (See section K, #17)
Unforgettable Judy Garland (See section K, #18)
The Magic of Judy Garland (See section L, #8)
The Immortal Judy Garland (See section L, #11)

The Legendary Judy Garland
   (See section L, #18)
Albums with "Maybe I'll Come Back":
Just for Openers (See section K, #1)

---

2 October 6, 1963

GUESTS

The Smothers Brothers
Barbra Streisand
Ethel Merman

SONGS

"Once in a Lifetime" (Judy Garland)
"Be My Guest" (Judy Garland, Barbra
   Streisand, The Smothers Brothers)
"Just in Time" (Judy Garland)
"I Talk to the Trees" (The Smothers
   Brothers)
"Dance, Boatmen, Dance" (The Smothers
   Brothers)
Simultaneously:
   "Happy Days Are Here Again" (Barbra
      Streisand)
   "Get Happy" (Judy Garland)

"There's No Business Like Show Business"
(Judy Garland, Barbra Streisand, Ethel
Merman)
"You're Just in Love" (Judy Garland, Ethel
Merman)
"Happy Harvest" (Judy Garland, singers,
dancers)
Judy Garland, Barbra Streisand Medley:
"Hooray for Love" (Judy Garland,
Barbra Streisand)
"After You've Gone" (Judy Garland)
"By Myself" (Barbra Streisand)
" 'S Wonderful" (Judy Garland)
"How About You?" (Judy Garland,
Barbra Streisand)
"Lover, Come Back to Me" (Barbra
Streisand)
"You and the Night and the Music"
(Judy Garland)
"It All Depends on You" (Judy Garland,
Barbra Streisand)
"Bewitched, Bothered and Bewildered"
(Barbra Streisand)
"Down with Love" (Barbra Streisand)
Trunk sequence: Judy Garland
"You Made Me Love You"
"For Me and My Gal"
"The Trolley Song"
Closing: Judy Garland
"Maybe I'll Come Back"

ADDENDA

★ This was the ninth show to be taped.

ALBUMS

The Garland/Streisand duets are on *The
Great Garland Duets* [Paragon 1001
(33⅓)].

Albums with "Once in a Lifetime":
All of Judy (See section K, #10)
Star Eyes (See section K, #15)
The Magic of Judy Garland
(See section L, #8)
The Immortal Judy Garland
(See section L, #11)
Albums with "Just in Time":
Unforgettable Judy Garland
(See section K, #6)
Judy Garland. Live! From Hollywood, vol.
2 (See section K, #14)
Albums with "You Made Me Love You":
Judy in Hollywood (See section K, #3)
The Magic of Judy Garland
(See section L, #8)
Albums with "The Trolley Song":
Judy in Hollywood (See section K, #3)
The Magic of Judy Garland
(See section L, #8)

3. October 13, 1963

Producer: George Schlatter
Director: Bill Hobin
Writers:
John Bradford
Tom Waldman
Frank Waldman

GUESTS

Terry-Thomas
Lena Horne

SONGS

"Day In, Day Out" (Judy Garland, Lena
Horne)
"Come Rain or Come Shine" (Judy
Garland, Lena Horne)

Lena Horne Medley:
   "I Want to Be Happy"
   "Where Is Love?"
   "He Loves Me"
Terry-Thomas sketch
"A Foggy Day" (Judy Garland)
Judy Garland, Lena Horne Medley:
   "Honeysuckle Rose" (Judy Garland)
   "Meet Me in St. Louis, Louis" (Lena
     Horne)
   "Deed I Do" (Judy Garland)
   "Zing! Went the Strings of My Heart"
     (Lena Horne)
   "It's All Right with Me" (Judy Garland)
   "The Trolley Song" (Judy Garland,
     Lena Horne)
   "Love" (Judy Garland, Lena Horne)
"Mad Dogs and Englishmen" (Judy Gar-
   land, Lena Horne, Terry-Thomas)
Trunk sequence: Judy Garland
   "The Man That Got Away"
Closing: Judy Garland
   "Maybe I'll Come Back"

ADDENDA

★ Lena Horne and Garland both appeared in *The Ziegfeld Follies of 1946*. Lennie Hayton, who conducted and arranged many of Garland's recordings while she was at MGM, was Lena Horne's husband. Garland's second husband, Vincente Minnelli, directed Horne in her first major motion picture, *Cabin in the Sky,* in 1943. It was also Minnelli's first feature film.

★ This show was production number four.

ALBUMS

Albums with "Day In, Day Out":
Judy. Judy Garland (See section K, #16)
The Judy Garland Deluxe Set
   (See section L, #2)
Albums with "Come Rain or Come
   Shine":
Judy (See section K, #2)
Judy Garland Concert (See section K, #11)
Star Eyes (See section K, #15)
Judy Garland. The Collection. Live!
   (See section K, #17)
Unforgettable Judy Garland
   (See section K, #18)
The Hits of Judy Garland
   (See section L, #1)
The Judy Garland Deluxe Set
   (See section L, #2)
Judy Garland—Her Greatest Hits
   (See section L, #4)
Judy Garland Over the Rainbow
   (See section L, #5)
The Magic of Judy Garland
   (See section L, #8)
The Immortal Judy Garland
   (See section L, #11)
20 Hits of a Legend (See section L, #14)
Judy Garland Recital (See section L, #19)
Albums with "A Foggy Day":
Judy Garland—Over the Rainbow
   (See section K, #8)
Judy Garland Concert (See section K, #11)
The Pick of Judy Garland
   (See section K, #12)
Judy Garland. Live! From Hollywood,
   vol. 2 (See section K, #14)
The Magic of Judy Garland
   (See section L, #8)
The Immortal Judy Garland
   (See section L, #11)

Judy Garland—20 Hits
(See section L, #13)
20 Hits of a Legend (See section L, #14)
Albums with "The Man That Got Away":
Judy's Greatest Hits (See section K, #5)
All of Judy (See section K, #10)
Star Eyes (See section K, #15)
Judy Garland. The Collection. Live!
(See section K, #17)
The Magic of Judy Garland
(See section L, #8)
The Immortal Judy Garland
(See section L, #11)
Judy Garland—20 Hits
(See section L, #13)

4 **October 20, 1963**

Producer: Gary Smith

GUESTS

George Maharis   The Dillards
Jack Carter   Leo Durocher

SONGS

"Alexander's Ragtime Band" (Judy
Garland)
"Be My Guest" (Judy Garland, Jack
Carter, George Maharis)
"I Wish You Love" (Judy Garland)
Production number (Jack Carter):
"Funny Thing Happened"
"Bob White" (interpolation)
"Goodbye" (George Maharis)
Dialogue spot with Judy Garland, George
Maharis, including "The Party's Over"
"Side by Side" (Judy Garland, George
Maharis)

Dialogue spot ("Tea for Two") (with Leo
Durocher, including "Take Me Out to
the Ball Game")
"Buckin' Mule" (The Dillards)
Full cast Medley:
"Y'All Come"
"Way Back Home"
"Crawfishin' "
"Somebody Touched Me"
"Ain't Nobody's Business but My Own"
"John Saw the Holy Number"
Trunk sequence: Judy Garland
"Swanee"
"Maybe I'll Come Back"

ADDENDA

★ This was the eighth show to be taped.

ALBUMS

Albums with "Alexander's Ragtime Band":
All of Judy (See section K, #10)
The Pick of Judy Garland
(See section K, #12)
Judy. Judy Garland (See section K, #16)
Judy Garland. The Collection. Live!
(See section K, #17)
Unforgettable Judy Garland
(See section K, #18)
Judy Garland—20 Hits
(See section L, #13)
Albums with "I Wish You Love":
Just for Openers (See section K, #1)
Albums with "Swanee":
All of Judy (See section K, #10)
Judy Garland Concert (See section K, #11)
Judy Garland. Live! From Hollywood, vol.
2 (See section K, #14)
Judy Garland. The Collection. Live!
(See section K, #17)

Unforgettable Judy Garland
  (See section K, #18)
The Hits of Judy Garland
  (See section L, #1)
The Judy Garland Deluxe Set
  (See section L, #2)
The Magic of Judy Garland
  (See section L, #8)
The Immortal Judy Garland
  (See section L, #11)

---

5 October 27, 1963

Producer: Gary Smith
Director: Bill Hobin
Choreographer: Ernest Flatt
Writers:
  Arnie Sultan
  Marvin Worth
  Bernard Rothman
  William Nichols

GUESTS

June Allyson
Steve Lawrence

SONGS

"Life Is Just a Bowl of Cherries" (Judy
  Garland)
"Happiness Is Just a Thing Called Joe"
  (Judy Garland)
"Time After Time" (Steve Lawrence)
"I've Got You Under My Skin" (Steve
  Lawrence)
"Be My Guest" (Judy Garland, Steve
  Lawrence)
Production number   (June Allyson):
  "Doodlin' Song"
"Tea for Two" (comedy number) (Judy
  Garland, June Allyson)

Dialogue spot with Judy Garland, June Al-
  lyson, including "Just Imagine"
  (Garland, Allyson)
"I'm in the Mood for Love" (Steve
  Lawrence)
Judy Garland, June Allyson, Steve
  Lawrence Medley:
  "Buckle Down, Winsocki" (dancers)
  "Honey" (June Allyson)
  "Cleopatterer" (Judy Garland, June
    Allyson, dancers)
  "Thou Swell" (Steve Lawrence)
Judy Garland, June Allyson, Steve
  Lawrence Medley:
  "Till the Clouds Roll By"
  "Look for the Silver Lining"
  "April Showers" (interpolation)
Trunk sequence: Judy Garland
  "San Francisco"
Closing: Judy Garland
  "Maybe I'll Come Back"

ADDENDA

★ This was June Allyson's debut on a television variety show.
★ June Allyson and Judy Garland were
  both at Metro at the same time. Allyson's pregnancy was the cause of Garland being scheduled to play opposite
  Fred Astaire in *Royal Wedding*. Garland
  never made the picture.
★ This was the fifth show aired and the
  sixth show taped.

ALBUMS

The Garland/Allyson numbers are on *Judy
  Garland: The Greatest Duets* [Broadcast
  Tributes BTRIB 0002 (33 ⅓)].
Albums with "Life Is Just a Bowl of
  Cherries":
Judy. Judy Garland (See section K, #16)

I Feel a Song Coming On
    (See section L, #3)
The Magic of Judy Garland
    (See section L, #8)
The Immortal Judy Garland
    (See section L, #11)
Albums with "Happiness Is Just a Thing
    Called Joe":
Star Eyes (See section K, #15)
I Feel a Song Coming On
    (See section L, #3)
Judy Garland—Her Greatest Hits
    (See section L, #4)
The Magic of Judy Garland
    (See section L, #8)
Albums with "San Francisco":
Judy (See section K, #2)
Judy's Portrait in Song (See section K, #7)
All of Judy (See section K, #10)
Judy Garland Concert (See section K, #11)
The Magic of Judy Garland
    (See section L, #8)
The Immortal Judy Garland
    (See section L, #11)
20 Hits of a Legend (See section L, #14)

---

6 **November 3, 1963**

Producer: Gary Smith
Director: Bill Hobin
Choreographers:
    Marc Breaux
    Dee Dee Wood
Writers:
    Arnie Sultan
    Marvin Worth
    William Nichols
    Bernard Rothman

GUESTS

Vic Damone
George Jessel
Zina Bethune

SONGS

"From This Moment On" (Judy Garland)
"Be My Guest" (Judy Garland, Vic
    Damone, Zina Bethune)
"Moon River" (Judy Garland)
"Getting to Know You" (Judy Garland,
    Zina Bethune)
Production number   (Vic Damone,
    dancers):
    "On the Street Where You Live"
    "Let's Take an Old-Fashioned Walk"
Judy Garland, Vic Damone Medley from
    Porgy and Bess:
    "Summertime"
    "It Ain't Necessarily So"
    "I Got Plenty of Nothin' "
    "Bess, You Is My Woman"
    "There's a Boat That's Leavin' Soon for
        New York"
Dialogue spot with Judy Garland, George
    Jessel, including:
    "My Mother's Eyes" (George Jessel)
    "Bill"
Judy Garland, Vic Damone, Zina Bethune
    Medley:
    "Auld Lang Syne"
    "Easter Parade"
    "Dear Old Donegal"
    "Brother, Can You Spare a Dime?"
    "Yankee Doodle"
    "You're a Grand Old Flag"
    "Happy Birthday to You"
    "Thank Heaven for Little Girls"
    "Me and My Shadow"
    "Mother"

"Seasons Greetings"
"Deck the Halls"
Trunk sequence: Judy Garland
   "Rock-a-Bye Your Baby with a Dixie
      Melody"
   "Smile"
Closing: Judy Garland
   "Maybe I'll Come Back"

ADDENDA

★ George Jessel was the cause of Judy
   Garland's name being changed from
   Frances Gumm. Judy was appearing
   with her sister as "The Gumm Sisters"
   at the Oriental Theater, Chicago, in
   1934. Jessel was the master of ceremonies, and he found that their name was
   causing the audience to giggle. He suggested the name "Garland," as he remembers it, because he had just been
   on the phone with the critic Robert
   Garland. Judy then took the name
   "Judy" from the Hoagy Carmichael
   song.
★ This was the twelfth show to be taped.

ALBUMS

Albums with "From This Moment On":
Judy's Portrait in Song (See section K, #7)
Judy Garland Concert (See section K, #11)
Judy Garland. The Collection. Live!
   (See section K, #17)
Albums with "Moon River":
Judy Garland Concert (See section K, #11)
Star Eyes (See section K, #15)

Albums with "Rock-a-Bye Your Baby with
   a Dixie Melody":
All of Judy (See section K, #10)
Judy Garland Concert (See section K, #11)
Judy. Judy Garland. (See section K, #16)
Judy Garland. The Collection. Live!
   (See section K, #17)
Unforgettable Judy Garland
   (See section K, #18)
The Hits of Judy Garland
   (See section L, #1)
The Magic of Judy Garland
   (See section L, #8)
A Garland for Judy (See section L, #9)
The Immortal Judy Garland
   (See section L, #11)
20 Hits of a Legend (See section L, #14)
Albums with "Smile":
Judy (See section K, #2)
All of Judy (See section K, #10)
Judy Garland Concert (See section K, #11)
The Pick of Judy Garland
   (See section K, #12)
Star Eyes (See section K, #15)
Judy Garland. The Collection. Live!
   (See section K, #17)
The Magic of Judy Garland
   (See section L, #8)
The Immortal Judy Garland
   (See section L, #11)
Judy Garland—20 Hits
   (See section L, #13)
20 Hits of a Legend (See section L, #14)

7 November 10, 1963

Producer: George Schlatter
Director: Bill Hobin
Choreographer: Nick Castle
Writers:
  John Bradford
  Tom Waldman

GUESTS

Count Basie
Mel Tormé
Judy Henske (folksinger)

SONGS

Opening numbers: Judy Garland, Count
  Basie Band
  "I Hear Music"

"The Sweetest Sounds"
"Strike Up the Band"
"Fascinating Rhythm" (Mel Tormé)
"Memories of You" (Judy Garland,
  Count Basie)
Production number   (Chorus, dancers):
  "God Bless the Child" (Judy Henske)
Comedy number with Mel Tormé, Jerry
  Van Dyke, and Judy Henske:
  "Walk Right In"
  "Low Down Alligator"
  "Lemon Tree"
Count Basie numbers:
  "One O'Clock Jump"
  "I Can't Stop Loving You"
"I've Got My Love to Keep Me Warm"
  (Judy Garland, Basie Band)
"Don't Dream of Anyone but Me"
  (Mel Tormé, Basie Band)

"April in Paris" (Judy Garland, Mel
    Tormé, Basie Band)
Judy Garland Medley:
    "A Cottage for Sale"
    "Hey, Look Me Over"
Closing: Judy Garland
    "Maybe I'll Come Back"

ADDENDA

★ Mel Tormé was responsible for "special
    musical arrangements" for "The Judy
    Garland Show." He and Garland had
    appeared together in the 1948 film
    Words and Music.
★ This was the second show to be taped.

ALBUMS

The Garland/Basie numbers are on *The
    Great Garland Duets* [Paragon 1001
    (33 ⅓)].
Albums with "Memories of You":
The Legendary Judy Garland
    (See section L, #18)
Albums with "A Cottage for Sale":
Judy Garland. Live! From Hollywood,
    vol. 1 (See section K, #13)
Star Eyes (See section K, #15)
Albums with "Hey, Look Me Over":
Judy (See section K, #2)
Judy Garland Concert (See section K, #11)
Judy Garland. The Collection. Live!
    (See section K, #17)
Unforgettable Judy Garland
    (See section K, #18)
Judy Garland—20 Hits
    (See section L, #13)

---

8 November 17, 1963

Producer: George Schlatter
Director: Bill Hobin
Choreographer: Danny Daniels
Writers:
    John Bradford
    Frank Waldman
    Tom Waldman

GUESTS

Liza Minnelli
Soupy Sales
The Castro Brothers

SONGS

"Liza" (Judy Garland)
"Come Rain or Come Shine" (Judy Gar-
    land)
"Together" (Judy Garland, Liza Minnelli)
Production number (Liza Minnelli,
    dancers):
    "Put On a Happy Face"
"I'm Calm" (Soupy Sales, Jerry Van Dyke)
Judy Garland, Liza Minnelli Medley:
    "We Could Make Such Beautiful
        Music"
    "The Best Is Yet to Come"
    "Bye, Bye, Baby"
    "Bob White"
    "You Are for Loving"
"Malagueña" (The Castro Brothers)
"You Make Me Feel So Young" (The Cas-
    tro Brothers)
Trunk sequence: Judy Garland
    "As Long as He Needs Me"
"Let Me Entertain You" (Liza Minnelli)
"Two Lost Souls" (Judy Garland, Liza
    Minnelli)
Closing: Judy Garland, Liza Minnelli
    "Maybe I'll Come Back"

ADDENDA

★ Liza Minnelli, of course, is Judy Garland's eldest daughter. This was their first professional appearance together.

★ This segment was the third show taped.

ALBUMS

Some of the Garland/Minnelli duets are on *The Great Garland Duets* [Paragon 1001 (33⅓)].

Albums with "Liza":

All of Judy (See section K, #10)

Judy Garland Concert (See section K, #11)

Judy. Judy Garland (See section K, #16)

Albums with "Come Rain or Come Shine":

(See the October 13, 1963, show.)

Albums with "As Long as He Needs Me":

Just for Openers (See section K, #1)

Judy in Hollywood (See section K, #3)

Star Eyes (See section K, #15)

The Legendary Judy Garland (See section L, #18)

The November 24, 1963, program was preempted because of President Kennedy's assassination.

---

9 **December 1, 1963**

Producer: Gary Smith
Director: Bill Hobin
Choreographers:
  Marc Breaux
  Dee Dee Wood
Writers:
  John Bradford
  Tom Waldman
  Frank Waldman

GUESTS

Peggy Lee
Jack Carter
Carl Reiner ("surprise" guest)

SONGS

"It's a Good Day" (Judy Garland)
"Never Will I Marry" (Judy Garland)
"Kids" (Jack Carter)
"When the World Was Young" (Peggy Lee)
Judy Garland, Peggy Lee Medley:
  "I Love Being Here with You"
  with interpolations of:
  "It's a Good Day"
  "Over the Rainbow"
  "Under the Bamboo Tree"
Judy Garland, Jack Carter Medley:
  "That Could Have Been Us"
  "My Defenses Are Down"
  "They Say It's Wonderful"
  "This Nearly Was Mine"
  "I'm Gonna Wash That Man Right Outta My Hair"
  "I've Grown Accustomed to Her Face"
  "Hymn to Him"
  "Wouldn't It Be Loverly"
  "Too Close for Comfort"
  "Mr. Wonderful"
Dialogue spot with Judy Garland and Carl Reiner
"San Francisco" (Judy Garland)
Judy Garland, Peggy Lee Medley:
  "I Like Men"
  "You Make Me Feel So Young"
  "Tess's Torch Song"
  "Fever"
  "It's So Nice to Have a Man Around the House"

"I'm Just Wild About Harry"

"Charlie, My Boy"

"Oh, Johnny, Oh, Johnny, Oh"

"Big Bad Bill Is Sweet William Now"

"Bill Bailey, Won't You Please Come Home"

Trunk sequence: Judy Garland

"How About Me?"

"When You're Smiling"

Closing: Judy Garland

"Maybe I'll Come Back"

ADDENDA

★ The song "It's a Good Day" was written by Peggy Lee and David Barbour.

★ This was the thirteenth show taped.

ALBUMS

Garland and Lee singing "I Love Being Here with You" is on *Judy Garland: The Greatest Duets* [Broadcast Tributes BTRIB 0002 (33 ⅓)].

Albums with "It's a Good Day":

Just for Openers (See section K, #1)

Albums with "Never Will I Marry":

Judy's Portrait in Song (See section K, #7)

Judy Garland. The Collection. Live!

(See section K, #17)

Judy Garland—20 Hits

(See section L, #13)

Albums with "San Francisco":

(See the October 27, 1963 show.)

Albums with "How About Me?":

Judy in Hollywood (See section K, #3)

Star Eyes (See section K, #15)

Judy Garland—20 Hits

(See section L, #13)

Albums with "When You're Smiling":

Judy Garland Concert (See section K, #11)

The Hits of Judy Garland

(See section L, #1)

Judy Garland Over the Rainbow

(See section L, #5)

The Magic of Judy Garland

(See section L, #8)

The Immortal Judy Garland

(See section L, #11)

---

10 December 8, 1963

Producer: George Schlatter

Director: Bill Hobin

Choreographer: Nick Castle

Writers:

John Bradford

Tom Waldman

Frank Waldman

GUEST

Mickey Rooney

SONGS

Opening Overture:

"Rock-a-Bye Your Baby with a Dixie Melody"

"By Myself"

"You Made Me Love You"

"Swanee"

"I Can't Give You Anything But Love"

"I Feel a Song Comin' On" (Judy Garland)

"All I Need Is the Girl" (Mickey Rooney)

Production number   (Mickey Rooney):

"When I'm Not Near the Girl I Love"

"Man Such As I"

"Girls"

"Thank Heaven for Little Girls"

"When the Sun Comes Out" (Judy Garland)

"Awakening" (Judy Garland)

Judy Garland, Mickey Rooney Medley:
  "Where or When"
  "How About You?"
  "But Not for Me"
  "Fascinating Rhythm"
  "God's Country"
  "Could You Use Me?"
  "Our Love Affair"
"You're So Right for Me" (Judy Garland,
  Mickey Rooney)
Judy Garland Medley:
  "Too Late Now"
  "Who Cares?"
  "Old Man River"
Closing: Judy Garland
  "Maybe I'll Come Back"

ADDENDA

★ Rooney and Garland were teamed in a series of films at MGM between 1937 and 1948.

★ This was the first show taped for the series. Among those in the audience for the inaugural program taping were Nick Adams, Max Baer, Lucille Ball, Jack Benny, Pamela Britton, Clint Eastwood, Van Heflin, William Hopper, Glynis Johns, Nancy Kulp, Sheldon Leonard, Dick Martin, Ross Martin, Roddy McDowall, Jimmy McHugh, Sid Melton, Gary Morton, Irene Ryan, Dick Van Dyke, Cara Williams, Natalie Wood.

ALBUMS

The Garland/Rooney numbers are on *Judy Garland: The Greatest Duets* [Broadcast Tributes BTRIB 0002 (33⅓)].
Albums with "I Feel a Song Comin' On":
Judy's Greatest Hits (See section K, #5)
Judy Garland. The Collection. Live! (See section K, #17)
Unforgettable Judy Garland (See section K, #18)
I Feel a Song Coming On (See section L, #3)
Judy Garland—Her Greatest Hits (See section L, #4)
The Magic of Judy Garland (See section L, #8)
The Immortal Judy Garland (See section L, #11)
Albums with "When the Sun Comes Out":
All Alone (See section K, #9)
Star Eyes (See section K, #15)
Judy Garland—20 Hits (See section L, #13)
Albums with "Too Late Now":
Star Eyes (See section K, #15)
Albums with "Who Cares?":
Judy. Judy Garland (See section K, #16)
The Magic of Judy Garland (See section L, #8)
The Immortal Judy Garland (See section L, #11)

11 December 15, 1963

Producer: George Schlatter
Director: Bill Hobin
Writers:
  John Bradford
  Tom Waldman
  Frank Waldman

G U E S T S

Tony Bennett
Dick Shawn
Steve Allen

S O N G S

"If Love Were All" (Judy Garland)
Production number (Judy Garland,
  Tony Bennett, Dick Shawn, dancers,
  singers):
  "Yes, Indeed"
  with interpolations of:
  "Nancy's Blues"
  "Dee Jay's Blues"
  "Fran's Blues"
"Honestly Sincerely" (Dick Shawn, Jerry
  Van Dyke)

Tony Bennett Medley:
"True Blue Lou"
"Keep Smiling at Trouble"
Production number (Judy Garland, Tony Bennett, singers, dancers):
"Night Train" (Chorus)
"Lullaby of Broadway" (Tony Bennett)
"Clear the Track" (Chorus)
"Carolina in the Morning" (Judy Garland)
"Pickin' Up Speed" (Chorus)
"Kansas City" (Tony Bennett)
"High Ballin' " (Chorus)
"When the Midnight Choo-Choo Leaves for Alabam' " (Judy Garland)
"Didn't We Tour" (Chorus)
"I Left My Heart in San Francisco" (Tony Bennett)
"Above the Blue Pacific Shore" (Judy Garland) (as countermelody to "San Francisco")
Production number (Judy Garland, Jerry Van Dyke, dancers, singers):
"One for My Baby"
"That's All"
"Happy Birthday to You"
Comedy spot with Judy Garland and Dick Shawn, including:
"My Buddy" (Dick Shawn)
"Every Evening" (Judy Garland) (as countermelody to "My Buddy")
"From This Moment On" (Dick Shawn)
"Me and My Shadow" (Dick Shawn)
"La Danza" (Dick Shawn)
"Rock-a-Bye Your Baby with a Dixie Melody" (Dick Shawn)
"Piccolo Pete" (Dick Shawn)
Trunk sequence: Judy Garland
"Stormy Weather"
"Alone Together"
"Maybe I'll Come Back"

ADDENDA

★ This was the fifth show taped.

ALBUMS

Albums with "If Love Were All":
Judy Garland. Live! From Hollywood, vol. 2 (See section K, #14)
Star Eyes (See section K, #15)
20 Hits of a Legend (See section L, #14)
Albums with "Stormy Weather":
Star Eyes (See section K, #15)
The Magic of Judy Garland (See section L, #8)
The Immortal Judy Garland (See section L, #11)
Albums with "Alone Together":
Star Eyes (See section K, #15)
The Judy Garland Deluxe Set (See section L, #2)

---

12 December 22, 1963

Producer: William Colleran
Director: Dean Whitmore
Choreographer: Peter Gennaro
Writers:
John Bradford
Frank Peppiat
John Aylesworth

GUESTS

Jack Jones	Liza Minnelli
Lorna Luft	Mel Tormé
Joe Luft	Tracy Everitt

SONGS

"Have Yourself a Merry Little Christmas" (Judy Garland)

"Consider Yourself" (Judy Garland, Lorna
  Luft, Joe Luft)
"Where Is Love?" (Joe Luft)
"Steam Heat" (Liza Minnelli, Tracy
  Everitt)
"Little Drops of Rain" (Judy Garland)
"Wouldn't It Be Loverly" (Jack Jones)
"Lollipops and Roses" (Jack Jones)
"Santa Claus Is Coming to Town" (Lorna
  Luft)
"Sweet Little Alice Blue Gown" (Liza
  Minnelli)
Judy Garland, Liza Minnelli, Jack Jones
  Medley:
  "Jingle Bells"
  "Sleigh Ride"
  "Not a Hayride"
  "It Happened in Sun Valley"
  "Winter Wonderland"
"Here We Come A'Caroling" (Mel Tormé,
  chorus)
"All Through the Year" (Judy Garland,
  Mel Tormé)
"The Christmas Song" (Judy Garland,
  Mel Tormé)
"Wassaling Song" (Judy Garland,
  Mel Tormé)
Ensemble Medley:
  "Caroling, Caroling"
  "What Child Is This?"
  "God Rest Ye Merry Gentlemen"
  "Hark, the Herald Angels Sing"
  "Good King Wenceslas"
  "It Came Upon a Midnight Clear"
  "Silent Night"
  "Deck the Halls"
Closing: Judy Garland
  "Over the Rainbow"

ADDENDA

★ In 1938, Judy Garland played opposite
  Jack Jones's father, Allan Jones, in
  Everybody Sing, one of her early MGM
  films.
★ Lorna Luft and Joe Luft are Judy's chil-
  dren.
★ "The Christmas Song" was written by
  Mel Tormé and Bob Wells.
★ This show was number fifteen in the
  taping schedule.

ALBUMS

Albums with "Sweet Little Alice Blue
  Gown":
Judy's Portrait in Song (See section K, #7)
Judy Garland. The Collection. Live!
  (See section K, #17)
Albums with "Over the Rainbow":
Judy's Greatest Hits (See section K, #5)
Judy Garland—Over the Rainbow
  (See section K, #8)
All of Judy (See section K, #10)
Judy Garland Concert (See section K, #11)
Star Eyes (See section K, #15)
Judy. Judy Garland (See section K, #16)
Judy Garland. The Collection. Live!
  (See section K, #17)
Unforgettable Judy Garland
  (See section K, #18)
The Judy Garland Deluxe Set
  (See section L, #2)
Judy Garland—Her Greatest Hits
  (See section L, #4)
Judy Garland Over the Rainbow
  (See section L, #5)
The Magic of Judy Garland
  (See section L, #8)

A Garland for Judy (See section L, #9)
The Immortal Judy Garland
  (See section L, #11)
Judy Garland—20 Hits
  (See section L, #13)
20 Hits of a Legend (See section L, #14)

---

13 December 29, 1963

Producer: William Colleran
Director: Dean Whitmore
Writers:
  John Bradford
  Frank Peppiat
  John Aylesworth

GUESTS

Bobby Darin
Bob Newhart
The Mighty Mites

SONGS

Football Medley: Judy Garland
  "Buckle Down, Winsocki"
  "You Gotta Be a Football Hero"
  "Jamboree Jones"
"Sing, Sing, Sing with a Swing" (comedy version) (Judy Garland, Bobby Darin, Bob Newhart)
"Michael Row the Boat Ashore" (Bobby Darin)
"Canaan's Land" (Bobby Darin)
"More" (Judy Garland)
Train Medley: Judy Garland, Bobby Darin
  "Sentimental Journey"
  "Going Home Train"
  "Chattanooga Choo-Choo"
  "On the Atchison, Topeka and the Santa Fe" (Judy Garland)

"Some of These Days" (Bobby Darin)
"Bye, Bye, Blackbird" (Judy Garland)
"Toot, Toot, Tootsie" (Bobby Darin)
"Beyond the Blue Horizon" (Judy Garland)
"I Know That You Know" (Bobby Darin)
"We've Been Swingin' on the Railroad"
"Lonesome Road"
Dance number: Peter Gennaro Dancers
Trunk sequence: Judy Garland
  "Do It Again"
  "Get Me to the Church on Time"
"Maybe I'll Come Back"

ADDENDA

★ Bobby Darin and Judy Garland were both in the movie *Pepe* in 1960.
★ The Mighty Mites were a children's football team from Venice, California.
★ The show was number fourteen in the taping schedule.

ALBUMS

The Garland/Darin numbers are on *Judy Garland: The Greatest Duets* [Broadcast Tributes BTRIB 0002 (33⅓)].
Albums with "Jamboree Jones":
Just for Openers (See section K, #1)
Albums with "More":
Judy—The Legend (See section K, #4)
All of Judy (See section K, #10)
Judy Garland Concert (See section K, #11)
Judy Garland. The Collection. Live!
  (See section K, #17)
Albums with "Do It Again":
Judy (See section K, #2)
Star Eyes (See section K, #15)
The Magic of Judy Garland
  (See section L, #8)

The Immortal Judy Garland
  (See section L, #11)
Albums with "Get Me to the Church on
  Time":
Just for Openers (See section K, #1)
The Magic of Judy Garland
  (See section L, #8)
The Immortal Judy Garland
  (See section L, #11)

---

14 **January 5, 1964**

Producer: Gary Smith
Director: Bill Hobin
Choreographer: Ernest Flatt
Writers:
  Arnie Sultan
  Marvin Worth
  Bernard Rothman
  William Nichols

GUESTS

Steve Allen
Jayne Meadows
Mel Tormé

SONGS

"Opening number: Judy Garland"
  "For Me and My Gal"
  "Judy's Gonna Give"
  "This Could Be the Start of Something
    Big"
Judy Garland, Steve Allen, Jayne
    Meadows, Mel Tormé Medley:
  "Be My Guest"
  "Hyde Park School Song"
  "Chicago" (partial)
  "San Francisco" (partial)
  "Maine Stein Song" (special lyrics)
  "Are You from Dixie?" (special lyrics)
"Here's That Rainy Day" (Judy Garland,
  dancers)
Steve Allen's "One-Man Show":
  "One-Man Show"
  "Take Me Out to the Ball Game"
  "All Alone"
  "Phone Book"
  "We're Shook"
  "Things for Sale"
  "Mister Allen, Will You"
Judy Garland, Steve Allen Medley:
  "I Love You Today" (Judy Garland,
    Steve Allen)
  "When I'm in Love" (Judy Garland,
    Steve Allen)
  "I'll Show Them All" (Judy Garland)
Production number   (Mel Tormé,
  chorus):
  "Goin' Home Baby"
"The Party's Over" (Judy Garland, Mel
  Tormé)

"Song Writers' Spot" (Judy Garland,
Steve Allen, Mel Tormé):
 "It's Bert Pomeroy for President"
 "Every Day's a Holiday"
Judy Garland, Steve Allen, Mel Tormé
Medley:
 "Ain't Misbehavin' "
 "Makin' Whoopee"
 "Glory of Love"
 "Wrap Your Troubles in Dreams"
 "You Took Advantage of Me"
 "Mean to Me"
 "Girl Friend"
 "Tiptoe Through the Tulips"
 "Truckin' "
 "Gypsy in My Soul"
 "Nice Work If You Can Get It"
 "Let's Do It"
 "My Heart Stood Still"
 "Hit the Road to Dreamland"
 "Way Back Home"
Trunk sequence: Judy Garland
 "Island in the West Indies"
 "Through the Years"
"Maybe I'll Come Back"

ADDENDA

★ The song "This Could Be the Start of
Something Big" was written by Steve
Allen.
★ The songs "I Love You Today," "When
I'm in Love," and "I'll Show Them All"
were also written by Steve Allen, for the
1963 Broadway show *Sophie*, based on
the life of Sophie Tucker.
★ This show was the eleventh taped.

ALBUMS

The Garland/Allen numbers are on *Judy
Garland: The Greatest Duets* [Broadcast
Tributes BTRIB 0002 (33⅓)].
Albums with "This Could Be the Start of
Something Big":
All of Judy (See section K, #10)
Albums with "Here's That Rainy Day":
Judy—The Legend (See section K, #4)
Star Eyes (See section K, #15)
Albums with "I'll Show Them All":
Unforgettable Judy Garland
 (See section K, #6)
Albums with "Island in the West Indies":
Just for Openers (See section K, #1)
Unforgettable Judy Garland
 (See section K, #6)
The Magic of Judy Garland
 (See section L, #8)
The Immortal Judy Garland
 (See section L, #11)
Albums with "Through the Years":
Judy—The Legend (See section K, #4)
Unforgettable Judy Garland
 (See section K, #6)

---

15 **January 12, 1964**

Producer: William Colleran
Director: Dean Whitmore
Choreographer: Peter Gennaro
Writers:
 John Bradford
 Frank Peppiat
 John Aylesworth

GUESTS

Ethel Merman
Shelley Berman
Peter Gennaro

SONGS

Production number (Judy Garland, Ethel
  Merman, Shelley Berman, Peter
  Gennaro):
  "Everybody's Doin' It"
  with interpolations of "Let's Do It"
"Come on Five" (Shelley Berman,
  dancers)
Dialogue spot with Shelley Berman,
  including:
  "You'll Never Walk Alone"
"I Got Rhythm" (Judy Garland)
Introduction to Ethel Merman
"Gee, but It's Good to Be Here" (Ethel
  Merman)
"I Get a Kick out of You" (Ethel Merman)
Production number (Peter Gennaro,
  dancers):
  "I Love a Parade"
"Oh, Shenandoah" (Judy Garland)
"Rollalong" (Judy Garland)
Dance number (Judy Garland, Peter
  Gennaro):
  with "Makin' Whoopee" (vocal by
  Shelley Berman)
Judy Garland, Ethel Merman Medley:
  "Friendship"
  "Let's Be Buddies"
  "You're the Top"
  "You're Just in Love"
  "It's De-Lovely"
  "Together"

Trunk sequence: Judy Garland
  "A Pretty Girl Milking Her Cow"
  "Puttin' on the Ritz"
  "The Battle Hymn of the Republic"
"Maybe I'll Come Back"

ADDENDA

★ Judy Garland had been a friend and
  staunch supporter of JFK. She had
  campaigned for him with the servicemen overseas, and they spoke frequently on the phone. She was
  devastated by his assassination. She
  proposed to dedicate "The Battle Hymn
  of the Republic" to his memory. The
  idea was opposed by a CBS executive
  who explained that in a few months no
  one would remember him anyway. She
  fought to have the song included in the
  show.
★ This was the sixteenth show in the series to be taped.

ALBUMS

The Garland/Merman Medley is on *The
  Great Garland Duets* [Paragon 1001
  (33⅓)] and *Judy Garland: The Greatest
  Duets* [Broadcast Tributes BTRIB 0002
  (33⅓)].
Albums with "Oh, Shenandoah":
All of Judy (See section K, #10)
Judy Garland. The Collection. Live!
  (See section K, #17)
Albums with "A Pretty Girl Milking Her
  Cow":
Judy in Hollywood (See section K, #3)
Judy Garland—Her Greatest Hits
  (See section L, #4)

Judy Garland Over the Rainbow
  (See section L, #5)
The Magic of Judy Garland
  (See section L, #8)
The Immortal Judy Garland
  (See section L, #11)
Albums with "Puttin' on the Ritz":
Judy in Hollywood (See section K, #3)
Judy. Judy Garland (See section K, #16)
The Magic of Judy Garland
  (See section L, #8)
The Immortal Judy Garland
  (See section L, #11)
The Legendary Judy Garland
  (See section L, #18)
Albums with "The Battle Hymn of the
  Republic":
Just for Openers (See section K, #1)
Unforgettable Judy Garland
  (See section K, #6)
All Alone (See section K, #9)
All of Judy (See section K, #10)
Judy Garland. The Collection. Live!
  (See section K, #17)
Unforgettable Judy Garland
  (See section K, #18)
The Magic of Judy Garland
  (See section L, #8)
The Immortal Judy Garland
  (See section L, #11)

---

16 January 19, 1964

Producer: William Colleran
Director: Dean Whitmore
Writers:
  John Bradford
  Frank Peppiat
  John Aylesworth

GUESTS

Vic Damone   Louis Nye
Chita Rivera   Ken Murray

SONGS

"They Can't Take That Away from Me"
  (Judy Garland)
"I Got a Feelin' You're Foolin' " (Judy
  Garland)
"I Believe in You" (Judy Garland, Chita
  Rivera)
Comedy monologue by Louis Nye
"Someone to Watch Over Me" (Judy
  Garland)
Introduction to Vic Damone
"You're Nobody Till Somebody Loves
  You" (Vic Damone)
Production number (Chita Rivera):
  "I Got Plenty of Nothin' "
"By Myself" (Judy Garland)
Judy Garland, Vic Damone Medley from
  West Side Story:
  "Maria"
  "Something's Coming"
  "Somewhere"
  "Tonight"
"Home Movies" spot with Judy Garland,
  Ken Murray
Trunk sequence: Judy Garland
  "Better Luck Next Time"
  "It's Almost Like Being in Love"
  "This Can't Be Love"
"Maybe I'll Come Back"

ADDENDA

★ Vic Damone and Chita Rivera were also Judy's guests on September 3, 1966, when she hosted "The Hollywood Palace." Damone also appeared on this series on November 3, 1963, and March 15, 1964.

★ This show was number seventeen in the production schedule.

ALBUMS

The Garland/Damone *West Side Story* Medley is on *Judy and Her Partners in Rhythm and Rhyme* [Star-Tone 213 (33⅓)].

Albums with "By Myself":

Judy (See section K, #2)

All Alone (See section K, #9)

All of Judy (See section K, #10)

Judy. Judy Garland (See section K, #16)

I Feel a Song Coming On
(See section L, #3)

The Magic of Judy Garland
(See section L, #8)

The Immortal Judy Garland
(See section L, #11)

Albums with "It's Almost Like Being in Love"/"This Can't Be Love":

Judy—The Legend (See section K, #4)

Judy's Portrait in Song (See section K, #7)

Judy Garland Concert (See section K, #11)

Judy. Judy Garland (See section K, #16)

Judy Garland. The Collection. Live!
(See section K, #17)

Unforgettable Judy Garland
(See section K, #18)

17 January 26, 1964

Producer: William Colleran
Director: Dean Whitmore
Choreographer: Wally Siebert
Writers:
   John Bradford
   Frank Peppiat
   John Aylesworth

GUESTS

Martha Raye	Ken Murray
Peter Lawford	Rich Little

SONGS

"76 Trombones" (Judy Garland)

"Parade of the Instruments" (Judy Garland)

"Tonight" (Mel Tormé)

Introduction of guests

Rich Little mimics well-known stars by reciting the lyrics to "The Man That Got Away"

"Taking a Chance on Love" (Martha Raye)

"It's So Nice to Have a Man Around the House" (Peter Lawford)

"I'm Old-Fashioned" (Judy Garland)

Glenn Miller Medley: Judy Garland, Martha Raye
   "I've Heard That Song Before"
   "Moonlight Cocktail" (Judy Garland)
   "Pennsylvania 6-5000"
   "Elmer's Tune"
   "At Last" (Judy Garland)
   "St. Louis Blues"

"Home Movies" spot with Judy Garland,
    Ken Murray
"Hit Parade of 1964" number: Judy
    Garland, Martha Raye, Peter Lawford
    "Be True to Your School"
        with interpolations of:
        "The Boy Next Door"
        "Dumb Head"
        "Nitty Gritty"
        "That Wonderful Year"
Trunk sequence: Judy Garland
    "All Alone"
    "Oh Lord, I'm on My Way"

ADDENDA

★ Peter Lawford and Judy Garland ap-
    peared together in 1948 in *Easter Pa-
    rade*. It was through Lawford that she
    first met Jack Kennedy.

★ This show was number eighteen on the
    production schedule.

ALBUMS

The Garland/Raye numbers are on *Judy
    Garland: The Greatest Duets* [Broadcast
    Tributes BTRIB 0002 (33⅓)] and *Judy
    and Her Partners in Rhythm and Rhyme*
    [StarTone 213 (33⅓)].
Albums with "76 Trombones":
Unforgettable Judy Garland
    (See section K, #6)
Albums with "I'm Old-Fashioned":
Judy's Portrait in Song (See section K, #7)
Judy Garland. The Collection. Live!
    (See section K, #17)
Albums with "All Alone":
Judy (See section K, #2)
All Alone (See section K, #9)

Martha Raye and Judy.

Judy Garland—20 Hits
    (See section L, #13)
Albums with "Oh, Lord, I'm on My Way":
Judy—The Legend (See section K, #4)

18   **February 2, 1964**

Producer: William Colleran
Director: Dean Whitmore
Writers:
    John Bradford
    Frank Peppiat
    John Aylesworth

GUESTS

Louis Jourdan
Kirby Stone Four
Ken Murray

SONGS

"San Francisco" (Judy Garland)
Production number (Judy Garland, Kirby
    Stone Four, chorus):
    "Baubles, Bangles, and Beads"
        (Kirby Stone Four)
    "You Do Something to Me" (Kirby
        Stone Four)
    "Whispering" (Judy Garland, Kirby
        Stone Four)
    "Baubles, Bangles, and Beads" (reprise)
"I Want a Girl (Just Like the Girl That
    Married Dear Old Dad)" (Louis
    Jourdan)
"Paris Is a Lonely Town" (Judy Garland)
"Smoke Gets in Your Eyes" (Judy Garland
    and four men dressed as firemen)
"Shall We Dance" (Judy Garland)
Introduction to dancers
"Home Movies" spot with Judy Garland,
    Ken Murray, including "Louise"

Cartoon Medley: Judy Garland, Louis Jourdan
  "Popeye the Sailor Man" (Judy Garland)
  "Huckleberry Hound" (Louis Jourdan)
  "Give a Little Whistle"
  "Little Lulu" (Louis Jourdan)
  "When You Wish upon a Star"
  "Who's Afraid of the Big Bad Wolf" (Louis Jourdan)
  "Zip-A-Dee-Doo-Dah"
  "Some Day My Prince Will Come" (Judy Garland)
Trunk sequence: Judy Garland
  "What'll I Do?"
  "Battle Hymn of the Republic"
Closing: Judy Garland
  "Maybe I'll Come Back"

ADDENDA

★ This was the nineteenth show to be taped.
★ The Garland/Jourdan Cartoon Medley is on *Judy and Her Partners in Rhythm and Rhyme* [StarTone 213 (33⅓)].

ALBUMS

Albums with "San Francisco":
(See the October 27, 1963, show.)
Albums with "Paris Is a Lonely Town":
Unforgettable Judy Garland
  (See section K, #6)
Albums with "What'll I Do?":
Judy—The Legend (See section K, #4)
All of Judy (See section K, #10)
The Pick of Judy Garland
  (See section K, #12)
Star Eyes (See section K, #15)

Albums with "The Battle Hymn of the Republic":
(See the January 12, 1964, show.)

---

19 February 9, 1964

"Judy in Concert"
Producer: Gary Smith
Director: Dean Whitmore
Choreographer: Wally Siebert
Writers:
  Frank Peppiat
  John Aylesworth
  Johnny Bradford

Concert format, with orchestra onstage.

SONGS

"Swing Low, Sweet Chariot"
"He's Got the Whole World in His Hands"
"When Johnny Comes Marching Home"
"There's a Long, Long Trail"
"Keep the Home Fires Burning"
"Give My Regards to Broadway"
"Boy of Mine"
"My Buddy"
"Oh, How I Hate to Get Up in the Morning"
"Over There"
"It's a Grand Old Flag"
"That's Entertainment"
"Make Someone Happy"
"Liza"
"Happiness Is Just a Thing Called Joe"
"Lorna"
"Rock-a-Bye Your Baby with a Dixie Melody"
"A Couple of Swells"
"America the Beautiful"

ADDENDA

★ This was the first of three programs in which Judy Garland did a concert format with no guest stars. It was number twenty in the production schedule.

★ This show was the introduction of the song "Lorna." The music was written by Mort Lindsey and used as the theme music for "The Judy Garland Show." The words were written by Johnny Mercer so that there would be a song Judy could sing for each of her children.

ALBUMS

Albums with "Swing Low, Sweet Chariot"/ "He's Got the Whole World in His Hands":

Judy Garland. Live! From Hollywood, vol. 2 (See section K, #14)

Albums with World War I songs:

All of Judy (See section K, #10)

Judy Garland. Live! From Hollywood, vol. 2 (See section K, #14)

Albums with "That's Entertainment":

Judy in Hollywood (See section K, #3)

Judy—The Legend (See section K, #4)

All of Judy (See section E, #10)

Judy Garland. The Collection. Live! (See section K, #17)

Unforgettable Judy Garland (See section K, #18)

The Judy Garland Deluxe Set (See section L, #2)

Judy Garland—Her Greatest Hits (See section L, #4)

The Magic of Judy Garland (See section L, #8)

The Immortal Judy Garland (See section L, #11)

Judy Garland—20 Hits (See section L, #13)

The Legendary Judy Garland (See section L, #18)

Albums with "Make Someone Happy":

Judy Garland—Over the Rainbow (See section K, #8)

Star Eyes (See section K, #15)

The Magic of Judy Garland (See section L, #8)

I Could Go On Singing Forever (See section L, #12)

Judy Garland—20 Hits (See section L, #13)

Albums with "Liza":

(See the November 17, 1963, show.)

Albums with "Happiness Is Just a Thing Called Joe":

Star Eyes (See section K, #15)

I Feel a Song Coming On (See section L, #3)

The Magic of Judy Garland (See section L, #8)

Albums with "Rock-a-Bye Your Baby with a Dixie Melody":

(See the November 3, 1963, show.)

Albums with "A Couple of Swells":

Judy in Hollywood (See section K, #3)

The Pick of Judy Garland (See section K, #12)

Judy. Judy Garland (See section K, #16)

Albums with "America the Beautiful":

All of Judy (See section K, #10)

20 February 16, 1964

Producer: Gary Smith
Director: Dean Whitmore
Choreographer: Wally Siebert
Writers:
  John Bradford
  Frank Peppiat
  John Aylesworth

GUESTS

Diahann Carroll
Mel Tormé

SONGS

"Hey, Look Me Over" (Judy Garland)
"Smile" (Judy Garland)
"I Can't Give You Anything but Love"
  (Judy Garland)
"After You've Gone" (Judy Garland)
"Alone Together" (Judy Garland)
"Come Rain or Come Shine" (Judy
  Garland)
Judy Garland, Mel Tormé Medley:
  "Stranger in Town" (Judy Garland)
  "Blues in the Night" (Mel Tormé)
  "The Trolley Song" (Judy Garland),
    with interpolation of "I Got a Wife
    and Kids" by Tormé
"Quiet Nights" (Diahann Carroll)
"Goody, Goody" (Diahann Carroll)
Judy Garland, Diahann Carroll Medley:
  "Let's Call the Whole Thing Off"
    (special lyrics)
  "It's Only a Paper Moon" (Judy
    Garland)
  "Dancing on the Ceiling" (Diahann
    Carroll)
  "That Old Black Magic" (Judy Garland)
"The Gentleman Is a Dope" (Diahann
  Carroll)
"Ill Wind" (Judy Garland)
"It Might as Well Be Spring" (Diahann
  Carroll)
"Hit the Road to Dreamland" (Judy
  Garland)
"Surrey with the Fringe on Top"
  (Diahann Carroll)
"Let's Take the Long Way Home"
  (Judy Garland)
"The Sweetest Sounds" (Diahann
  Carroll)
"Any Place I Hang My Hat Is Home"
  (Judy Garland, Diahann Carroll)
Trunk sequence: Judy Garland
  "Don't Ever Leave Me"
  "It's Gonna Be a Great Day"

ADDENDA

★ This show was number twenty-one in
  the production schedule.

ALBUMS

The Garland/Carroll Medley is on *The
  Great Garland Duets* [Paragon 1001
  (33⅓)].
Albums with "Hey, Look Me Over":
(See the November 10, 1963, show.)
Albums with "Smile":
(See the November 3, 1963, show.)
Albums with "I Can't Give You Anything
  but Love":
Judy (See section K, #2)
Judy Garland. The Collection. Live!
  (See section K, #17)
Unforgettable Judy Garland
  (See section K, #18)
Judy Garland—Her Greatest Hits
  (See section L, #4)

Judy Garland Over the Rainbow
   (See section L, #5)
The Magic of Judy Garland
   (See section L, #8)
The Immortal Judy Garland
   (See section L, #11)
20 Hits of a Legend (See section L, #14)
Albums with "After You've Gone":
Judy (See section K, #2)
Judy Garland Concert (See section K, #11)
Judy Garland. The Collection. Live!
   (See section K, #17)
The Immortal Judy Garland
   (See section L, #11)
Albums with "Alone Together":
(See the December 15, 1963, show.)
Albums with "Come Rain or Come
   Shine":
(See the October 13, 1963, show.)
Albums with "Don't Ever Leave Me":
Judy—The Legend (See section K, #4)
Star Eyes (See section K, #15)
Albums with "It's Gonna Be a Great Day":
Judy (See section K, #2)
Judy. Judy Garland (See section K, #16)

---

21 **February 23, 1964**

Producer: Gary Smith
Director: Dean Whitmore
Writers:
   John Bradford
   Frank Peppiat
   John Aylesworth

GUESTS

Jack Jones
Ken Murray

SONGS

"Swanee"
Medley:
   "It's Almost Like Being in Love"
   "This Can't Be Love"
"Just in Time"
"A Foggy Day"
"If Love Were All"
"Just You, Just Me"
"Last Night When We Were Young"
Palace Medley:
   "Shine On, Harvest Moon"
   "Some of These Days"
   "My Man"
   "I Don't Care"
"Love with the Proper Stranger" (Jack
   Jones)
"Wives and Lovers" (Jack Jones)
"Home Movies" spot with Judy Garland,
   Ken Murray
Jeanette MacDonald/Nelson Eddy
   Medley: Judy Garland, Jack Jones
   "San Francisco" (introduction—
      partial)
   "Will You Remember" (Judy Garland,
      Jack Jones)
   "Rosalie" (Jack Jones)
   "I'll See You Again" (Judy Garland,
      Jack Jones)
   "Lover, Come Back to Me" (Judy
      Garland)
   "Donkey Serenade" (Judy Garland,
      Jack Jones)
Trunk sequence: Judy Garland
   "When The Sun Comes Out"
Closing: Judy Garland
   "Maybe I'll Come Back"

ADDENDA

★ This was show number twenty-two in
   production.

ALBUMS

The Garland/Jones Medley is on *The Great Garland Duets* [Paragon 1001 (33⅓)].

Albums with "Swanee":
(See the October 20, 1963, show.)

Albums with "It's Almost Like Being in Love"/"This Can't Be Love":
(See the January 19, 1964, show.)

Albums with "Just in Time":
(See the October 6, 1963, show.)

Albums with "A Foggy Day":
(See the October 13, 1963, show.)

Albums with "If Love Were All":
(See the December 15, 1964, show.)

Albums with "Just You, Just Me":
Judy Garland. Live! From Hollywood, vol. 2 (See section K, #14)
The Judy Garland Deluxe Set (See section L, #2)
The Magic of Judy Garland (See section L, #8)
The Immortal Judy Garland (See section L, #11)

Albums with "Last Night When We Were Young":
Unforgettable Judy Garland (See section K, #6)
Star Eyes (See section K, #15)
The Judy Garland Deluxe Set (See section L, #2)
The Magic of Judy Garland (See section L, #8)
The Immortal Judy Garland (See section L, #11)
The Legendary Judy Garland (See section L, #18)

Albums with the Palace Medley:
Judy—The Legend (See section K, #4)
Judy Garland. Live! From Hollywood, vol. 2 (See section K, #14)

Albums with "When the Sun Comes Out":
(See the December 8, 1963, show.)

22 March 1, 1964

Producer: Gary Smith
Director: Bill Hobin
Choreographer: Ernest Flatt
Writers:
   Arnie Sultan
   Marvin Worth
   Bernard Rothman
   William Nichols

GUESTS

Ray Bolger
Jane Powell

SONGS

"I've Got a Lot of Living to Do (Judy Garland)"
"Be My Guest (Mel Tormé)"
"That's All (Judy Garland)"
"One for My Baby (Judy Garland, cast)"
Production number   (Ray Bolger):
   "Margie"
   "Sweet Lorraine"
   "Cecilia"
   "Lady in Red"
   "Maria"
   "When I'm Not Near the Girl I Love"
   "K-K-Katy"
   "I Love the Girls"
"On the Sunny Side of the Street" (Judy Garland, Ray Bolger)
Production number   (Jane Powell, dancers):
   "Dear Friend"
Judy Garland, Jane Powell, Jerry Van Dyke Medley:
   (Jerry Van Dyke lip-synchs to the voices of famous musical stars)

"Romantic Duets"

"Leading Men"

"Meant for Two"

"I Remember It Well" (Judy Garland)

"There Was a Role" (Jane Powell)

"Make Believe" (Jane Powell)

"Will You Remember?" (Jane Powell, with Judy lip-synching)

"All Aboard for Movieland"

Dialogue spot with Judy Garland, Ray Bolger, including:

"If I Only Had a Brain . . ."

"We're Off to See the Wizard"

Production number (Judy Garland, Jane Powell, Ray Bolger, dancers):

"Jitterbug"

Trunk sequence: Judy Garland

"When Your Lover Has Gone"

"Some People"

"Maybe I'll Come Back"

ADDENDA

★ This show had originally been scheduled for November 24, 1963. It was preempted, and rescheduled for February 16, 1964, due to President Kennedy's assassination. It was rescheduled again and finally aired on March 1, 1964. It was the tenth in the series to be taped.

★ Ray Bolger and Judy Garland first appeared together in 1939 in *The Wizard of Oz*. They also worked together in *The Harvey Girls* in 1946.

★ The third time is the charm. Jane Powell finally played the June Allyson/Judy Garland role in *Royal Wedding* opposite Fred Astaire.

ALBUMS

The Garland/Powell and Garland/Bolger numbers are on *Judy Garland: The Greatest Duets* [Broadcast Tributes BTRIB 0002 (33⅓)].

Albums with "I've Got a Lot of Living to Do":

Judy. Judy Garland (See section K, #16)

Albums with "That's All":

Judy Garland—Over the Rainbow (See section K, #8)

Judy Garland—20 Hits (See section L, #13)

Albums with "When Your Lover Has Gone":

Judy Garland. Live! From Hollywood, vol. 1 (See section K, #13)

Star Eyes (See section K, #15)

Judy Garland. The Collection. Live! (See section K, #17)

Albums with "Some People":

Just for Openers (See section K, #1)

Judy Garland. The Collection. Live! (See section K, #17)

The Magic of Judy Garland (See section L, #8)

The Immortal Judy Garland (See section L, #11)

23 March 8, 1964

"Judy in Concert"

Producer: William Colleran

Director: Dean Whitmore

Choreographer: Wally Siebert

Writers:

John Bradford

Frank Peppiat

John Aylesworth

Concert format, with orchestra onstage

SONGS

"Once in a Lifetime"
"I Feel a Song Coming On"
"If I Had a Talking Picture of You"
"Toot, Toot, Tootsie"
"Dirty Hands, Dirty Face"
"Carolina in the Morning"
"Love of My Life"
"The Boy Next Door"
"On the Atchison, Topeka and the Santa Fe"
"You're Nearer"
"Alexander's Ragtime Band"
"How Long Has This Been Going On?"
"Steppin' Out with My Baby"
"I'm Always Chasing Rainbows"
"I'm Nobody's Baby"
"The Man That Got Away"
"Be a Clown"
"Once in a Lifetime" (reprise)

ADDENDA

★ This concert show was the twenty-third in production.

ALBUMS

Albums with "Once in a Lifetime":
(See the October 6, 1963, show.)
Albums with "I Feel a Song Coming On":
(See the December 8, 1963, show.)
Albums with "If I Had a Talking Picture of You":
Judy in Hollywood (See section K, #3)
Albums with "Toot, Toot, Tootsie":
All of Judy (See section K, #10)
Albums with "Dirty Hands, Dirty Face":
Judy in Hollywood (See section K, #3)
Albums with "Love of My Life":
Judy in Hollywood (See section K, #3)

Albums with "The Boy Next Door":
Judy in Hollywood (See section K, #3)
All of Judy (See section K, #10)
Star Eyes (See section K, #15)
The Magic of Judy Garland
    (See section L, #8)
Albums with "On the Atchison, Topeka and the Santa Fe":
All of Judy (See section K, #10)
Judy. Judy Garland (See section K, #16)
Albums with "You're Nearer":
All of Judy (See section K, #10)
The Magic of Judy Garland
    (See section L, #8)
The Immortal Judy Garland
    (See section L, #11)
20 Hits of a Legend (See section L, #14)
Albums with "Alexander's Ragtime Band":
(See the October 20, 1963, show.)
Albums with "How Long Has This Been Going On?":
The Judy Garland Deluxe Set
    (See section K, #2)
The Legendary Judy Garland
    (See section K, #18)
Albums with "Steppin' Out with My Baby":
All of Judy (See section K, #10)
Judy Garland. Live! From Hollywood,
    vol. 1 (See section K, #13)
Judy. Judy Garland (See section K, #16)
Albums with "I'm Always Chasing Rainbows":
Judy Garland—Over the Rainbow
    (See section K, #8)
All Alone (See section K, #9)
The Pick of Judy Garland
    (See section K, #12)
Star Eyes (See section K, #15)
Judy Garland. The Collection. Live!
    (See section K, #17)

Judy Garland—20 Hits
(See section L, #13)
20 Hits of a Legend (See section L, #14)
Albums with "I'm Nobody's Baby":
Judy—The Legend (See section K, #4)
Judy's Greatest Hits (See section K, #5)
All Alone (See section K, #9)
All of Judy (See section K, #10)
Star Eyes (See section K, #15)
Judy Garland. The Collection. Live!
(See section K, #17)
Unforgettable Judy Garland
(See section K, #18)
Albums with "The Man That Got Away":
(See the October 13, 1963, show.)
Albums with "Be a Clown":
Judy Garland Concert (See section K, #11)
Judy. Judy Garland (See section K, #16)

---

24 March 15, 1964

Producer: William Colleran
Director: Dean Whitmore
Choreographer: Wally Siebert
Writers:
John Bradford
Frank Peppiat
John Aylesworth

Concert format, with orchestra onstage.

GUEST

Vic Damone

SONGS

Garland Medley:
"This Is My Lucky Day"
"Sweet Danger"
"Do I Love You?"
"I Love You"
"When Your Lover Has Gone"

"Down with Love"
"Old Devil Moon"
"Never Will I Marry"
"Any Place I Hang My Hat Is Home"
"Chicago"
"Who Are You Now? (Vic Damone)"
"I'm Gonna Miss You" (Vic Damone)
Judy Garland, Vic Damone Medley:
"Night of My Nights"
"He's in Love"
"And This Is My Beloved"
Trunk sequence: Judy Garland
"Lost in the Stars"

ADDENDA

★ This was the twenty-fourth show to be taped.

ALBUMS

Albums with "This Is My Lucky Day":
Unforgettable Judy Garland
(See section K, #6)
The Magic of Judy Garland
(See section L, #8)
The Immortal Judy Garland
(See section L, #11)
The Legendary Judy Garland
(See section L, #18)
Albums with "Sweet Danger":
Judy's Portrait in Song (See section K, #7)
Judy Garland. The Collection. Live!
(See section K, #17)
Albums with "Do I Love You?":
Judy—The Legend (See section K, #4)
Judy Garland. Live! From Hollywood,
vol. 1 (See section K, #13)
The Judy Garland Deluxe Set
(See section L, #2)
I Feel a Song Coming On
(See section L, #3)
Judy Garland—Her Greatest Hits
(See section L, #4)

The Magic of Judy Garland
(See section L, #8)
The Immortal Judy Garland
(See section L, #11)
Albums with "I Love You":
Unforgettable Judy Garland
(See section K, #6)
Judy Garland. Live! From Hollywood, vol.
1 (See section K, #13)
Star Eyes (See section K, #15)
Albums with "When Your Lover Has
Gone":
(See the March 1, 1964, show.)
Albums with "Down with Love":
Judy. Judy Garland (See section K, #16)
The Judy Garland Deluxe Set
(See section L, #2)
Judy Garland—Her Greatest Hits
(See section L, #4)
Judy Garland Over the Rainbow
(See section L, #5)
The Magic of Judy Garland
(See section L, #8)
The Immortal Judy Garland
(See section L, #11)
Albums with "Old Devil Moon":
Judy Garland. Live! From Hollywood,
vol. 1 (See section K, #13)
Judy. Judy Garland (See section K, #16)
Judy Garland. The Collection. Live!
(See section K, #17)
The Judy Garland Deluxe Set
(See section L, #2)
Judy Garland—Her Greatest Hits
(See section L, #4)
Judy Garland Over the Rainbow
(See section L, #5)
The Magic of Judy Garland
(See section L, #8)
The Immortal Judy Garland
(See section L, #11)

The Legendary Judy Garland
(See section L, #18)
Albums with "Never Will I Marry":
Judy's Portrait in Song (See section K, #7)
Judy Garland—20 Hits
(See section L, #13)
Albums with "Any Place I Hang My Hat Is
Home":
Judy's Portrait in Song (See section K, #7)
Judy Garland. The Collection. Live!
(See section K, #17)
The Magic of Judy Garland
(See section L, #8)
The Immortal Judy Garland
(See section L, #11)
Albums with "Chicago":
(See the September 29, 1963, show.)
Albums with "Lost in the Stars":
Unforgettable Judy Garland
(See section K, #6)

25 March 22, 1964

Producer: William Colleran
Director: Dean Whitmore
Choreographer: Wally Siebert
Writers:
   John Bradford
   Frank Peppiat
   John Aylesworth

Concert format, with orchestra onstage.

GUEST
Bobby Cole

SONGS
"Sail Away"
"Comes Once in a Lifetime"
"I Am Loved"

"Life Is Just a Bowl of Cherries"
"Why Can't I?"
"I Gotta Right to Sing the Blues"
"Joey, Joey, Joey"
"Love"
"By Myself"
"Get Happy"
"As Long as He Needs Me"
"From This Moment On" (The Bobby
    Cole Trio)
"I Wonder What Became of Me"
    (The Bobby Cole Trio)
"The Lady's in Love with You"
    (The Bobby Cole Trio)
"Poor Butterfly" (Judy Garland,
    The Bobby Cole Trio)
Trunk sequence: Judy Garland
    "Old Man River"

ADDENDA

★ This was the next to the last show
  taped for the series.

ALBUMS

Albums with "Comes Once in a Lifetime":
The Immortal Judy Garland
    (See section L, #11)
Albums with "I Am Loved":
Star Eyes (See section K, #15)
Albums with "Life Is Just a Bowl of
    Cherries":
(See the October 27, 1963, show.)
Albums with "Why Can't I?":
All Alone (See section K, #9)
Albums with "Joey, Joey, Joey":
Judy. Judy Garland (See section K, #16)
20 Hits of a Legend (See section L, #14)
Albums with "I Gotta Right to Sing the
    Blues":
All Alone (See section K, #9)

The Magic of Judy Garland
    (See section L, #8)
The Immortal Judy Garland
    (See section L, #11)
The Legendary Judy Garland
    (See section L, #18)
Albums with "By Myself":
(See the January 19, 1964, show.)
Albums with "Get Happy":
Judy Garland Concert (See section K, #11)
Judy. Judy Garland (See section K, #16)
Albums with "As Long as He Needs Me":
(See the November 17, 1963, show.)
Albums with "Poor Butterfly":
All Alone (See section K, #9)

26 March 29, 1964

"Judy in Concert"
Producer: William Colleran
Director: Dean Whitmore
Choreographer: Wally Siebert
Writers:
    Frank Peppiat
    John Aylesworth
Special vocal arrangements by Bobby Cole

Concert format, with orchestra onstage.

SONGS

"After You've Gone"
"The Nearness of You"
"Time After Time"
"That Old Feeling"
"Carolina in the Morning"
"When You're Smiling"
Medley:
    "It's Almost Like Being in Love"
    "This Can't Be Love"

"By Myself"
"Last Dance"
"Suppertime"
"Just in Time"
"A Foggy Day"
"If Love Were All"
"Just You, Just Me"
Trunk sequence   Judy Garland:
    "When The Sun Comes Out"

ADDENDA

★ This was the last show taped for the series.

ALBUMS

Albums with "After You've Gone":
(See the February 16, 1964, show.)
Albums with "The Nearness of You":
Star Eyes (See section K, #15)
Albums with "Time After Time":
Star Eyes (See section K, #15)

Albums with "When You're Smiling":
(See the December 1, 1963, show.)
Albums with "It's Almost Like Being in Love"/"This Can't Be Love":
(See the January 19, 1964, show.)
Albums with "Suppertime":
All Alone (See section K, #9)
Judy. Judy Garland (See section K, #16)
Albums with "A Foggy Day":
(See the October 13, 1963, show.)
Albums with "If Love Were All":
(See the December 15, 1963, show.)
Albums with "Just You, Just Me":
(See the February 23, 1964, show.)
Albums with "When the Sun Comes Out":
(See the December 8, 1963, show.)

8
RECORDS: THE CONCERTS YEARS

———————— ★ ————————

". . . fine shadings were there that mark the line between talent and genius . . ."

Mrs D. W. Griffith, *When The Movies Were Young*

———————— ★ ————————

"When I write a lyric, I like to think how Judy Garland would sing it."

Oscar Hammerstein II, [at an introduction to a show-business dinner]

———————— ★ ————————

From her signing with Metro-Goldwyn-Mayer in 1935, until she was fired in 1950, Judy Garland's singing and recording career had been guided and dominated by the studio to amplify her screen image. Nourished as she developed her skills, Judy was also circumscribed with limits defined by executive judgments of the marketplace. It was a safe and secure niche.

Finding herself suddenly unemployable by Hollywood standards, Garland was equally suddenly stripped of all the services and support with which studios insulated their major stars. She had, quite literally, to sing for her supper. And she had to rely more fully than ever before on her instincts—musically and in terms of how she would relate to her audiences.

Garland gambled.

She broke with her Metro-defined image and style. She reinterpreted the emotional content of her standard songs and reinvented them for herself vocally. She created new standards, deepened the intensity of her style, and gave herself a whole new audience and range of admirers. Without ever sacrificing the naturalness, friendliness, wit, or need with which she sang during her Metro tenure, she added a fire and impact that was new.

Just as *A Star Is Born* revealed a more complex and formidable performer than MGM had allowed on the screen, so the Garland style of her concert years was marked by an ability to give songs an emotional depth and shading rarely seen outside of straight acting.

Garland fans generally divide into two overlapping groups: those who prefer her performances from her film years and those who prefer the later Garland. The former find the mixture of visual memory, nostalgia, and the image of the wistful girl and vulnerable young woman appealing. Within the energy, there is an innocence and gentleness about the early voice that suggests a reaching out, and the humor of the Metro years contained a youthful ebullience, a bubbling over of high spirits. Early Judy Garland evokes a protectiveness on the part of her audience, and protectiveness implies that the protector is stronger, more worldly.

By the fifties, Judy's voice had deepened and matured. Her style remained innocent of artifice, but her voice bespoke no innocence of experience. Her vocal power was controlled, not suppressed, and she married it to an increasingly elegant technique.

In so doing, Garland went beyond expressing a song's content. She gave her renditions an open emotional intensity that commands rather than seeks a listener's attention. Further, she draws from the listener an active response to the song's values, creating a dialogue of sensibilities.

That is why reviewers of her concerts talked about being embarrassed by their tears. Entertainment usually implies a passivity on the part of the entertained. Judy Garland's mature vocal style invites emotional participation.

If in her film years Judy bridged the distance between composer/lyricist and audience, her mature style eliminated it. Garland seemed to sing with her defenses down. But her reading of a song infiltrates a listener's personal experience with an artistry of such subtlety, sophistication, and force that, in fact, the listener finds his heart on her sleeve. The passionate attachment of the later Garland fans, the Garland "cult," is, in part, a measure of devotion for one who can say—out loud, in public—what most people can only feel and not describe, and certainly not describe out loud.

With her concert version of "Over the Rainbow," Judy Garland immediately declared her independence as a vocal stylist, and the ground on which she would henceforth meet her audiences. Her MGM version, from *The Wizard of Oz,* had become a classic long before she left the studio. To many, it was Judy: Judy, the vulnerable; Judy, the wistful; Judy, the child-woman. Her 1939 voice was sweet and pure. More to the point, however, she sang the song with a total vocal simplicity that suited the role of Dorothy to perfection. The power behind the voice was completely restrained. She sang in the upper part of her register—indeed, in its farthest reaches to emphasize the final "Why can't I?"—which thinned her voice, lending an even greater dimension of vulnerability. And she used no tremolo, no fluctuations of loudness and softness of breath passing over the vocal cords. For Judy used her tremolo to convey sadness or tenderness, and these emotions would have intruded on the unaffected wistfulness of the performance.

There is nothing wistful about the adult Garland version of "Over the Rainbow." It is a song of longing and ache, of happiness denied, of hope diminished. It is a song of haunting sadness, but sadness without self-pity, for Judy makes it a song of striving as well. In the very first phrase, for example, "Somewhere over the rainbow," she puts a force behind "somewhere" that was missing previously, while "rainbow" comes out in tremolo, giving the voice under the word a restrained trembling quality. Then, in the phrases "skies are blue" and "dreams that you dare to dream," she lengthens the notes under "are" and "dare," emphasizing their importance and conveying a sense that the apparently unattainable does exist.

When the lyric reads "away above the chimney tops / that's where you'll find me," she uses an increasing level of power and sings "find" in an extended vibrato, a rapid fluctuation of pitch around a tone. This adds a brilliance to the note and heightens the impact of the word it carries. And she ends the song using her full vocal force, adding increasing power to each successive syllable in "why / oh why / can't I?" and sings "can't" with the pulsating strength of vibrato, the "I" being swallowed in the increasing power of the orchestra. The force of the ending seems to be a cri de coeur. But Garland extends the impact by consistently putting the emotional center of phrases next to—but not on—each successive "me" or "I." The sadness is haunting because she has universalized it.

Both Garland's voice and her musical skills continued to deepen throughout the fifties and early sixties. As the MGM years receded, she worked with increasingly sophisticated arrangements and adopted and adapted a greater range of jazz-inflected techniques. She continued to work with Roger Edens and Kay Thompson, a formidable jazz stylist in her own right. Throughout the fifties, however, her arrangers were now musicians who had largely developed their skills with the Big Bands during the height of the Swing Era.

The first nonconcert recordings Judy made when she was on her own, in 1953, were with the Paul Weston Orchestra, with Weston doing the arrangements. Skip Martin, who arranged "The Man That Got Away" and the other songs for A Star Is Born, had been with the Charlie Barnet band. Harold Mooney, who did the arrangements for the Miss Show Business album, had arranged for Jimmy Dorsey. Nelson Riddle, one of the most brilliant arrangers in the business, who arranged both the Judy and Judy In Love albums for her, had played the trombone and arranged for Charlie Spivak and Tommy Dorsey. Gordon Jenkins, another brilliant arranger, arranged and conducted the Alone album; Jenkins had played and arranged for Isham Jones. And in 1960, Mort Lindsey picked up the baton and worked with her through her television series and her last film, *I Could Go On Singing.*

These are the prime Garland years. When she sang backed by these professionals of skill, sensitivity, and sophistication, her songs actually glow with a sheer gladness of talent and joy in performance. (Indeed, one suspects that a large part of the reason Judy cries while singing "Over the Rainbow" on the *Palace Two-A-Day* album, recorded in 1952, is frustration at the backup she's getting from an orchestra playing too lushly and dragging behind her, with Hugh Martin at the piano playing flourishes and trills.)

Music, be it pop, jazz, or classical, is an ensemble art form. What the listener hears is the more or less delicate blending and melding of the visions and talents of composer, arranger, and performing musicians. A vocalist is the soloist of the ensemble, just as, for example, a trumpet might be the soloist in a jazz group or a violin the soloist in a concerto.

Judy Garland's acting career, then, and her ever developing ability to bring depth and meaning to her roles, is pertinent to her singing career. For film is also an ensemble medium, the best pictures embodying a happy confluence of fine writing, directing, art direction, lighting, and editing, in addition to skilled screen performances. When an actor is speaking his lines, he is the soloist of the ensemble, no matter how small the part. The listener and viewer focus on the soloist, and it is against the rules to steal attention away from him, for his success defines, in part, the success of the whole.

Judy, during her Metro years, learned ensemble acting simultaneously with de-

veloping her ability to get beyond the words in the scripts to present human beings expressing sentiments and thoughts. She later described acting as understanding, thinking, and feeling the silences between the lines on the page, between the words the character says.

So, too, in music. As a singer, Judy never lost sight of the unity of words and music, of the content of the lyrics as well as the rhythms of the notes. She conveyed the same intangible qualities of these silences between the lines through pacing, tremolo, modulation, and vibrato. Listen, in her 1939 "Over the Rainbow," to the way she thinned her voice by judiciously moving to the upper end of her register or how in "Better Luck Next Time" she slowed key passages to a conversational pace and emphasized vocal trembling.

By 1950, Judy Garland was a skilled vocalist, able to carry solos with panache and, as she showed during her middle MGM period, able to successfully blend her vocal range and power into a conventional whole without sacrificing her interpretation of a lyric's emotional content. She merged into the group at the end of "The Trolley Song," for example; she softened her voice and style for duets with Gene Kelly and Fred Astaire.

In the fifties and sixties, Garland took the concepts of vocalist as actress and soloist/ensemble to a higher plane. Increasingly, instead of blending with the band or orchestra behind her, she added another dimension to both the music and the meaning of the lyrics by floating vocally over arrangements. In effect, floating adds another layer of orchestration as the singer develops a melodic line separate, but complementary, to the one the instrumentalists are playing. Rather than simply improvising around notes, float is an interpretive improvisation around the whole score.

Judy had experimented with float as early as 1939, with "Fascinating Rhythm," but the sophistication of this approach did not fit with the image MGM was defining for her. Garland's use of it came into full prominence later, particularly in the albums she did with Nelson Riddle and the *Alone* album with Gordon Jenkins, allowing these skilled arrangers to create more sophisticated accompaniments than she had sung with in the forties. And by floating over these arrangements, Garland gained greater freedom to employ all the other techniques at her disposal.

Listen, for instance, to her rendition of "Blue Prelude" (1957). This song was written primarily as an instrumental and is a difficult vocal number. Judy floats over the instrumental arrangement (probably the only intelligent way to sing it). She modulates from one end of her register to the other and back again, extending and playing with individual notes along the way, and goes from tremolo to vibrato. But, in addition, by singing in parallel but not in conformity, with the instruments, she adds what is, in effect, another section to the orchestra—and a jazz-inflected duet with a melancholy trumpet playing countermelody. She then amplifies the emotional intensity of the final "got the blues" by joining with the arrangement, and trails off into "what can I lose / Goodbye," with lengthened notes and diminishing power. The result is a song of numbing sadness, developed with such

subtlety of technique that the music and lyrics are virtually fused.

Garland's ability to sell sad is well known. Less recognized in the popular mythology, however, is her ability to sing upbeat numbers, not merely with a smile but with an almost audible grin in her voice.

In some ways, it is easier to sing these songs than sad or tender ones. The tempos are usually faster, and the arrangements louder, which can disguise vocal inadequacies. There are fewer silences between the lines in a happy lyric, for happiness seems to need less explanation, and there is less need for technique because the inherent rhythms of the melodic line can carry a singer.

What makes Garland's renditions all the more joyful, then, is her characteristic intensity and depth of lyrical interpretation, allied to a musically sophisticated integration of technique with score. She took no shortcuts. In songs such as "Carolina in the Morning" (1955), "Life Is Just a Bowl of Cherries" (1956), "This Is It" (1958), or "I've Got a Lot of Living to Do" (1963, from her TV show), the listener is virtually assaulted with a vocal zest and contagious enthusiasm for living.

Judy Garland is an anomaly to the average music critic. It is considered appropriate—indeed, the highest form of art— for an actress on the screen or stage to give characterizations that manipulate a viewer's or listener's emotions. We willingly accede to this manipulation and call it a "suspension of disbelief." The artistry of the actress, however, is vaguely illegitimate and suspect when employed by the singer.

Yet to the listener, the result is songs with an evocative richness that never bores. Garland was once described as having an almost uncanny ability to delve deeper and deeper into the meaning of a lyric. She also had the ability to involve the listener in the process.

Her songs work on multiple levels. There is, of course, some of the loveliest singing in the realm of American popular music. But because she used all the skills available to her as both an extraordinary musician and a brilliant actress, there is also a story, a story told by one person to another, a story with an implied history—just as there was with each of her film characterizations. The listener, then, can accept the song and story and enjoy the performance. Or, as one often does with film characterizations, one can internalize and personalize them. Or, again as with film, the listener can explore the technical virtuosity and elegance that brought them to life. Better yet, you can do all three.

Art in its highest form appears effortless and is both emotionally and intellectually stirring. Judy Garland's enduring greatness was her ability to seamlessly fuse words and music into an organic whole. Her genius was to engage her audience, both moving and involving them, while leaving the casual observer bemused by just how.

G. SINGLES

1 "Send My Baby Back to Me"
[Bob Hillard, Milton Delugg (1953)]
"Without a Memory"
[J. M. Robinson]

Label:
Columbia 40010 (78)
Columbia 4-40010 (45)
Columbia Canadian Records 2204 (78)
Released: 1953

ADDENDA

★ Garland recorded both of these numbers on April 3, 1953, with Paul Weston's Orchestra. They were arranged and conducted by Paul Weston. (They were released on May 4, 1953.)

★ "Send My Baby Back to Me," "Without a Memory," "Go Home, Joe," and "Heartbroken" were recorded as a result of a four-song contract with Columbia Records. The Columbia release of A Star Is Born was a separate deal.

2 "Go Home, Joe"
[I. Gordon]
"Heartbroken"
[P. Springer, Fred Ebb]

Label:
Columbia 40023 (78)
Columbia Canadian 2237 (78)
Released: 1953

ADDENDA

★ These songs were recorded on April 3, 1953, and released June 29. They were recorded with the Paul Weston Orchestra. Weston arranged and conducted.

3 "The Man That Got Away"
[Ira Gershwin, Harold Arlen (1954)]
"Here's What I'm Here For"
[Ira Gershwin, Harold Arlen (1954)]

Label:
Columbia 40270 (78)
Columbia 4-40270 (45)
Released: 1954

ADDENDA

★ Both songs were written for, and sung by, Judy Garland in A Star Is Born (1954).

★ Judy's interpretation of "The Man That Got Away" caused some initial controversy on the set of A Star Is Born. Hugh Martin was originally her vocal coach for the picture. That ended when Garland refused to bow to Martin's insistence that she sing the song sweet and in a lower key. (The soundtrack and single-release versions are in C.)

Lawrence Stewart, who was present at the confrontations, reports: "After much difficulty, the song was recorded both ways [Garland's and Martin's], and Judy's preference was adopted for the picture, because the lower and sweeter version lacked brilliance and all those dramatic qualities which had to be developed in the song, not only in terms of itself but, more particularly, in terms of its function in the story." (Quoted in R. Haver, *A Star Is Born.* New York: Alfred A. Knopf, 1988, p. 94.)

Martin stormed off the set and left for New York.

★ "The Man That Got Away" sold more than a million copies and went gold in 1954. The song was nominated for an Academy Award as best song. (It lost to "Three Coins in the Fountain," by Jule Styne and Sammy Cahn, from the film of the same name.)

★ Both songs were recorded in 1954 with the Ray Heindorf Orchestra. The arrangements were by Ray Heindorf and Skip Martin.

---

4 **"Gotta Have Me Go with You"**
[Ira Gershwin, Harold Arlen (1954)]
"Lose That Long Face"
[Ira Gershwin, Harold Arlen (1954)]

Label: Columbia 8005 (78)
Released: 1954

ADDENDA

★ These are Garland songs from *A Star Is Born* (1954). The orchestra was conducted by Ray Heindorf, with arrangements by Heindorf and Martin.

---

5 **"The Man That Got Away"**
"Someone at Last"
[Ira Gershwin, Harold Arlen (1954)]

Label: Columbia 8006 (78)
Released: 1954

ADDENDA

★ "Someone at Last" is from *A Star Is Born* (1954). The orchestra for both sides was conducted by Ray Heindorf. Arrangements were by Heindorf and Martin.

---

6 **"Someone at Last"**
"Born in a Trunk" Medley

Label: Columbia 8007 (78)
Released: 1954

---

7 **"It's a New World"**
[Ira Gershwin, Harold Arlen (1954)]
"Born in a Trunk" Medley

Label: Columbia 8008 (78)
Released: 1954

ADDENDA

★ "It's a New World" is from *A Star Is Born.* The orchestra was conducted by Ray Heindorf, with arrangements by Heindorf and Martin.

8 **"Here's What I'm Here For"**
"Born in a Trunk" Medley

Label: Columbia 8009 (78)
Released: 1954

9 **"Maybe I'll Come Back"**
[Charles L. Cooke, Howard C. Jeffrey]
"Over the Rainbow"
[E. Y. Harburg, Harold Arlen (1939)]

Label: Capitol 6128 (45)
Released: 1956

A rare behind-the-scenes shot of discussion
surrounding "The Man That Got Away" number.

ADDENDA

★ Judy Garland used "Maybe I'll Come
Back" as the closing theme to her
weekly TV show, "The Judy Garland
Show." This version was recorded in
1956 with the Nelson Riddle Orchestra.

★ This version of "Over the Rainbow" is
the concert version that Garland introduced in the United States at the Palace
in 1951. It was recorded in 1955 with
the Jack Cathcart Orchestra.

10 **"It's Lovely to Be Back in London"**
[Roger Edens (1957)]
"By Myself"
[Howard Dietz, Arthur Schwartz (1937)]

Label: EMI CL 14791 (45) (U.K.)
Released: 1957

A D D E N D A

★ "By Myself" was one of the songs she sang later, in the movie *I Could Go On Singing* (1963). It was introduced by Jack Buchanan in the Broadway show *Between the Devil,* in 1937. This song was Howard Dietz's favorite among his own lyrics.

★ Both songs were recorded in 1957.

11 **"Zing! Went the Strings of My Heart"**
[James F. Hanley (1935)]
"Rock-a-Bye Your Baby with a Dixie Melody"
[Sam M. Lewis, Joe Young, Jean Schwartz (1918)]

Label: Capitol 4624 (45)
Released: 1961

A D D E N D A

★ "Zing! Went the Strings of My Heart" was first recorded by Judy Garland for the 1938 film *Listen, Darling.*

★ Both songs were recorded in 1961 with Mort Lindsey conducting.

12 **"San Francisco"**
[Gus Kahn, Bronislau Kaper (1936)]
"Chicago"
[Fred Fisher (1922)]

Label: Capitol 6125 (45)
Released: 1961

A D D E N D A

★ "San Francisco" was the title song of the 1936 movie, starring Jeanette MacDonald, Clark Gable, and Spencer Tracy.

★ "Chicago" was the music behind the titles to Judy Garland's 1949 film *In the Good Old Summertime.*

13 **"The Man That Got Away"**
"April Showers"
[Buddy DeSylva, Louis Silvers (1921)]

Label: Capitol 6126 (45)
Released: 1961

A D D E N D A

★ "The Man That Got Away" was recorded in 1961 with the Mort Lindsey Orchestra.

★ "April Showers" was recorded in 1956 with the Nelson Riddle Orchestra. The song comes from the Broadway show *Bombo* (1921), starring Al Jolson.

14 "Come Rain or Come Shine"
[Johnny Mercer, Harold Arlen (1946)]
"Rock-a-Bye Your Baby with a Dixie Melody"

Label: Capitol 6127 (45)
Released: 1961

ADDENDA

★ "Come Rain or Come Shine," which became a Garland standard, was introduced in the Broadway show *St. Louis Woman* (1946). It is an unusual song. It starts in one key and ends in another. It also has no introductory verse.

15 "Maybe I'll Come Back"
"Over the Rainbow"

Label: Capitol 6128 (45)
Released: 1961

16 "Swanee"
[Irving Caesar, George Gershwin (1919)]
"That's Entertainment"
[Howard Dietz, Arthur Schwartz (1953)]

Label: Capitol 6129 (45)
Released: 1961

ADDENDA

★ Judy Garland first recorded "Swanee" in 1939. It became permanently associated with her after her tour de force performance in the "Born in a Trunk" sequence in *A Star Is Born* in 1954.

★ "That's Entertainment" was introduced by Jack Buchanan, Oscar Levant, Fred Astaire, Nanette Fabray, and later, in the reprise with Cyd Charisse (dubbed by India Adams) in *The Band Wagon* (1953). It was the only song written expressly for the movie.

★ Both songs were recorded with the Mort Lindsey Orchestra in 1961.

17 "Little Drops of Rain"
[E. Y. Harburg, Harold Arlen (1962)]
"Paris Is a Lonely Town"
[E. Y. Harburg, Harold Arlen (1962)]

Label: Warner Bros. 5310 (45)
Released: 1962

ADDENDA

★ Garland introduced both songs in *Gay-Purr-ee* (1962). Garland sang "Little Drops of Rain" and "Paris Is a Lonely Town" on the soundtrack. They were recorded in 1962 with the Mort Lindsey Orchestra.

18 "Once in a Lifetime"
[Leslie Bricusse, Anthony Newley (1961)]
"Sweet Danger"
[Robert Wright, George Forrest (1961)]

Label: Capitol 4656 (45)
Released: 1962

ADDENDA

★ These songs were recorded in 1962 with the Mort Lindsey Orchestra.

★ "Once in a Lifetime" comes from the 1962 Broadway show *Stop the World— I Want to Get Off*.

19 **"Hello, Bluebird"**
[Cliff Friend (1926)]
"I Could Go On Singing"
[E. Y. Harburg, Harold Arlen (1963)]

Label: Capitol 4938 (45)
Released: 1963

ADDENDA

★ Judy Garland introduced "I Could Go On Singing" in the 1963 film of the same name. Mort Lindsey conducted.

20 **"Hello, Dolly!"**
[Jerry Herman (1964)]
"He's Got the Whole World in His Hands" (with Liza Minnelli)
[Geoff Love (1957)]

Label: Capitol 5497 (45)
Released: 1964

ADDENDA

★ "Hello, Dolly!" was introduced by Carol Channing in the 1964 Broadway musical of that name. The song won a Grammy as best song of the year.
★ Garland recorded these songs with Harry Robinson conducting the orchestra.

H.   ALBUMS FROM RECORDING SESSIONS

1 **Miss Show Business**

Label:
    Capitol W 676 (33⅓)
    Capitol DW 676 (33⅓)
    Capitol EDM 2-676 (45)
    Capitol CDP 92344 (CD)
Released: 1955

SIDE ONE
"This Is the Time of the Evening"
    (Chorus)
    [Roger Edens, Leonard Gershe (1955)]
"While We're Young"
    [Alec Wilder, Morty Palitz, Bill
        Engvick (1943)]
Garland Medley:
    "You Made Me Love You"
        [James V. Monaco, Joe McCarthy
        (1913)]
    From *Broadway Melody of 1938*—
    1937

"For Me and My Gal"
  [George W. Meyer, Edgar Leslie,
    E. Ray Goetz (1917)]
  From *For Me and My Gal*—1942
"The Boy Next Door"
  [Ralph Blane, Hugh Martin (1944)]
  From *Meet Me In St. Louis*—1944
"The Trolley Song"
  [Ralph Blane, Hugh Martin (1944)]
  From *Meet Me in St. Louis*—1944
"A Pretty Girl Milking Her Cow"
  [Adaptation by Roger Edens (1940)]
  From *Little Nellie Kelly*—1940
"Rock-a-Bye Your Baby with a Dixie
    Melody"
  [Schwartz, Lewis, Young (1918)]
"Happiness Is Just a Thing Called Joe"
  [E. Y. Harburg, Harold Arlen (1942)]

SIDE TWO

Palace Medley:
  "Judy at The Palace"
    [Roger Edens (1951)]
  "Shine On, Harvest Moon"
    [Nora Bayes, Jack Norworth
      (1908)]
  "Some of These Days"
    [Shelton Brooks (1910)]
  "My Man"
    [Maurice Yvain, English lyrics by
      Channing Pollock (1921)]
  "I Don't Care"
    [Harry O. Sutton, Jean Lennox
      (1905)]
"Carolina in the Morning"
  [Walter Donaldson, Gus Kahn (1922)]
"Danny Boy"
  [Fred W. Weatherly (1913)]
  Garland first sang this song in *Little
    Nellie Kelly*—1940

"After You've Gone"
  [Henry Creamer, Turner Layton
    (1918)]
  From *For Me and My Gal*—1942
"Over the Rainbow"
  [E. Y. Harburg, Harold Arlen (1939)]
  From *The Wizard of Oz*—1939

ADDENDA

★ The orchestra and chorus were under
  the direction of Jack Cathcart. Arrangements were by Harold Mooney. The
  songs were recorded on August 25, 26,
  and 30, 1955. The album was released
  on September 26, 1955.
★ The master number for these songs, in
  order of appearance on the LP, are
  14359, 14360 through 14363 (Garland
  Medley), 14365, 14364, 14407, 14390
  (Palace Introduction), 14367 through
  14370 (Palace Medley), 14371, 14372,
  and 14373.
★ Despite the interpolations surrounding
  the Palace Medley, Al Jolson never
  played the Palace. He played the Winter Garden Theater.
★ *Miss Show Business* was in the Top 40
  for seven weeks.
★ The CD, released in June 1989, does
  not contain "On the Atchison, Topeka
  and the Santa Fe." This was recorded
  on August 30, 1955, at the same sessions as the other songs on *Miss Show
  Business* but has not been released. The
  master number is 14366.

SONG ADDENDA

★ "While We're Young" was introduced
  by Mabel Mercer. The first recording of
  this song was by Fred Waring and his
  Pennsylvanians.

★ "Rock-a-Bye Your Baby with a Dixie Melody" was a Jolson standard. He introduced it on Broadway in 1918 in the show *Sinbad.* He stopped the show with it.

★ "Happiness Is Just a Thing Called Joe" was introduced by Ethel Waters in *Cabin in the Sky* (1943). It was nominated for an Academy Award for best song.

★ Judy Garland became determined to someday record this song when she heard the Woody Herman recording with Frances Wayne doing the vocal (1945).

★ "Shine On, Harvest Moon" was Nora Bayes's trademark.

★ "Some of These Days" was introduced by Sophie Tucker in Chicago in 1910. From then on, it was her theme song.

★ "My Man" was introduced into the United States by Irene Bordoni. It became associated with Fanny Brice after she sang it on Broadway in the *Ziegfeld Follies of 1921.* She also sang it in her talking picture debut, *My Man* (1929).

★ "I Don't Care," which Judy Garland sang in her 1949 movie *In the Good Old Summertime,* was associated with Eva Tanguay.

★ "Carolina in the Morning" was introduced in the Broadway revue *The Passing Show of 1922.*

2 Judy

Label:
  Capitol T-734 (33⅓)
  Capitol DT-734 (33⅓)
  Capitol EAP 1/2/3-734 (45)
  Capitol LCT 6121 (33⅓) (U.K.)
  Capitol CDP 92345 (CD)
Released: 1956

SIDE ONE

"Come Rain or Come Shine"
  [Johnny Mercer, Harold Arlen (1946)]
"Just Imagine"
  [Buddy DeSylva, Lew Brown, Ray
    Henderson (1927)]
"I Feel a Song Coming On"
  [Jimmy McHugh, Dorothy Fields,
    George Oppenheimer (1935)]
"Last Night When We Were Young"
  [E. Y. Harburg, Harold Arlen (1936)]
"Life Is Just a Bowl of Cherries"
  [Ray Henderson, Lew Brown (1931)]
"April Showers"
  [Buddy DeSylva, Louis Silvers (1921)]

SIDE TWO

"I Will Come Back (Maybe I'll Come Back)"
[Charles L. Cooke, Howard C. Jeffrey]
"Dirty Hands, Dirty Face"
[James V. Monaco, Edgar Leslie (1923)]
"This Is My Lucky Day"
[Buddy DeSylva, Lew Brown, Ray Henderson (1926)]
"Memories of You"
[Eubie Blake, Andy Razaf (1930)]
"Any Place I Hang My Hat Is Home"
[Johnny Mercer, Harold Arlen (1946)]

ADDENDA

★ The songs on this album were arranged and conducted by Nelson Riddle. They were recorded on March 19, 26, and 31, 1956. The album was released October 10, 1956.
★ *Judy* was in the Top 40 for five weeks.
★ Garland discovered "Last Night When We Were Young" when she was about sixteen and fell in love with it. She tried to get it into *In the Good Old Summertime,* and went as far as recording it, but it was dropped from the film.
★ In 1988, Tony Bennett was asked to name his ten all-time favorite recordings. Garland's "Last Night When We Were Young," from this album, was on the list.
★ Garland's rendition of "Memories of You" on this album is, to my mind, the definitive vocal. Compare her interpretation to Clyde Hurley's easy jazz trumpet improvisations on it (on *Paul Weston: Mood for 12,* Columbia CL 693). Hurley, incidentally, was with the MGM orchestra for six years.

★ The master numbers of the songs on this album, in order of their appearance, are 15301, 15271, 15109, 15303, 15302, 15108, 15121, 15105, 15274, 15273, and 15304.
★ The compact disk, released on June 20, 1989, contains "I'm Old Fashioned," recorded on March 26, 1956 (master number 15272). It had not been released previously.

SONG ADDENDA

★ "Come Rain or Come Shine" is from the 1946 Broadway musical *St. Louis Woman.*
★ "Just Imagine" was introduced by Shirley Vernon, Mary Lawlor, and Ruth Mayon in 1927 in the Broadway musical *Good News.*
★ "I Feel a Song Coming On" is from the 1935 film *Every Night at Eight.* It was introduced by Frances Langford.
★ "Last Night When We Were Young" was published as an independent number.
★ "Life Is Just a Bowl of Cherries" was originally an Ethel Merman number in Broadway's *George White's Scandals of 1931.*
★ "April Showers" was an Al Jolson specialty. He first sang it in 1921 at the Winter Garden Theater in New York in *Bombo.*
★ "Dirty Hands, Dirty Face" was also associated with Jolson. He sang it in *The Jazz Singer* (1927).
★ "This Is My Lucky Day" was introduced by Harry Richman in Broadway's *George White's Scandals of 1926.*

★ "Memories of You" was introduced by Ethel Waters in the all-black Broadway revue *Blackbirds of 1930*.

★ "Any Place I Hang My Hat Is Home" was introduced in the Broadway musical *St. Louis Woman* in 1946.

★ "I'm Old-Fashioned" [Johnny Mercer and Jerome Kern (1942)] was introduced in the 1942 film *You Were Never Lovelier* by Fred Astaire and Nan Wynn (dubbing for Rita Hayworth).

CONTEMPORARY COMMENTS

The American Record Guide, July 1957
. . . contains one of the finest renditions to be had of the Harold Arlen/E. Y. Harburg song, "Last Night When We Were Young," among other choice numbers.

---

3 **Alone**

Label:
    Capitol T-835 (33⅓)
    Capitol DT-835 (33⅓)
    Capitol EAP-835 (45)
    Capitol EAP 1/2/3-835 (45)
    Capitol CDP 92346 (CD)
Released: 1957

SIDE ONE

"By Myself"
    [Howard Dietz, Arthur Schwartz (1937)]
"Little Girl Blue"
    [Lorenz Hart, Richard Rodgers (1935)]
"Me and My Shadow"
    [Billy Rose, Dave Dreyer, Al Jolson (1927)]

"Among My Souvenirs"
    [Edgar Leslie, Horatio Nicholls (1927)]
"I Gotta Right to Sing the Blues"
    [Ted Koehler, Harold Arlen (1932)]
"I Get the Blues When It Rains"
    [Marcy Klauber, Harry Stoddard (1928)]

SIDE TWO

"Mean to Me"
    [Roy Turk, Fred E. Ahlert (1929)]
"How About Me?"
    [Irving Berlin (1926)]
"Just a Memory"
    [Buddy DeSylva, Lew Brown, Ray Henderson (1927)]
"Blue Prelude"
    [Joseph Bishop, Gordon Jenkins (1933)]
"Happy New Year"
    [Gordon Jenkins (1949)]

ADDENDA

★ "Alone" was in the Top 40 for three weeks.
★ The songs for this album were recorded at sessions on February 6 and 22, and March 6, 1957. They were arranged, and the orchestra conducted, by Gordon Jenkins. The album was released on May 6, 1957.
★ The CD, released on June 20, 1989, contains "Then You've Never Been Blue." This song was recorded on March 6, 1957, but was not previously released (master number 16629).
★ For a good example of Garland's increasing technical virtuosity throughout the fifties, compare her "Mean to Me" from 1951 (on *Frances Ethel Gumm and Harry Lillis Crosby*, Legend 1973) with this rendition from 1957.
★ The master numbers, in order of appearance on the LP, are 16627, 16573, 16576, 16683, 16681, 16574, 16626, 16575, 16684, 16628, and 16682.

SONG ADDENDA

★ "Little Girl Blue" comes from the 1935 Broadway musical *Jumbo*. It was introduced by Gloria Grafton. *Jumbo* was the last show produced at the New York Hippodrome.
★ "Me and My Shadow" was originally written for Frank Fay, who introduced it in 1927 in *Harry Delmar's Revels*. It was popularized by Al Jolson.
★ "I Gotta Right to Sing the Blues" comes from the *Earl Carroll Vanities of 1932*. This is one of the few Harold Arlen songs written in an authentic blues style. Jazz trombonist Jack Teagarden used it as his band's theme song.

★ "Just a Memory" was originally published as an independent number. It was then used on Broadway in *Manhattan Mary* (1927).
★ "Blue Prelude" was introduced by Isham Jones and His Orchestra. It was the theme song of Woody Herman and His Orchestra. It was intended primarily to be an instrumental and is an exceedingly difficult vocal number. (Garland's rendition on this album is stunning.)
★ "Then You've Never Been Blue" [Sam Lewis, Joe Young, Ted Fiorito (1935)] was introduced by Frances Langford in the film *Every Night at Eight* (1935).

CONTEMPORARY COMMENTS
The American Record Guide, July 1957
"Alone" contains a good collection . . . vibrantly and feelingly sung.

4 Judy in Love

Label
    Capitol T-1036 (33⅓)
    Capitol ST-1036 (33⅓)
    Capitol EAP 1/2/3-1036 (45)
    Capitol EAP-1636 (45)
Released: 1958

SIDE ONE

"Zing! Went the Strings of My Heart"
    [James F. Hanley (1935)]
    Garland sang this in the 1938 film
        Listen, Darling.
"Do It Again"
    [Buddy DeSylva, George Gershwin
        (1922)]

"I Concentrate on You"
  [Cole Porter (1939)]
"Do I Love You?"
  [Cole Porter (1939)]
"I Am Loved"
  [Cole Porter (1950)]
"More Than You Know"
  [Billy Rose, Edward Eliscu, Vincent
    Youmans (1929)]

SIDE TWO

"This Is It"
  [Dorothy Fields, Arthur Schwartz
    (1939)]
"Day In, Day Out"
  [Johnny Mercer, Rube Bloom (1939)]
"I Can't Give You Anything but Love"
  [Dorothy Fields, Jimmy McHugh
    (1928)]
"I'm Confessin' "
  [A. J. Neiburg, Doc Daugherty, Ellis
    Reynolds (1930)]
"I Hadn't Anyone Till You"
  [Ray Noble (1938)]

ADDENDA

★ This album is with Nelson Riddle and
  His Orchestra. Riddle also did the arrangements. The songs were recorded
  at sessions on May 19 and 26 and June
  17, 1958. The album was released on
  November 3, 1958.
★ The master numbers, in order of appearance on the album, are 19148,
  19400, 19403, 19401, 19402, 19195,
  19147, 19146, 19197, 19196, and
  19194.

SONG ADDENDA

★ "Do It Again" was introduced on Broadway by Irene Bordoni in 1922 in *The
  French Doll.*

★ "I Concentrate On You" was introduced
  by Douglas McPhail (a regular cast
  member from Garland's "Let's put on a
  show!" series of films) in the film
  Broadway Melody of 1940.
★ "Do I Love You?" was introduced on
  Broadway by Ethel Merman and Ronald
  Graham in 1939 in *Du Barry Was a
  Lady.*
★ "I Am Loved" comes from the 1950
  Broadway musical *Out of This World,*
  where it was sung by Priscilla Gillette.
★ "More Than You Know" was written for
  the Broadway musical *Great Day*
  (1929).

  According to Polly Rose Gottlieb in
  her biography of her brother, *The Nine
  Lives of Billy Rose,* "[Billy] felt that for
  the first time he wasn't just another Tin
  Pan Alley writer of pop songs. Youmans was such a giant among compos-
  ers that Billy thought the name Billy
  Rose wasn't dignified enough. So on
  the three all-time hits from the show,
  'Without a Song,' 'Great Day,' and
  'More Than You Know,' Billy's credit
  read: William Rose."

  The show lasted thirty-six performances.
★ "This Is It" was introduced by Ethel
  Merman on Broadway in 1939 in *Stars
  in Your Eyes.*
★ "I Can't Give You Anything but Love"
  was introduced by Patsy Kelly in *Harry
  Delmar's Revels* (1927). It died in the
  show. It was then used in *Blackbirds of
  1928,* where it was sung by Adelaide
  Hall. It became the first big hit for the
  team of Fields and McHugh.

  Fields and McHugh got their inspiration for it when they were walking on
  Fifth Avenue in New York. Outside Tif-

fany's, Dorothy Fields overheard a man saying, "I'd love to buy that for you, baby, but I ain't got anything but love to give you."

★ "I'm Confessin'" was originally introduced and recorded by Fats Waller and his Buddies with other lyrics, under the title "Lookin' for Another Sweetie."

5 The Letter

Label: Capitol S/TAO 1188 (33⅓)
Released: 1959
A drama, with music, written by Gordon Jenkins, with John Ireland, the Ralph Brewster Singers, and the Gordon Jenkins Orchestra

SONGS

"Beautiful Trouble"
"Love in the Village"
"The Worst Kind of Man"
"That's All There Is, There Isn't Any More"
"Love in Central Park"
"The Red Balloon"
"The Fight"
"At the Stroke of Midnight"
"Come Back"

ADDENDA

★ The original release came with "the letter," which has become a collector's item.

★ It was rereleased in 1963 as *Our Love Letter*, on Capitol ST 1941 (33⅓).

CONTEMPORARY COMMENTS

The American Record Guide, August 1959
Judy Garland . . . sings gloriously in the

My dearest dear,

I write this letter because I have no other choice. Life without you is intolerable. I tried to fill my world with all kinds of distractions—sports, travel, stupid hobbies—but it's no use. My restless mind keeps running back to the good days, the bright days, when our incredible affair first began. Most introductions are only a jumble of polite words, but ours was the Fourth of July and Christmas morning—at least it was to me. Knowing you as I do now, I'm sure you must have felt somewhat the same.

I am sitting by our special window, looking out over the town that loved us so. New York has changed since it was ours. As I walk through Greenwich Village, it seems smaller now, and the arch at Washington Square hardly big enough to hold two people as happy as we were. As I write to you, and think back through the years, I hear music. Our life together seems almost like a concert, with music accenting each scene. Music greeting us all along our way, and sometimes we'd stop and listen to it awhile. When we felt like hearing music that smiled back at us, we went to Nick's. And if the music changed, we changed with it, and held hands a little tighter, as the blues went by. They play other people's music at Nick's now, not ours. Our music always needs two to be heard, and if the loudest drum sounded to us like a love song, well, that's the way it was, and that's the way it should be.

It's been a long time now between letters, but it has taken me that long to realize how much I need you, how necessary you are to my happiness. At the time, it was almost impossible to answer your last letter.

I can't find the right words to end this letter. It must be because the thoughts it holds can have no end. It must be as clear to you as it is to me... we belong together, and will be, <u>have</u> to be together. There just isn't anything else to say—

Paul

album. Unfortunately, there is really little that deserves such fine singing in the album . . . I couldn't take it, frankly. But I must admit I was impressed with the Garland voice.

6 Judy! That's Entertainment

Label:
   Capitol T-1467 (33⅓)
   Capitol ST-1467 (33⅓)
   Capitol SLER-6528 (33⅓)
   Capitol SM 11876 (33⅓)
   Capitol CCM 7-48426 (CD)
Released: 1962

SIDE ONE

"That's Entertainment"
   [Arthur Schwartz, Howard Dietz
      (1953)]
"Who Cares?"
   [Ira Gershwin, George Gerschwin
      (1931)]
"I've Confessed to the Breeze"
   [Otto Harbach, Vincent Youmans
      (1925)]
"If I Love Again"
   [R. Oakland, J. Murray (1932)]
"Yes"
   [D. Langdon, André Previn (1962)]
"Puttin' on the Ritz"
   [Irving Berlin (1929)]

SIDE TWO

"Old Devil Moon"
   [E. Y. Harburg, Burton Lane (1946)]
"Down with Love"
   [E. Y. Harburg, Harold Arlen (1937)]
"How Long Has This Been Going On?"
   [Ira Gershwin, P. G. Wodehouse,
      George Gershwin (1928)]

"It Never Was You"
   [Maxwell Anderson, Kurt Weill
      (1938)]
"Just You, Just Me"
   [Raymond Klages, Jesse Greer (1929)]
"Alone Together"
   [Arthur Schwartz, Howard Dietz
      (1932)]

ADDENDA

★ Capitol SM 11876 (33⅓) is an abridged version of this album. "I've Confessed to the Breeze" and "How Long Has This Been Going On?" are not on the shortened version. Capitol CCM 7-48426 contains all the original releases.

★ The orchestra is conducted by Jack Marshall. The songs were recorded on June 8, 9, and 17, 1960. The album was released on October 31, 1960.

★ Judy Garland introduced "Yes."

★ *That's Entertainment,* on initial release, contained a dozen songs Garland had not previously recorded.

★ The master numbers for these renditions, in order of appearance on the album, are 34010, 33950, 34012, 33934, 34026, 33951, 34011, 33935, 33036, 33952, and 34013.

SONG ADDENDA

★ "I've Confessed to the Breeze" was written for the 1925 Broadway show *No, No, Nanette,* but was dropped from the New York production.
★ "Puttin' on the Ritz" was introduced in 1930 by Harry Richman in the picture of the same name. In 1946, it was reintroduced by Fred Astaire, with new lyrics, in the film *Blue Skies.*
★ "Old Devil Moon" comes from the 1947 Broadway show *Finian's Rainbow,* where it was sung by Ella Logan and Donald Richards.
★ "Down with Love" comes from the 1937 Broadway musical *Hooray for What!*
★ "How Long Has This Been Going On?" was introduced by Bobbe Arnst in the 1928 Broadway show *Rosalie.* It had originally been written for *Funny Face* but was dropped during out-of-town tryouts.
★ "It Never Was You" was introduced by Richard Kollmar and Jeanne Madden in 1938 in the Broadway musical *Knickerbocker Holiday.* It became a permanent Garland number after she sang it in *I Could Go On Singing* (1963).
★ "Alone Together" was introduced by Clifton Webb and Tamara Geva in the 1932 Broadway show *Flying Colors.*

CONTEMPORARY COMMENTS

The American Record Guide, February 1961
What can you say about a Judy Garland collection of songs beautifully sung? Two-word review of the record: Get it.

7 Judy in London

Label:
  Capitol 94407 (33⅓)
  Capitol SLB 8099 (33⅓)
Released: 1961

SIDE ONE

"This Is My Lucky Day"
Garland Medley:
  "You Made Me Love You"
  "For Me and My Gal"
  "The Trolley Song"
"Happiness Is Just a Thing Called Joe"
"Rock-a-Bye Your Baby with a Dixie Melody"
"Stormy Weather"
  [Ted Koehler, Harold Arlen (1933)]

SIDE TWO

"The Man That Got Away"
"San Francisco"
"I Can't Give You Anything but Love"
"Chicago"
"Do It Again"

SIDE THREE

"Over the Rainbow"
"After You've Gone"
"I Happen to Like New York"
  [Cole Porter (1930)]
"Why Was I Born?"
  [Oscar Hammerstein II, Jerome Kern (1929)]
"You Go to My Head"

SIDE FOUR

Palace Medley:
  "Shine On, Harvest Moon"
  "Some of These Days"
  "My Man"
  "I Don't Care"

"It's a Great Day for the Irish"
   [Roger Edens (1940)]
   From *Little Nellie Kelly*—1940
"Come Rain or Come Shine"
"Swanee"
"You'll Never Walk Alone"
   [Oscar Hammerstein II, Richard
      Rodgers (1945)]

ADDENDA

★ The orchestra was conducted by Norrie
   Paramor. The songs were recorded in
   England on August 2, 3, 4, 5, and 8,
   1960. The album was not released until
   October 23, 1961.
★ The master numbers, in order of appearance on the album, are 34439,
   34449 (Garland Medley), 34451,
   34452, 34440, 34445, 34447, 34454,
   34437, 34438, 34448, 34455, 34441,
   34444, 34450, 34453 (Palace Medley),
   34456, 34446, 34442, and 34443.

SONG ADDENDA

★ "I happen to like New York" was writ-
   ten for the 1930 Broadway musical *The
   New Yorkers*.
★ "Why Was I Born?" was written for,
   and introduced by, Helen Morgan in
   the 1929 Broadway show *Sweet Adeline*.
   Variety selected the song for its "Fifty-
   Year Hit Parade."

---

8 The Garland Touch

Label:
   Capitol W-1710 (33⅓)
   Capitol W1-1710 (33⅓)
   Capitol SW-1710 (33⅓)
Released: 1962

SIDE ONE

"This Is My Lucky Day"
"I Happen to Like New York"
"Comes Once in a Lifetime"
   [Betty Comden, Adolph Green, Jule
      Styne (1961)]
Palace Medley:
   "Shine on Harvest Moon"
   "Some of These Days"
   "My Man"
   "I Don't Care"

SIDE TWO

"Happiness Is Just a Thing Called Joe"
"Sweet Danger"
   [Robert Wright, George Forrest
      (1961)]
"You'll Never Walk Alone"
"Do I Love You?"
   [Cole Porter (1939)]
"More Than You Know"
   [Billy Rose, Edward Eliscu, Vincent
      Youmans (1929)]
"It's a Great Day for the Irish"

ADDENDA

★ *The Garland Touch* was in the Top 40 for five weeks. It was released July 30, 1962.

★ The album was released in the United Kingdom under the title *You'll Never Walk Alone*, World Record Club T/ST 675 (33⅓).

★ *The Garland Touch* is a "pick-up" album; it is made from recording studio tracks from a variety of sessions, with the songs not planned for a specific LP.

"This Is My Lucky Day," "I Happen to Like New York," "You'll Never Walk Alone," "Happiness Is Just a Thing Called Joe," the Palace Medley, and "It's a Great Day for the Irish" were recorded in England on August 2, 3, and 8, 1960. (Master numbers 34439, 34441, 34443, 34451, 34453, and 34456). [These renditions are also on the *Judy in London* album (Capitol SLB-8099).]

"Once in a Lifetime" and "Sweet Danger" were recorded in New York on October 13, 1961.

"More Than You Know" and "Do I Love You?" were recorded on May 26 and June 17, 1958 (master numbers 19195 and 19401). [They are also on the *Judy in Love* album (Capitol ST-1036).]

CONTEMPORARY COMMENTS

The American Record Guide, October 1962 "The Garland Touch" is as certain and irresistible as ever.

9 **Maggie May**

Label: Capitol CL 14791 (45)
Released: 1964

SIDE ONE

"Maggie, Maggie May"
"There's Only One Union"

SIDE TWO

"It's Yourself"
"The Land of Promises"

ADDENDA

★ These songs, from Lionel Bart's *Maggie May,* were from Garland's last recording sessions with Capitol. They were recorded on August 1, 1964. The album was not released in the United States.

10 **Judy Garland "Live"**

Label: Capitol CDP·92343 (CD)
Released: 1989

SONGS

"Sail Away"
  [Noel Coward (1950)]
"Something's Coming"
  [Stephen Sondheim, Leonard
    Bernstein (1957)]
"Get Me to the Church on Time"
  [Alan Jay Lerner, Frederick Loewe
    (1956)]

"Hey, Look Me Over"
  [Carolyn Leigh, Cy Coleman (1960)]
"Just in Time"
  [Betty Comden, Adolph Green (1956)]
"Never Will I Marry"
  [Frank Loesser (1956)]
"Some People"
  [Stephen Sondheim, Jule Styne
    (1959)]
"Joey, Joey, Joey"
  [Frank Loesser (1956)]
"The Party's Over"
  [Betty Comden, Adolph Green (1956)]
"It's a Good Day"
  [Peggy Lee, David Barbour (1946)]
"That's All"
  [Alan Brandt, Bob Haymes (1952)]
"Fly Me to the Moon"
  [Bart Howard (1954)]
"I Wish You Love"
  [Charles Trenet, Albert A. Beach
    (1955)]
"As Long as He Needs Me"
  [Lionel Bart (1962)]

ADDENDA

★ This disk contains nine original tracks recorded on April 25 and 26, 1962, for an album that was to be called *Judy Takes Broadway*. Garland felt that she sounded hoarse during the recording sessions, and it was decided not to release them at that time.

★ The final five tracks are from Judy's television series and were previously released on *Just for Openers* [Capitol W/ DW 2062 (33⅓)].

SONG ADDENDA

★ "Sail Away" was introduced in the London musical *Ace of Clubs* by Graham Payn.

★ "Get Me to the Church on Time" was introduced on Broadway in *My Fair Lady* (1956).

★ "Hey, Look Me Over" was introduced by Lucille Ball and Paula Stewart in the 1960 show *Wildcat*. The melody was later used by Louisiana State University for its official song (under the title "Hey, Fighting Tigers").

★ "Never Will I Marry" comes from the show *Greenwillow*. It was introduced to Broadway in 1960 by Anthony Perkins.

★ "Fly Me to the Moon" was originally called "In Other Words." With that title it didn't get off the ground. The U.S. space program provided the inspiration for the new title, and the song became a major success.

★ "I Wish You Love" was popular in France before it was imported. Its introduction to the United States, with English lyrics, was by Keely Smith.

★ "As Long As He Needs Me" was sung by Georgia Brown in the 1963 production of *Oliver*.

I. CONCERT ALBUMS

1 **Judy Garland "Live" at the Palace February 1952: An Evening of Song, Dance and Conversation**

Label: Classic International Theatremusic C.I.T. 2001 (33 ⅓)
Released: 1952

SIDE ONE

Introduction (by Judy's 8 Boy Friends)
"Tonight's the Night"
Palace Medley:
  "Shine On, Harvest Moon"
    [Nora Bayes, Jack Norworth
      (1908)]
  "Some of These Days"
    [Shelton Brooks (1910)]
  "My Man"
    [Maurice Yvain, Channing Pollock
      (1921)]
  "I Don't Care"
    [Harry O. Sutton, Jean Lennox
      (1905)]
"Rock-a-Bye Your Baby with a Dixie
  Melody"
  [Sam M. Lewis, Joe Young, Jean
    Schwartz (1918)]
Garland Medley:
  "You Made Me Love You"
    From *Broadway Melody of 1938*—
      1937
  "For Me and My Gal"
    From *For Me and My Gal*—1942
  "The Boy Next Door"
    From *Meet Me in St. Louis*—1944
  "The Trolley Song"
    From *Meet Me in St. Louis*
"Get Happy"
  From *Summer Stock*—1950

SIDE TWO

"A Couple of Swells"
  From *Easter Parade*—1948
"Over the Rainbow"
  From *The Wizard of Oz*—1939
"Love"
  [Ralph Blane, Hugh Martin (1945)]
"A Pretty Girl Milking Her Cow"
  From *Little Nellie Kelly*—1940
"Liza"
  [Ira Gershwin, Gus Kahn, George
    Gershwin (1929)]

Judy performing at the Palace, 1951.

Introduction to Lauritz Melchior
"Auld Lang Syne" (audience singing to
Judy)

ADDENDA

★ Hugh Martin was at the piano.
★ This was the American introduction of
Garland's concert version of "Over the
Rainbow."
★ Despite the interpolations in the Palace
Medley, Al Jolson never played the Pal-
ace. He played the Winter Garden.
★ Vincente Minnelli, in his autobiography, *I Remember It Well,* takes credit for
suggesting that Garland sing "Rock-a-
Bye Your Baby with a Dixie Melody" at
her London Palladium concert in 1951.
He reports himself as saying: "People
have always said you're the greatest entertainer since Jolson. Why don't you
sing one of his songs? It'll give them
some basis of comparison. I came up
with one song idea: 'Rock-a-Bye Your
Baby With a Dixie Melody.' "
★ It was a tradition at the Palace, at the
closing night performance, that the
headliner of the next show be introduced. After Garland's show finally
closed, Lauritz Melchior was scheduled
to open.

SONG ADDENDA

★ "Liza" comes from Florenz Ziegfeld's
1929 Broadway musical *Show Girl.* Liza
Minnelli was named for this song.

2 Judy Garland at the Grove

Label:
    Capitol T-1118 (33⅓)
    Capitol ST-1118 (33⅓)
    Capitol 26-0007-1 (33⅓)
    Capitol 26-0007-4 (cassette)
    EMI 26007 (33⅓) (U.K.)
Released: 1958

SIDE ONE

"Garland Overture" (instrumental)
"When You're Smiling"
    [Mark Fisher, Joe Goodwin, Larry
        Shay (1928)]
"Zing! Went the Strings of My Heart"
    [James F. Hanley (1935)]
    From *Listen, Darling*—1938
"Purple People Eater"
    [Sheb Wooley (1958)]
Garland Medley:
    "You Made Me Love You"
        [Joseph McCarthy, James V.
            Monaco (1913)]

"For Me and My Gal"
    [Edgar Leslie, E. Ray Goetz, George
        W. Meyer (1917)]
"The Trolley Song"
    [Ralph Blane, Hugh Martin (1944)]

SIDE TWO

"When the Sun Comes Out"
    [Ted Koehler, Harold Arlen (1941)]
"Rock-a-Bye Your Baby with a Dixie
    Melody"
    [Sam M. Lewis, Joe Young, Jean
        Schwartz (1918)]
"Over the Rainbow"
    [E. Y. Harburg, Harold Arlen (1939)]
    From *The Wizard of Oz*—1939
"After You've Gone"
    [Henry Creamer, Turner Layton
        (1918)]
    From *For Me and My Gal*— 1942
"A Pretty Girl Milking Her Cow"
    [Adaptation by Roger Edens (1940)]
    From *Little Nellie Kelly*—1940
"Swanee"
    [Irving Caesar, George Gershwin
        (1919)]
    From *A Star Is Born*—1954

ADDENDA

★ The concert, and the recording, were
with Freddy Martin and His Orchestra.
The tracks were taken by remote recording hook-up on August 6, 1958.

★ The master numbers (in order of appearance on the record) are 30175 (instrumental), 30176, 30177, 30178,
30179 (Garland Medley), 30180,
30181, 30182, 30183, 30184, 30185.

3 Long-Lost Holland Concert

This contains tracks beyond the songs
    sung at this concert.
    (See Anthology Albums, Section L)

4 Judy Garland in Holland, vol. 2

This contains tracks beyond the songs
    sung at this concert.
    (See Anthology Albums, Section L)

5 Judy Garland in Holland, vol. 3

This contains tracks beyond the songs
    sung at this concert.
    (See Anthology Albums, Section L)

6 Judy at Carnegie Hall

Label:
    Capitol WBO-1569 (33⅓)
    Capitol SWBO-1569 (33⅓)
    Capitol EAP-1569 (45)
    Capitol 4X2K-01569 (cassette)
    Capitol C2-90013 (CD)
Released: 1961

SIDE ONE

Overture:
    "The Trolley Song"
    "Over the Rainbow"
    "The Man That Got Away"
"When You're Smiling"
    [Mark Fisher, Joe Goodwin, Mark
        Shay (1928)]

Medley:
  "It's Almost Like Being in Love"
    [Alan Jay Lerner, Frederick Loewe
    (1947)]
  "This Can't Be Love"
    [Lorenz Hart, Richard Rodgers
    (1938)]
"Do It Again"
  [Buddy DeSylva, George Gershwin
  (1922)]
"You Go to My Head"
  [Haven Gillespie, J. Fred Coots
  (1938)]
"Alone Together"
  [Howard Dietz, Arthur Schwartz
  (1932)]

SIDE TWO

"Who Cares?"
  [Ira and George Gershwin (1931)]
"Puttin' on the Ritz"
  [Irving Berlin (1929)]
"How Long Has This Been Going On?"
  [Ira and George Gershwin (1927)]
"Just You, Just Me"
  [Raymond Klages, Jesse Greer (1929)]
"The Man That Got Away"
  [Ira Gershwin, Harold Arlen (1954)]
"San Francisco"
  [Gus Kahn, Bronislau Kaper (1936)]
"I Can't Give You Anything but Love"
  [Dorothy Fields, Jimmy McHugh
  (1928)]
"That's Entertainment"
  [Howard Dietz, Arthur Schwartz
  (1953)]

SIDE THREE

"Come Rain or Come Shine"
  [Johnny Mercer, Harold Arlen (1946)]
"You're Nearer"
  [Lorenz Hart, Richard Rodgers (1939)]

"A Foggy Day"
  [Ira and George Gershwin (1937)]
"If Love Were All"
  [Noel Coward (1929)]
"Zing! Went the Strings of My Heart"
  [James F. Hanley (1935)]
  From Listen, Darling—1938
"Stormy Weather"
  [Ted Koehler, Harold Arlen (1933)]

SIDE FOUR

Garland Medley:
  "You Made Me Love You"
  "For Me and My Gal"
  "The Trolley Song"
"Rock-a-Bye Your Baby with a Dixie
  Melody"
"Over the Rainbow"
"Swanee"
"After You've Gone"
"Chicago"
  [Fred Fisher (1922)]

ADDENDA

★ This is a complete recording of the live concert at Carnegie Hall in New York City on April 23, 1961.

Rumors abound that this recording contains rerecorded songs or versions from other performances. According to the Capitol Records' "Artist Performance Record" for Judy Garland, all the songs were recorded on April 23, 1961. Master numbers (in order of appearance on the album) are 23724 (Overture), 23725, 23726 (Medley), 23727, 23728, 23729, 23730, 23731, 23732, 23733, 23734, 23735, 23736, 23737, 23738, 23739, 23740, 23741, 23742, 23743, 23744 (Garland Medley), 23745, 23746, 23747, 23748, 23749.

★ The orchestra was conducted by Mort Lindsey.

★ This album was number one in the United States for thirteen consecutive weeks. It was on the best-seller list for eighty-five weeks. It sold half a million copies by 1962 and well over a million subsequently. It was the largest-selling two-record set released up until that time.

★ *Judy at Carnegie Hall* won Grammy Awards for Best Engineering Contribution (Popular Recording) and Best Album Cover for 1961.

★ It won the Gold Disc Award R.I.A.A. in 1962.

★ An abridged version of this concert was released on Capitol CDP 46470 (CD) under the title *Live at Carnegie Hall.* It was a short-lived release due to consumer fury at the cuts. In 1989, Capitol released C2-90013 (CD). This not only restored the cuts, but added approximately twenty minutes of Garland interaction with the audience.

SONG ADDENDA

★ "Almost Like Being in Love" was introduced on Broadway in the 1947 musical *Brigadoon* by David Brooks and Marion Bell. In the 1954 movie of the same name, it was sung by Gene Kelly, Garland's costar in *For Me and My Gal* (his first movie), *The Pirate,* and *Summer Stock.*

★ "This Can't Be Love" comes from the 1938 Broadway show *The Boys from Syracuse.*

★ "Do It Again" comes from the 1922 Broadway show *The French Doll.* It was introduced by Irene Bordoni.

★ "You Go to My Head" was written two years before it was actually published. Most of the leading music publishers turned it down.

★ "Alone Together" comes from the 1932 Broadway revue *Flying Colors.*

★ "You're Nearer" comes from the 1939 Broadway show *Too Many Girls.*

★ "A Foggy Day" was introduced by Fred Astaire in the 1937 film *A Damsel in Distress.*

★ "If Love Were All" comes from the 1929 Broadway show *Bitter Sweet.*

★ "Stormy Weather" was originally written for Cab Calloway, who did not sing it in the Cotton Club Revue as planned. Ethel Waters was persuaded not to carry out her threats to retire and sang it in the next Revue. She created a sensation, and the song became closely associated with her.

CONTEMPORARY COMMENTS

The New York Times, September 24, 1961
. . . The potentially commanding singing talent of Judy Garland came into sure, consistent focus in the last year as she gave concert after concert at which she was able to give full rein to her instinctive showmanship.

There are, basically, two sides to Miss Garland as a singer—the lusty voiced belter, craftily adept at a theatrical type of projection that stems from the days before microphones, and the easy, casual singer who works on intimate terms with her audience. Both roles are played here.

—John S. Wilson

The American Record Guide, October 1961
As exciting a set as anyone has released
this year . . . , a two-record set actually recorded at the historic concert in April.
Generally, I don't "understand" these lo-
cation albums, but this one is something
else again. Not only is Miss Garland . . .
in superb voice but she also sings a wonderful collection of songs and is given a
brilliant orchestral accompaniment by
Mort Lindsey.

7 **Judy Garland and Liza Minnelli,
Live at The Palladium**

Label:
    Capitol WBO-2295 (33⅓)
    Capitol SWBO-2295 (33⅓)
    World Record Club ST-764/5 (33⅓)
    (U.K.)
Released: 1964

SIDE ONE

Overture
    "The Man That Got Away"
    "The Travelin' Life" (Minnelli)
    "Gypsy in My Soul" (Minnelli)
    "Hello, Dolly!" (with Minnelli)
        [Jerry Herman (1964)]
    "Together" (with Minnelli)
        [Buddy DeSylva, Lew Brown, Ray
            Henderson (1926)]
Medley (with Minnelli):
    "We Could Make Such Beautiful
        Music Together" (with Minnelli)
        [Robert Sour, Henry Manners
            (1940)]
    "Bob White"
        [Johnny Mercer, Bernard Hanighen
            (1937)]

SIDE TWO
Medley (with Minnelli):
    "Hooray for Love"
        [Leo Robin, Harold Arlen (1948)]
    "After You've Gone"
    "By Myself" (Minnelli)
    " 'S Wonderful"
        [Ira and George Gershwin (1927)]
    "How About You?" (with Minnelli)
        [Ralph Freed, Burton Lane (1941)]
    "Lover, Come Back to Me" (Minnelli)
        [Oscar Hammerstein II, Sigmund
            Romberg (1928)]
    "You and the Night and the Music"
        [Howard Dietz, Arthur Schwartz
            (1934)]
    "It All Depends on You" (with
        Minnelli)
        [Buddy DeSylva, Lew Brown, Ray
            Henderson (1925)]
"Who's Sorry Now?" (Minnelli)
    [Bert Kalmar, Harry Ruby, Ted Snyder
        (1923)]

"Smile"
   [John Turner, Geoffrey Parsons,
      Charles Chaplin (1936)]
"How Could You Believe Me?" (Minnelli)
   [Burton Lane, Alan Jay Lerner (1951)]
"What Now, My Love?"
   [Gilbert Becaud, Delanoe, English
      lyrics by Carl Sigman (1962)]

SIDE THREE

Medley (special lyrics) (Minnelli):
   "Take Me Along"
   "If I Could Be with You"
   "Tea for Two"
   "Who?"
   "They Can't Take That Away from Me"
   "By Myself"
   "Mammy"
"Make Someone Happy"
   [Betty Comden, Adolph Green, Jule
      Styne (1960)]
"Pass That Peace Pipe" (Minnelli)
   [Roger Edens, Hugh Martin, and
      Ralph Blane (1943)]
"His Is the Only Music That Makes Me
   Dance"
   [Bob Merrill, Jule Styne (1964)]
Garland Medley (with Minnelli):
   "When the Saints Go Marching In"
   "He's Got the Whole World in His
      Hands"
   [Geoff Love (1957)]

SIDE FOUR

"Never Will I Marry"
   [Frank Loesser (1960)]
"Swanee" (with Minnelli)
"Chicago" (with Minnelli)
"Over the Rainbow"
"San Francisco" (with Minnelli)

ADDENDA

★ These concerts were recorded with
   Harry Robinson conducting The Pal-
   ladium Orchestra.
★ In 1965, these same tracks were rere-
   leased under the title *The Judy Garland/
   Liza Minnelli Concert at The London
   Palladium* [Capitol EM 1249 (33⅓) and
   TCEM 1249 (cassette)].
★ Neither of these releases contains the
   full concert.

SONG ADDENDA

★ "Together, Wherever We Go" was in-
   troduced by Ethel Merman, Sandra
   Church, and Jack Klugman in the 1959
   Broadway stage production of *Gypsy*.
★ "Hooray for Love" was introduced by
   Tony Martin in the 1948 film *Casbah*.
★ "'S Wonderful" was introduced by
   Allen Kearns and Adele Astaire in the
   1927 Broadway show *Funny Face*.
★ "How About You?" was introduced by
   Judy Garland and Mickey Rooney in
   the film *Babes on Broadway* in 1941.
★ "Lover, Come Back to Me" was intro-
   duced on Broadway by Evelyn Herbert
   in the 1929 operetta *The New Moon*.
★ "You and the Night and the Music" was
   introduced by Georges Metaxa and
   Libby Holman in the 1934 Dietz and
   Schwartz show *Revenge with Music*.
★ "It All Depends on You" comes from
   the 1925 show *Big Boy*, where it was
   introduced by Al Jolson.
★ "Who's Sorry Now?" was introduced in
   1923 by Van and Schenck and used in
   the 1950 film *Three Little Words*, sung
   by Gloria DeHaven.

★ "How Could You Believe Me?" (also called "The Liar's Song") comes from the 1951 movie *Royal Wedding,* sung by Fred Astaire and Jane Powell. (The song had been written with Judy Garland in mind, but she did not make the movie.)

★ "Pass That Peace Pipe" was originally written for a Fred Astaire/Gene Kelly number in *Ziegfeld Follies.* It was not used until 1947 when Joan McCracken introduced it in the movie *Good News.*

★ "Never Will I Marry" was introduced on Broadway in 1960 by Anthony Perkins in *Greenwillow.*

---

8 Judy Garland/Liza Minnelli "Live" at the London Palladium

Label: Capitol ST-1191 (33⅓)
Released: 1973
abridged version

SIDE ONE

"Together" (with Minnelli)
    [Jule Styne, Stephen Sondheim
        (1959)]
"The Man That Got Away"
"Who's Sorry Now" (Minnelli)
    [Ted Snyder, Bert Kalmar, Harry Ruby
        (1923)]
Medley:
    "Hooray for Love" (with Minnelli)
    "After You've Gone"
    "By Myself (Minnelli)
    " 'S Wonderful"
    "How About You?" (with Minnelli)
    "Lover, Come Back to Me" (Minnelli)
    "You and the Night and the Music"

"It All Depends on You" (with Minnelli)
"What Now, My Love?"

SIDE TWO

"Hello, Dolly!" (with Minnelli)
"Gypsy in My Soul" (Minnelli)
    [Clay Boland, Moe Jaffe (1937)]
"Swanee" (with Minnelli)
"Over the Rainbow"
Medley (with Minnelli):
    "When the Saints Go Marching In"/
        "Brotherhood of Man"
        [Frank Loesser (1961)]
    "He's Got the Whole World in His
        Hands"

SONG ADDENDA

★ "Gypsy in My Soul" was introduced in the University of Pennsylvania's Mask and Wig Club production of the revue *Fifty-Fifty.*

---

9 Judy Garland in Concert: San Francisco

Label: Mark 56 Records 632 (33⅓)
Released: 1973

SIDE ONE

Overture
"I Feel a Song Coming On"
Garland Medley:
    "You Made Me Love You"
    "For Me and My Gal"
    "The Trolley Song"
"Do It Again"
"The Man That Got Away"
"Rock-a-Bye Your Baby with a Dixie
    Melody"

SIDE TWO

"I Can't Give You Anything but Love"
"Purple People Eater"
"Liza"

---

10 Judy Garland at Home at The Palace Opening Night

Label:
  ABC 620 (33⅓)
  ABCS 620 (33⅓)
Released: 1967

SIDE ONE

Overture
"I Feel a Song Coming On"
  [Jimmy McHugh, Dorothy Fields,
    George Oppenheimer (1935)]
Medley:
  "It's Almost Like Being in Love"
  "This Can't Be Love"
Garland Medley:
  "You Made Me Love You"
  "For Me and My Gal"
  "The Trolley Song"
"What Now, My Love?"

SIDE TWO

"Bob White (Watcha Gonna Swing
  Tonight)" (with Lorna Luft)
  [Johnny Mercer, Bernie Hanighen
    (1937)]
"Jamboree Jones" (with Lorna Luft)
  [Johnny Mercer (1937)]
"Together" (with Lorna Luft, Joe Luft)
"Over the Rainbow" (instrumental)
"Old Man River"
  [Oscar Hammerstein II, Jerome Kern
    (1927)]

"That's Entertainment"
"I Loved Him, but He Didn't Love Me"
  [Cole Porter (1929)]
"Rock-a-Bye Your Baby with a Dixie
  Melody"
"Over the Rainbow" (instrumental)

ADDENDA

★ Recorded live at the Palace Theatre,
  1967.
★ ABC released this same album later
  under the title *Judy Garland. The ABC
  Collection* [ABC 30007 (33⅓)].

SONG ADDENDA

★ "I Loved Him, but He Didn't Love Me"
  comes from the 1929 English revue
  Wake Up and Dream.

CONTEMPORARY COMMENTS

Saturday Review, September 30, 1967
... the Garland voice is unstable....
where once there was smoothness, now
there is strain.

  To go below the top layer of performance is another matter. The sharpness
and excitement of youth may be gone
from Miss Garland's efforts, but the intrinsic spark remains. If you involve yourself with her for a little while, you *really*
hear her and discover the artistic justifi-
cation for the continuing phenomenon.
                            —Burt Kovall

11 Judy Garland. The Last Concert

Label: Paragon 1003 (33 ⅓)

ADDENDA

★ This is a recording of Garland's 1968 Boston appearance. It was not her last concert, of course.

12 Judy. London. 1969

Label:
Juno S 1000 (33⅓)
Sunset Records 50196 (33⅓) (U.K.)
Released: 1969

SIDE ONE

"I Belong to London"
[Ross Parker, special lyrics by Stan Freeman]
"Get Happy"
"The Man That Got Away"
"I'd Like to Hate Myself in The Morning"
[John Meyer (1968)]

SIDE TWO

"Just in Time"
[Betty Comden, Adolph Green, Jule Styne (1956)]
Garland Medley:
"You Made Me Love You"
"For Me and My Gal"
"The Trolley Song"
"For Once in My Life"
[Ronald Miller, Orlando Murden (1963)]
"San Francisco"
"Over the Rainbow"

ADDENDA

★ This was not actually a concert per se. It was a London cabaret appearance.
★ The liner notes suggest that this version of "Over the Rainbow" was the last song Judy sang in public; that is obviously incorrect.

J. SOUNDTRACKS AND SOUNDTRACK SELECTIONS

1 A Star Is Born

Label:
Columbia CL 1101 (33⅓)
(DeLuxe Box Set, with booklet— mono)
Columbia BL 1201 (33⅓)
Columbia BM 1201 (78)
Columbia BA 1201 (45)
Columbia CS 8740 (33⅓)
Columbia Harmony HS 11366 (33⅓)
Columbia CL 6200 (33⅓)
Philips BBL 7007 (33⅓) (U.K.)
CBS Realm RM 5206 (33⅓) (U.K.)
CBS Realm RMS 5206 (33⅓)
Hallmark SHM 654 (33⅓)
Hall of Fame EP B 2580
CBS JST 44380 (cassette)
Columbia CK 44380 (CD)

ADDENDA

★ Two musical sequences were cut from the film two months after its release, but the recordings remained uncut and intact.
★ The soundtrack album was recorded in Hollywood on August 4, 5, and 6, 1954. It was released by Columbia Rec-

ords on September 2, 1954 (on CL 1101), in mono. It was then released as an electronically remastered stereo LP. The original package was a deluxe box set, with booklet. It was then issued as a regular album.

★ Hall of Fame EP-B-2580, released on October 11, 1954, consists of the "Born in a Trunk" sequence of songs.

★ In 1988, the *original soundtrack* of *A Star Is Born,* recorded in stereo at the studio, was released on compact disc (Columbia CK 44380) and cassette (CBS JST 44380). Grab it.

This is the only version out that has both the original stereo of the film itself and the background noises and "bits"

that enhance the performance. All previous "original soundtrack" recordings were made in a recording studio, and previous "stereo" versions were electronically remastered from mono.

2 Pepe

Label:
 Colpix CP 507 (33⅓)
 Colpix CPS 507 (33⅓)
 Pye International NPL 28015 (33⅓) (U.K.)

3 Gay Purr-ee

Label:
 Warner Bros. B-1479 (33⅓)
 Warner Bros. BS-1479 (33⅓)
 Warner Bros. W-802 (33⅓)
 Warner Bros. WS-802 (33⅓)

CONTEMPORARY COMMENTS

The American Record Guide, November 1962

To compound the felicity the songs are sung by Judy Garland, who now has at least two more great ones for her repertoire . . . The two are "Little Drops of Rain" and "Paris Is a Lonely Town." . . . the latter is done to a fare thee well.

4 I Could Go On Singing

Label:
 Capitol W-1861 (33⅓)
 Capitol WS-1861 (33⅓)

K. ALBUMS FROM "THE JUDY GARLAND SHOW"

---

1 **Just for Openers**

Label:
    Capitol W-2062 (33⅓)
    Capitol DW-2062 (33⅓)

SIDE ONE

"It's A Good Day"
    [David Barbour, Peggy Lee (1946)]
    December 1, 1963, show
"That's All"
    [Bob Haymes, Alan Brandt (1952)]
    March 1, 1964, show
"Some People"
    [Jule Styne, Stephen Sondheim
        (1959)]
    March 1, 1964, show
"More"
    [N. Oliviero, Riz Ortolani, M. Giorgio-
        lini, English lyrics by Norman
        Newell (1963)]
    December 29, 1963, show

"Island in the West Indies"
    [Ira Gershwin, Vernon Duke (1935)]
    January 5, 1964, show
"As Long as He Needs Me"
    [Lionel Bart (1962)]
    November 17, 1963, show

SIDE TWO

"Get Me to the Church on Time"
    [Alan Jay Lerner, Frederick Loewe
        (1956)]
    December 29, 1963, show
"Fly Me to the Moon (In Other Words)"
    [Bart Howard (1954)]
    September 29, 1963, show—series
        premiere
"I Wish You Love"
    [Charles Trenet, Albert A. Beach
        (1955)]
    October 20, 1963, show
"Jamboree Jones"
    [Johnny Mercer (1937)]
    December 29, 1963, show
"The Battle Hymn of the Republic"
    [Julia Ward Howe, William Steffe
        (1862)]
    January 12, 1964, and February 2,
        1964, shows
"Maybe I'll Come Back"
    [Charles L. Cooke, Howard C. Jeffrey]
    closing theme for "The Judy Garland
        Show"

ADDENDA

★ This is the first album to appear from
  the soundtrack of "The Judy Garland
  Show." Mort Lindsey conducts.
★ Garland used "Maybe I'll Come Back"
  as her weekly closing theme.

SONG ADDENDA

★ "More" is the theme from the 1963 movie *Mondo Cane*.

★ "Island in the West Indies" was introduced by Gertrude Niesen, and danced by Josephine Baker, in the Broadway revue *Ziegfeld Follies of 1936*.

★ "Some People" comes from the 1959 musical *Gypsy*. It was introduced by Ethel Merman.

2 Judy

Label: Radiant 711-0101 (33⅓)

SIDE ONE

"Come Rain or Come Shine"
[Johnny Mercer, Harold Arlen (1946)]
October 13, 1963, and February 16, 1964, shows

"Smile"
[John Turner, Geoffrey Parsons, Charles Chaplin (1936)]
November 3, 1963, and February 16, 1964, shows

"I Can't Give You Anything but Love"
[Dorothy Fields, Jimmy McHugh (1928)]
February 16, 1964, show

"Hey, Look Me Over"
[Carolyn Leigh, Cy Coleman (1960)]
November 10, 1963 and February 16, 1964 shows

"By Myself"
[Howard Dietz, Arthur Schwartz (1937)]
January 19, 1963, show and March 22, 1964, shows

SIDE TWO

"San Francisco"
[Gus Kahn, Bronislau Kaper (1936)]
October 27, 1963, December 1, 1963, and February 2, 1964, shows

"Fly Me to the Moon"
September 29, 1963—series premiere

"Do It Again"
[Buddy DeSylva, George Gershwin (1922)]
December 29, 1963, show

"After You've Gone"
From *For Me and My Gal*—1942
February 16, 1964, show and March 29, 1964—last show of series

"All Alone"
[Irving Berlin (1924)]
January 26, 1964, show

"It's Gonna Be a Great Day"
[Billy Rose, Edward Eliscu, Vincent Youmans (1929)]
February 16, 1964, show

ADDENDA

★ The cuts on this album are from the original soundtrack of "The Judy Garland Show." Mort Lindsey conducts.

SONG ADDENDA

★ The music for "Smile" was used for the background in Chaplin's 1936 film, *Modern Times*.

3 Judy in Hollywood

Label: Radiant 711-0102 (33⅓)

SIDE ONE

"Love of My Life"
From *The Pirate*—1948
March 8, 1964, show
"A Couple of Swells"
From *Easter Parade*—1948
February 9, 1964, show
"That's Entertainment"
February 9, 1964, show
"The Boy Next Door"
From *Meet Me in St. Louis*—1944
March 8, 1964, show
"How About Me?"
[Irving Berlin (1928)]
December 1, 1963, show
"If I Had a Talking Picture of You"
[Buddy DeSylva, Ray Henderson
(1929)]
March 8, 1964, show
"Toot, Toot, Tootsie"
[Gus Kahn, Ernie Erdman, Dan Russo
(1922)]
March 8, 1964, show

SIDE TWO

"You Made Me Love You"
From *Broadway Melody of 1938*—1937
October 6, 1963, show
"For Me and My Gal"
From *For Me and My Gal*—1942
October 6, 1963, show
"The Trolley Song"
From *Meet Me in St. Louis*
October 6, 1963, and February 16,
1964, shows

"As Long As He Needs Me"
[Lionel Bart (1963)]
November 17, 1963, and March 22,
1964, shows
"Dirty Hands, Dirty Face"
[Edgar Leslie, James V. Monaco
(1923)]
March 8, 1964, show
"A Pretty Girl Milking Her Cow"
From *Little Nellie Kelly*—1940
January 12, 1964, show
"Puttin' on the Ritz"
[Irving Berlin (1929)]
January 12, 1964, show

ADDENDA

★ The cuts on this album are from the
original soundtrack of "The Judy Garland Show." Mort Lindsey conducts.

SONG ADDENDA

★ "If I Had a Talking Picture of You" was
introduced by Janet Gaynor and
Charles Farrell in the 1929 film *Sunny
Side Up.*
   Gaynor played the Garland role in
the 1937 version of *A Star Is Born.*
★ "Toot, Toot, Tootsie" was sung by Al
Jolson in *Bombo* in 1922. It became one
of his specialty numbers.

4 Judy—The Legend

Label: Radiant 711 0103 (33⅓)

SIDE ONE

"Do I Love You?"
[Cole Porter (1939)]
March 15, 1964, show

"What'll I Do?"
   [Irving Berlin (1924)]
   February 2, 1964, show
"Oh Lord, I'm on My Way"
   January 26, 1964, show
"Unless You've Played the Palace"
   (Palace Medley)
   February 23, 1964, show
"Don't Ever Leave Me"
   [Oscar Hammerstein II, Jerome Kern
      (1929)]
   February 16, 1964, show

SIDE TWO

"I'm Nobody's Baby"
   From *Andy Hardy Meets Debutante*—
      1940
   March 8, 1964
"That's Entertainment"
   February 9, 1964, show
"More"
   December 29, 1964, show
"Chicago"
   [Fred Fisher (1922)]
   September 29, 1963, show—series
      premiere—and March 15, 1964,
      show
Medley:
   "It's Almost Like Being in Love"
      [Alan Jay Lerner, Frederick Loewe
         (1947)]
   "This Can't Be Love"
      [Lorenz Hart, Richard Rodgers
         (1937)]
      January 19, 1964, show and March
         29, 1964—last show of the series
"Here's That Rainy Day"
   [Johnny Burke, Jimmy Van Heusen
      (1953)]
   January 5, 1964, show

"Through the Years"
   [Edward Heyman, Vincent Youmans
      (1931)]
   January 5, 1964, show

ADDENDA

★ The cuts on this album are from the
original soundtrack of "The Judy Garland Show." Mort Lindsey conducts.

SONG ADDENDA

★ "Don't Ever Leave Me" was introduced
by Helen Morgan in the 1929 Broadway
musical *Sweet Adeline*.
★ "Here's That Rainy Day" was introduced by John Raitt in the 1953 Broadway musical *Carnival in Flanders*.
★ "Through the Years" comes from the
1932 Broadway show of the same
name. It was introduced by Natalie Hall
and Michael Bartlett. This was a favorite of Vincent Youmans's among his
own compositions; he described it as
his best creation.

---

5 **Judy's Greatest Hits**

Label: Radiant-711 0104 (33⅓)
Incomplete listing

SONGS

"I'm Nobody's Baby"
   From *Andy Hardy Meets Debutante*—
      1940
   March 8, 1964, show
"Over the Rainbow"
   From *The Wizard of Oz*—1939
   December 22, 1963, show

"The Man That Got Away"
From *A Star Is Born*—1954
March 8, 1964, show
"I Feel a Song Comin' On"
December 8, 1963, and March 8, 1964,
shows

ADDENDA

★ The cuts on this album are from the
original soundtrack of "The Judy Garland Show." Mort Lindsey conducts.

---

6 Unforgettable Judy Garland

Label: Radiant 711-0105 (33⅓)

SIDE ONE

"This Is My Lucky Day"
[Buddy DeSylva, Lew Brown, Ray
Henderson (1926)]
March 15, 1964, show
"Lost in the Stars"
[Maxwell Anderson, Kurt Weill
(1949)]
March 15, 1964, show
"I'll Show Them All"
[Steve Allen (1963)]
January 5, 1964, show
"Paris Is a Lonely Town"
From "Gay Purr-ee—1962
February 2, 1964, show
"Through the Years"
January 5, 1964, show
"Island in the West Indies"
January 5, 1964, show
Medley:
"There's a Long, Long Trail"
[Stoddard King, Zo Elliott (1913)]

"Give My Regards to Broadway"
[George M. Cohan (1904)]
February 9, 1964, show

SIDE TWO

"This Could Be the Start of Something
Big"
[Steve Allen (1956)]
January 5, 1964, show
"I Love You"
[Cole Porter (1943)]
March 15, 1964, show
"Last Night When We Were Young"
[E. Y. Harburg, Harold Arlen (1936)]
February 23, 1964, show
"Just in Time"
[Betty Comden, Adolph Green, Jule
Styne (1956)]
October 6, 1963, and February 23,
1964, shows
"76 Trombones"
[Meredith Willson (1957)]
January 26, 1964, show
"The Battle Hymn of the Republic"
January 12, 1964, and February 2,
1964, shows

ADDENDA

★ The cuts on this album are from the
original soundtrack of "The Judy Garland Show." Mort Lindsey conducts.

SONG ADDENDA

★ *Lost in the Stars* was the title song to
the 1949 Broadway show. The song
was introduced by Todd Duncan.
★ "I'll Show Them All" was written for
the 1963 Broadway show *Sophie,* based
on the life of Sophie Tucker.

★ "There's a Long, Long Trail" was a popular World War I ballad. It was written and published before the war started.

★ "Give My Regards to Broadway" was introduced in 1904 by George M. Cohan, playing the title role in *Little Johnny Jones*.

★ "I Love You" was introduced on Broadway by Wilbur Evans in *Mexican Hayride* in 1944.

Porter wrote the song on a bet. Mike Todd bet him that he could take the most clichéd title around and write a hit song around it.

★ "Just in Time" was introduced by Judy Holliday and Sidney Chaplin in the 1956 Broadway show *The Bells Are Ringing*.

★ "76 Trombones" was introduced on Broadway in 1957 by Robert Preston in *The Music Man*.

---

7 Judy's Portrait in Song

Label: Radiant 711 0106 (33⅓)

SIDE ONE

"From This Moment On"
[Cole Porter (1950)]
November 3, 1963 show
"Sweet Little Alice Blue Gown"
[Joseph McCarthy, Harry Tierney (1919)]
"San Francisco"
October 27, 1963, December 1, 1963, and February 2, 1964, shows
"Sweet Danger"
[Robert Wright, George Forrest (1961)]
March 15, 1964, show

"When Your Lover Has Gone"
[E. A. Swan (1931)]
March 1, 1964, and March 15, 1964, shows
"Oh, Shenandoah"
January 12, 1964, show

SIDE TWO

"A Couple of Swells"
From "Easter Parade"—1948
February 9, 1964, show
Medley:
"Almost Like Being in Love"
"This Can't Be Love"
February 9, 1964, and March 22, 1964, shows
"Free and Easy" ("Any Place I Hang My Hat Is Home")
[Johnny Mercer, Harold Arlen (1946)]
March 15, 1964, show
"Never Will I Marry"
[Frank Loesser (1960)]
December 1, 1963, and March 15, 1964, shows
"I'm Old-Fashioned"
[Johnny Mercer, Jerome Kern (1942)]
January 26, 1964, show
"Old Devil Moon"
[E. Y. Harburg, Burton Lane (1947)]
March 15, 1964, show

ADDENDA

★ The cuts on this album are from the original soundtrack of "The Judy Garland Show." Mort Lindsey conducts.

SONG ADDENDA

★ "From This Moment On" was written for the 1950 Broadway show *Out of This World*. It was dropped during the out-of-town tryouts before reaching Broadway. Three years later, it made it to the screen in the film *Kiss Me, Kate,* where it was sung by Ann Miller and Tommy Rall.

★ "Sweet Little Alice Blue Gown" was introduced in the 1919 show *Irene* by Edith Day.

★ "When Your Lover Has Gone" was used on the soundtrack for the 1931 film *Blonde Crazy,* starring James Cagney and Joan Blondell.

★ "I'm Old-Fashioned" was introduced by Fred Astaire in the film *You Were Never Lovelier.*

8 Judy Garland—Over the Rainbow

Label: Radiant 711-0107 (33⅓)
Incomplete listing

SONGS

"I'm Always Chasing Rainbows"
    March 8, 1964, show
"Make Someone Happy"
    [Betty Comden, Adolph Green (1960)]
    February 9, 1964, show
"That's All"
    March 1, 1964, show
"A Foggy Day"
    [Ira and George Gershwin (1937)]
    October 13, 1963, and February 23,
    1964, shows

ADDENDA

★ The cuts on this album are from the original soundtrack of "The Judy Garland Show." Mort Lindsey conducts.

9 All Alone

Label: Tucker TLP 201 (33⅓)

SIDE ONE

"I'm Always Chasing Rainbows"
    From *Ziegfeld Girl*—1941
    March 8, 1964, show
"I'm Nobody's Baby"
    From *Andy Hardy Meets Debutante*—
    1940
    March 8, 1964, show
"The Man That Got Away"
    From *A Star Is Born*—1954
    March 8, 1964, show
"The Battle Hymn of the Republic"
    January 12, 1964, and February 2,
    1964, shows
"Poor Butterfly"
    [John Golden, Raymond Hubbell
    (1916)]
    March 22, 1964, show
"All Alone"
    [Irving Berlin (1924)]
    January 26, 1964, show

SIDE TWO

"When The Sun Comes Out"
    [Ted Koehler, Harold Arlen (1940)]
    December 8, 1963, and February 23,
    1964, shows, and March 29, 1964—
    last show of series
"Stormy Weather"
    [Ted Koehler, Harold Arlen (1933)]
    December 15, 1963, show
"Suppertime"
    [Irving Berlin (1933)]
    March 29, 1964—last show of the
    series

"I Gotta Right to Sing the Blues"
[Ted Koehler, Harold Arlen (1932)]
March 22, 1964, show
"Why Can't I?"
[Lorenz Hart, Richard Rodgers (1929)]
March 22, 1964, show

"By Myself"
[Howard Dietz, Arthur Schwartz
(1937)]
January 19, 1964, show, and March 29,
1964—last show of series

SONG ADDENDA

★ Irving Berlin wrote "All Alone by the Telephone" for Grace Moore in 1924. According to Cole Porter, "Grace could never move very well on stage, so Berlin wrote [it so that] . . . she could sit and sing enchantingly and never have to get about." (Quoted in *The Cole Porter Story,* as told to Richard C. Hubler. New York: World Publishing Co., 1965, p. 19.)

★ "Supper Time" was introduced by Ethel Waters in the 1933 revue *As Thousands Cheer.*

★ "Why Can't I?" was introduced by Lillian Taiz and Inez Courtney in the 1929 show *Spring Is Here.*

---

10 **All of Judy**

Label: Telebrity 1228 (33⅓)

SIDE ONE

"That's Entertainment"
    February 9, 1964, show
"Make Someone Happy"
    February 9, 1964, show
"Liza"
    [Ira Gershwin, Gus Kahn, George
        Gershwin (1929)]
    November 17, 1963, and February 9,
        1964, shows
"Steppin' Out with My Baby"
    [Irving Berlin (1948)]
    March 8, 1964, show
"I'm Always Chasing Rainbows"
    From *Ziegfeld Girl*—1941
    March 8, 1964, show
"I'm Nobody's Baby"
    From *Andy Hardy Meets Debutante*—
        1940
    March 8, 1964, show

"The Man That Got Away"
    From *A Star Is Born*—1954
    March 8, 1964, show

SIDE TWO

"Once in a Lifetime"
    [Leslie Bricusse, Anthony Newley
        (1961)]
    October 6, 1963, show
"Love of My Life"
    From *The Pirate*—1948
    March 8, 1964, show
"The Boy Next Door"
    From *Meet Me in St. Louis*—1944
    January 26, 1964, and March 8, 1964,
        shows
"On the Atchison, Topeka and the Santa
    Fe"
    From *The Harvey Girls*—1946
    March 8, 1964, show
"You're Nearer"
    [Lorenz Hart, Richard Rodgers (1940)]
    March 8, 1964, show
"Toot, Toot, Tootsie"
    March 8, 1964, show
"Alexander's Ragtime Band"
    [Irving Berlin (1911)]
    October 20, 1963, show

SIDE THREE

"When Johnny Comes Marching Home"
    [Louis Lambert (1863)]
    February 9, 1964, show
"There's a Long, Long Trail"
    February 9, 1964, show
"Keep the Home Fires Burning"
    [Lena Guilbert Ford, Ivor Novello
        (1915)]
    February 9, 1964, show
Medley:
    "I am a Yankee Doodle Boy"
        [George M. Cohan (1904)]

"You're a Grand Old Flag"
   [George M. Cohan (1906)]
"Boy of Mine"
   [J. Kiern Brennan, Ernest R. Ball
      (1918)]
   February 9, 1964 show
"My Buddy"
   [Gus Kahn, Walter Donaldson (1922)]
   February 9, 1964, show
"Oh, How I Hate to Get Up in the
   Morning"
   [Irving Berlin (1918)]
   February 9, 1964, show
"Over There"
   [George M. Cohan (1917)]
   February 9, 1964, show
"America the Beautiful"
   [Katherine Lee Bates, Samuel A. Ward
      (1895)]
   February 9, 1964, show

SIDE FOUR

"From This Moment On"
   November 3, 1963, show
"This Could Be the Start of Something
   Big"
   January 5, 1964, show
"Here's That Rainy Day"
   January 5, 1964, show
"Fly Me to the Moon"
   September 29, 1963—series premiere
"What'll I Do?"
   February 2, 1964, show
"Smile"
   November 3, 1963, and February 16,
      1964, shows

SIDE FIVE

"A Couple of Swells"
   From Easter Parade—1948
   February 9, 1964, show

"San Francisco"
   October 27, 1963, December 1, 1963,
      and February 2, 1964, shows
"Rock-a-Bye Your Baby with a Dixie
   Melody"
   [Sam M. Lewis, Joe Young, Jean
      Schwartz (1918)]
   November 3, 1963, and February 9,
      1964, shows
"Swanee"
   From A Star Is Born—1954
   October 20, 1963, and February 23,
      1964, shows
"Over the Rainbow"
   From The Wizard of Oz—1939
   December 22, 1963, show

SIDE SIX

Medley:
   "It's Almost Like Being in Love"
   "This Can't Be Love"
      February 9, 1964, and March 22,
         1964, shows
"By Myself"
   January 19, 1964, and March 22, 1964,
      shows
"Oh, Shenandoah"
   January 12, 1963, show
"The Battle Hymn of the Republic"
   January 12, 1964, and February 2,
      1964, shows

ADDENDA

★ "Make Someone Happy" was intro-
   duced by Nancy Dussault and John
   Reardon in the 1960 Broadway show
   Do Re Mi.
★ "Steppin' Out with My Baby" was a
   Fred Astaire number in the 1948 film
   Easter Parade.

★ "When Johnny Comes Marching Home" was written and popularized during the Civil War. It was even more popular during the Spanish-American War. Louis Lambert is thought to be the pen name of Patrick Gilmore, the country's number one bandleader before John Philip Sousa.

11 Judy Garland Concert

Label: Trophy TR 7-2145 (33⅓)

SIDE ONE

"Liza"
    November 17, 1963, and February 9, 1964, shows
"After You've Gone"
    From *For Me and My Gal*—1942
    February 16, 1963, show and March 29, 1964—last show of the series
"San Francisco"
    October 27, 1968, and February 2, 1964, shows
"A Foggy Day"
    [Ira and George Gershwin (1937)]
    October 13, 1963, and February 23, 1964, shows
"From This Moment On"
    November 3, 1963, show
Garland Medley
    "You Made Me Love You"
        From *For Me and My Gal*
    "For Me and My Gal"
        From *For Me and My Gal*
    "The Trolley Song"
        From *Meet Me in St. Louis*—1944
    October 6, 1963, show

SIDE TWO

"Come Rain or Come Shine"
    October 13, 1963, and February 16, 1964, shows
"I'm Always Chasing Rainbows"
    From *Ziegfeld Girl*—1941
    March 8, 1964, show
"Alexander's Ragtime Band"
    October 20, 1963, show
"Moon River"
    [Johnny Mercer, Henry Mancini (1961)]
    November 3, 1963, show
"Hey, Look Me Over"
    November 10, 1963, and February 16, 1964, shows
Medley:
    "Swing Low, Sweet Chariot"
    "He's Got the Whole World in His Hands"
    February 9, 1964, show

SIDE THREE

"Be A Clown"
    From *The Pirate*—1948
    March 8, 1964, show
"Smile"
    November 3, 1963, and February 16, 1964, shows
"When You're Smiling"
    December 1, 1963, show and March 29, 1964—last show of the series
"Swanee"
    From *A Star Is Born*—1954
    October 20, 1963, and February 23, 1964, shows
"Rock-a-Bye Your Baby with a Dixie Melody"
    November 3, 1963, and February 23, 1964, shows

"Get Happy"
    From *Summer Stock*—1950
    March 22, 1964, show

SIDE FOUR

"That's Entertainment"
    February 9, 1964, show
"Zing! Went the Strings of My Heart"
    From *Listen, Darling*—1938
"More"
    December 29, 1963, show
Medley:
    "It's Almost Like Being in Love"
    "This Can't Be Love"
        January 19, 1964, and March 22,
        1964, shows
"Chicago"
    September 29, 1963, show—series
        premiere—and March 15, 1964,
        show
"Over the Rainbow"
    From *The Wizard of Oz*—1939
    December 22, 1963, show

SONG ADDENDA

★ "Moon River" was the theme song of
the 1961 nonmusical film *Breakfast at
Tiffany's*. It was sung behind the titles
by Andy Williams.

12 The Pick of Judy Garland

Label: CBS BT-18051 (cassette)

SIDE ONE

"Alexander's Ragtime Band"
    October 20, 1963, show
"I'm Always Chasing Rainbows"
    From *Ziegfeld Girl*—1941
    March 8, 1964, show
"A Couple of Swells"
    From *Easter Parade*—1948
    February 9, 1964, show
"Make Someone Happy"
    February 9, 1964, show
"That's All"
    March 1, 1964, show

SIDE TWO

"Over the Rainbow"
    From *The Wizard of Oz*—1939
    December 22, 1963, show
"The Man That Got Away"
    From *A Star Is Born*—1954
    March 8, 1964, show
"What'll I Do?"
    February 2, 1964, show
"Smile"
    November 3, 1963, and February 16,
        1964, shows
"A Foggy Day"
    October 13, 1963, and February 23,
        1964, shows

ADDENDA

★ This consists of rerecorded tracks.

13 Judy Garland. Live! From Hollywood, vol. 1

Label: Golden Circle CC-37117
(cassette)

SIDE ONE

"This Is My Lucky Day"
March 15, 1964, show
"Sweet Danger"
March 15, 1964, show
"Do I Love You?"
[Cole Porter (1939)]
March 15, 1964, show
"When Your Lover Has Gone"
March 1, 1964, and March 15, 1964,
shows
"I Love You"
March 15, 1964, show
"Free and Easy" ("Any Place I Hang My
Hat Is Home")
March 15, 1964, show

SIDE TWO

"Down with Love"
[E. Y. Harburg, Harold Arlen (1937)]
March 15, 1964, show
"Old Devil Moon"
March 15, 1964, show
"Never Will I Marry"
December 1, 1963, and March 15,
1964, shows
"Chicago"
September 29, 1963—series premiere
—and March 15, 1964, shows
"A Cottage for Sale"
[Willard Robinson, Larry Conley
(1930)]
November 10, 1963, show

"Hey, Look Me Over"
November 10, 1963, and February 16,
1964, shows
"Steppin' Out with My Baby"
March 8, 1964, show

ADDENDA

★ "Never Will I Marry" is misnamed
"Born to Wander" in the liner notes.

14 Judy Garland. Live! From Hollywood, vol. 2

Label: Golden Circle CC-37118
(cassette)

SIDE ONE

"Swanee"
October 20, 1963, and February 23,
1964, shows
Medley:
"Swing Low, Sweet Chariot"
"He's Got the Whole World in His
Hands"
February 9, 1964, show
"When Johnny Comes Marching Home"
February 9, 1964, show
"Give My Regards to Broadway"
February 9, 1964, show
"Boy of Mine"
February 9, 1964, show
"My Buddy"
February 9, 1964, show
"Oh, How I Hate to Get Up in the
Morning"
February 9, 1964, show
"Over There"
February 9, 1964, show
"It's Almost Like Being in Love"
January 19, 1964, and March 22, 1964,
shows

SIDE TWO

"Just in Time"
    October 6, 1963, show
"A Foggy Day"
    October 13, 1963, and February 16,
    1964, shows
"If Love Were All"
    [Noel Coward (1929)]
    December 15, 1963, and February 23,
    1964, shows
"Just You, Just Me"
    February 23, 1964, show
Palace Medley:
    "You Made Me Love You"
        From *Broadway Melody of 1938*—
        1937
    "For Me and My Gal"
        From *For Me and My Gal*—1942
    "The Trolley Song"
        From *Meet Me in St. Louis*—1944
    October 6, 1963, show

ADDENDA

★ "Just You, Just Me" is misnamed "Lovers' Knot" in the liner notes.

---

15 **Star Eyes**

Label: Audiofidelity AFE 3-4 (33⅓)

RECORD ONE, SIDE ONE

"Moon River"
    November 3, 1963, show
"The Boy Next Door"
    From *Meet Me in St. Louis*—1944
    March 8, 1964, show
"I'm Nobody's Baby"
    From *Andy Hardy Meets Debutante*—
    1940
    March 8, 1964, show

"If Love Were All"
    December 15, 1963, and February 23,
    1964, shows
"I'm Always Chasing Rainbows"
    From *Ziegfeld Girl*—1941
    March 8, 1964, show

SIDE TWO

"Make Someone Happy"
    February 9, 1964, show
"Alone Together"
    December 15, 1963, show
"Do It Again"
    December 29, 1963, show
"Too Late Now"
    [Alan Jay Lerner, Burton Lane (1951)]
    December 8, 1963, show
"I Love You"
    [Cole Porter (1943)]
    March 15, 1964, show

RECORD TWO, SIDE ONE

"Don't Ever Leave Me"
    February 16, 1964, show
"Come Rain or Come Shine"
    November 17, 1963, and February 16,
    1964, shows
"Last Night When We Were Young"
    February 23, 1964, show
"The Nearness of You"
    [Ned Washington, Hoagy Carmichael
    (1940)]
    March 29, 1964—last show of the
    series
"Once in a Lifetime"
    October 6, 1963, show

SIDE TWO

"I Am Loved"
    [Cole Porter (1950)]
    March 22, 1964, show

"Time After Time"
   [Sammy Cahn, Jule Styne (1947)]
   March 29, 1964—last show of the
   series
"I Can't Give You Anything but Love"
   February 16, 1964, show
"Happiness Is Just a Thing Called Joe"
   October 27, 1963, and February 9,
   1964, shows
"As Long as He Needs Me"
   November 17, 1963, and March 22,
   1964, shows

RECORD THREE, SIDE ONE

"What'll I Do?"
   February 2, 1964, show
"How About Me?"
   December 1, 1963, show
"When Your Lover Has Gone"
   March 1, 1964, and March 15, 1964,
   shows
"A Cottage for Sale"
   November 10, 1963
"Here's That Rainy Day"
   January 5, 1964

SIDE TWO

"Stormy Weather"
   December 15, 1963, show
"The Man That Got Away"
   From *A Star Is Born*—1954
   March 8, 1964, show
"Smile"
   November 3, 1963, and February 16,
   1964, shows
"When the Sun Comes Out"
   December 8, 1963, and February 23,
   1964, shows, and March 29, 1964—
   last show of the series
"Over the Rainbow"
   December 22, 1963, show

SONG ADDENDA

★ "Too Late Now" was introduced by
Jane Powell in the 1951 film *Royal
Wedding*.

★ "The Nearness of You" was introduced
by Gladys Swarthout in the 1938 film
Romance in the Dark. It was one of Carmichael's favorites among his own
songs. Glenn Miller popularized it.

★ "Time After Time" was introduced by
Frank Sinatra in the 1947 film *It Happened in Brooklyn*.

16 Judy. Judy Garland

Label: Audiofidelity AFE 3-5 (33 ⅓)

RECORD ONE, SIDE ONE

"By Myself"
    January 19, 1964, and March 22, 1964,
    shows
"I Feel a Song Coming On"
    December 8, 1963, and March 8, 1964,
    shows
"Alexander's Ragtime Band"
    October 20, 1963, show
"Rock-a-Bye Your Baby with a Dixie
    Melody"
    November 3, 1963, and February 9,
    1964, shows
"Swanee"
    October 20, 1963, and February 23,
    1964, shows

SIDE TWO

"Liza"
    November 17, 1963, and February 9,
    1964, shows
"On the Atchison, Topeka and the Santa
    Fe"
    March 8, 1964, show
"Life Is Just a Bowl of Cherries"
    October 27, 1963, show
"From This Moment On"
    November 3, 1963, show
"San Francisco"
    October 27, 1963, December 1, 1963,
    and February 2, 1964, shows

RECORD TWO, SIDE ONE

"Get Happy"
    March 22, 1964, show

"When You're Smiling"
    December 1, 1963, show and March 29,
    1964—last show of the series
"Old Devil Moon"
    March 15, 1964, show
"Day In, Day Out"
    [Johnny Mercer, Rube Bloom (1939)]
    October 13, 1963, show
"Steppin' Out with My Baby"
    March 8, 1964, show

SIDE TWO

"It's Gonna Be a Great Day"
    February 16, 1964, show
"Puttin' on the Ritz"
    January 12, 1964, show
"Supper Time"
    March 29, 1964—last show of the
    series
"Who Cares?"
    December 8, 1963, show
"I Happen to Like New York"
    [Cole Porter (1930)]

RECORD THREE, SIDE ONE

"Give My Regards to Broadway"
    February 9, 1964, show
"Joey, Joey, Joey"
    [Frank Loesser (1956)]
    March 22, 1964, show
"Down with Love"
    March 15, 1964, show
"A Couple of Swells"
    February 9, 1964, show
"Get Me to the Church on Time"
    December 29, 1963, show

SIDE TWO

"Hey, Look Me Over"
    November 10, 1963, and February 16,
    1964, shows

Medley:
> "It's Almost Like Being in Love
> This Can't Be Love"
>> February 9, 1964, show, and March
>> 29, 1964 —last show of series

"I've Got a Lot of Living to Do"
> March 1, 1964

"Be a Clown"
> March 8, 1964

"Over the Rainbow"
> December 22, 1963

ADDENDA

★ Garland's singing of "Life Is Just a Bowl of Cherries" on this album is significantly different from the same song on the *Judy* album [Capitol T-734 (1956), See Records: The Concert Years, Section H, #2]. Not only has her voice deepened, but by 1963, she gives the song a slightly darker interpretation.

★ "I Happen to Like New York" is misattributed on the album cover.

---

17 Judy Garland. The Collection. Live!

Label: Castle CCSLP 129 (33⅓)

RECORD ONE, SIDE ONE

"The Man That Got Away"
> From *A Star Is Born*—1954
> March 8, 1964, show

Medley:
> "For Me and My Gal"
> "The Trolley Song"
>> October 6, 1963, show

"Swanee"
> From *A Star Is Born*
> October 20, 1963, and February 23, 1964, shows

"I'm Nobody's Baby"
> From *Andy Hardy Meets Debutante*—1940
> March 8, 1964, show

"After You've Gone"
> From *For Me and My Gal*—1942
> February 16, 1963, and March 29, 1964 —last show of the series

"Alexander's Ragtime Band"
> October 20, 1963, show

"Over the Rainbow"
> From *The Wizard of Oz*—1939
> December 22, 1963, show

"I Feel a Song Comin' On"
> December 8, 1963, and March 8, 1964, shows

SIDE TWO

"Rock-a-Bye Your Baby with a Dixie Melody"
> November 3, 1963, and February 9, 1964, shows

"I'm Always Chasing Rainbows"
> From *Ziegfeld Girl*—1941
> March 8, 1964, show

"From This Moment On"
> November 3, 1963, show

"Sweet Little Alice Blue Gown"
"Sweet Danger"
> March 15, 1964, show

"When Your Lover Has Gone"
> March 1, 1964, and March 15, 1964 shows

"Some People"
> March 1, 1964, show

RECORD TWO, SIDE ONE

"Oh, Shenandoah"
> January 12, 1964, show

"Free and Easy" ("Any Place I Hang My Hat Is Home")"
> March 15, 1964, show

Medley:

"It's Almost Like Being in Love"

"This Can't Be Love"

January 19, 1963, show and March 29, 1964—last show of the series

"Never Will I Marry"

December 1, 1963, and March 15, 1964, shows

"I'm Old-Fashioned"

[Johnny Mercer, Jerome Kern (1942)]

January 26, 1964, show

"Old Devil Moon"

March 15, 1964, show

"Fly Me to the Moon"

September 29, 1963, show—series premiere

"That's Entertainment"

February 9, 1964, show

RECORD TWO, SIDE ONE

"More"

December 29, 1963, show

"Chicago"

September 29, 1963, show—series premiere and March 15, 1964, show

"The Battle Hymn of the Republic"

January 12, 1964, and February 2, 1964, shows

"Come Rain or Come Shine"

October 13, 1963, and February 16, 1964, shows

"Smile"

November 3, 1963, and February 16, 1964, shows

"I Can't Give You Anything but Love"

February 16, 1964, show

"Hey, Look Me Over"

November 10, 1963, and February 16, 1964, shows

SONG ADDENDA

★ "I'm Old-Fashioned" was introduced by Fred Astaire in the 1942 film *You Were Never Lovelier*.

---

18 **Unforgettable Judy Garland**

Label:

Castle UNLP-001 (33 ⅓)

Castle UNMC-001 (cassette)

SIDE ONE

Medley:

"For Me and My Gal"

"The Trolley Song"

October 6, 1963, show

"Swanee"

From *A Star Is Born*—1954

October 20, 1963, and February 23, 1964, shows

"I'm Nobody's Baby"

From *Andy Hardy Meets Debutante*—1940

March 8, 1964

"Alexander's Ragtime Band"

March 8, 1964, show

"Over the Rainbow"

From *The Wizard of Oz*—1939

December 22, 1963, show

"I Feel a Song Comin' On"

December 8, 1963, and March 8, 1964, shows

"Rock-a-Bye Your Baby with a Dixie Melody"

November 3, 1963, and February 9, 1964, shows

Medley:

"It's Almost Like Being in Love"

"This Can't Be Love"

January 19, 1964, show and March 29, 1964—last show of the series

SIDE TWO

"Fly Me to the Moon"
   September 29, 1963—series premiere
"That's Entertainment"
   February 9, 1964, show
"Chicago"
   September 29, 1963—series premiere
      —and March 15, 1964, show
"The Battle Hymn of the Republic"
   January 12, 1964, and February 2,
      1964, shows
"Come Rain or Come Shine"
   November 17, 1963, and February 16,
      1964, shows
"I Can't Give You Anything but Love"
   February 16, 1964, show
"Hey, Look Me Over"
   November 10, 1963, and February 16,
      1964, shows

ADDENDA

★ This is an abbreviated version of *Judy Garland. The Collection. Live!,* Castle CCSLP-129.

---

19 Judy Garland: Her Greatest Hits

Label: TRIP 16-9 (33 ⅓)

SIDE ONE

"Over the Rainbow"
   December 22, 1963, show
"A Foggy Day"
   October 13, 1963, and February 16,
      1964, shows
"Make Someone Happy"
   December 15, 1963, show
"When the Sun Comes Out"
   December 8, 1963, and February 23,
      1964, shows, and March 29, 1964—
      last show of the series

"Smile"
   November 3, 1963, and February 16,
      1964, shows
"I'm Always Chasing Rainbows"
   March 8, 1964, show
"How About Me?"
   December 1, 1963, show
"That's All"
   March 1, 1964, show

SIDE TWO

"Alexander's Ragtime Band"
   October 20, 1963, show
"Any Place I Hang My Hat Is Home"
   March 15, 1964, show
"The Man That Got Away"
   March 8, 1964, show
"Don't Ever Leave Me"
   February 16, 1964, show
"Never Will I Marry"
   December 1, 1963, and March 15,
      1964, shows
"A Couple of Swells"
   February 9, 1964, show
"What'll I Do?"
   February 2, 1964, show

---

20 The Great Garland Duets

Label: Paragon 1001 (33 ⅓)
Includes:
with Count Basie:
   "I Hear Music"
   "The Sweetest Sounds"
   "Strike Up the Band"
      November 10, 1963, show
with Ethel Merman:
   "Friendship"
   "Let's Be Buddies"
   "You're the Top"

"You're Just in Love"
"It's De-Lovely"
"Together"
January 12, 1964, show
with Diahann Carroll:
"It's Only a Paper Moon" (Judy
Garland)
"Dancing on the Ceiling" (Diahann
Carroll)
"That Old Black Magic" (Judy
Garland)
"The Gentleman Is a Dope" (Diahann
Carroll)
"Ill Wind" (Judy Garland)
"It Might as Well Be Spring" (Diahann
Carroll)
"Hit the Road to Dreamland" (Judy
Garland)
"Surrey with the Fringe on Top"
(Diahann Carroll)
"Let's Take the Long Way Home"
(Judy Garland)
February 16, 1964, show
with Liza Minnelli:
"We Could Make Such Beautiful
Music"
"The Best Is Yet to Come"
November 17, 1963, show
with Frank Sinatra and Dean Martin:
"Let There Be Love"
"You're Nobody Till Somebody Loves
You"
February 25, 1962, Special
with Jack Jones:
"Will You Remember"?
"Rosalie" (Jack Jones)
"I'll See You Again"
"Lover, Come Back to Me" (Judy
Garland)
"Donkey Serenade"
February 23, 1964, show

with Barbra Streisand:
"Get Happy" (Judy Garland)
"Happy Days Are Here Again" (Barbra
Streisand)
"Hooray for Love"
"After You've Gone" (Judy Garland)
"By Myself" (Barbra Streisand)
" 'S Wonderful" (Judy Garland)
"How About You"?
"Lover, Come Back to Me" (Barbra
Streisand)
"You and the Night and the Music"
(Judy Garland)
"It All Depends on You"
October 6, 1963, show

---

21 **Judy and Her Partners
in Rhythm and Rhyme**

Label: Star-Tone ST 213 (33⅓)

SIDE   ONE

"76 Trombones" (Judy Garland)
January 26, 1964, show
Garland/Damone duets
January 19, 1964, show
"They Can't Take That Away from Me"
(Judy Garland)
January 19, 1964, show
Garland/Raye duets
January 26, 1964, show
"Maybe It's Because" (with Bing Crosby)
Radio: October 5, 1949

SIDE   TWO

Garland/Rooney duets
December 8, 1963, show
"The Day After Forever" (with Dick
Haymes)
Provenance undetermined

"All Through the Day" (with Gene Kelly)
    Rehearsal check from MGM years
    Garland/O'Connor duets
    September 29, 1963, show—series
      premiere
"Too Late Now" (Judy Garland)
    December 8, 1963, show
    Garland/Jourdan Cartoon Medley
    February 2, 1964, show

L. ANTHOLOGY ALBUMS

This is a representative, not comprehensive, listing of Garland anthology albums.

1 The Hits of Judy Garland

Label:
    Capitol T-1999 (33⅓)
    Capitol ST-1999 (33⅓)
    Capitol SY/8XY-4605 (33⅓)
    Capitol SN-16175 (33⅓)
    Capitol SN-1-16175 (33⅓)
    Capitol 4N-16175 (cassette)

SIDE ONE

Garland Medley:
    "You Made Me Love You"
    "For Me and My Gal"
    "The Trolley Song"
      Orchestra conducted by Mort
        Lindsey
"Over the Rainbow"
    Chorus and orchestra conducted by
      Jack Cathcart
"Swanee"
    Orchestra conducted by Freddy Martin

"Come Rain or Come Shine"
    Orchestra conducted by Nelson Riddle
"The Man That Got Away"
    Orchestra conducted by Mort Lindsey

SIDE TWO

"Chicago"
    Orchestra conducted by Mort Lindsey
"I Can't Give You Anything but Love"
    Orchestra conducted by Nelson Riddle
"Zing! Went the Strings of My Heart"
    Orchestra conducted by Freddy Martin
"April Showers"
    Orchestra conducted by Nelson Riddle
"Rock-a-Bye Your Baby with a Dixie
    Melody"
    Orchestra conducted by Freddy Martin
"When You're Smiling"
    Orchestra conducted by Mort Lindsey

2 The Judy Garland Deluxe Set

Label: Capitol STCL 2988 (33⅓)

SIDE ONE

"Over the Rainbow"
"Rock-a-Bye Your Baby with a Dixie
  Melody"
"April Showers"
"Last Night When We Were Young"
"That's Entertainment"

SIDE TWO

"If I Love Again"
"Puttin' on the Ritz"
"Old Devil Moon"
"Down with Love"
"How Long Has This Been Going On?"

SIDE THREE

"It Never Was You"
"Just You, Just Me"
"Alone Together"
"Maybe I'll Come Back"
"Zing! Went the Strings of My Heart"

SIDE FOUR

"I Can't Give You Anything but Love"
"It Never Was You"
"More Than You Know"
"I Am Loved"
"I Hadn't Anyone Till You"

SIDE FIVE

"I Concentrate on You"
"I'm Confessin' "
"Do I Love You?"
"Do It Again"
"Come Rain or Come Shine"

SIDE SIX

"Day In, Day Out"
"Just Imagine"
"Swanee"
"The Man That Got Away"
"Chicago"

3 I Feel a Song Coming On

Label:
  Capitol PRO 1391 (33⅓)
  Pickwick PC 3053 (33⅓)

SIDE ONE

"I Feel a Song Coming On"
"Among My Souvenirs"
"Do I Love You?"
"It's a Great Day for the Irish"
"Happiness Is Just a Thing Called Joe"

SIDE TWO

"Little Girl Blue"
"By Myself"
"I Concentrate on You"
"Life Is Just a Bowl of Cherries"
"Any Place I Hang My Hat Is Home"

ADDENDA

★ The same album released on Sears Roe-
  buck SP 430 (33⅓) is called *By Myself*.

4 Judy Garland—Her Greatest Hits

Label:
Pickwick PC 2010 (33⅓)
Capitol CDP 46622 (CD)

SIDE ONE

"I Feel a Song Coming On"
"Among My Souvenirs"
"Do I Love You?"
"It's a Great Day for the Irish"
"Happiness Is Just a Thing Called Joe"

SIDE TWO

"Little Girl Blue"
"By Myself"
"I Concentrate on You"
"Life Is Just a Bowl of Cherries"
"Any Place I Hang My Hat Is Home"

SIDE THREE

"Over the Rainbow"
"Come Rain or Come Shine"
"Just You, Just Me"
"A Pretty Girl Milking Her Cow"
"When You're Smiling"

SIDE FOUR

"Old Devil Moon"
"I Can't Give You Anything but Love"
"Down with Love"
"It Never Was You"
"That's Entertainment"

5 Judy Garland Over the Rainbow

Label: Pickwick PC 3078 (33⅓)

SIDE ONE

"Over the Rainbow"
"Come Rain or Come Shine"
"Just You, Just Me"
"A Pretty Girl Milking Her Cow"

SIDE TWO

"When You're Smiling"
"Old Devil Moon"
"I Can't Give You Anything but Love"
"Down with Love"
"It Never Was You"

ADDENDA

★ The contents of this album have not been personally verified.

6 Judy Garland

Label: Capitol LSY 5217 (33⅓)

SIDE ONE

"I Feel a Song Coming On"
"Come Rain or Come Shine"
"Who Cares?"
"Stormy Weather"
Garland Medley:
    "You Made Me Love You"
    "For Me and My Gal"
    "The Trolley Song"
"Rock-a-Bye Your Baby with a Dixie
    Melody"
"Swanee"
"Chicago"

ADDENDA

★ These tracks were previously released on the *Judy* [Capitol T-734], *Judy in London* [Capitol SBL 8099], and *Judy at Carnegie Hall* [Capitol SWBO 1569] albums.

---

7 Title unidentified

Label: Capitol SY 5218 (33⅓)

SONGS

"April Showers"
"I Hadn't Anyone Till You"
"I'm Confessin'"
"A Pretty Girl Milking Her Cow"
"This Is My Lucky Day"
"I Can't Give You Anything but Love"
"You're Nearer"
"Chicago"
"Comes Once in a Lifetime"
"The Battle Hymn of the Republic"

ADDENDA

★ This album contains renditions previously released on *Judy* [Capitol T-734], *Garland at the Grove* [Capitol T-1118], *Judy in London* [Capitol SLB-8099], *The Garland Touch* [Capitol SW-1701], and *Just for Openers* [Capitol W-2062].

---

8 The Magic of Judy Garland

Label:
    Capitol DNFR-7632 (33⅓)
    Capitol DNFR-1-7632 (33⅓)

RECORD ONE, SIDE ONE

"That's Entertainment"
"I Can't Give You Anything but Love"
"Comes Once in A Lifetime"
"I'm Confessin' "
"By Myself"

SIDE TWO

"A Foggy Day"
"Stormy Weather"
"When You're Smiling"
"San Francisco"
"A Pretty Girl Milking Her Cow"

RECORD TWO, SIDE ONE

"Come Rain or Come Shine"
"You're Nearer"
"Swanee"
"After You've Gone"
"The Man That Got Away"

SIDE TWO

"Puttin' on the Ritz"
"Do It Again"
"Old Devil Moon"
"Down with Love"
"Just You, Just Me"

RECORD THREE, SIDE ONE

"Get Me to the Church on Time"
"Fly Me to the Moon"
"Some People"
"Island in the West Indies"
"The Battle Hymn of the Republic"

SIDE TWO

"Life Is Just a Bowl of Cherries"
"Among My Souvenirs"
"Just Imagine"
"Me and My Shadow"
"It Never Was You"

RECORD FOUR, SIDE ONE

"You Made Me Love You"
"For Me and My Gal"
"The Boy Next Door"
"The Trolley Song"
"Any Place I Hang My Hat Is Home"

SIDE TWO

"Last Night When We Were Young"
"I Feel A Song Coming On"
"April Showers"
"Little Girl Blue"
"I Gotta Right to Sing the Blues"

RECORD FIVE, SIDE ONE

"I Concentrate on You"
"Do I Love You?"
"More Than You Know"
"It's a Great Day for the Irish"
"You'll Never Walk Alone"

SIDE TWO

"Happiness Is Just a Thing Called Joe"
"This Is It"
"Zing! Went the Strings of My Heart"
"I Am Loved"
"I Hadn't Anyone Till You"

RECORD SIX, SIDE ONE

"I Could Go On Singing"
"What Now, My Love?"
"Smile"
"The Music That Makes Me Dance"
"Make Someone Happy"

SIDE TWO

"Lucky Day"
"Chicago"
"Rock-a-Bye Your Baby with a Dixie
    Melody"
"Who Cares?"
"Over the Rainbow"

ADDENDA

★ This six-record set is a compilation of
recordings previously released on the
Capitol label. It includes concert performances at the London Palladium,
Carnegie Hall in New York, and the
Cocoanut Grove in Los Angeles, and
selections from the *Miss Show Business,
Alone, Judy in Love, The Garland Touch,*
and *I Could Go On Singing* albums.

9 A Garland for Judy

Label: Capitol EAP-20051 (45)

SIDE ONE

"Over the Rainbow"
"Rock-a-Bye Your Baby with a Dixie
    Melody"

SIDE TWO

Garland Medley:
    "You Made Me Love You"
    "For Me and My Gal"
    "The Trolley Song"
    "The Boy Next Door"

ADDENDA

★ The contents of this album have not
been personally verified.

10 Over the Rainbow with Judy Garland

Label: Music for Pleasure MFP 1237
(33⅓)

11 The Immortal Judy Garland

Label: Longines SY 5217/18/19/20/21
(33⅓)

RECORD ONE, SIDE ONE

"Stormy Weather"
"The Man That Got Away"
"Chicago"
"Rock-a-Bye Your Baby with a Dixie
  Melody"
"Over the Rainbow"

SIDE TWO

"Last Night When We Were Young"
"I Feel A Song Coming On"
"Who Cares?"
"Life Is Just a Bowl of Cherries"
"By Myself"

RECORD TWO, SIDE ONE

"The Battle Hymn of the Republic"
"I Can't Give You Anything but Love"
"Comes Once in a Lifetime"
"A Pretty Girl Milking Her Cow"
"You're Nearer"

SIDE TWO

"This Is My Lucky Day"
"I'm Confessin' "
"April Showers"
"I Hadn't Anyone Till You"
"Come Rain or Come Shine"

RECORD THREE, SIDE ONE

"Zing! Went the Strings of My Heart"
"A Foggy Day"
"Swanee"
"I Am Loved"
"Me and My Shadow"

SIDE TWO

"After You've Gone"
"What Now, My Love?"
"Smile"
"Little Girl Blue"
"I Gotta Right to Sing the Blues"

RECORD FOUR, SIDE ONE

"Get Me to the Church on Time"
"Fly Me to the Moon"
"It's a Great Day for the Irish"
"San Francisco"
"Some People"

SIDE TWO

"Puttin' on the Ritz"
"Do It Again"
"Island in the West Indies"
"Any Place I Hang My Hat Is Home"
"You'll Never Walk Alone"

RECORD FIVE, SIDE ONE

"I Concentrate on You"
"Do I Love You?"
"Just You, Just Me"
"The Music That Makes Me Dance"
"It Never Was You"

SIDE TWO

"That's Entertainment"
"Old Devil Moon"
"Down with Love"
"More Than You Know"
"When You're Smiling"

ADDENDA

★ The contents of this album have not been personally verified.

12 I Could Go On Singing Forever

Label: Longines SY 5222 (33⅓)

SIDE ONE

"I Could Go On Singing"
Garland Medley:
  "You Made Me Love You"
  "For Me and My Gal"
  "The Boy Next Door"
  "The Trolley Song"

SIDE TWO

"Happiness Is Just a Thing Called Joe"
"This Is It"
"Among My Souvenirs"
"Just Imagine"
"Make Someone Happy"

13 Judy Garland—20 Hits

Label: Phoenix P20 624 (33⅓)

SIDE ONE

"Over the Rainbow"
"A Foggy Day"
"Make Someone Happy"
"When the Sun Comes Out"
"Smile"
"I'm Always Chasing Rainbows"
"How About Me?"
"That's All"
"Don't Ever Leave Me"
"Chicago"

SIDE TWO

"That's Entertainment"
"Hey, Look Me Over"
"Alexander's Ragtime Band"
"Free and Easy"
"The Man That Got Away"
"All Alone"
"I'm Nobody's Baby"
"Never Will I Marry"
"A Couple of Swells"
"What'll I Do?"

14 20 Hits of a Legend

Label: Nostalgia 22004/42004 (33⅓)

SIDE ONE

"Over the Rainbow"
"Rock-a-Bye Your Baby with a Dixie
  Melody"
"Limehouse Blues"
"Isle of Capri"
"How Could You Believe Me?"
"Swanee"
"It's a Great Day for the Irish"
"After You've Gone"
"The Party's Over"
"Some People"

SIDE TWO

"San Francisco"
"I Can't Give You Anything but Love"
"Come Rain or Come Shine"
"I'm Always Chasing Rainbows"
"A Foggy Day"
"Zing! Went the Strings of My Heart"
"Smile"
"If Love Were All"
"You're Nearer"
"Joey, Joey, Joey"

ADDENDA

★ Side one is from Judy Garland's film years. Most of the tracks are from radio shows she did with Bing Crosby.

15 Long-Lost Holland Concert

Label: Obligato GIH-60 (33⅓)

SIDE ONE

Overture
"When You're Smiling"
"Sail Away"
"It's Almost Like Being in Love"
"This Can't Be Love"
"Do It Again"
"You Go to My Head"
"Something's Coming"
"Alone Together"

SIDE TWO

"Who Cares?"
"Puttin' on the Ritz"
"Just You, Just Me"
"How Long Has This Been Going On?"
"Just in Time"
"The Man That Got Away"
"San Francisco"
"Get Me to the Church on Time"
"That's Entertainment"

ADDENDA

★ The concert was with Norrie Paramor.

16 Judy Garland in Holland, vol. 2

Label: Obligato GIH-610 (33⅓)

SIDE ONE

"I Can't Give You Anything but Love"
"Come Rain or Come Shine"
"You're Nearer"
"If Love Were All"
"Never Will I Marry"
"If Love Were All" [sic]
"A Foggy Day"
"For Me and My Gal"

SIDE TWO

"Joey, Joey, Joey"
"Zing! Went the Strings of My Heart"
"The Trolley Song"
"Hey, Look Me Over"
"You Made Me Love You"
"Rock-a-Bye Your Baby with a Dixie
    Melody"
"Stormy Weather"
"Over the Rainbow"

ADDENDA

★ The *Holland Concert* albums contain tracks not recorded at this concert.

17 Judy Garland in Holland, vol. 3

Label: Obligato GIH-6100 (33⅓)

SIDE ONE

"Swanee"
"It's a Great Day for the Irish"
"After You've Gone"
"The Party's Over"
"Some People"
"San Francisco"

ADDENDA

★ Side one was recorded live in Holland.
★ Side two is from 1951 Bing Crosby radio programs.

---

18 The Legendary Judy Garland

Label:
Capitol SM SLB-9346 (33⅓)
Pair PDL 2-1127 (33⅓)
Pair PDK 2-1127 (cassette)

SIDE ONE

"That's Entertainment"
"I Could Go On Singing"
"How Long Has This Been Going On?"
"Get Me to the Church on Time"

SIDE TWO

"Puttin' on the Ritz"
"You'll Never Walk Alone"
"I Gotta Right to Sing the Blues"
"Fly Me to the Moon"

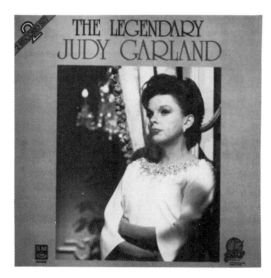

SIDE THREE

"Lucky Day"
"It Never Was You"
"Old Devil Moon"
"Memories of You"

SIDE FOUR

"Among My Souvenirs"
"As Long as He Needs Me"
"If I Love Again"
"Last Night When We Were Young"

---

19 Judy Garland Recital

Label: EMI [54] 2604091 (33⅓)

SIDE ONE

Garland Medley:
"You Made Me Love You"
"For Me and My Gal"
"The Trolley Song"
Orchestra conducted by Mort
Lindsey
"Over the Rainbow"
Orchestra conducted by Jack Cathcart
"Swanee"
Orchestra conducted by Freddy Martin
"April Showers"
Orchestra conducted by Nelson Riddle
"Rock-a-Bye Your Baby with a Dixie
Melody"
Orchestra conducted by Freddy Martin

SIDE TWO

"That's Entertainment"
Orchestra conducted by Jack Marshall
"Chicago"
Orchestra conducted by Mort Lindsey
"Zing! Went the Strings of My Heart"
Orchestra conducted by Freddy Martin

"When You're Smiling"
Orchestra conducted by Mort Lindsey
"Come Rain or Come Shine"
Orchestra conducted by Nelson Riddle
"Just You, Just Me"
Orchestra conducted by Jack Marshall

ADDENDA

★ The tracks on this album have all been previously released on the Capitol label. They are from *Miss Show Business, Judy, That's Entertainment, Garland at the Grove,* and *Judy at Carnegie Hall.*

---

20 Judy Garland: More Than a Memory

Label:
    Stanyan SR 1095 (33⅓)
    Stanyan POW 3001 (33⅓)

SIDE ONE

"Fascinating Rhythm"
"Figaro"
"Last Call for Love"
"Don't Tell Me That Story"
"Heartbroken"
"Go Home, Joe"

SIDE TWO

"Without a Memory"
"Send My Baby Back to Me"
"Roses Red, Violets Blue"
"Take My Hand, Paree"
"Paris Is a Lonely Town"
"Little Drops of Rain"

ADDENDA

★ The first four songs on this album are from Judy's MGM years. "Heartbroken," "Go Home, Joe," "Without a Memory," and "Send My Baby Back to Me" were recorded in April 1953 with Paul Weston as singles and released on the Columbia label. The final four songs on this album are from the 1962 film *Gay Purr-ee.*

---

21 Judy! Judy! Judy!

Label: Star-Tone ST 224 (33⅓)

SIDE TWO

Cole Porter Medley:
    "Night and Day"
    "I Get a Kick Out of You"
    "You're the Top"
    "Let's Do It"
    "Don't Fence Me In"
    "You'd Be So Nice to Come Home To"
    "It's De-Lovely"
    "My Heart Belongs to Daddy"
    "So in Love"
    "I Love You"
    "From This Moment On"
    "Night and Day (reprise)"
        From the Academy Awards Show of
        April 1965
"What the World Needs Now"
"Give My Regards to Broadway"
"It's All for You"
    From "The Tonight Show Starring
        Johnny Carson"—December 17,
        1968

"Till After the Holidays"
From "The Tonight Show Starring
Johnny Carson"—December 17,
1968
"I'd Like to Hate Myself in the Morning"
From "The Merv Griffin Show"—
December 1968

ADDENDA

★ Side one is from Garland's MGM
years.

---

22 Frank Sinatra and Judy Garland

Label: ZAFIRO ZV 892 (33⅓)

SIDE ONE

Garland Medley (instrumental)
TV: "The Judy Garland Show"—
February 25, 1962
"You're Nobody Till Somebody Loves
You" (Judy Garland, Frank Sinatra,
Dean Martin)
TV: "The Judy Garland Show"—
February 25, 1962
"I Can't Give You Anything but Love"
(Judy Garland)
TV: "The Judy Garland Show"
—February 25, 1962
"The One I Love" (Frank Sinatra, Dean
Martin)
TV: "The Judy Garland Show"—
February 25, 1962
"Gotta Be This or That"
(Judy Garland, Frank Sinatra)
Radio: "The Danny Kaye Show"—
October 5, 1945

SIDE TWO

"Get Me to the Church on Time" (Frank
Sinatra)
"That's Judy" (Frank Sinatra)
"My Romance" (Judy Garland, Frank
Sinatra)
Radio: "The Danny Kaye Show"—
October 5, 1945
"Just in Time" (Judy Garland)
TV: "The Judy Garland Show"—
February 25, 1962
"How Deep Is the Ocean?" (Judy
Garland)
Radio: "The Danny Kaye Show"—
October 5, 1945

---

23 Judy Garland: America's Treasure

Label: Dunhill Compact Discs GRZ 013
(CD)
1.   "Swanee"
2.   "San Francisco"
3.   "You Made Me Love You"
4.   "For Me and My Gal"
5.   "The Trolley Song"
6.   "The Man That Got Away"
7.   "After You've Gone"
8.   Dialogue
9.   "Happiness Is Just a Thing Called Joe"
10.   "Chicago"
11.   "I Can't Give You Anything but
Love"
12.   "Come Rain or Come Shine"
13.   Dialogue
14.   "Stormy Weather"
15.   "Rock-a-Bye Your Baby with a Dixie
Melody"
16.   "Over the Rainbow"
17.   Reprise

24 Judy Garland. Over the Rainbow

Label: NCB AR30064 (33⅓)
[picture disc]

SIDE ONE

"Over the Rainbow"
"Rock-a-Bye Your Baby with a Dixie
    Melody"
"Limehouse Blues"
"Isle of Capri"
"How Could You Believe Me?"
"Swanee"
"It's a Great Day for the Irish"
"After You've Gone"
"The Party's Over"
"Some People"

SIDE TWO

"San Francisco"
"I Can't Give You Anything but Love"
"Come Rain or Come Shine"
"I'm Always Chasing Rainbows"
"A Foggy Day"
"Zing! Went the Strings of My Heart"
"Smile"
"If Love Were All"
"You're Nearer"
"Joey, Joey, Joey"

ADDENDA

★ This album contains cuts from 1951
   Bing Crosby shows.

25 Judy Garland: The Greatest Duets

Label: Broadcast Tribute BTRIB 0002
    (33⅓)

SIDE ONE

"Rock-a-Bye Your Baby with a Dixie
    Melody" (Garland alone)
    1951 radio broadcast tribute to Bing
    Crosby
with Bobby Darin
    "The Judy Garland Show," December
    29, 1963
with Steve Allen
    "The Judy Garland Show," January 5,
    1964
with June Allyson
    "The Judy Garland Show," October 27,
    1963
with Peggy Lee
    "The Judy Garland Show," December
    1, 1963
with Mickey Rooney
    "The Judy Garland Show," December
    8, 1963

SIDE TWO

with Van Johnson
    Provenance undetermined
with Jane Powell
    "The Judy Garland Show," March 1,
    1964
with Ray Bolger
    "The Judy Garland Show," March 1,
    1964
with Ethel Merman
    "The Judy Garland Show," January 12,
    1964
with Martha Raye
    "The Judy Garland Show," January 26,
    1964
with Donald O'Connor
    "The Judy Garland Show," September
    29, 1963

26 The Legendary Judy Garland

Label: Time-Life Music SLGD 12 (33⅓)

SONGS

"Over the Rainbow"
"Last Night When We Were Young"
"I Hadn't Anyone Till You"
"Puttin' on the Ritz"
"Memories of You"
"I Feel a Song Coming On"
"Come Rain or Come Shine"
"It Never Was You"
"Zing! Went the Strings of My Heart"
"More Than You Know"
"Life Is Just a Bowl of Cherries"
"When You're Smiling"
"Just a Memory"
"How Long Has This Been Going On?"
"Blue Prelude"
"Little Girl Blue"
"Down with Love"
"Happiness Is Just a Thing Called Joe"
"I Can't Give You Anything but Love"
"You'll Never Walk Alone"
"I Gotta Right to Sing the Blues"
"The Man That Got Away"

ADDENDA

★ This is a two-record set composed of recordings Garland made for Capitol between 1955 and 1961.

27 Judy Garland. For Collectors Only

Label: Paragon 1002 (33⅓)

ADDENDA

★ This is a rare instance of an album title being totally accurate and informative about a record's contents.

M. MISCELLANEOUS ALBUMS WITH GARLAND SELECTIONS

1 Greatest Hits of the 30s

Label: Capitol ST 23032 (33⅓)

2 Greatest Hits of the 40s

Label: Capitol ST 23049 (33⅓)

3 World's Best-Loved Songs

Label: Capitol ST 23090 (33⅓)
Includes "I Can't Give You Anything But Love"

4 The Stereo Collector's Set, vol. 7

Label: Capitol SL 6603 (33⅓)

5 Collector's Best— The Legendary Song Stylists

Label: Capitol SL 6706 (33⅓)

6 Greatest Artists of Our Time— Judy Garland/Dinah Shore

Label: Capitol SL 6752 (33⅓)
Includes:
    "I Concentrate on You"
    "Over the Rainbow"

7 The Stereo Collector's Set, vol. 2: Broadway and Hollywood Show Stoppers

Label: Capitol 4XL 6612 (33⅓)

8 The Best of the Great Song Stylists

Label: Capitol 4XL 6617 (33⅓)

9 Showstoppers

Label: Capitol SL 6524 (33⅓)
Includes:
  "I Concentrate on You"
  "Zing! Went the Strings of My Heart"

10 Broadway and Hollywood Showstoppers

Label: Capitol 4XL 6591 (33⅓)

11 Popular Gold Album

Label: Capitol T 972 (33⅓)
Includes: "Over the Rainbow"

12 More Stars in Stereo

Label: Capitol SW 1162 (33⅓)
Includes: "I'm Confessin' "

13 What's New, Volume One

Label: Capitol SN 1 (33⅓)
Includes: "That's All There Is, There Isn't Any More"
  From "The Letter"—1959

14 Three Billion Millionaires

Label:
  United Artists UXS-54 (33⅓)
  UXL-4 (33⅓)
Includes: "One More Lamb" (with children's chorus)
Released: 1964
Narrator: Arnold Michaelis

S T A R R I N G

Jack Benny	Sammy Davis, Jr.
Carol Burnett	George Maharis
Wally Cox	Judy Garland
Bing Crosby	Terry-Thomas
Danny Kaye	

Special Guest: Adlai Stevenson

A D D E N D A

★ Profits from this album were donated by the performers to the United Nations.
★ The album was billed as "the first musical comedy ever created expressly for the record medium."

15 Golden Moments from the Silver Screen

Label: Harmony H 30549 (33⅓)
Includes: "The Man That Got Away"
From *A Star Is Born*—1954

16 Fifty Years of Film Music

Label: Warner Bros. 3xx 2736 (33⅓)
Includes: "The Man That Got Away"
The song, with some dialogue, from the movie soundtrack of *A Star Is Born*

17 Fifty Years of Film

Label: Warner Bros. 3xx 2737 (33⅓)
Includes: "The Man That Got Away"
Dialogue with James Mason and parts of the song from the movie soundtrack of *A Star Is Born*

18 International Stars of The Talk of the Town

Label: EMI DUO 117 (33⅓)

19 Here's Johnny: Magic Moments from The Tonight Show

Label: Casablanca SPNB 1296 (33⅓)
Includes: "The Man That Got Away"

20 Star Shine

Label: Pickwick SPC 3253 (33⅓)
Includes: "Over the Rainbow"

21 Hollywood's Golden Era: All Singing!!!

Label: DRG CDXp 2103 (compact disc only)
Includes:
Palace Medley:
    "Judy at The Palace"
    "Shine On, Harvest Moon"
    "Some Of These Days"
    "My Man"
    "I Don't Care"
    "The Trolley Song"

22 Hollywood. Hollywood

Label: EMI [54] 2605151 (33⅓)
Includes:
    "That's Entertainment"
    "Over the Rainbow"

GARLAND BIBLIOGRAPHY

―――――――★―――――――

This bibliography does not include the fan magazine literature or the publicity releases issued by MGM.

BOOKS

Dahl, David. *Young Judy*. New York: Mason/Charteris, 1975.

Deans, Mickey, and Pinchot, Ann. *Weep No More, My Lady*. New York: Hawthorn, 1972.

DiOrio, Al. *Little Girl Lost. The Life and Hard Times of Judy Garland*. London: Coronet, 1973.

Dyer, Richard. *Heavenly Bodies: Film Stars and Society*. New York: St. Martin's Press, 1986.

Edwards, Anne, *Judy Garland*. New York: Simon and Schuster, 1975.

Finch, Christopher. *Rainbow: The Stormy Life of Judy Garland*. New York: Grosset & Dunlap, 1975.

Fordin, Hugh. *The Movies' Greatest Musicals*. New York: Frederick Ungar, 1984.

Frank, Gerold. *Judy*. New York: Harper & Row, 1975.

Fricke, John, Scarfone, Jay, and Stillman, William. *The Wizard of Oz: The Official Fiftieth Anniversary Pictorial History*. New York: Warner Books, 1989.

Glickmann. *Judy Garland*. Paris: Pensée Universelle, 1981.

Harmetz, Aljean. *The Making of The Wizard of Oz*. New York: Limelight Editions, 1984; New York: Delta-Dell, 1989, with new preface.

Harnne, Howard, ed. *The Judy Garland Souvenir Songbook*. New York: Chappell Music, 1975.

Haver, Ronald. *A Star Is Born. The Making of the 1954 Movie and Its 1983 Restoration*. New York: Alfred A. Knopf, 1988.

Hill, Norman, ed. *The Lonely Beauties*. New York: Popular Library, 1971.

Juneau, James. *Judy Garland*. New York: Pyramid Publications, 1975.

Melton, David. *Judy. A Remembrance*. Hollywood, Cal.: Stanyan Press, 1972.

Meyer, John. *Heartbreaker*. Garden City, N.Y.: Doubleday, 1983.

Minnelli, Vincente, with Hector Arce. *I Remember It Well*. New York: Doubleday, 1974.

Morella, Joe, and Epstein, Edward. *Judy. The Films and Career of Judy Garland*. New Jersey: Citadel Press, 1969.

Parrish, James Robert. *Liza!* New York: Pocket Books, 1975.

Pleasants, Henry. *The Great American Popular Singers*. New York: Simon and Schuster, 1974.

Smith, Lorna. *Judy—with Love. The Story of "Miss Show Business."* London: Robert Hale and Company, 1975.

Spada, James. *Judy & Liza.* New York: Doubleday/Dolphin, 1983.

Steiger, Brad. *Judy Garland.* New York: Ace, 1969.

St. Johns, Adela Rogers. *Some Are Born Great.* New York: New American Library, 1974.

Tormé, Mel. *The Other Side of the Rainbow. With Judy Garland on the Dawn Patrol.* New York: William Morrow, 1970.

Watson, Thomas J., and Chapman, Bill. *Judy. Portrait of An American Legend.* New York: McGraw-Hill, 1986.

ARTICLES

Barber, R. "The Eternal Magic of Judy Garland." *Good Housekeeping,* January 1962.

Bel, R. S. "Garland Displays Her Old Form at Concert." *Billboard* 77:12, July 31, 1965.

Benchley, N. "Offstage." *Theatre Arts,* February 1952.

Brinson, P. "The Great Come Back." *Films and Filming,* December 1954.

Brown, T. "The Famous Came to Cheer Judy." *Melody Maker* 32:11, October 19, 1957.

Brown, T. "Stage Fright? Of Course Says Judy Garland." *Melody Maker* 35:6–7, July 23, 1960.

Castan, S. "Liza Minnelli: Judy's Daughter Bows In." *Look,* May 21, 1963.

Cedrone, L. "Judy Garland's Socko $65,000 Balto Week as Prelude to Her Met Stand." *Variety* 214:49, May 6, 1959.

———. "Only One Boo in Baltimore Almost Ends Judy's Act but Garland Cultists Win Out." *Variety* 250:2, February 21, 1968.

Clurman, Harold. "Theatre." *The Nation* 183:314–15, October 13, 1956.

Crowther, Bosley. "Rebirth of a Star." *New York Times,* Section 2, October 17, 1954.

Davidson, B. "Judy: Another Look at the Rainbow." *McCall's,* January 1962.

Davidson, M., ed. "My Mom and I" (interview with Liza Minnelli), *Good Housekeeping,* July 1968.

Deans, Mickey. "Judy Garland: Her Last Tragic Months." *Look,* October 7, 1969.

English, H. "Judy Garland—a 'New Voice,' a New Film, a New Career." *Down Beat* 21:3, January 13, 1954.

Fadiman, Clifton. "Judy and Juan: Two High Moments." *Holiday,* March 1952.

Garland, Judy. "A Poet—with the Stature of a Giant; a Tribute to Oscar Hammerstein II." *Melody Maker* 35:4, August 27, 1960.

———. "There'll Always Be an Encore." *McCall's* January 1964 and February 1964.

Glenn, L. " 'Purr-ee' à la Garland." *New York Times,* Section 2, December 10, 1961.

Goldman, W. "Judy Floats." *Esquire,* January, 1969.

Green, A. "Judy Garland and Her Brood Very Much 'At Home at the Palace'—at $9.90 top." *Variety* 247:47, August 2, 1967.

Green, S. "With Judy at Carnegie Hall (recording)." *Hi Fi Review* 7:73, October 1961.

Grevatt, R. "No Gimmicks for Me—Says Judy Garland." *Melody Maker* 32:11, October 12, 1957.

Hamilton, J. "Four for Posterity." *Look,* January 16, 1962.

Henderson, R. "Judy Garland." *Emmy: The Magazine of Television Arts and Sciences,* May/June, 1983.

Henshaw, L. "Judy—'A Talent That Couldn't Be Learned.' " *Melody Maker* 44:23, June 28, 1969.

Higham, C., and Greenberg, J. "North Light and Cigarette Bulb." *Sight and Sound* 36, Autumn 1967.

Hopper, Hedda. "No More Tears for Judy!" *Woman's Home Companion,* September 1954.

Hotchner, A. E. "Judy Garland's Rainbow." *Reader's Digest,* August 1952.

Hutton, J. "Caught in the Act." *Melody Maker* 44:6, January 4, 1969.

Hyams, J. ed. "Real Me." *McCall's,* April 1957.

Jenkins, G. "Judy Is a Miraculous Person!" *Melody Maker* 32:11, November 16, 1957.

Korall, B. "The Garland Phenomenon." *Saturday Review* 50:66, September 30, 1967.

Levinson, L. "Judy Pulls Nice 27G in Captivating Her Cult at Gotham's New Felt Forum." *Variety* 249:42, December 27, 1967.

Lewis, R. W. "TV Troubles of Judy Garland." *The Saturday Evening Post* 236:92–5, December 7, 1963.

Lewis, T. "Judy Garland at Home at The Palace." *America* 117:208, August 26, 1967. (Inside back cover.)

Litman, L. "Judy Pulls Sweet $74,027 in Pitt, Rochester, Despite Sound Systems." *Variety* 224:56, October 25, 1961.

Livingston, G. "Judy Burns 2,000 Buffs in No Show for 2nd Night of 2 Concert Hub Date." *Variety* 251:2, May 29, 1968.

Lucraft, H. "A Star Reborn." *Melody Maker* 31:15, March 5, 1955.

———. "A Crush on Gable." *Melody Maker* 31:15–16, March 12, 1955.

———. "Cruel Publicity." *Melody Maker* 31:17, March 19, 1955.

MacKaye, M. "Mighty Atoms of Hollywood." *Ladies' Home Journal,* September 1940.

McAndrew, J. "Star Studded Shellac (Judy Garland as a Recording Star)." *Record Changer* 11:12, January 1952.

McVay, D. "Judy Garland." *Films and Filming,* October 1961.

Masters, K. "Judy Irked at Aussie Audience; Will Play Anywhere Except Melbourne." *Variety* 235:76, June 3, 1964.

Morella, Joe. "22,000 in Line: Garland's Final 'Standing Ovation.'" *Variety* 255:4, July 2, 1969.

Murphy, A. D. "Judy Garland's Dull 21G Abortive LA Stand Stirs Greek Theatre Woes." *Variety* 240:61, September 22, 1965.

Pacheco, Patrick. "Whatever Happened to Baby Gumm?" *After Dark,* June 1975.

Poirier, N. "Momma's Girl: Judy Garland's Daughter." *The Saturday Evening Post* 236:30–1, October 5, 1963.

Richards, D. "Judy Garland SRO 12G in 1st of Two Sun. Night London Palladium Shows." *Variety* 220:49, September 7, 1960.

———. "Judy's Showstopper Ignites London's 'Night of 100 Stars' Benefit at Palladium." *Variety* 235:96, July 29, 1964.

Rosterman, R. "Judy Garland." *Films in Review,* April 1952.

Schoenfeld, H. "Judy, in the Pink, Fights Weather but Pulls Solid 55G at Forest Hills Fest." *Variety* 239:54, July 21, 1965.

Schulberg, Budd. "A Farewell to Judy." *Life* 67:26–8, July 11, 1969.

Shipp, Cameron. "Star Who Thinks Nobody Loves Her." *The Saturday Evening Post,* 227:28–9, April 2, 1955.

Sorel, R. "Judy Garland Takes L.I. Fair Audience by Storm." *Billboard* 79:22, July 1, 1967.

———. "Judy Garland Dies at 47—Singing and Acting Great." *Billboard* 81:8, July 5, 1969.

Stanley, R. "Judy Garland's Melbourne Concert Fiasco Dulls Her Aussie BO Rainbow." *Variety* 235:55, May 27, 1964.

Traube, L. "Judy Garland Hits B'way Big, Hard; Looks Bit Wagnerian at Met Opera." *Variety* 214:1, May 13, 1959.

Tynan, Kenneth. "The Theatre: Engagement at the Metropolitan Opera House." *The New Yorker* 35:75–6, May 23, 1959.

Wilson, J. S. "Two Song Belters (Recordings)." *New York Times,* Section 2, September 24, 1961.

Zhito, L. "Judy Crowns London, NY Successes with Triumphant LA Homecoming." *Billboard* 64:3, May 3, 1952.

Billboard. "Judy Garland Sues CBS for $1.3 mil" (69:15, March 23, 1957).

———. "Garland Stint Rates Superlatives" (71:11, May 18, 1959).

———. "Garland in Cincy Fadeout" (77:12, June 12, 1965).

———. "Judy: 'The Finest Male Entertainer in the World Today'" (80:T30, November 30, 1968).

Billboard Music Week. "Artists' Biographies" (73:14, October 16, 1961).

———. "Today's Top Record Talent" (April 7, 1962).

Cash Box. "Judy Garland Suffers Stroke in Hong Kong" (25:7, June 6, 1964).

Coronet. "How Not to Love a Woman" (37:41–4, February 1955).

Current Biography. 1941 (The H. W. Wilson Company, New York).

———. December 1952.

Dance Magazine. "Judy at The Palace" (30:29–31, November 1956).

Down Beat. "Judy Holds Stud Hand in Unions" (19:13, March 7, 1952).

———. "'Recording Artists' Roster" (21:99, June 30, 1954).

———. "Tormé Sues Judy Garland for $22,500 on TV Pact" (31:13, April 23, 1964).

———. "Judy Garland Ordered Back to U.S. to Answer Tormé Suit" (31:13, December 17, 1964).

Film Careers. "Judy Garland," vol. 1, no. 2 (March 1964).

Films and Filming. "Judy Garland" (October 1961).

Good Housekeeping. "Three Little Girls Grow Up" (129:168, September 1949).

Hi Fi. "Judy (recording 'Judy at Carnegie Hall')" (11:112–13, October 1961).

Ladies' Home Journal. "Plot Against Judy Garland" (84:64–5, August 1967).

Life. (cover) December 11, 1944.

———. "Judy Goes Boom" (30:49, April 23, 1951).

———. "Judy Comes Back" (31:105–6, October 29, 1951).

———. (cover) September 13, 1954.

———. "Judy and Mickey Reunited" (55:47, July 19, 1963).

———. "Triumph of Judy's Liza" (58:82–84, May 28, 1965).

Look. "A Star Is Reborn" (18:63–6, May 18, 1954).

———. "Stars of the Year: Judy Garland. Bing Crosby" (cover story) (March 22, 1955).

National Review. "Cult of Judy: Two-record album of her triumphant Carnegie Hall concert" (13:154–55, August 28, 1962).

Newsweek. "Judy's Symphonic Jive" (22:80, July 12, 1943).

———. "Judy Couldn't Relax" (36:14–15, July 3, 1950).

———. "Judy's Triumph" (39:90, March 10, 1952).

———. "Triumph in Hollywood" (44:86, November 1, 1954).

———. "Judy at the Met" (53:112, May 11, 1954).

———. "Question Mark" (62:70, November 4, 1963).

———. "Over the Rainbow" (74:18–19, July 7, 1969).

New York Times Magazine. "Little Girl, Big Voice" (January 24, 1954).

The New Yorker. Obituary (45:19, July 5, 1969).

Redbook. "Redbook Dialogue" (118:60–61, November, 1961).

The Saturday Evening Post, portrait (226:101, September 26, 1953).

Screen Greats. "Judy Garland and Mickey Rooney," no. 9 (no date).

Senior Scholastic. "Second Generation, Garland Style" (84:14, January 31, 1964).

Sight and Sound. "Star Turn: Judy Garland" (20, June 1951).

Skywald Publishing. "Judy Garland. A Special Tribute Issue" (no date).

Time. "Baby Nora Bayes" (42:90, December 27, 1943).

———. "Working Girl" (54:101, November 14, 1949).

———. "Over and Over the Rainbow" (77:52, May 5, 1961).

———. "New New Garland" (80:57, November 16, 1962).

———. "Two Old Pros" (83:44, May 29, 1964).

———. "Seance at The Palace" (90:40, August 18, 1967).

———. "End of the Rainbow" (94:64 5, July 4, 1969).

Variety. "Judy's Scores at NY Palace: 19 weeks, 750G" (185:1, February 20, 1952).

———. "Judy Garland Made Show Biz History in Many Ways During Her Palace Run" (185:1, February 27, 1952).

———. " 'Star' Outstanding Presold Pic of Recent Times due to Garland Aura" (195:29, September 1, 1954).

———. "New Frontier, Las Vegas" (203:52, July 18, 1956).

———. "Judy—She Makes a Brill Bldg. Lyric Sound Like a Shakespeare Sonnet" (204:75, October 3, 1956).

———. "Judy May Bring Vaude Back to Winter Garden" (198:1, March 30, 1955).

———. "Flamingo, Las Vegas" (206:61, May 8, 1957).

———. "Dominion, London" (208:67, October 23, 1957).

———. "Fontainebleau, M.B'ch." (213:55, February 25, 1959).

———. "Judy 190G Booty; Who Gets What?" (214:1, May 20, 1959).

———. " 'Revitalized' Judy Garland to Star in London Musical Prior to B'way" (221:1, December 21, 1960).

———. "Fields Day for a Comeback; Judy with a New Agent" (221:1, January 18, 1961).

———. "Judy Garland Grosses Pot o' Gold over Dallas, Houston BO Rainbow" (222:80, March 1, 1961).

———. " 'Judy at Carnegie' Capacity $20,000; Star Surcharged Gotham Comeback" (222:200, April 26, 1961).

———. "Judy Packs Hub Garden for Wow Take of $49,534" (224:69, November 1, 1961).

———. "Sahara, Las Vegas" (228:61, September 26, 1962).

———. "Harrah's, Lake Tahoe" (229:60, February 20, 1963).

———. "Judy Exits Her Harrah's, Tahoe Date: 'Exhaustion' " (229:57, February 20, 1963).

———. "Fontainebleau, M.B." (238:88, March 17, 1965).

———. "Thunderbird, Las Vegas" (239:69, June 23, 1965).

———. "Sahara, Las Vegas" (241:59, December 8, 1965).

———. "Diplomat Hotel, Fla" (241:52, February 9, 1966).

———. "Judy's Mexico City Fiasco Stirs Lotsa Heated Overtones" (244:2, August 31, 1966).

———. "Unique Manifestation of Judy Garland Cult" (247:1, June 21, 1967).

———. "Judy Garland Outdraws Hot Red Sox by 3 to 1 in Cuffo Hub Concert" (248:47, September 6, 1967).

———. "Her Show 'No Casualty,' Judy Garland Says in Detroit, 'It's a Calamity' " (248:2, October 4, 1967).

———. "Caesar's Palace" (249:52, December 6, 1967).

———. "Hotel St. Moritz, NY Locks Out Judy Garland for $1,800 Unpaid Bills" (251:2, May 22, 1968).

———. "Judy Garland's Fall on NJ Stage but No Fracture" (251:51, June 3, 1968).

———. "Talk of Town. London" (253:82, January 15, 1969).

———. "Judy the Talk of Town in London" (253:2, January 29, 1969).

———. "Garland and Ray Bow New Act in Sweden" (254:96, March 19, 1969).

———. "Sue Judy over Disks Cut at London Cafe" (254:2, April 2, 1969).

———. "Judy Garland Sues over 'Conversion' of Swedish Tour Film" (254:2, April 23, 1969).

———. "Charisma of Judy Garland Reflected in Global Press on Her Death at 47" (255:4, June 25, 1969).

———. "Judy at the Palace" (255:4, June 25, 1969).

———. "The Judy Garland Cult" (255:4, July 2, 1969).

———. "MGM Awaits W7 Experience with Garland Revival" (255:18, July 9, 1969).

———. "Judy Remembered in Disk, Tape Issues" (255:2, July 30, 1969).

———. "2 Disk Tape Cos. Sue Over Rights to Judy's TV'er" (256:51, August 20, 1969).

DISCOGRAPHIES

Kinkle, Roger D. *The Complete Encyclopedia of Popular Music and Jazz, 1900–1950,* vol. 2 (New Rochelle, N.Y.: Arlington House, 1974).

Lynch, Richard C. "A Judy Garland Movie Songbook," *Kastlemusick Monthly Bulletin,* vol. 5, no. 9 (September, 1980).

Munn, R. C. "Judy Garland. Her Soundtracks in the Fifties" *Goldmine* (May 20, 1988).

Pitts, Michael R., and Harrison, Louis H. *Hollywood on Record: The Film Stars' Discography* (Metuchen, N.J.: Scarecrow Press, 1978).

Rust, Brian. *The Complete Entertainment Discography, 1890s to 1942* (New Rochelle, N.Y.: Arlington House, 1973).

GARLAND SONG INDEX

★

This index contains only songs that Judy Garland performed. While part of the accepted Garland mythology is that she had a limited repertoire, it is interesting to note that more than 700 songs are cited in this book and listed below. Numbers in italics refer to the interpretative text in chapters 1 to 8.

NAME INDEX

★

CREDITS

★